THE INSIDERS' ® GUIDE TO

Boca Raton & the Palm Beaches

INCLUDING DELRAY BEACH, BOYNTON BEACH AND LAKE WORTH

THE INSIDERS' GUIDE TO

Boca Raton & the Palm Beaches

INCLUDING DELRAY BEACH, BOYNTON BEACH AND LAKE WORTH

by
Stephanie Murphy
and
Cynthia Thuma

The Insiders' Guides Inc.

Co-published and marketed by:
Boca Raton News, Inc.
33 SE Third Street
Boca Raton, FL 33432
(407)395-8300

Co-published and distributed by:
The Insiders' Guides Inc.
The Waterfront • Suites 12 &13
P.O. 2057
Manteo, NC 27954
(919) 473-6100

•

FIRST EDITION
1st printing

•

Copyright ©1995
by Boca Raton News, Inc.

•

Printed in the United States
of America

•

ISBN 0-912367-77-6

Boca Raton News, Inc.

President & Publisher
Roger Coover

Vice President/Advertising
Wayne Ezell

Account Executives
Lisa Freedman
Lynne Levine

Contributing Editor
Lesley Tarpinian

The Insiders' Guides® Inc.

Publisher/Managing Editor
Beth P. Storie

President/General Manager
Michael McOwen

Vice President/Advertising
Murray Kasmenn

Creative Services Director
Mike Lay

Partnership Services Director
Giles Bissonnette

Project Editor
Dan DeGregory

Project Artist
Stephanie Myers

On Line Services Director
David Haynes

Fulfillment Director
Gina Twiford

Sales and Marketing Director
Julie Ross

Managing Editor
Theresa Chavez

Controller
Claudette Forney

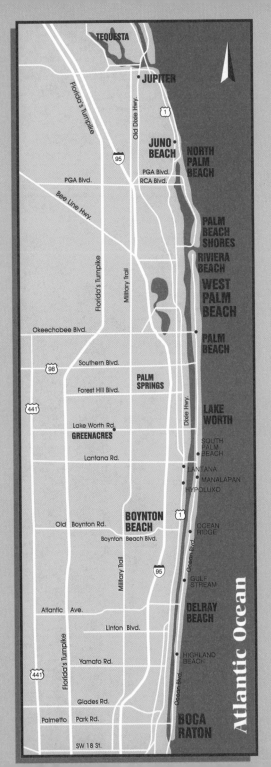

Eastern Palm Beach County

Greater West Palm Beach

Hood Rd.

Old Dixie Hwy.

Prosperity Farms Rd.

Federal Hwy.

PGA Blvd.

Bee Line Hwy.

Lake Park Rd. West

PALM BEACH GARDENS

RCA Blvd.
Burns Rd.

95

Old Dixie Hwy.

NORTH PALM BEACH

Northlake Blvd.

LAKE PARK

N Ocean Blvd.

Blue Heron Blvd.

PALM BEACH SHORES

Inlet Ave.

RIVIERA BEACH

Florida's Turnpike

Haverhill Rd.

Military Trail

45 St. Ext.

LAKESIDE GREEN

95

Congress Ave.

Broadway

45 St.
36 St.

Australian Ave.

N Dixie Hwy.

N Ocean Blvd.

N County Rd.

WEST PALM BEACH

Okeechobee Blvd.

CENTURY VILLAGE

GOLDEN LAKES

HAVERHILL

S Dixie Hwy.

S County Rd.

PALM BEACH

Belvedere Rd.

GOLFVIEW

Southern Blvd.

CLOUD LAKE

Summit Blvd.

441

S Ocean Blvd.

Atlantic Ocean

Greater
Boca Raton

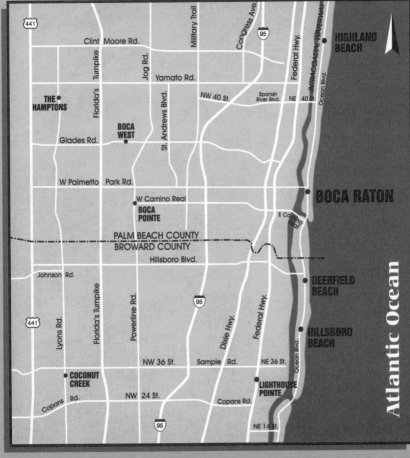

Table of Contents

Directory of Maps

Preface

If you follow the travel brochures, you'll find that Gainesville, in the north-central part of the state is "the Real Florida." Broward County, whose seat is Fort Lauderdale, will make you "feel brand new."

Their claims and those of all other areas in the Sunshine State may well be true; this is one awesome state. But no other part of Florida is quite like Palm Beach County, whose promise to our visitors is simple and best reflected in the motto of the Tourist Development Council: The Best of Everything.

That's quite a promise, but Palm Beach County delivers. From our fabulous beaches on the eastern edge that help make our's one of the world's greatest resort areas to the rich dark soil in the western reaches around Lake Okeechobee that makes us a respected agricultural area, Palm Beach County has much to offer; and the quality of the offerings is undeniable.

An arrogant boast? No. It's great to be a tourist here, but even greater to live here year round and enjoy the temperate climate, excellent beaches, world-class shopping, fabulous dining, first-rate schools and colleges and hundreds of annual festivals, attractions and cultural events.

But there's a bonus: Neighboring Broward and Dade counties also have much to offer. Both counties are nearby and a snap to reach via interstate highways, Florida's Turnpike or our tri-county rail system, aptly named Tri-Rail.

We urge you to sample the good life we Palm Beach countians enjoy daily. We love it here and believe you will too.

So get into the mood: Take off your shoes. Try a mango. Head for the beach. Slap a Nestor Torres or Roberto Perera tape into the boom box and stretch out on your beach recliner. Order a tall, icy glass of orange juice or a frozen Rum Runner. Pass the time with a good book by an author who knows our little corner of Florida well, such as Cherokee Paul McDonald, Carl Hiaasen or Edna Buchanan. Smell the salt spray mingling with coconut-scented tanning oil. Feel the warmth of the sun's rays on your skin. Enjoy.

We wish you the best of everything too. Come join us on our tour.

How to Use This Book

When we sat down to plan the chapters for *The Insiders' Guide® to Boca Raton & the Palm Beaches*, we knew we had a formidable task before us.

First we recognized that Boca Raton and the Palm Beaches are part of a culturally diverse tri-county area

TRI-COUNTY TELEPHONE AREA CODES

One important bit of information is the matter of telephone area codes in the tri-county area. Palm Beach County's area code is 407. Dade's is 305. And as of mid-September 1995, Broward County will have its own 954 area code. Previously in the 305 area, Broward's new code will be phased in as follows:

• Starting mid-September 1995, long-distance callers will be able to access Broward County phone customers by dialing either 954 or 305.

• Starting January 1, 1996, long-distance calls to pagers in Broward County will require the use of 954.

• As of June 1, 1996, it will be mandatory to use the 954 area code for all residential and business long-distance calls. The only exception will be cellular phones.

• Area code 954 will become mandatory for long-distance calls to cellular phones on January 1, 1997 Although some residents of southern Palm Beach County (a.k.a. South County,) can dial into parts of the 305 area without first dialing the area code, we have tried to simplify matters by inserting the 305 code for all phone numbers listed within that calling area. Phone numbers without listed area codes are 407 numbers. Be aware, however, that depending on where you are calling from and to, even numbers in the same area code may be long distance calls and may require you to dial the area code with the number.

that includes Dade and Broward counties. Throughout this book we refer you to places and events in these counties as well as our own, but our primary focus always is Palm Beach County. One important point to note: We often refer to the geographic area of Palm Beach County south of Boynton Beach as "South County" (please refer to our maps of Palm Beach County, Greater Boca Raton and Greater West Palm Beach). We figure you'll likely encounter locals who adhere to this vernacular . . . so we just want to avoid any confusion!

In this book, we present chapters on a variety of topics of special interest to visitors and new and old residents alike. This book is not intended to be read from cover to cover to make sense of it. Although you would derive maximum benefit from doing so, we wanted to create a guide you'll want to keep handy so you can consult it frequently and usefully. Feel free to write in the margins and generally mark up the text — that's what this book is meant for. Also jot down any comments you might wish to share with us for our annual updates — we are always interested in your impressions and suggestions.

We have an expression here in Florida for those who come for a visit but end up spending a lifetime here. We say that they "have sand in their shoes."

Here's hoping your shoes fill quickly.

About the Authors

Stephanie Murphy, a native Floridian and 25-year resident of Boca Raton, is a journalist with more than 20 years experience with Florida newspapers and magazines. She was a columnist, reporter and editor with *The Boca Raton News* for 15 years, a reporter with the *Fort Lauderdale News* and a copy editor at the *Orlando Sentinel-Star* and *The Palm Beach Post.*

Since 1992, she has been a freelance journalist and independent marketing consultant for businesses, agencies and nonprofit cultural organizations. Her feature articles have appeared in *Culture* magazine, *Palm Beach Illustrated*, Broward County's *Cultural Quarterly*, *South Florida Business Journal,* and *Quality Cities*, a publication of the Florida League of Cities Inc.

A journalism graduate of the University of Florida, she spent most of her childhood living on Santa Rosa Island — a once-remote barrier island in the Florida Panhandle, now a tourist destination off Pensacola.

Murphy and a Labrador Retriever/ghostwriter named Lemonade live in Boca Raton. Her twentysomething sons, Travis and Ryan Brown, grew up between the lines of "The Brown Bag," "Murphy's Law" and "People Mean Business," various long-running columns she wrote for *The News.*

Though she's had the chance to visit much of the world, the only place in it **Cynthia Thuma** can imagine calling home is southeastern Florida. A native of Fort Lauderdale, the only time Cynthia has lived away from Florida's Gold Coast was during her two years in Tallahassee at Florida State University, where she received her Bachelor of Science degree and developed a fierce loyalty for her beloved Seminoles.

The remainder of Cynthia's schooling took place in Fort Lauderdale at Broward Community College, where she earned an Associate in Arts degree, and at Nova Southeastern University, where she's completing work on her Master of Arts degree.

On those infrequent occasions when she and her husband, Jim, a research analyst, have substantial free time together, they enjoy traveling, sidewalk art shows and the many cultural festivals around South Florida. When she's got free time alone, Cynthia heads for the nearest bookstore or library or takes her Rottweiler, Doogie, for long nature walks.

She has worked as a staff writer and editor at *The News* in Boca Raton and *The Hollywood Sun.* After *The Sun* closed, Cynthia tried the freelance writing market until landing her present position as communications coordinator at her alma mater, Broward Community College.

Acknowledgments

Cynthia...

Many, many kind and helpful folks have provided information, shared their experiences and fortified me with encouragement as I worked on this book. All of their suggestions and nuggets of wisdom are appreciated.

First, to my husband, Jim, my mother and my brother Joe, who showed relentless good humor, considerable patience and overlooked my unpredictable moods as deadlines approached.

To my father, for passing along his passion for research, his attention to detail and his wanderlust.

My brother and Dean Bender, both professional anglers, provided much of the information for the chapter on fishing.

Sara Stevenson, marketing director for the South Florida Golf Tour and a longtime friend who knows where the bunkers are on every course in South Florida, assisted in preparation of the golf chapter.

Ann Romer, a longtime friend and fellow bibliophile, helped provide historical perspective, information in a variety of areas and moral support by the truckload.

Thanks, too, to Beth Storie, publisher of The Insiders' Guides, and

The News' Wayne Ezell, for granting me this learning opportunity. And, by gosh, I have learned far, far more from the opportunity than I ever anticipated.

To Dan DeGregory, our project editor at The Insiders' Guides, a man of unflagging good humor, patience and tact.

And finally, to coauthor Stephanie Murphy, who I respected but didn't know well at the start of this project. Now that I know her better, I respect her and her work even more.

Stephanie...

Collectively, I'm grateful to the Floridians I've interviewed whose life experiences shaped the process of listening and stringing together words about this incomparable region. Thanks to Publisher Beth Storie for selecting me to tell the stories we've chosen for *The Insiders' Guide® to Boca Raton & the Palm Beaches*.

A monumental thank you to coauthor Cynthia Thuma for her professionalism, good humor, moral support and delightfully readable writing.

Muchas gracias to editor Dan DeGregory for his encouragement, patience and unfailing focus while

Photo: Stephanie Murphy

West Palm Beach's modern skyline serves as the backdrop for the tents of Sun Fest along Flagler Drive.

weaving together a liquid logic of a saga that was changing while he wrapped it in readability. Many times this year, Dan probably pleaded with Palm Beach County to sit still just a minute, and of course it didn't.

Appreciation to project manager Wayne Ezell for keeping all the tops spinning at the same time he was playing father of the bride.

Sally McGraw remains a true sister. Thanks to Gregory Crawford, for his encouragement, caring and understanding; Ruth Morell for her charm and boundless good cheer; Dick Buntrock, a captain extraordinaire; Jennifer and Jim Wilson, for adding a RAM doubler before we "maxed out" our memory.

My son Travis, for his priceless ability to find a pulse whenever my sense of humor fell into a coma.

And my son Ryan, for his special flair for reconnaissance. Also for assimilating the knack to whip up a killer pasta from a bare cupboard to patch us through that 11th hour of writing.

Many thanks to the people who said outrageous and meaningful things. I'll begin with Millie Drozda, for her unabashed explanation of how she and husband Cliff couldn't resist the move to Boca Raton in early '95: "We listened to the universe and it said Boca Raton."

Numerous experts: Will Ray of the Palm Beach Cultural Council; Laura Hochman at Adolph and Rose Levis Jewish Community Center; Lily Appel of Pineapple Productions; Skip Sheffield, Kay Anderson, Eadie Steele and Kathleen Cronin.

Numerous authors whose works illuminate:

Wilma Bell Spencer, *Palm Beach: A Century of Heritage*; Louis Simms, *In Place of Pearls;* Dr. Arthur S. Evans Jr. and David Lee, *Pearl City, Florida*; William Olendorf and Robert Tolf, *Addison Mizner Architect to the Affluent*; National Geographic Society's *The World of the American Indian*; Donald W. Curl, *Palm Beach County, An Illustrated History*; Curl and John P. Johnson, *Boca Raton, A Pictorial History*; Alva Johnston, *The Legendary Mizners*; and Jim Sheeran, coauthor of *The Palm Beach Book of Facts and Firsts*.

Publications such as *Palm Beach Jewish Times, The Palm Beach Post, The Boca Raton/Delray Beach News,* South Florida Newspaper Network.

Thanks to Tom Wenham, the guru who figured out how to move things like the law library without mixing up the books or shelving them too soon; University of Florida Bureau of Economic and Business Research; historian extraordinaire Peg McCall, for her priceless memory and charming recollections of black cats and such; Buck Buchholz and Marti Mattila, the "dirt-movers deluxe;" Betty Withrow, for her grand anecdotes; Jean Spence, for defining gracious behavior; Clay Calello and Teresa Vogt, for their humor, wisdom and loyalty; Dottie Patterson of the Delray Beach Historical Society; Foto Apel . . . the entire staff gets the congeniality award; Rusty Cobb, for being always genuine; Zane Emerson, for his humor and lovability; Cindy Stofft, for remaining unique in a copycat world; and Helen and Dennis Dallas, for demonstrating how to cash out early and well.

Inside
History

In a walk through Boca Raton history, the safest course is with perspective in tow. Like the dominant nose of an iceberg with other features you scarcely notice, big names trip you up. So take your time to fathom the lesser reputations that complement firsts and foremosts.

The first Big Names to disregard are 7-foot-tall Indians. Coastal tribes — of moderate physique in fact — subsisted on bear and venison, shellfish, water fowl and the primitive crops they cultivated in sandy marshes.

Also contrary to myth, Boca Raton does not mean "mouth of the rat" and probably isn't a literal translation of any one word or phrase. A reference to *Boca Ratones* appears on 16th-century maps of Biscayne Bay but shifts to the Palm Beach County site by 1823. Boca is Spanish for "mouth," and natives in Raton, Mexico, say the word means "rocks." One historic reference mentions a Tequesta clan living on Rio Rattones, or "river of rocks," at Biscayne.

The one Big Name at the hub of all else is society architect Addison Mizner. An Insider's profile appears separately in the Addison Mizner chapter.

Prominent characters who shaped the pace of growth and the flavor of development are first settlers Thomas Moore Rickards and his wife, Lizzie; citrus growers George and Katie Long; real estate promoter Harley Gates; railroad tycoon Henry Morrison Flagler; utilities magnate Clarence Geist; wartime general Henry "Hap" Arnold; hotelier J. Meyer Schine and his wife, Hildegarde; Alcoa founder Arthur Vining Davis; banker Thomas Fleming; builder George Snow; ex-Mayor Norman Wymbs; real estate developers John Temple and Tom Crocker; Yamato Colony founder Jo Sakai and pineapple farmer George Morikami; farmer Alex Hughes (the first settler in Pearl City); IBM's first site manager Howie Davidson; City Councilwoman Ann Cassady; Bob and Gloria Drummond, a prominent local family who, as a result of the tragic death of their two children, spearheaded the establishment of Boca Raton's first hospital; and Count Adolph and Countess Henrietta de Hoernle.

For this inaugural edition of *The Insiders' Guide® to Boca Raton & the Palm Beaches*, it's tempting to single out a cluster of milestones: the 100th anniversary of Henry Flagler's railroad reaching Boca Raton; the 70th anniversary of Addison Mizner's exercise to escape ennui after dressing up Palm Beach; the 50th anniversary of the end of World War II, when the military commandeered the Boca Raton Hotel for a "satin-sheet" barracks to house officers stationed at the Army Air Corps base; and the sesquicentennial of Florida statehood, which mattered little in the then-languid life of this coastal wilderness.

The Florida East Coast Canal, completed in 1894 and popularly known as the Intracoastal Waterway, is operated by the U.S. Army Corps of Engineers. Its link into Lake Worth from the north opened in 1883, expediting access to points south. Until engineers connected the dots of ponds and lagoons, Boca was still playing hard to get behind a spine of dunes and a rocky inlet masking a pair of lakes.

Pirates of the 16th century enjoyed its hole-in-the-wallness as they plotted raids on Spanish ships sailing north along the coast from Havana, Cuba, and Santo Domingo, Dominican Republic.

"New World" Explorers Find "Old World" Tribes

When Ponce de Leon landed in Florida in 1513 and Hernando de Soto detailed expeditions around 1540, modest-size settlements of Tequesta and Jeaga Indians existed slightly inland and along the coast of what would become Palm Beach County.

Pedro Menendez de Arvila represented Spanish interests in Florida for King Charles V. Menendez de Arvila extolled the tropical lushness he found after combing the coastline and the banks of its natural harbor in 1565,

searching for a son lost during a voyage from Havana.

The Tequestas — enterprising mound builders who subsisted mostly on shellfish — had ties to the Calusas who likely migrated from Florida's southwest coast toward Lake Okeechobee. Thanks to Jeaga civility 300 years ago, merchant Jonathan Dickinson was merely detained and not consumed in their village near Jupiter Inlet, following his family's shipwreck. The Englishman penned a journal about the group's deliverance after they arrived in Philadelphia around 1699. The Quaker author is the historic namesake for Jonathan Dickinson State Park — now situated just over the Martin County line — and the subject of a play *The Vanished People*, produced in 1994 at the Palm Beach Shakespeare Festival.

By the 1770s, the Seminoles were developing a name for themselves, literally, as a unit that shared Muskogean language and culture with the vast nations of the Creek confederacy in Alabama and Georgia. The Spanish called them *cimarron* for their stubborn independence from established ways. Their Miccosukee cousins coined the term Seminole or "wild one."

The Seminoles headed toward Florida to avoid encroachment as the Creeks lost more and more land to American colonists. The Seminole War of 1837 decided the fate of most survivors; Seminoles were among the Five Civilized Tribes that were relocated to the Indian Territory west of the Mississippi River. A tiny band of Miccosukee fled south to join ren-

This sculpture is outside Temple Beth El, the first synagogue in South County —
established in 1967. Note the young people at the tree of learning.

egade Seminoles holed up in compounds deep in the Everglades. The Creeks had been named for their river-bank affinity, which may explain how scant clusters of Seminoles survived for decades in the formidable 5,000-square-mile swamp without anyone's knowledge, permission or blessing.

Thriving today, the tribe holds an annual festival at Big Cypress Reservation and runs what may be the world's largest year-round, floating bingo game, perched as it is on the proverbial "river of grass."

Early settlers who reached the Boca wilderness encountered the occasional "wild one," as well as hardships the Indians had tamed or transcended: oppressive heat and humidity, voracious mosquitoes, poisonous snakes, carnivores and no place to hide. The Seminoles — who lived in open-sided chickee huts thatched with palmetto fronds and supported with trees — were agreeable traders who bartered bear steaks for baubles. Desolate but promising, the area was called *estahakee,* or "beautiful scene," by Seminoles camped inland along the Hillsboro River, that borders what is now Broward County.

Toward the end of the Second Seminole War, a U.S. military commander established Fort Jupiter, where Congress commissioned a lighthouse to be erected at the confluence of the Loxahatchee and Indian rivers. It was dismantled for security reasons during the Civil War and reassembled in 1866; postwar lighthouse keepers were among the area's prominent early settlers.

Lake Worth, 22 miles long and named for a military commander, was the favored destination of most visitors or settlers in South Florida prior to the 1880s. The Dimick clan of Illinois settled east of the lake on the toy island that would become Palm Beach.

Footprints in the Sand

Before the era immortalized by author Theodore Pratt in *The Barefoot Mailman,* letters traveled by schooner from Key West to Cuba, by steamer to New York, then south by train and various sloops along the Indian River to Jupiter. In 1875, the point man for South Florida civilization was the carrier who hoofed it along parts of the shoreline between Lake Worth and Miami, the only postal connections in the region. Ships sailed from Fort Pierce toward Jupiter Lighthouse, scooted into the Inlet and tied up, handing mail pouches to the carrier who walked to the north end of Lake Worth. Sailing down the lake to the post office — about a mile from Palm Beach — the carrier made the transfer, then sailed to the south end of Lake Worth at Hypoluxo Island. A three-day trek along the shore — punctuated with rowboat rides across the inlets at Boynton, Boca, Hillsboro and points south — ended at the north end of Biscayne Bay, where the mailman sailed on to the post office in Miami.

Houses of refuge built by the government to shelter shipwreck victims served the postmen and the intrepid passersby they guided for a $5 fee. One, called Orange Grove House, was built in 1876 north of Boca in neighboring Linton — later renamed Delray Beach.

Steamboats changed the pace of life in the region, once workers linked the network of swamps and lagoons to form the East Coast Canal — today part of the Intracoastal Waterway. And while water transport was as reliable then as it is today, it was the iron horse that forever altered the pace and potential of South Florida.

Rail to the Rescue

The year 1884 marked the arrival of our first notable New Yorker, Henry Morrison Flagler. After acquiring a tumble-down railway that hiccupped its way south from Jacksonville, Flagler refurbished the line and nudged it down the coast to Palm Beach — then on to Boca and Delray by 1895. The Florida East Coast Railway eventually made it to Miami and Key West, making it easier for passengers to reach the nine resort hotels Flagler built along 500 miles of coastline.

Pineapples and Panthers

T. M. Rickards, a civil engineer who migrated to Florida in 1876, was commissioned by the state and Flagler's Model Land Co. to examine various land parcels, including some pineapple fields Flagler bought. Before the FEC line reached Boca, Rickards was acquiring riverfront property as far south as the New River in Fort Lauderdale and the Hillsboro River at Boca's caboose. When the Model Land Co. hired Rickards to in-

spect its groves and represent Flagler's interests, he moved his family here.

Rickards settled on the east side of the Intracoastal Waterway at the north shore of Lake Boca Raton, near Palmetto Park Road. He named his land Black Cat Plantation, after the lithe panthers that roamed the area. In 1897, Rickards surveyed the city and divided it into 10-acre tracts. Pineapples were planted on 500 acres, and parcels were sold to Northern speculators. J.E. Ingraham, vice president of the railroad, also bought a grove.

Rickards' second house, just east of the tracks on Royal Palm Road, was larger and more splendid than anything else in the pioneer outpost. By the time George A. Long and family arrived in 1902, Long's friend Rickards offered them the waterfront place. By then, crops were plentiful and wildlife abundant. What the settlers didn't grow, shoot or trap for themselves, they acquired from Seminole traders poling along in cypress dugouts.

In 1903, new settlers Bert and Annie Raulerson arrived with her brother Perry Purdom and his wife, Florence. The Raulersons built a bungalow on W. Palmetto Park Road in 1914; the restored cottage was moved to S.W. Second Avenue in 1987.

Frank and Jeannette Chesebro bought 60 acres from Model Land Co. to farm pineapples, tomatoes, beans and turnips. This included the beachfront site that became The Cabana Club and some high-profile acreage that interested Addison Mizner 20 years later. The Chesebro's home perched east of the tracks, just south of Camino Real.

The Hero of Yamato Colony

By 1903, Ingraham and others interested in accelerating the area's agriculture production accepted the proposal of young Japanese farmers eager to settle an area between Boca and Delray. Their leader, Jo Sakai, had a business degree from New York University and visions of opening doors for enterprising Japanese. Florida business leaders and politicians encouraged them, confident the Japanese horticulturists could conquer the sandy pine hammock. Cultivating land donated by Model Land Co., supervised by Rickards, they called the settlement *Yamato*, an ancient phrase for "large peaceful country."

Nineteen-year-old George Morikami joined the colony in 1906, during Yamato's heyday, before a blight paralyzed crop production and competition from Cuba destroyed the domestic pineapple market. Many colonists returned to Japan after the blight, but Morikami instead switched crops and began wholesaling winter vegetables on a grand scale. He also judiciously collected tiny parcels of land that, sewn together and donated to Palm Beach County upon his death in 1976, form the majestic grounds of Morikami Park and Japanese Gardens in Delray Beach — the only museum in America devoted exclusively to Japanese culture. Look for more information on this 200-acre county park in our chapters on Attractions, Parks and Festivals.

By 1906, the Rickards relocated to North Carolina, ending a decade in which he dominated events in Boca Raton while managing his own plantation, investments by northern speculators and the Model Land Co. George Long assumed his post, bought the Rickards' house and set up a packing house in the old FEC Railway distribution center. In 1908, Long's Packing House became Boca's pulse, serving as the first school, election poll and meeting hall for the Board of Trade. For the next dozen years, Boca was a respected produce hub, shipping vegetables — especially peppers — by train.

When Alex Hughes, the first resident of Pearl City, arrived for work at Yamato Colony in 1914, he found a very diverse compound: a dozen white men, six Japanese and six Bahamians. George Long donated several acres east of Dixie Highway and north of Palmetto Park Road for black farm workers to build their homes. In 1923, Hughes succeeded in opening Roadman Elementary in Pearl City, so named for pearl pineapples. Its first church, the Macedonia A.M.E., still stands on N.E. 11th Street.

Around 1914, William and Mamie Myrick built a frame cottage at 301 S.W. First Avenue, which they sold in '17. The new owners' daughter, Lillian Race Williams, later named the house "Singing Pines" for the sound of the wind blowing around its eaves. In 1975, the restored house moved to Crawford Boulevard as the Children's Museum.

In 1915, Bill and Peggy Young opened the first grocery store, and the Board of Trade's 10 members put in a phone line from Delray. By 1917, a wooden drawbridge on Palmetto Park Road over the East Coast Canal linked the beach area with crushed-shell roads to the farms. A concrete bridge replaced the wooden structure in 1923 (the present-day span was installed in 1987). Truck farmer John Brown, who became the first mayor, hauled the shell and rock used to widen Dixie Highway in 1916, a year before the water plant was constructed.

Early homesteaders Harley and Harriett Gates chose a West Indies-style ornamental-block bungalow as the centerpiece of their Palmetto Park Plantation on the west side of the Intracoastal. The namesake of Boca's main east-west thoroughfare became Casa Rosa in 1923. (This remained a local landmark until new owners razed it in 1980 to build the Wildflower waterway cafe.)

Gates, Long and Raulerson comprised one of the town's first real estate consortia, advertising properties of the Boca Raton Land Company in *The Delray News-Journal* and *The Miami Herald*.

Promoting the town on a trip to Miami in 1922, Gates encountered Alabama land baron Lafayette Cooke and persuaded him to inspect the plum parcels in Boca. Cooke's daughter, Floy, and her husband, Jones Cleveland Mitchell, arrived in 1923 to oversee the 500 acres Cooke had bought through his new enterprise, the Southeast Coast Land Company. The acreage includes what is now

Royal Palm Country Club and the land north along Dixie Highway to Palmetto. At the southwest corner of the Dixie-Palmetto intersection, the Mitchells built Boca's first commercial building, the Arcade, in 1926. The two-story structure, with perpendicular halls on the first floor, served as an office, store and apartment building. A majestic banyan tree planted there in the early 1930s was a landmark for more than a half-century until Palm Beach County leveled its limbs to widen Dixie Highway in 1987 (fire had gutted the Arcade earlier that year).

While Gates busied himself parlaying Boca real estate, Long dwelled on upgrading the town's base. He promoted incorporation as the ticket to bond financing for roads and utilities, and Florida granted township status in 1924.

By then, a fixed wooden bridge spanned the Inlet, and fun-seekers came to dance, swim and fish at an early pavilion, Boca Ratone By the Sea. Clarence Geist replaced the span in 1930 with a one-lane, manually operated drawbridge to please yacht owners drawn to his private club. (The present-day concrete Inlet Bridge was constructed in 1963.) In 1980, Arvida Corp. developed the contemporary Boca Beach Club — the beachside presence of the Boca Raton Resort and Club — on the site of that early shore recreation area.

After roads and bridges made Boca easier to reach, tourism picked up; everyone was driving a car. Winter in South Florida, after all, was just as appealing to Northerners then as it is now. The '20s were one of the few times in history that "middle-class" had much in common with Boca Raton. Until then, visitors were primarily affluent, and most folks who lived here had service jobs keeping wealthy tourists content.

Boom to Bust to Crash

The rest of South Florida progressed well ahead of Boca, with "boom" the buzzword up and down the coast. But 1925 may be remembered as the year obscurity abandoned Boca Raton — when Addison Mizner and a Palm Beach syndicate of high-rollers bought a three-quarter-mile strip of oceanfront land.

Mizner Development Corp. bought some 12-passenger Pullman buses to bring real estate prospects from "bustling" Palm Beach and Miami. They were quite the ride — carpeting, curtains and wicker seats.

Mizner's "grand design" was a goner by late 1926, when the Dawes brothers assumed management of the syndicate's assets. The Chesebro family filed a lawsuit seeking a court-ordered sale of land parcels to recover what Mizner Development owed them from its purchase in 1925. Trustees accepted the bid of Philadelphia utilities mogul Clarence Geist, one of the charter investors of Mizner Development, to acquire the assets, including the Cloister Inn, the Administration Building, numerous houses and acreage. Geist bid less than $75,000 and assumed a $7 million debt arbitration.

Familiar with Mizner's vision and confident of another boom, Geist expanded the Cloister Inn into a private haven for golfers and yachtsmen. Following $3.5 million worth of luxurious improvements designed by Schultze and Weaver, the Cloister Inn opened in 1930 as the Boca Raton Club.

Geist also took Mizner's lead to construct a depot grand enough to serve as the gateway from El Camino Real to his exclusive Boca Raton Club. Quite unlike the standard "cracker-shack" stations the Florida East Coast Railway established elsewhere, Geist's 1930 interpretation of Mizner's depot suited the grand design.

The FEC Railway abandoned passenger service in the 1960s, and agreed to donate the depot to the Historical Society if it would buy the land. The Community Redevelopment Agency helped coordinate acquisition financing with local banks, and private donors took the lead on restoration funds. Seen today on Dixie Highway just north of Camino Real, the restored Count Adolph de Hoernle Pavilion reflects the generosity of this local philanthropist.

Dr. William O'Donnell became house physician at the Boca Raton Club in the 1930s; meanwhile, his civic-minded wife, Dottie, distributed a mimeographed news bulletin called *The Pelican*.

Having invested $8 million in the Boca Raton Club, Geist obsessively dominated events in Boca until his death in 1938, when his estate provided a trust to maintain the property.

In 1933, Fort Lauderdale farmer August Butts acquired acreage in the vicinity of what is now Town Center Mall and installed a sophisticated irrigation system. Green beans were the cash crop. At one time, the Butts fam-

Photo: Cynthia Thuma

Memorial Park, on South County Road in Palm Beach, was designed by Addison Mizner. The park has the Memorial Fountain, plaques honoring the town's war dead and a reflecting pool.

Photo:Delray CRA

Sundy House is one of many historical homes in Delray Beach.

ily controlled more than 3,000 acres and had their own freight loading dock.

In 1935, Boca got serious about the need for an airport: Club members who owned planes started lobbying management for a convenient landing strip; despite plenty of land, there weren't any stretches suitable for setting down planes in an emergency. Geist's executive convinced the city to target a northwest site with taxes owed by the old Model Land Co. Once the city acquired a quitclaim deed, the state requested federal funds from the WPA, a New Deal agency geared toward creating jobs.

Boca bent the rules a bit, stalling other WPA projects to concentrate available manpower on the airstrip, which was operational by 1937.

Once World War II began, J.C. Mitchell visited Washington to lobby for a military installation in Boca. He caught the attention of Gen. Henry "Hap" Arnold, who was committed to expanding U.S. air power beyond the Army Air Corps' limited role of protecting ground forces. Boca won its bid once Arnold experienced the climate and saw the vacant land and the existing airstrip. After acquiring more than 5,000 acres, the Air Corps opened a radar school and air base. In 1942, the military commandeered the Boca Raton Club to serve as a barracks for soldiers stationed at the radar base.

One of these soldiers was Roy Withrow, whose wife, Betty, still lives on Boca Raton Road. Mrs. Withrow, who turned 80 years old in June 1995, remembers her husband, a military policeman, marching the first troops into town. The Withrows' son, Jack, grew up and was a lifeguard here before he joined the Navy, settled down here with his wife, Liz, raised their four children and spent three decades with the fire department — including 17 years as chief.

Jack Withrow is credited with distinguished leadership in bridging the transition from a small-town, volunteer-style fire department to a modern fire-rescue operation that wins national awards. A victim of cancer, he died in 1995 at age 61.

Wartime flyboy Allen Logan Lake, a Californian stationed on Florida's west coast during the war, visited cousin Herbert Hayes, who was billeted at the Boca Raton Club while stationed at the radar base. Lake's widow was so enamored with the area, she returned here in the 1960s to live. When a construction crew from Shaw Trucking arrived in early 1995 to demolish the house on Golden Harbour Drive to make way for the new owner's waterfront estate, they found Lake's Army-issue pilot's navigation kit in the garage — complete with dogtags, service record, postcards from Lake's parents and his lieutenant's insignia. Staring at a view of the Intracoastal, unchanged since World War II, the demolition crew read Lake's memoir of his final mission — a flight from London, the bombing of Rotterdam and a crash landing in May 1944.

The Schine Era

J. Meyer Schine, an immigrant entrepreneur who owned more than 150 theaters around the country, began acquiring hotels, including the Roney Plaza on Miami Beach and the Ambassador in Los Angeles. He and his wife,

Hildegarde, shaped Miami's cultural beginnings, initiating the first community opera company, an orchestra for the University of Miami and a music hall on Collins Avenue. They bought the Boca Raton Club in 1944 for $2.2 million and spent a dozen years refining its reputation as a world-class resort. In 1946, the Schines renamed the resort the Boca Raton Hotel and Club. The Schines also acquired oceanfront land north and south of Palmetto Park Road, in addition to the Cabana Club, the golf courses and other acreage.

J. Meyer Schine died in 1971. Hildegarde Schine's death in 1994 at age 91 closed a half-century of cultural activism in Boca Raton. She was instrumental in founding the city library, the art guild which foreran the Boca Raton Museum of Art, and a half-dozen music study clubs.

Fond of sharing anecdotes, Hildegarde once compared notes with Marta Batmasian about their husbands' affinity for shopping centers. She is credited with democratizing the Boca Raton Hotel for locals who hadn't been inside the gates during Geist's reign. In one humorous account, Hildegarde explained how she and a friend hosted a series of music recitals to raise money to build a church on land donated by the Chesebros. When the minister announced financing was in place, her friend commented on the good news for "you Methodists."

Hildegarde said, "Not me, I'm Jewish. I did it for you." Whereupon her friend said, "Me neither, I'm Presbyterian."

Insiders who visit the Boca Raton Historical Society, today housed at Old Town Hall, will find in its gift shop an art deco desk that belonged to J. Meyer Schine. The late Doris Schine Maxwell, one of the Schine's four children, donated the piece.

Post-War House Cleaning

After the war, Joe Moore negotiated the sale and lease of Boca's old Army facilities. One taker was Domina Jalbert, a scientist who set up an aeronautics lab on N.W. 20th Street to test his world-famous parafoil.

Another was Ira "Doc" Eshleman, a Miamian with a radio ministry who built the Bibletown Winter Conference Center (see our Worship chapter). Hundreds of visitors spent winters here attending religious lecture series, and Eshleman even sold lots to people who wanted to move here.

In 1946, author Theodore Pratt abandoned the congestion of Lake Worth to live in Floresta, where he penned many of his historical novels about Florida. In 1958, still looking for quietude, Pratt vacated bustling Boca and moved to Delray Beach.

A devastating hurricane in 1947 demolished many buildings at the air base, leaving Mizner's sturdy stucco bungalows in Floresta like a separate island surrounded by wilderness and fractured military parcels.

In 1949, Miami real estate broker Harold R. Davis proposed a mile-wide industrial district for land north of the air base. The forerunner of modern corporate citizens who came for Boca's accessibility to sea, land and air transport, Davis saw the potential for being wired to markets in the Caribbean Basin. And he intuited a need for a service industry and light manufacturing for long-term economic stability. Davis' research was on the money, but the project never materialized.

The attraction Africa U.S.A. arrived almost two decades before Disney World reinvented Orlando. John Pederson, a Fort Lauderdale Realtor and a fan of African wildlife, spent three years planning and executing plans for a 177-acre theme park in Camino Gardens. He developed a landscaped park with tropical flora to make wild animals comfortable. They roamed freely, similar to Lion Country Safari, but visitors rode motorized trains to sight-see instead of viewing animals from their cars. The forerunner of safari attractions elsewhere, Africa U.S.A. became the region's largest tourist attraction. It appeared on the cover of *Life* magazine in 1960 but had to be closed a year later after officials discovered an African red tick infestation. Many animals were quarantined, others were destroyed, and still others were sold to zoos. Several tropical birds escaped to wander surrounding neighborhoods. Descendants of Africa U.S.A.'s Muscovy

Photo: Sophie Brandstrom

A Delray Beach parade participant is decked out in a period costume.

ducks still decorate Camino Gardens.

The Next Generation

In 1956, Arthur Vining Davis, chairman and founder of Alcoa Aluminum, bought the Boca Raton Hotel and Club from the Schines for $22 million. The letters of Davis' name form the corporate identity of Arvida, another compelling dimension in Boca's evolution. (Read more about Davis and Arvida in our Real Estate chapter.)

As of the early 1960s, Boca Raton had no hospital (Bethesda Memorial in Boynton Beach was the closest facility). In 1962, Debbie and Randy Drummond, two children of a prominent family, died of poisoning. This prompted a debate about whether closer medical facilities might have saved them. An outpouring of sympathy and contributions from all over the country flowed into Boca, launching a campaign to raise money for a community hospital. In 1967, Boca Raton Community Hospital (see our Health Care chapter), known as the Miracle on Meadows Road, opened its doors thanks to the Debbie-Rand Memorial Service League.

Prior to 1963, when Boca Raton High School opened, local teens traveled to school in Delray Beach.

Photo: Stephanie Murphy

Rocks and water elements are intricate details at Morikami Park. Land for the 200 acre site was donated by one of the Yamato colonists.

Delray Beach — The First 100 Years

If your mule got a toothache or your child needed a sling — and for many other crises in 1895 — Boca folks hoofed it up the road to Delray Beach, nee Linton, a more established community with sophisticated services many pioneer villages lacked.

Delray remains progressive and community-minded in the year of its centennial. A hundred years from now, people may still be talking about the 1995 centennial and a celebration that lasted all year.

The Centennial Committee planned nostalgia events, with activities coordinated by the Delray Beach Joint Venture — a collaboration of the Community Redevelopment Agency, the Chamber of Commerce and the Downtown Development Authority.

A centennial logo was created to highlight the downtown restoration and relocation of a portion of the town's 1895 Florida East Coast Railway Depot. The logo design makes you think of an old photo, with corner slots and ruffled edges. It shows the old depot, which was sitting in a pasture after being rescued from demolition. Depending on when you're reading this, you might still have time to get in on some of the activities. If not, maybe this rundown of events that were part of the celebration will provide enjoyment enough.

A complete Centennial Calendar has been prepared by the Delray Beach Joint Venture. For details, contact the Chamber office, 278-0424, or the Joint Venture, 279-1381.

All the 100-year-old residents were invited for a party in Worthing Park at the depot. Restaurants baked separate "railroad cars" into a "train cake."

History Month

May of 1995 was History Month, so Palm Beach County history teachers were invited for a history lesson by Spencer and Ruth Pompey, descendants of a pioneer family. The Joint Venture geared its Fourth of July festivities — a parade, picnic, three-legged race and fireworks from a barge offshore — to include the diverse groups with early Delray experiences: Seminole Indians, Japanese and Bahamian farmers, blacks who migrated south to look for jobs after Reconstruction, and colonial settlers who moved from northern Florida or other states.

Delray scheduled a croquet match and tennis and golf tournaments played in knickers and other period dress. An awards program honored businesses with longevity. And for entertainment, descendants of pioneer families were guests of honor at the performance of a comedy written by Ernie Simon, a third-generation resident. Other activities that patted Delray on the back included a dance contest for the Charleston, the Peabody and the Lindy, a Gay Nineties fashion show, a Farmer's Market during fall Harvest Fest, a Haitian band performing during Heritage Month at the Tennis Center, a horticulture tour guided by a 101-year-old still-active gardener, a gospel celebration during the 18th Annual Roots Festival.

For the holidays, Light Up Delray showcases a 100-foot tree on the grounds of Old School Square.

Police officers wore exaggerated "period" badges all year, and the fire department planned an elaborate "muster" reminiscent of the days volunteers had to race the flames for water hookups.

The Treasure Coast Women's Political Group staged a "protest" on the courthouse steps to reenact the era of women's suffrage — dressed, of course, as suffragettes.

For a finale, the 60-year-old Colony Hotel throws a formal dinner-dance on New Year's Eve.

Historic Bicycle Tour

October is Heritage Month in Delray, often marked with a bicycle tour of the city's historic district. Dozens of sites provide visitors with a bevy of information about Delray Beach's early years. Follow us.

At the east end of Atlantic Avenue, a Beach Pavilion was erected in 1986 to illustrate historic designs significant to Delray. Just north of the pavilion is the Orange Grove House of Refuge Marker for the first building in town — a house for shipwrecked sailors built by the U.S. government in 1876. Nearby is the Linton Marker for pioneer settlers of the Town incorporated as Linton in 1895.

South of the public beach is the Delray Wreck Marker designating the offshore site of a 1903 shipwreck that today delights local divers and snorkeling buffs. The SS *Inchulva*, a British steamer rigged for secondary power as a schooner, went down in a storm on its way from Galveston, Texas, to Newport News, Virginia, and eventually Hamburg, Germany. Lost were nine crew members and most of *Inchulva's* cargo of wheat, cotton, cottonseed meal, brewer's grain, pine lumber and ixtle — a textile fiber derived from tropical bromeliads and amaryllis.

Old School Square at 51 N. Swinton Avenue is comprised of the 1913 and 1926 Delray Beach Elementary School buildings — restored in 1992 and converted into a museum, theater and archive center. More about national award-winning Old School Square and its role in the Renaissance of Downtown appears in the Delray portion of the Arts chapter.

Architecture

Numerous historic residences are being restored, showcasing a variety of early architectural styles:

Cason Cottage, 5 N.E. First Avenue, a 1915 residence, is restored as a museum and houses the Delray Historical Society. Nanny's Attic, 124 N. Swinton Avenue, is a 1910 foursquare-style house converted into an arts

1895 - DELRAY BEACH - 1995

F.E.C. Railway Depot - 1895

Centennial

and crafts shop. The Clark House, 102 N. Swinton Avenue, is an 1898 pioneer-style residence that was converted into an office.

Mediterranean Revival structures proliferated in the wake of designer Addison Mizner and include, from 1925, the former Arcade Tap Room at 411 E. Atlantic Avenue; the Turner House at 145 N.E. Sixth Avenue; the Scott House at 19 Andrews Avenue; the Barwick Building, a 1924 storefront at 222 E. Atlantic Avenue; and the 1938 Marine Villas on Marine Way. St. Paul's Episcopal Church, 188 S. Swinton Avenue, dates to 1929.

Banker's Row is a 1920s district with houses along the west side of N.E. First Avenue between Second and Third streets. On the east side of the street is the 1938 cottage-style development of Mackle Cottages.

Tarrimore House, 52 N. Swinton Avenue, began as a bungalow in 1924 and now draws celebrities and other diners to Damiano's Restaurant. Another example of the bungalow style is the Community Redevelopment Agency offices in a 1925 house at 24 N. Swinton Avenue.

Mission style is reflected at The Palm Apartments, 119 N.E. Seventh Avenue, a 1928 multifamily layout; the American Legion post of 1923, at 263 N.E. Fifth Avenue — under consideration by the National Registry of Historic Places; the 1926 Colony Hotel at 525 E. Atlantic Avenue; and the 1924 First Presbyterian Church at 36 Bronson Avenue.

The Historic Preservation Board of Palm Beach County acquired a 1939 Monterey for its headquarters at 20 N. Swinton Avenue.

Seabreeze Avenue has sported rows of royal palms since the 1930s.

Pioneer-style (metal roof and wood siding) Blank House, 85 S.E. Sixth Avenue, was built in 1907.

Also pioneer style, the Methodist Church Rectory, 14 S. Swinton Avenue, was the pastor's home in 1912.

Cathcart House, 38 S. Swinton Avenue, is a 1902 Bahamian-style house. The vernacular-style Cathcart Building, 135 E. Atlantic Avenue, dates to 1912. Sundy House, also 1902, is a stick-style house restored and converted into a tea-style restaurant and antique shop.

The brick exterior of The Green Owl, 333 E. Atlantic Avenue, complemented commercial structures of 1928 Downtown. Today it's a cafe.

The City Marina public boat docks on Marine Way date to 1936.

Atlantic Avenue Bridge over the Intracoastal Waterway was rebuilt in 1952. The gateway's first bridge dates to 1911.

Boston's on the Beach has operated for 16 years as a hotel-restaurant-nightclub at 40 S. Ocean Boulevard. The shell was built in 1939. Several blocks south is the Seagate Club, a 1935 beachfront hotel-restaurant. Nassau Street Historic District is noted for its 1936 Colonial Revival-style cottages.

Art Moderne influences show up at the 1948 Ocean City Laundry building, 200 N.E. Third Avenue; the 1940 Presidential at 700 E. Atlantic Avenue; and the Boyd Building, 836 E. Atlantic Avenue.

Also from 1948 is the Wideman Building, 400 W. Atlantic Avenue, a Caribbean Deco-style commercial building renovated in the early 1990s.

Doc's Soft-Serv at 10 N. Swinton Avenue was an ice cream shop from 1951 until the '90s, when it closed and then reopened as Doc's All American, complete with red-white-and-blue neon signage.

In 1964, banker Thomas Fleming — son of a Fort Lauderdale attorney and son-in-law of August Butts — convinced the Board of Regents that the next state university belonged in Boca. Fleming also persuaded his friend, President Lyndon B. Johnson, to give the dedication address for Florida Atlantic University.

Boca credits Fleming with establishing its first bank, First Bank and Trust Co. in 1956, and founding its first real newspaper, *The Boca Raton News*, a weekly that first appeared in December 1955. Until then, the city relied upon mimeographed tidbits in *The Pelican* for news.

IBM Corporation altered Boca in another direction in 1967, when the decision was made to build a manufacturing facility on Yamato Road. Within a year, the site expanded with a research and development operation that produced many of IBM's signature products: The PC, for example, involved landmark technology that put Boca Raton on IBM's corporate map and "Big Blue" in the world's view.

To grow or not to grow was *not* the question in 1972. The city instituted a growth cap of 40,000 dwelling units — a bold, pull-up-the-ladder-Jack effort to keep Boca a boutique-size cocoon and to avoid the congestion swallowing Broward and Dade counties. Though voters approved the growth cap, a Palm Beach County Circuit Court judge struck down the measure as arbitrary. When the U.S. Supreme Court refused to hear Boca's appeal, the issue died.

Photo: Stephanie Murphy

PODOCARPUS

The Bonsai Gardens are a popular area at Morikami Museum and Japanese Gardens.

Also in '72, Minnesotan Kenneth Dahlberg, who wintered at the Royal Palm Yacht Club, admitted his regret over the attention surrounding a $25,000 check drawn on his account at Boca Raton National Bank — tagged as a campaign contribution to reelect President Richard Nixon. Footage from *All The President's Men*, a film about the Watergate scandal, shows a close-up of the check.

Business and economic forces that shaped the 1980s are addressed in our Business chapter, including the arrival of W.R. Grace, Motorola, Sony, Sensormatic and Office Depot.

Look for a separate chapter on Mizner Park, including the **International Museum of Cartoon Art** (also in Arts and Culture) and **Jacobson's Department Store** (also in Business).

Inside
Addison Mizner

Irony rode the coattails of a 1970s housing phenomenon: the California-style townhouse that shaped Florida subdivisions like cookie dough. Developers introduced progressive "new" designs here years after they defined yuppie neighborhoods on the West Coast. But much earlier, California gave Boca Raton more than vanilla villas — a legacy for all seasons from the autumn years of favorite son Addison Mizner.

With the exception of Oak Park, Illinois, early laboratory of Frank Lloyd Wright, you won't find a town anywhere whose signature is so dominated by architecture — let alone by one designer — to the extent that Boca Raton spells Addison Mizner. Wright once commented on many architects having imagination, "but only Mizner had the courage to let his out of the cage." Once out, his exaggerations projected pure environmental theater starring the past, present and future of Boca Raton.

Mizner's controversial preoccupation with the past gives gainsayers something to argue about 62 years after his death. But debate doesn't alter the combination to the safe. Imaginary tumblers click in sequence and doors open because Mizner possessed a fortunate alignment of certain elements: He was born into a prominent

family living a privileged lifestyle; while young, he traveled through exotic territory that stimulated his creative passions; grown up and technically unschooled, he capitalized on family ties for timely entree to an affluent clientele whose need to show off provided the perfect stage to showcase his designs. With such situational magic, Addison wasn't likely to miss.

Born in 1872 into a pioneer family in Benicia, California — a hamlet northeast of San Francisco — Addison grew up in genteel eccentricity allowed the town's most celebrated family. California's aristocratic young ladies attended exclusive private schools in Benicia and often dined at the Mizner compound. Officers from the town barracks rounded out this slice of courtly civilization framed by heritage.

Addison's dad was Lansing Bond Mizner — lawyer, land speculator, "permanent" state senator and close friend of President Benjamin Harrison. Addison and his younger brother, Wilson, were teenagers when their father was appointed Envoy Extraordinary and Minister Plenipotentiary to five nations in Central America in 1889.

Only a slight upgrade from their Benicia digs, the diplomatic household in Guatemala City introduced the boys to Spanish tutors, personal servants and university archives on Spanish art and architecture. After two years exploring exotic culture in the Tropics — and a tedious academic detour to San Francisco — Addison attended the University of Salamanca, Spain, absorbing the ancient Spanish and Moorish footprints that influenced his vision. This cemented his determination to be an artist, fracturing the agenda of a family steeped in Establishment perks. They dismissed Addison to China, where he learned to love Oriental creatures, Asian art and silk pajamas.

Back in San Francisco, he worked for then-poor architect Willis Polk, whose early innovations foreran the California bungalow. On-the-job training with craftsmen gained Addison the awareness and appreciation for architectural detailing that would characterize his most celebrated designs in Palm Beach and Boca Raton.

In debt and dreaming of a Nob Hill cocoon, Addison took a powder in 1897 to join Wilson in the Klondike, casually sketching bonanza town layouts as he panned his way to a respectable stake. Solvent again, but on the outs with the arbiters of San Francisco society, he put his profits into a trust fund and spent a few years wandering the Pacific and Indian oceans, hawking his artwork, restoring portraits for Polynesian royalty and collaborating with Ethel Mumford on a literary grenade of satire, *The Cynic's Calendar*. A descendant of English portrait artist Sir Joshua Reynolds and a Watson on his mother's side, Addison also toured Australia, hustling prize fighters under the moniker "Whirlwind Watson."

Addison returned to San Francisco — intent on reclaiming his social station, possibly marrying wealth if it would stand still long enough. It jumped instead from a middle-floor balcony at the Waldorf-Astoria while Addison was on a coffee campaign in Guatemala. He focused anew on another gold mine: Guatemala's abundance of cathedral splendor. Its poor were blessed with antiques and elaborate, historic trappings of early Catholic missions. His penchant for bartering went so well, Addison landed in New York in 1904 with a sideshow of sacred accoutrements and a mission of his own: to become a society architect.

Happily, his springboard into New York society included familiar faces and newcomers from the Old West, namely Tessie Fair Oelrichs, who arranged a shop on Fifth Avenue to popularize Addison's altar relics. Glib and charming, he won the favor of old money, new money, showbiz celebrities and pretenders to the throne. Through one doyenne of opera, he gained a commission to remodel a home for Mrs. Stephen Brown. Mrs. William K. Vanderbilt Sr. underwrote spicy soirees at Addison's digs, and his frequent companions were Broadway favorites Marie Dressler and her accompanist Jerome Kern. Society architect Stanford White befriended Addison as well, throwing him an occasional bone from his stable of plum commissions.

Addison Mizner

Fashionably in debt, Addison persisted in his global odysseys to collect cathedral finery. Along the way he sketched buildings, streetscape elements and construction detailing that would later distinguish his designs. Home from one of his sojourns, he bought a waterfront place at Port Washington to house his collection and a growing menagerie. Branching out among the barons of Long Island, he cornered the market on unusual landscapes for indulgent clients with expansive grounds. Styles varied with his whims, from Asian to English to Mediterranean. Among a handful of homes he designed for his Long Island neighbors, the I. Townsend Burden residence of 1916 survives today as the Admissions Building of the New York Institute of Technology.

A series of events — the death of his mother in 1915, the wartime demise of his practice, shaky health and complications from an adolescent leg injury — led to a lengthy illness, causing Addison to ponder an escape to his beloved Antigua. He detoured instead to Palm Beach, waiting to die while his stimulating world travels conspired to cheat him from martyrdom. He got well about the time he decided to remake Palm Beach in the Mizner image and dabble in the vision of a custom backyard of his own down the road in Boca Raton.

Debate continues whether Addison Mizner deserves the title stage designer or architect, because he lacked the formal education required in modern times to practice the most scientific discipline of the arts. But no one disputes the genius of his vision,

the beauty of his well-proportioned buildings or the integrity of his craftsmanship. Without Mizner, there would be no "Palm Beach look" as we know it — occasionally coined "Bastard-Spanish-Moorish-Romanesque-Gothic-Renaissance-Bull-Market-Damn-The-Expense Style"; most certainly, Boca Raton would not be the unique mecca of Mizneresque Mediterranean Revival. Nor would certain existing landmarks verify his paper vision of "a happy combination of Venice and Heaven, Florence and Toledo, with a little Greco-Roman glory and grandeur thrown in."

His real-life buildings took direction from his Muse, who occasionally forgot whether the tale reflected Addison's imagination or a dream sequence inspired by his travels. Either one worked for his Palm Beach clients, bored with their tame Victorian surroundings and intrigued by the suggestive scenarios that all but danced off the quasi-blueprints of his palatial stage-sets.

Affable, fluent in Spanish and proficiently profane, he was popular with workers, especially when laboring beside them with sleeves rolled to the elbows of beefy arms. Tall, blond, blue-eyed and muscular, Addison was saved from being sloppy by shoulders as broad as his paunch. A life of excesses gave him the perfect torso to display waistcoat, watch fob and a go-to-hell gaze.

Paris Singer, French-born heir to the fortune of Isaac Singer, was the index of Palm Beach society during and after World War I. He acquired a tourist trap known as Joe's Alligator

Photo: Smith & Knibbs, Inc.

Shops, offices and apartments line Plaza Real in Mizner Park.

Farm and arranged for buddy Mizner to begin its transformation into Worth Avenue — its centerpiece, a convalescent hospital for injured soldiers that would be suitable to recycle as a future private club. Near completion, with the priority already shifted to social den, the never-clinic opened in 1919 as the majestic Everglades Club — Singer's private repository of respectability.

Resort-goers had a choice between public hotels — though stylish — and Singer's enchanting private stronghold perched on the east flank of Lake Worth. Palm Beach winters were a must in New York social circles, and membership demand skyrocketed the first season. Singer personally regulated the rolls by whim each year.

El Mirasol

Married to a partner with J.P. Morgan & Co. in Philadelphia, where the family residence Whitemarsh Hall

made "an important architectural statement," Eva Stotesbury was immune to Paris Singer's stance of take-no-prisoners in Palm Beach. Coveting a winter home that would stun the locals, she scrapped her Philly designer and his blueprints after she saw The Everglades Club. Addison Mizner's 1920 creation for her, the 37-room El Mirasol, endures in memory only as the pivotal jewel of his early Palm Beach mansions, and his entree to dozens of commissions along the ivory tower Island. In its day, Stotesbury's Spanish-Moorish estate defined Palm Beach etiquette and blessed a daughter's marriage to Gen. Douglas MacArthur.

For oil tycoon Joshua Cosden, Mizner offered Playa Riente, the largest and most imposing playpen in the resort. In 1923, its 70 rooms garnered $1.8 million; a year later, the widow of auto magnate Horace Dodge paid another $1 million premium. Mizner designed a smallish house for himself at 720 S. Ocean Boulevard, then sold it on demand to Harold S. Vanderbilt. In modern times, Yoko Ono owned and restored the residence, known as El Salano.

Other famous clients included Charles Munn, John Phipps and his brother Henry, Rodman Wanamaker II and Edward Shearson. A compound he designed for the Wanamakers leapt to national consciousness as the Palm Beach White House during the Kennedy presidency and more recently as the setting for the scandal surrounding William Kennedy Smith's après-Au Bar rendezvous.

Bankrolled initially by Singer, the designer started Mizner Industries to shape the clay roof tiles, flooring and other building materials shorted by World War I. Later, the enterprise merged with Las Manos, where workers fashioned "antique" furniture, stained glass, stone castings and other accessories by hand.

Mizner came to Palm Beach about five years after the death of Henry Flagler, whose luxury "hotel civilization" for the captains of commerce dotted the coast from St. Augustine to Key West. By the time Mizner's coterie of investors set their cap on a make-over of wild, wooly, unspoiled Boca Raton, Palm Beach was a civilized hamlet of Mizneresque mansions that triggered whispers of walled Moorish compounds punctuating powerful old Spain and graceful Venetian waterways. A handful of commercial structures and the Embassy Club portion of the Society of the Four Arts rank with the unspoiled magnificence of Worth Avenue to preserve Mizner's legacy in Palm Beach. On streets parallel to Worth Avenue — where his own five-story apartment rose above Via Mizner, down from Via Parigi — he also contributed more modest homes.

South of Palm Beach in Gulf Stream, Mizner created the Golf and Polo Club for John Phipps in 1923. A few years later, Mizner gave Boynton Beach its Woman's Club; like many of his surviving creations, it is listed on the National Register of Historic Places.

Boca Joins the Florida Boom

Spring 1925: Mizner headed a syndicate of Palm Beachers who bought a strip of Atlantic-front land along the same Boca dunes that enticed pioneer Frank Chesebro in 1903. The investors' clout squashed any doubt that Boca was destined for greatness, claiming ties to a third of the nation's wealth: Gen. T. Coleman du Pont, Rodman Wanamaker II, a pair of Vanderbilts, Elizabeth Arden, Paris Singer and Irving Berlin, to name a few. Having acquired several thousand acres, including a couple of precious miles on the ocean, Mizner Development Corporation set a record of more than $2 million in first-day land sales and beat its own game several times during its first month in Boca. Some accounts say Mizner and Wilson, the corporate treasurer, sold $11 million worth of land during the first six months; others suggest the 1925 sales volume was more than double that amount. With a feeding frenzy under way in the West Palm and Miami offices, branches opened in Chicago and every major city on the eastern seaboard.

Mizner circulated hints about a magic city, beginning with a monumental Spanish-style hotel to be built on the north side of the Inlet. Luxury accents included a casino, yacht basin, golf courses, polo fields, residential villages and a castle for himself. His reputation and the infectious fever of boom-time speculation drew a commitment from the Ritz-Carlton chain to take over the hotel. Mizner's attention segued to a 300-acre plum for the west side of Lake Boca Raton — the $1.5 million 100-room Cloister Inn that would flank the world's widest, lushest boulevard, El Camino Real.

February 6, 1926: Mizner's fabled Ritz-Carlton Cloister Inn opened its doors and cracked the portals of what some observers believe is the single most important element in Boca history. Five hundred of the nation's glitterati beamed themselves up for the party, many of whom bore a striking resemblance to the figures described in outrageous advertising about Boca Raton: "World leaders in finance, society and the arts establish international resort on Florida's East Coast." Ace publicist Harry Reichenbach garnered $3,000 a week for such purple prose but ended his career stranded in his own hype and debt.

General du Pont became annoyed at having his reputation exploited and began to renounce the deal through negative headlines from New York.

People who bought land on speculation from Mizner Development defaulted on loan payments, thus straining Addison's own cash flow. Economic forces compounded the bad press spoiling Mizner's promotion, as a railroad embargo on building materials stalled construction projects up and down the coast. A Danish vessel floundered in Miami's harbor and blocked the port for six weeks, scuttling efforts to skirt the rail crisis with offshore shipping.

Before the boom started its downhill slide, city officials named Mizner town planner so he could plat the rest of the city as he penciled in his own projects. His 1925 Administration Building at the corner of Camino Real and Dixie Highway housed executives and consultants. Restored in 1988, the two-story Mediterranean Revival masterpiece — reflecting Mizner's awe over the home of El Greco in Toledo, Spain — today houses Addison's Restaurant, several shops, service businesses and professional offices.

Overextended on millions in loans, Mizner turned over management of the company to a Chicago firm headed by Rufus Dawes, brother of then U.S. Vice President Charles Dawes.

Still, the land boom peaked without a nod to Mizner, delaying his "grand design" and plans for Boca's first municipal building. Delray architect William Alsmeyer modified the concept for Town Hall, using Mizner's design to finish the building that housed city offices from 1927 to 1983. Restored by the Boca Raton Historical Society in 1984, Old Town

Photo: Cynthia Thuma

The Everglades Club was the first building that Addison Mizner designed in Florida, and its success was a springboard for his career as a society architect in South Florida.

Hall, 71 N. Federal Highway, is a distinctive, golden-domed Mediterranean Revival structure. The Historical Society operates the facility and accomplished its listing on the National Register of Historic Places.

Both Town Hall and the Administration Building afford authentic examples of the architectural details Mizner favored: arched entrances, Palladian windows, tile flooring mixed with durable Dade County pine planks, cypress ceilings, barrel-tile roofs and wrought-iron grill work.

Lower in profile but still grand are his 29 bungalows that pepper a neighborhood renamed Old Floresta for its historic significance to the Mizner era. Many owners restored these bungalows, some with Mizner-inspired additions.

An original investor in Mizner's grand scheme for Boca, utilities magnate Clarence Geist positioned himself to tidy up after Mizner Development went belly-up in 1927. Geist's Spanish River Land Company bought the Cloister Inn and other Mizner assets from the Dawes brothers, bankrolled a $3.5-million expansion of the original property, and reopened the former Cloister Inn as the private Boca Raton Club in 1930.

Though out of step after the boom, Mizner continued to create landmark structures that match the splendor of his Palm Beach mansions. A second Cloister Inn, commissioned by resort developers at Sea Island, Georgia, dressed up Savannah's barrier island.

Some of Mizner's grandest mansions appeared in Manalapan and St. Petersburg, at Bryn Mawr outside Philadelphia, and in Colorado Springs. Home again in California, Mizner added a brilliant gem to his crown with Casa Bienvenida, built in Montecito near Santa Barbara for New Yorker Albert Elliot Dieterich.

Hurricanes ravished lesser structures throughout the decades, and death confiscated Addison Mizner in February 1933. Many of his inspired creations fared better and remind us, in their restored majesty, that believing leads to seeing.

Photo: Aerial Visions Inc.

This aerial view shows the Congress Avenue interchange of I-95 just north of Yamato Road. In the center is the Park-and-Ride area. A new Tri-Rail depot is planned for 1996.

Inside
Getting Around

Boca Raton and the Palm Beaches are blessed with accessibility, regardless of your favorite ride: Wing it into nearby international or executive airports, sail into town from the Atlantic Ocean or the Intracoastal Waterway, book a train berth, lose the cruise-control on your ragtop or vroom by on a Harley hog.

In-town, you may also jog, pedal or in-line skate, hop the county transit bus, Palm Tran, or kick back on Tri-Rail. If word associations are helpful, remember "TWA" for street layouts: terraces, ways and avenues run north and south, while streets, courts and places run east and west. A major exception is Atlantic Avenue, the east-west gateway to Delray Beach.

Boca Raton once took a bit of ribbing over the "Palmetto Pretzel," a nickname for the spaghetti-bowl 12th Avenue intersection of Palmetto Park Road just east of Interstate 95.

Redesigned, the "Pretzel" unraveled its knotting effect on traffic.

Dixie Highway and Palmetto Park Road are the city's north-south and east-west dividers. One of four I-95 exits for the Boca area, Palmetto Park goes east to the ocean at U.S. Highway A1A and all the way west of U.S. Highway 441 (also called State Road 7) to nudge the Everglades. Dixie runs parallel to U.S. Highway 1 (also called

Federal Highway) throughout Palm Beach County; in a few areas, Old Dixie and Federal are the same. In Delray Beach, part of Dixie Highway is called Swinton Avenue.

The other interstate exits at Boca are Congress Avenue near the Delray Beach line, Yamato Road and Glades Road — by far the most heavily traveled at peak hours. As Boca's exit from Florida's Turnpike, Glades is a main artery to suburbs west of I-95 and regional shopping destinations. Completed last year, the Congress Avenue Exit funnels traffic from the interstate to northern business corridors and neighborhoods.

Yamato Road, also known as 51st Street, exits much farther east than most links to I-95, so drivers who like to trim their time in the fast lane often take Yamato east into the city or west to the Tri-Rail station. Named for the Japanese farming colony established here in the early 1900s, Yamato evolved from a railhead for crops to the "Silicon Beach" address of IBM and other high-tech firms who followed Big Blue's lead in the 1970s.

Anyone who makes it to the beach reaches Highway A1A, a two-lane coastal ribbon known as Ocean Boulevard in street addresses. Most people who don't live on the ocean use other main arteries to navigate; but by all means, don't neglect a tour of the county along this lovely strip.

You'll glimpse the ocean and pristine beaches interspersed with dunes, seagrape and other protected native flora, expensive high-rise condominiums and winding, wooded drives leading to multimillion-dollar estate homes. In some narrow areas, you'll pass yachts docked along the Atlantic Intracoastal Waterway, a scant pebble-toss from a mansion on the ocean side of Highway A1A.

Airports

Palm Beach International Airport (PBIA) is 25 miles north of Boca Raton between Southern Boulevard and Belvedere Road on Australian Avenue in West Palm Beach. PBIA handles regular flights to major U.S. cities, Canada and the Caribbean Basin. Check individual carriers for flight and fare details; call 471-7403 to inquire about airport facilities.

Inside the airport you'll find car-rental counters for Alamo, Avis, Budget, Dollar, National and Value. On the baggage claim level is a kiosk with literature about area cultural attractions, hotels, restaurants and limousines. Also, Level 2 has a currency exchange and a small business center open weekdays from 8:30 AM to 4:30 PM.

To reach Boca from PBIA, take Australian south to Southern, then east to the southbound ramp for I-95. Boca exits follow the one for Linton Boulevard in Delray Beach. For a peek around Palm Beach, take Australian north to Okeechobee Boulevard, then head east across the Intracoastal Waterway.

Only 20 miles south of Boca is **Fort Lauderdale-Hollywood International Airport**, also well-connected to U.S. hubs, Central and South America, Canada and the Caribbean. Call (305)359-1200 for general information.

The airport is accessible via I-95, taking Exit 26 onto I-595 eastbound to Exit 12B.

You may also take Florida's Turnpike to Fort Lauderdale south, Exit 54 at I-595, for a 75¢ toll. To reach Boca from the Fort Lauderdale airport, follow signs outside the terminal to I-595 and go west to either I-95 or the turnpike.

Miami International Airport, (305)876-7000, 47 miles south of Boca Raton, offers daily flights to Europe and South America. Some airlines quote fare discounts for various domestic destinations. The airport is accessible from I-95 or the turnpike to State Road 836, the Dolphin Expressway.

Boca Raton Airport is a busy noncommercial hub for private pilots, executive travelers and heli-

A park-and-ride lot at the Congress Avenue Exit of I-95 provides easy access for commuters who want to share a ride.

copter charters to other airports. Adjacent to Florida Atlantic University on Airport Road, just east of I-95 and north of Glades Road, the site was an Army airstrip during World War II. For information, call 368-1110.

Highways

No, I-95 isn't for sissies. Trips are manageable during non-peak hours, and mastering the interstate is essential to navigating South Florida. Boca interchanges on I-95 are Exit 38 at Palmetto Park Road, Exit 39 at Glades Road, Exit 40 at Yamato Road and Exit 40C at Congress Avenue. Glades Road in Boca Raton is Florida's Turnpike Exit 75. Road expansion projects were completed in the past few years, and work will begin this year on sound barrier walls throughout Palm Beach County.

The Turnpike, once called the Sunshine State Parkway, runs for 313 miles from Miami-Homestead north to Wildwood. South of Ocala, it merges with I-75. Exit numbers correlate with mile markers for easy navigating. Nicknamed "Florida's Main Street," the toll-road operates on a ticket system northward from Lantana and on coin-collection elsewhere. South of Broward County is the Turnpike's 47-mile Homestead Extension around urban arteries in Dade County, with a bypass to the Florida Keys. Turnpike tolls from Boca to Fort Lauderdale Airport are 75¢.

South of Boca, the turnpike connects with the Sawgrass Express-way, a toll road that opened in 1986 as a bypass of urban traffic in Broward. The Sawgrass merges with I-75 westbound to Naples at the same point it links with I-595 eastbound to the Lauderdale airport. East of the turnpike, the Sawgrass connects with I-95 Exit 36C in Deerfield Beach.

The state Department of Transportation maintains and operates the turnpike, which has eight service plazas — most within 35 miles of one another. Each plaza has fast-food vendors such as Burger King, Taco Viva, Sbarro, Nathan's and Popeye's; fuel and limited vehicle repair service; telephones, restrooms, information brochures and snack machines; and 24-hour armed security.

For motorists' convenience and safety, call boxes are located every mile in each direction, as well as on the Sawgrass Expressway. The radio report uses four-digit codes to distinguish medical emergencies from vehicle mishaps. The turnpike also has its own division of Florida Highway Patrol officers for further security and assistance.

Ground Transportation

Car Rentals

Unless otherwise noted, the following car rental agencies use a toll-free number for reservations. Local numbers and addresses are included for agencies with a Boca Raton center:

ALAMO RENT-A-CAR
(800) 327-9633

AVIS RENT-A-CAR
(800) 331-1212
1 N.W. Yamato Rd.
at Dixie Hwy.   *241-0705*

BUDGET CAR AND TRUCK RENTAL
(800) 527-0700
10 E. Boca Raton Rd.   *750-7369*
Complimentary pickup   *750-7411*

DOLLAR RENT-A-CAR
(800) 421-6868
1950 Glades Rd.   *368-4288*

ENTERPRISE RENT-A-CAR
(800) 325-8007
10018 Spanish Isles Blvd.   *852-0031*

HERTZ RENT-A-CAR
(800) 654-3131
181 N.W. 13th St.   *392-9082*
5150 Town Center Cir.
In the Marriott Hotel   *391-1029*

NATIONAL CAR RENTAL
(800) 227-7368
1300 N.W. First Ave.   *395-1050*

SEARS RENT-A-CAR
10 E. Boca Raton Rd.   *750-7371*

VALUE RENT-A-CAR
(800) 468-2583
2000 N.W. 19th St.
In the Sheraton of Boca Raton   *395-4051*

Limousine and Luxury Transport

The word "limousine" is not a casual item in these parts. The Yellow Pages has copious display ads touting approximately 50 stretch connections. The more established firms include Stan Brady's Gold Coast Transporta-

tion of Boca Raton Inc., 368-8833, and Rod Cunningham's Boca Raton Transportation, 750-7800. Many firms also offer airport shuttle charters.

Choose your wheels, from Rolls-Royce to stretch Cadillac, Town Car and Phantom Classic. Besides corporate specialists, weddings and night-club packages, some folks are chauffeured full-time.

Trains

Amtrak has daily passenger service northbound and southbound, with stops in Deerfield Beach and Delray Beach. For reservations, call (800) USA RAIL.

Tri-County Commuter Rail, or Tri-Rail, operates commuter train service from West Palm Beach to Miami, with 15 stops and shuttle-bus service to three airports. Boca Raton's station is off Yamato Road on the grounds of the Embassy Suites Hotel, just west of I-95. The Delray Beach stop is at 345 S. Congress Avenue, behind the South Palm Beach County Administrative Complex. Service is provided seven days a week year round except for Thanksgiving and Christmas.

Weekdays, for example, four trains leave Boca Raton for West Palm Beach, with 28 minutes as the time posted to arrive at the airport station.

Tri-Rail fare is $3 each way, and all-day tickets and commuter packages are available. Double-deck rail cars are air-conditioned and equipped with comfortable seats and restroom facilities. For information, call (800) TRI-RAIL.

Rules of the Road

Before you start tooling along Florida's highways, there are a few things that you should know:

    * State law requires that all drivers and front-seat passengers wear seat belts at all times. Although motorists cannot be stopped when the law is violated, if motorists are stopped for another infraction and are not wearing seat belts, police will issue the driver a ticket. If the front-seat passenger is not wearing a seat belt and is 15 or younger, the driver is ticketed. Any passenger 16 or older not wearing a seat belt is ticketed. The fine for not using a seat belt is $32.50.

    * Children 3 and younger always must be in a child-restraint seat, whether they are in the front or back seat. Four- and 5-year-olds must be in a child-restraint seat or seat belt in either the front or back seats. Violation of the child restraint law results in a $155 fine and a three-point deduction from the motorist's driver's license.

Buses

Palm Tran is Palm Beach County's mass transit line and runs Monday through Saturday, with routes serving the areas from Jupiter/Tequesta south to Boca Raton. Seniors and the disabled also have **Dial-A-Ride** service. For information, call toll-free, 930-5123.

Bus fare is $1 one way, and exact change is required. Reduced fare is 50¢ one way for children ages 3 to 18, permanently disabled citizens and folks age 60 and older. Monthly commuter passes are available for $37, or $18.50 for those eligible for reduced fare. Passes are available at Building S-1440 of the Palm Beach International Airport.

Bus schedules are available at the Greater Boca Raton Chamber of Commerce, 1800 N. Dixie Highway, Boca Raton; the Delray Beach Chamber of Commerce, 64 S.E. Fifth Avenue, Delray Beach; and the Governmental Center, 301 N. Olive Avenue, West Palm Beach.

Routes vary within each municipality. For example: Route No. 25 in Delray Beach stops at the public beach, Atlantic Avenue and Federal Highway, the South County Courthouse, Delray Square, the Lakes of Delray and the Village of Oriole.

Ports

We explore boat travel in our Boating chapter. Cruise ships, which operate from Port Everglades in Fort Lauderdale, the Port of Palm Beach and the Port of Miami, are detailed in our Daycations chapter.

Photo:Zwing Advertising

Enjoy fine dining throughout Palm Beach County.

Inside
Restaurants

Do not be concerned that New York is a three-hour flight away; you'll be just fine here. We asked a leading Boca Raton businessman — a guy who has traveled the world and eaten in the finest restaurants, hosting celebrities and billionaires at his table — to list his favorite area restaurants. Assuming he'd mention the ones he promotes for business reasons, we thought his answer an intriguing invitation for you to get started right away: "There are so many great restaurants, my list starts with how close to home and whether it's our night out or we're taking the kids along."

Not to be overlooked when eating out is the creature waiting at home for the take-out box you bring back. Considering a 90-pound Labrador princess with excellent taste, we think twice about where to dine.

As the crossroads of the Americas and as part of one of the world's great resort areas, it's a natural that South Florida is a fantastic place to go foraging with knife and fork . . . and maybe a little garlic salt.

The tastes of South Florida are many, influenced by settlers from the Bahamas, Cuba, the Caribbean, Central and South America and the rest of the world. The cuisine offered here is inspired by traditional Southern American cooking, with bursts of inspiration from the people of many countries who come to our shores. They each add a dash of their own special spice to South Florida flavor.

Our Palm Beach County restaurants provide a gastronomic world tour, where you'll enjoy Southern fare such as fried chicken and Okeechobee catfish, collards and grits as well as the finest French cuisine; from sushi and sashimi to spaetzle and sauerkraut, lip-smacking barbecue ribs to Key lime pie that's so tangy your lips will pucker. From Cuba, we offer sweet platinitos maduros; from Russia, pelmeni; from Italy, pasta primavera. The world comes together here; many tastes do too.

The restaurants listed here are but a small sampler of the area's top spots to eat. Some are downright inexpensive. A few are pricey. Most fall somewhere in between. But remember, this list is a start, not the complete list, of excellent restaurants available here. There are dozens more good — no make that great — restaurants out there, and we urge you to be adventuresome. Try some of those out-of-the-way and off-the-beaten-path spots; truth is, it's tough to get a bad meal here. Palm Beachers are discriminating diners. Restaurants that fail to deliver wither and blow away quickly.

All the full-service restaurants we include accept all major credit cards.

Below is a dollar-sign designation to give you an idea of cost. It's based on dinner for two with appetizer, dessert and soft drink, coffee or tea, excluding what you might spend on cocktails, beer or wine and gratuity.

Here's our price code:

$25 or less	$
$26 to $50	$$
$51 to $75	$$$
$75 or more	$$$$

Regarding tips, participate in the practice here even if it's not an accepted custom "at home." Certain private clubs add a gratuity to the customer's bill, but generally speaking, the amount of the tip is open. The best guideline is 15 percent: If you leave only 10 percent, it means you got poor service; 20 percent means you got exceptional service.

Bon appetit!

Palm Beach County

Boca Raton

ADDISON'S
2 E. Camino Real
$$ 391-9800

Housed in the 1920s Mizner Administration Building, Addison's specializes in Northern Italian delicacies in an Old World atmosphere patterned after the home of El Greco in Spain. Addison's is also wedding central, a popular destination for nuptials and wedding receptions in the majestic courtyard dominated by towering banyan trees. Sunday brunch is a lavish

tradition, especially on holidays. Addison's also serves lunch and hosts private luncheons in its many dining rooms. Reservations are suggested.

BACI
344 Plaza Real, Mizner Park
$$ 362-8500

If you visit Baci, you'll see purple neon and hear purple prose, '90s style, as glitter babies of both sexes run their games on each other. Baci boasts stark, cavernous ceilings as a backdrop for contemporary black and white accents against the purple. And the counterpoint to this contrived aura is Baci's splendid food: designer pastries, sinful sauces, progressive pastas and home-baked foccacia dusted with basil. Baci serves lunch and dinner, and the bar crowd stays late.

BISTRO L'EUROPE
346 Plaza Real, Mizner Park
$$ 368-4488

The younger sister of Cafe L'Europe opened with Mizner Park's debut in December 1990. See this chapter's Palm Beach section for more about the Worth Avenue legend right here in Boca. The Bistro is a favorite stop after a movie or shopping at Mizner Park, and it serves a continental cuisine. Lunch and dinner are served. Reservations are recommended.

BISTRO ZENITH
Regency Court
3011 Yamato Rd.
$ 997-2570

If you closed your eyes from the parking lot at Regency Court until you reached the doorway of Bistro Zenith, you might get the feeling you'd landed in a chic nightspot in Northern Eu-

rope or Scandinavia . . . maybe Helsinki or Copenhagen, even Stockholm's Old Town, where younger restaurateurs are carving out cosmopolitan cells of magnetism that draw diners for the food and the alternative destination value amid all those centuries of tradition.

Owners Karin and Craig Larson have scored a hit in their first year, with an open-kitchen, let's-order-some-of-that dynamism scooting around the room. A friendly staff enhances the feeling that "you've come to the right place."

Chef Joseph Hahn did his homework to begin with, completing college in South Carolina before joining the culinary team at Trump Taj Mahal in Atlantic City, New Jersey,

on his way to Boca. He likes to balance traditional American dishes with Oriental and Mediterranean influences . . . or Southwestern whenever the planets line up, as they do often at Bistro Zenith.

The decor is high-tech, with neon accents and a bemused sort of dish-ran-away-with-the-spoon attitude played out in a motif of sun, moon and stars. Go there hungry and be adventurous. There's plenty of seafood, meats, decadent desserts, daring appetizers and an ambitious wine list. Loaves of foccacia bread arrive promptly, and the chef has observed somewhere that true bistro hounds prefer to dip bread in olive oil rather than slather it with butter.

Lunch and dinner are served. Reservations are recommended.

BOCA RATON RESORT AND CLUB
501 E. Camino Real
$$$$ *395-3000, Ext. 3640*

Restaurants in The Cloister include the famous **Top of the Tower Italian Restaurant** for fine dining and panoramic views of the city, lunch and dinner; **Chauncey's Court** for more casual meals at lunch and dinner; the **Gazebo Bar** for lunch and cocktails; the **Lobby Espresso** for specialty beverages and snacks; the **El Lago Lounge** for cocktails; and the **Patio** for breakfast. Food quality is exceptional and service is legendary throughout this historic landmark.

At the Resort's nearby Boca Beach Club is fine oceanfront dining at **Nick's Fish Market**; the **Cabana Restaurant** with terrace seating available serving breakfast, lunch and a buffet dinner; **Cappy's Bar** for lunch and cocktails; and **Nick's Lounge** for cocktails and dancing. The Resort is available to hotel guests and membersof the Premier Club. Reservations are recommended.

CARIBBEAN GRILL
1300 N.W. Second Ave.
$-$$ *362-0161*

Boca Raton's Hispanic community comes to this tidy restaurant located on the northeast corner of Glades Road and Second Avenue for tasty Cuban food prepared and served with love.

Most folks are surprised to learn Cuban fare isn't like its spicy Mexican counterpart, but it is incredibly addicting. Typical Cuban dishes feature pork, beef and seafood specialties, lots of rice, beans and plantains, which are large fruits of the banana family, cooked and served several ways, all of them delicious. Another popular vegetable is the yuca, which tastes like a potato.

Caribbean Grill's entrees include a choice of side dishes, but be sure to opt for the platinitos maduros (sweet plantains) and congris, a beans-and-rice dish. Among the best of traditional Cuban cuisine is Ropa Vieja, a spicy beef dish that translates to "old clothes." The Bistec de Pallomilla, grilled thinly sliced round steak marinated in an oil-and-garlic sauce called mojo and served with grilled onions, is also a treat. Another favorite is Lechon Asado y Deshuesado, roast pork pulled apart, then doused with mojo and served with thinly sliced onions. Squeeze a little lime juice on it and send your taste buds to heaven.

Open for lunch and dinner.

CARMEN'S
Radisson Bridge Resort
999 E. Camino Real
$$$ *368-9500*

Panoramic views of the city and the ocean beyond complement the gorgeous food, whether it's Sunday brunch, a four-course prix-fixe dinner or the Tuesday night seafood buffet extravaganza (with mesquite-roasted prime rib for sissies). Live entertainment rounds out the package Wednesday through Saturday, and happy hour is Tuesday through Friday, featuring complimentary hors d'oeuvres and special drink prices.

There is a choice of self parking and valet service.

CARSON'S
5798 N. Federal Hwy.
$$ *995-RIBS*

Listen up, South Siders! Carson's is making another clean sweep. With six family-owned restaurants in Chicago, Dean Carson has opened his first Florida rib house. The place is squeaky clean, the food marvelous and served in generous portions. Delectables include the famous barbecue ribs, juicy pork chops, barbecue chicken and combo orders of ribs, chicken and filet mignon. Steak options are the 12-ounce filet and the 16-ounce and 22-ounce New York Strips. The Garbage Salad is terrific with hearts of palm; there's also Caesar, a classic Greek and a handful of custom dressings. Sandwiches include barbecue pork and beef, burgers and charbroiled chicken. Entrees and sandwiches come with cole slaw and a choice of baked potato, the outrageous double-baked, au gratin, potato skins or French fries. And you can have a garden salad or Caesar in place of the cole slaw for a small extra charge. Desserts are Eli's Cheesecake, apple pie à la mode, Blackout Cake and Gold Brick Sundae.

Carson's marinates meat in its own sauce then smokes it slowly in a hickory wood-burning pit. Ask your server for the nightly dinner specials. Carson's has a full-service bar with beer on tap. The restaurant is large with an open kitchen in the rear, comfortable booths, oak plank flooring and brick accents. The artwork is contemporary abstracts.

Be sure to check out Carson's take-out service . . . one look at the cartons and you know they're serious about those ribs. Whether you order them shipped around the country, (800) GIV-RIBS, or drive over to Carson's and pick them up, the container is heavy-duty cardboard, 11-by-15-inches, with printed instructions on the box for re-heating your meal. Carson's is now open for lunch and valet parking is available. Open for lunch and dinner Monday through Friday and dinner only Saturday and Sunday.

THE CHEESECAKE FACTORY
5530 Glades Rd.
$$ *393-0344*

What a place! Dating to its first operation opened in 1978 in Beverly Hills, The Cheesecake Factory created a stir. It actually started out with the owner's mother's cheesecake served with coffee. Today, there are 14 locations including the one that arrived in Boca Raton in February. A very extensive and eclectic lunch and dinner menu includes an elaborate Sunday Brunch, big luscious sandwiches, exotic salads, plenty of pastas and Oriental and Southwest specialties.

Did we mention cheesecake? Lunch alone has more than 30 varieties such as White Chocolate Raspberry Truffle, Kahlua Almond Fudge, Hugs 'N' Kisses, Chocolate Pecan Turtle and Double Chocolate Upside Down Jack Daniels. The Cheescake Factory ships them all over "next day air" if you call (800) 726-4225 between 9 AM and 4:30 PM Pacific Time. Friends who frequent the Newport Beach,

Photo: Four Seasons Ocean Grand Hotel

The Ocean Bistro at Palm Beach's Four Seasons Ocean Grand Hotel is a casually elegant poolside escape for breakfast or dinner.

California, location say it's not unusual for a two-hour wait. Which people seem not to mind because the 15-page menu keeps 'em occupied.

The Cheesecake Factory already needs to expand, with plans to spread out in the fall. The decor is knockout deco, very sophisticated and well-done. The only other Cheesecake Factory location in Florida is Coco Walk in Coconut Grove. This one in Boca Raton is a destination all by itself.

CHINESE CONNECTION RESTAURANT AND LOUNGE
2200 W. Glades Rd.
$$-$$$ 395-4858

Comfortably nestled in Glades Plaza, this gem of a restaurant is easy to miss, but it's a shame if you do. The food, service and prices are all excellent. The menu is extensive and diversified, with a wide variety of chef's specialties and Mandarin and Szechuan favorites.

It's open for lunch and dinner everyday, but it doesn't open until 3 PM on Sunday, so go for a late lunch or an early dinner.

THE CUBAN CAFE
3350 N.W. Boca Raton Blvd.
Plumtree Centre
$-$$
750-8860

From its oxblood-red tile floor and wrought-iron grill work to the extensive menu, Cuban Cafe takes the best of Old Cuba and brings it to Boca Raton.

All the Cuban specialties are offered here. For those who are not yet acquainted with Cuban fare, a great idea is one of the cafe's four sampler platters.

For seafood lovers, the Zarzuela de Mariscos is a treat, loaded with lobster, shrimp, scallops, cuttlefish, crab claws and fish fillets over a bed of rice. Also tasty is the Camarones al Ajillo, with huge shrimp sauteed in white wine and garlic.

For a delightful topper for your meal, try flan, a caramel custard that's rich, sweet and delightful and goes nicely with Cafe Cubano.

The Cuban Cafe is open for lunch and dinner Monday through Friday and for dinner only on Saturday and Sunday.

DIRTY MOE'S OYSTER BOAT
Spanish River Blvd.
$-$$ 395-3513

Quiet it's not. Quaint it's not. Its ambiance comes right off the docks, with barnacle-covered crawfish traps at the entrance, picnic tables and a few fish nets strung up around the bar. But for almost 15 years, Dirty Moe's has been about Florida's bounty from the seas, cold libations (be sure and try a Rum Runner) and camaraderie.

Some folks go no further on the menu than the appetizers, where they find Moe's wings, smoked marlin dip and conch fritters. There's even Louisiana crawfish sold by the pound.

Don't pass by the conch salad in the rush to try Moe's famed steamed rock shrimp. We recommend it unseasoned. Other seafood specialties include Maine or Florida lobster and crab, fish, oyster and clam dinners. Top off your meal with a slice of Key lime pie.

Dirty Moe's is open daily from 11 AM until late seven days a week.

THE GAZEBO
4199 N. Federal Hwy.
$$$ 395-6033

Tucked next to a branch bank, this tiny oasis of civility is pure delight for all who enter. Prominent civic leader Kathy Sellas has mastered a marvel of formal Continental fare that remains consistently exceptional over the years. Items in great demand include the Dover sole, that arrives fresh daily. Gazebo takes a late summer break, so it's best to call for Kathy's vacation schedule. There's plenty of parking and reservations are suggested.

HOUSTON'S
1900 Executive Center Cir.
$ 998-0055

Consistently good service and high-quality groceries make Houston's American menu extra popular year round. The restaurant serves lunch and dinner.

Diners like the crisp, casual surroundings and the quaint patio waiting area. You can't make reservations, but you'll be glad you waited for a table (usually about a half-hour). Fish is especially good here, and there's plenty to choose from in chicken, burgers, salads, superior soups and steaks. Parking is plentiful and valet service is available.

LA VIEILLE MAISON
770 E. Palmetto Park Rd.
$$$$ 391-6701

French for "the old house," this landmark establishment rests comfortably on some impressive laurels. Founded by Leonce Picot of Down Under fame in Fort Lauderdale, La Vieille Maison has been rated among

Florida's finest dining experiences since it opened. A restored historic two-story Mizneresque residence, it revels in the mystique of a Mediterranean villa. Ideal for special dinners and nods to civilized tradition, the restaurant specializes in prix-fixe multi-course meals, with two seatings a night. Wines and champagne selections are extensive. Reservations required.

LA VILLETTA

4351 N. Federal Hwy.
$$$ 362-8403

An inspired addition to the local Italian school, La Villetta arrived almost four years ago. It's tucked against the north side of a strip center on the west side of Federal Highway, so keep your eyes peeled. Be ready for marvelous, inventive vegetables and imaginative pasta pleasers, with a superb wine list to complement the meal. The chef is ingenious with entrees and decadent desserts. Reservations are suggested for this dinner-only spot.

MARIO'S OF BOCA

2200 Glades Rd.
$ 392-5595

Everyone goes to Mario's sooner or later, sometimes just for a fix of garlic rolls. A very busy place, especially in season, with droves of folks showing up for a tasty noontime buffet served Monday through Sunday. For dinner, there are plenty of pasta dishes, veal, chicken and seafood, as well as pizza and casual Italian fare. Tony Bova is the owner. Great value and tasty food make Mario's a winner for lunch and dinner. Mario's is in the Glades Plaza shopping center west of I-95.

MAX'S GRILLE

404 Plaza Real, Mizner Park
$$$$ 368-0080

"Eclectic" is the buzzword here, at a restaurant positively obsessed with being the best. Diners come out the big winners.

The Max's Grille staff takes some chances with its menu but turns out imaginative, superlative dishes presented artistically.

Among the appetizers, don't pass by the chicken wings with chili-lime peanut glaze. In this dish, the humble fowl's wing soars to new heights.

Among the entrees, some favorites to consider: maple mustard glazed salmon with baby spinach and citrus herbed couscous, and in homage to Japanese culinary tradition, the piquant yellowfin tuna with Basmati rice, vegetable stir-fry, mirin-soy glaze and wasabi cream. (Hint: Ask for it medium.)

Is there an entree more plain than meat loaf? Not at Max's. The Max's Grille meat loaf with spinach, smashed potatoes and wild mushroom cabernet sauce will change your mind forever.

As appetizing as the entrees are, try to save room for dessert. Max's offerings are delightful and sinfully indulgent.

Max's Grille is open for lunch and dinner, with a weekend brunch starting at 11:30 AM.

MIDO'S JAPANESE RESTAURANT

508 Via de Palmas, Ste. 76
Royal Palm Plaza
$$-$$$ 361-9683

For those who love sushi and sashimi, this is heaven. But Mido's is also heavenly for those who enjoy Japanese cuisine but can't quite accept the notion of eating raw fish.

The sushi and sashimi are available in many ways: à la carte for appetizers or in dinner combinations. Also available are chirashi, which is assorted raw fish on a bed of sushi rice, or the Norimaki dinner, featuring a California roll, tuna roll and vegetable roll. Even better yet are the sushi and sashimi platter or Mido's Boat, a wooden schooner (no, not a real one) filled with a special assortment of sushi and sashimi.

For those who prefer their Japanese food served steaming, there is plenty to choose from, including several varieties of teriyaki, an excellent tempura platter, sukiyaki, shabu-shabu and hibachi. Four special seasonal platters and three special platters — samurai steak, shogun platter and the Sea of Japan platter — round out the offerings. All dinners include a light, delicious miso and salad.

As it is with most Japanese restaurants, presentation is as important as taste, and both are superb at Mido's. Take for example, an item as simple and necessary as wasabi, the doughy green horseradish that accompanies sushi and sashimi. In most restaurants, your lump of it is deposited on your plate. Here, it is sculpted into the center of a cucumber cup cut to resemble a flower. It's a small touch but leaves a powerful impression.

Mido's is open for lunch and dinner.

MISSISSIPPI SWEETS BBQ Co.
2399 N. Federal Hwy.
$-$$ 394-6779

The sweet, lip-smacking barbecue sauce that's famous in southern Mississippi is what keeps folks coming back to this small restaurant on Federal Highway. So does the collection of roof-scorching hot sauces you can douse your pork or chicken with, for those who appreciate the yin and yang of fine Southern cuisine. The pork and chicken specialties are the stars and include a barbecued or rotisseried half-chicken or a full slab of baby back ribs. Each dinner is served with a pair of side dishes; make sure the deep-fried sweet potato slices are among yours. Ask about the day's homemade dessert specials, and don't miss the Snickers pie or the Mississippi Mudslide Eclair when it's offered.

Open for lunch and dinner Monday through Friday and for dinner on the weekend.

MYKONOS RESTAURANT
2499 N. Federal Hwy.
$$ 392-5258

Owners John Theodosakos and Pete Ziros welcome newcomers as if family were spending the day in their island village. Be hungry and festive, for musicians often entertain in the full-service lounge.

Start with a salad, as they're fresh and available in small or large sizes. The Village variety has tomatoes, onions, cucumbers, feta cheese, olive oil and Greek olives. There's a traditional Greek salad, the Athenian style with Romaine, scallions and dill, or you can tame it out with a Caesar, also small or large.

Succulent hot appetizers are Bakaliaro, crispy fried cod served with Skordalia (potatoes, garlic, olive oil and vinegar), Spanakopita (spinach pie), tender fried Kalamarakia (baby squid) and Oktapodaki Sharas (broiled octopus).

Greek delicacies include Arni Psito (roast lamb), Mousaka (layers of fried eggplant, sauteed ground meat, cheeses, topped with Bechamel sauce), Pastitsio (Greek macaroni with sauteed ground meat, cheeses and Bechamel sauce) and Mosharaki Fileto (young tender beef served with rice and a vegetable). Fish dishes include snapper, grouper, swordfish and sea scallops. The Scampi is delicious, with ample shrimp served tender and not overcooked. Shrimp à la Mykonos is sauteed with feta cheese in a light tomato sauce, and Poseidon's Platter is a fillet of snapper, shrimp, scallops and crab meat in a light feta and tomato sauce. Broiled items include lamb, beef or chicken shish kabobs; broiled lamb chops; broiled quail marinated in Greek herbs; Alexander's chicken, marinated and sauteed with broccoli, mushrooms and red peppers; Filetakia Sofrito, pieces of filet mignon sauteed in wine sauce and mushrooms. There's also plain American filet mignon, charcoal broiled.

Desserts are bakhlava, Greek surprises and cakes each day, plus homemade Greek yogurt with nuts and honey. Mykonos serves imported and domestic beer, champagnes, white and red Greek wines as well as those of France, Italy and California. The bar offers weekday happy hour specials from 3:30 to 7 PM. Mykonos is open seven days with a casually elegant environment for lunch and dinner. Lunch is weekdays from 11 AM to 3 PM.

PETE'S BOCA RATON
7940 Glades Rd.
$$ 487-1600

There's plenty to do at multidimensional Pete's, as we mention in the chapter on Nightlife. The surroundings invite the vacation frame of mind, while owner Pete Boinis gets serious about gourmet dining in the contemporary American style. He knows you don't all want seafood, although his kitchen is expert with poached salmon and such, so the menu has plenty of prime beef, New York strip, inventive pastas and salads, veal and chicken. Service is great, and valet parking is available. Live music keeps the joint jumping. Pete's serves lunch and dinner seven days a week.

RENZO'S OF BOCA
5999 N. Federal Hwy.
$$ 994-3495

Regular customers gladly wait for a table and a talk with the no-nonsense owner, Renzo Sciortino, who opened the restaurant five years ago. Some folks even drive down from Boynton Beach, where he had another place for five years. Renzo also is head of the family that operates this slice of home-style Italia with gourmet style and flavor. The crew includes Renzo, his wife, Sarah, their daughters, cousins and godfathers, maybe.

The emphasis is on fresh food, consistently prepared for people who

Photo: Delray Beach Community Redevelopment Agency

Beach-goers trek between the dunes to approach and leave the beach in Delray.

return again and again. Seating is limited to 95, so call ahead. The Caesar salad is one of the freshest in town, and very popular with the lunch crowd on weekdays. Great garlic bread comes to the table piping hot.

Among the most popular entrees is the Yellowtail Snapper Livornese, served in a sauce of white wine, onions, capers and a touch of marinara. Another favorite is the Shrimp Zingara, with mushrooms, green peppers, onions, garlic and marinara sauce. Top of the heap is Angel Hair Veneziana with shrimp, scallops and cognac cream in a light marinara over cappelini. Sides include crispy, nouveau-style fresh broccoli or spinach with garlic. Baked dishes are extra-good, including the lasagna with tiny peas. Do make room for a cappuccino with desserts, made fresh daily. Renzo serves fine wines, imported and domestic beer.

Dinner is served seven days a week, and reservations are recommended. The restaurant is in the Renzo Plaza on the west side of Federal Highway and just north of the light at Jeffrey Street. Valet parking is complimentary.

TOM'S PLACE
7251 N. Federal Hwy.
$-$$ 997-0920

Drop your voice a bit and speak with reverence when you say the name of South Florida's best ribs restaurant. There are many good barbecue joints and some superb ones in South Florida, but there is only one Tom's Place.

It wasn't all that many years ago that Tom and Helen Wright had folks lined a quarter-mile up Glades Road at Dixie Highway on Saturdays for their specialty ribs caressed with world-class sweet and spicy sauce. Tom's was just a take-out place then. Later, the building was renovated so folks could sit down and pig out on a daily basis. Now, the place has moved north to its more spacious present location.

Most dinner entrees are served with a choice of two vegetables. The collard greens, a Southern tradition, are always superb here. You can spice them up with a dash of hot sauce or the bottle of pepper vinegar that's on your table.

Two excellent dishes are the Rib Combo, with a half-rack of baby back ribs, a half-rack of St. Louis ribs and veggies or the Seafood Combo, featuring catfish or sole and shrimp. If you haven't tried catfish, do. It's a tender, mild fish that's fabulous when batter-fried. Southern side specialties include fried okra or hush puppies; and don't pass up the peach cobbler or the sweet potato pie to top off your meal.

Tom's is open Tuesday through Saturday for lunch and dinner and

---

Insiders' Tips

From December through March, Insiders go to their favorite restaurants before 6 PM to beat the seasonal crowds.

on Mondays for dinner during the season.

TooJay's

5030 Champion Blvd.	241-5903
3013 Yamato Rd.	997-9911
$ (both locations)	

TooJay's is known for its Killer Cake made with four kinds of chocolate, and there are 10 locations (look for them throughout this chapter) to test your will to live. Fresh, fresh, fresh ingredients and mounds of food at great prices are the signature of TooJay, a catchy deli-style upscale diner started by Mark J. Katzenberg and Jay Brown. Gourmet salads, pastries, cheesecake, even somebody's grandma's meat loaf now and then, plus nightly dinner specials and overstuffed deli sandwiches keep the fans packin' it in. Even if you don't know your way around Palm Beach County, you're likely to trip over a TooJay's. There are also locations in Stuart, 2440 S.E. Federal Highway, 287-6514; Hollywood, 4401 Sheridan Street, (305) 962-9909; and Altamonte Springs near Orlando, 515 E. Altamonte Drive, 830-1770.

WATERCOLORS CAFE

Radisson Bridge Resort of Boca Raton
999 E. Camino Real
$$ 368-9500

What a way to start the day! Outdoors overlooking the Intracoastal Waterway, breakfast is especially satisfying at Watercolors Cafe, one of two restaurants inside the Radisson Bridge Resort. Choices are light Continental fare, luscious omelettes, delectable Indian River French Toast and grilled blintzes, and fresh bakery items. For lunch Watercolors has soups and chowders for lunch; entree salads such as Thai chicken, Bridge Caesar and fajita taco salad; designer pizzas such as Grilled Vegetable, Apple Smoked Bacon with sea scallops, and the Boca Pizza with Maine lobster, shrimp, scallops and catch of the day. Specialties are fajitas and shrimp quesadillas.

On to dinner, with luscious appetizers, salads, sandwiches and entrees such as Fettuccini Nicole, Cavatelli, seafood grill and Key West Pepperpot with mahi mahi, shrimp and scallops in a basil tomato broth and served over cappelini.

Deerfield Beach

THE COVE

1754 S.E. Third Ct.
$-$$ (305) 421-9271

The Cove takes the term "greenhouse effect" to a new dimension. This open-air restaurant and marina is a breezy oasis for tired boaters and hungry landlubbers alike. Plants — hundreds of them — hang throughout, giving a restful feel. Enjoy one of the Cove's signature fruity frozen drinks to cool down, then consider the menu, which stays light and features homemade chowders and salad, seafood and sandwich entrees.

One lunchtime favorite is the Chicken Waldorf Salad, brimming with white-meat chicken, white grapes, apple chunks, walnuts and raisins. On the evening menu, the Abaco Dolphin, broiled in lemon, white wine and butter and topped with a mushroom-sherry sauce, is yummy.

The Cove is open throughout the week for lunch and dinner. On Sundays, you can also get breakfast. And those of you who like to stay out 'til the wee hours will find friends here.

Delray Beach

BOSTON'S ON THE BEACH
40 S. Ocean Blvd.
$$ *278-3364*

In 1994, it took a three-day birthday bash to celebrate the 15th anniversary of owner Perry Don Francisco's brainstorm to serve South Florida a modest crock of Beantown. The Worcester, Massachusetts, native was here on vacation with plans to complete his doctorate in education administration. Instead, he founded a textbook example of the successful eatery.

Just south of Atlantic Avenue on Highway A1A, a perky blue canopy over the veranda shades you from the rays while you sample the raw bar, the Smoked Fish Spread, a Boston basket of fried shrimp, chicken fingers, onion rings and French fries or maybe some fresh Ipswich steamers. Suds are on tap alongside the full bar. Unlike many tourist snares, the lobster trap here is a great idea, providing various sizes of live Maine lobster, the twin lobster special or stuffed lobster with a thick New York strip. Definitely come back for the swordfish, red snapper or dolphin and for the Nantucket, a shrimp and scallop combo in Scampi sauce over linguine. Also available are Worcester and Boston burgers, hot and cold sandwiches and New England-style rolls.

Inside is the famous bar and dining room, quaint and casual with worn woods, ceiling fans and a section of bar stool-height tables for the view outside and TV sports inside. Shorts is the uniform of choice in this climate. Usually a prominent stop during Art and Jazz festivals and Summer Nights on the Avenue, Boston's entertainment is described in the chapter on Nightlife.

Boston's on the Beach is open for lunch and dinner every day, and the restaurant serves a casual breakfast on the weekend.

BOSTON'S UPPER DECK
40 S. Ocean Blvd.
$$ *278-3364*

Bursting at the seams with the crowds downstairs, owner Perry Don Francisco and ace chef Felix Adams conjured up a whole new dining experience above Boston's on the Beach. A separate kitchen upstairs accommodates the new dining room and outdoor terrace with panoramic ocean views.

With any luck, the Upper Deck will continue Boston's Sunset Dinner for Two, available Sunday through Thursday: a starter of either New England clam chowder, Seafood Minestrone, house salad or Caesar; entree selections such as Chicken Oscar, New York strip, pork tenderloin and yellowtail snapper; dessert; espresso or cappuccino; and a bottle of wine, the Hess Chardonnay or Cabernet Sauvignon.

If you like fish, try the blackened swordfish with chilled mango sauce or the yellowtail snapper in beurre blanc (white butter) sauce. And if you don't prefer seafood, try Boston's New

York strip, served in a shallot/red wine/mushroom demi glaze, with the chef's famous garlic mashed potatoes and scrumptious sautéed vegetables. Bright crunchy pea pods, summer squash, carrots, broccoli and bok choy. Other nightly specials: grilled portabella pizza, Penne Bolognese, Cappelini Con Cinque Fungi Alfredo, Veal Chop Marsala, and Land and Sea — a petite filet mignon with Maine lobster. For dessert we recommend the white chocolate raspberry cheesecake. On the lighter side, there are frozen sorbets and double-dipped Sicilian cannolis.

The Upper Deck lunch menu includes some dinner-size salads including Chicken Caesar or Blackened Swordfish Caesar; hot and cold sandwiches; and entrees of chicken, pasta, shrimp, fish, New York strip, roast pork and the Tornados of Beef stuffed with crabmeat and Maine lobster.

Beverages include naughty tropical specialties, frozen concoctions Jimmy Buffett would sing about. After the dining room closes, people usually wander downstairs to hear the band.

Plan ahead, because it's usually sold out for the season — mostly to that cult clientele from Worcester. You'll find dinner every day of the week and lunch too on Friday, Saturday and Sunday.

BUSCH'S SEAFOOD RESTAURANT

840 E. Atlantic Ave.   278-7600
$$

Established in 1942, Busch's has been a mainstay in South County — most recently in Delray Beach, after moving from Ocean Ridge. Seafood is the specialty here and accounts for about 95 percent of the dishes served. But landlubbers can also find prime Angus beef on the menu.

Adding to the ambiance is Busch's location along the Intracoastal Waterway, affording every diner a view of the water. If you prefer to arrive by boat, docking is available. Indoor and terrace dining add to the experience. Typical attire is dressy casual. Busch's does not accept reservations.

Hours vary according to the season: In summer, the restaurant is open from 4:30 to 10 PM Monday through Friday and 11:30 AM to 10 PM on Saturday and Sunday. During the tourist season, Busch's extends its hours: It opens at 11:30 AM daily and closes at 10 PM Sunday through Thursday, 11 PM on Friday and Saturday.

ELWOOD'S DIXIE BARBECUE

301 Atlantic Ave.   272-7427
$

In the heart of downtown Delray Beach, Elwood's set up shop in an old gas station.

Patrons now fill the seats both inside the former garage and outside where car once pulled in for a fill-up. Specialties include ribs, chicken, barbecue, catfish and collards. This is not the place for folks who dislike loud noise, but fun-lovers will get a kick when trains pass on the railroad track next door.

Lunch is available Monday through Saturday from 11 AM to 3:30 PM. Dinner is served from 5 to 11 PM Monday through Saturday and 6 to 10 PM on Sunday. The outdoor bar is open until 2 AM.

FIFTH AVENUE GRILL

821 S. Federal Hwy.   265-0122
$$

Fifth Avenue Grill touts itself as a restaurant that will serve you the "best steak you've ever had." Under the same ownership as Boynton Beach's Banana Boat, this eatery draws large crowds for both lunch and dinner. Wood paneling and a large brick fireplace create a warm, New England club feel.

In addition to steak, menu items include seafood, pasta and sandwiches. Reservations are suggested for parties of six or more, but smaller groups cannot reserve tables.

The Grill is open for lunch from 11:30 AM Monday through Saturday and from noon on Sunday. It closes at 10 PM Sunday through Thursday and at 11 PM on Friday and Saturday.

THE LITTLE MERMAID RESTAURANT

505 N.E. Fifth Ave.   276-6900
$$$

For Scandinavian fare, this is the place to go. Delft porcelain decorates this cozy restaurant that is tucked away in a small strip mall. The menu items get their names from Hans Christian Anderson stories. Of course, salmon is big here; choices include gravlaks and The Golden Treasure, a salmon fillet that is split lengthwise, lightly battered and sautéed and served with grilled onions and béarnaise sauce. Also on the menu are lamb, veal, pork and, yes, Danish meatballs.

The restaurant is open Wednesday through Sunday from 5 to 9 PM.

Jupiter

TOOJAY'S

4050 U.S. Hwy. 1 S.
$ 627-5555

One of 10 South Florida locations, this deli-style eatery is a hit for the food and the prices. See the Boca Raton listing for details.

Lake Worth

COUCO PAZZO

915 Lake Ave.
$$ 585-0320

Funny thing about a secret weapon . . . they work best in the holster that fits. Fortunately, for diners who know where to look, Couco Pazzo is the perfect fit for chef/proprietor Marty Servidio.

Bigger than a breadbasket but not by much, Couco Pazzo has lace curtains, a handful of tables and a long list of people wanting to be called when a reservation opens up. Beverages include wine and beer.

The complimentary bruschetta is addictive, so you'll need some time to indulge an appetizer, perhaps sauteed shrimp, before the Caesar salad, an entree and dessert with a cappuccino. Marty has gills . . . how else to explain his way with fresh fish that flirts with almonds? You'll find yourself going back for the veal dishes, especially Saltimbocca, the Chicken Paillard, the great vegetables, noble pastas and irresistible desserts, including traditional tiramisu, profiteroles and a white chocolate cheesecake New York never experienced.

Photo: Insiders' Guide Inc. /RNI

Gourmet seafood dishes are served in many area restaurants.

L'ANJOU

717 Lake Ave.
$$$ 582-7666

Step inside off bustling Lake Avenue and, *voila*! You're suddenly whisked into a comfortable French country home, amid old friends and enjoying delicious meals that are neither *haute* nor haughty. The lacy, diaphanous curtains make downtown Lake Worth disappear. The pleasant surroundings allow those tight muscles to relax.

The menu is a solid one, built around fish, veal, beef and chicken entrees, many with a delightful poivre sauce with crushed peppercorns.

L'Anjou is open for dinner daily.

TOOJAY'S

419 Lake Ave.
$ 582-8684

Just one of 10 TooJay's throughout South Florida, this eatery scores big for its tempting food and prices. See the Boca Raton listing for details.

Lighthouse Point

CAP'S PLACE

2765 N.E. 28th Ct.
$$ (305) 941-0418

Eugene "Cap" Knight died in 1964, but the quaint restaurant that bears his name lives on.

Back during Prohibition, Cap's operated as a speakeasy and gaming club, but the restaurant's shining moment came in January 1942, when President Franklin D. Roosevelt and British Prime Minister Winston Churchill took a break from their secret war conferences nearby and dined at the restaurant. The notables and the notorious have found their way to

Cap's, among them Beatle George Harrison, slugger Joe DiMaggio, boxer Jack Dempsey and actress Susan Hayward.

Years back, Cap, attired in his customary bib overalls and flannel shirt, used to sit in his rocking chair by the kitchen door and check every plate. Cap's been gone a long time now, but this rustic bit of Floridiana lives on.

Next to the famed hearts-of-palm salad that accompanies each meal, sea fare is the strongest part of the menu at Cap's — although the fried chicken is delicious too. Your server will let you know what's in season and available.

The listed address is for Cap's dock. You'll need to take a boat ride to the spit of land the restaurant sits upon. Turn east off Federal Highway at N.E. 24th Street and follow the signs.

Cap's Place is open nightly for dinner until about 10 PM.

Palm Beach

CAFE L'EUROPE

The Esplanade
150 Worth Ave.
$$$ 655-4020

The restaurant combines the sophistication and tradition one expects from the Continent with a relaxed bistro mood. You'll enjoy being here, regardless of the occasion. The atmosphere mingles dark woods, snowy linens, fresh flowers and soft lighting; the dining room duplicates the European fine dining experience well.

For lunch the bistro offers magnificent pasta dishes, salads, soups and sandwiches. For a really decadent cap

Bistro L'Europe at Mizner Park offers indoor and outdoor dining.

to an afternoon of shopping, visit the Champagne & Caviar Bar. The Cafe bistro also serves aprés-luncheon fare and dinner. Cafe L'Europe is also ready for the after-theater crowd if you reserve in advance. Definitely make reservations for dinner.

Note: At press time (August 1995) Cafe L'Europe was in the process of moving a stone's throw away from Worth Avenue to a location at South County Road on the corner of Brazilian Avenue. Call for details about when they will reopen.

HAMBURGER HEAVEN
314 South County Rd.
$ 655-5277
Since 1945, Hamburger Heaven is where Palm Beach's beautiful people go when they're tired of glitzy and ditsy cuisine and hankering to hunker down over wonderful soups, salads and comfort food, such as the Heavenly Hamburgers, smothered with famed sweet pepper relish.

Be sure and check out the daily specials and the fabulous desserts.

Hamburger Heaven is open Monday through Saturday from 7:30 AM to 8 PM during the season, 7:30 AM to 4 PM during the summer. It's closed on Sunday.

JANEIRO RESTAURANT AND WINE BAR
191 Bradley Pl.
$$$ 659-5223
As saucy and sassy as Rio itself, Janeiro beckons you into the Zebra Room and the Main Dining Room, where even the chairs wear frocks of their own tied with sashes. Charming and imaginative, Janeiro serves such delicacies as pecan-crusted Chilean salmon, Brazilian white and black bean and potato-crusted snapper, Black Truffle Madiera Sauce on the Tournado, vegetables in lemon beurre blanc and a potato puree with roasted

garlic. Appetizers range from Carpaccio and Fricassee of Escargot to sesame-crusted seared rare tuna, gazpacho and Napoleons of grilled shiitake mushrooms with roasted peppers. Diners are entertained with a piano, saxophone and drum trio. Palm Beach's only wine bar, Janeiro serves 25 varieties by the glass and more than 175 bottles from around the world. Janeiro is just north of Bradley's Saloon. Valet parking is available. You may dine at lunch or dinner all week long.

THE OCEAN BISTRO
Four Seasons Ocean Grand Hotel
2800 S. Ocean Blvd.
$$$ 582-2800

More casual dining than at The Restaurant, described next, The Ocean Bistro serves breakfast, lunch and dinner inside and outdoors on the terrace under a canopy, poolside and overlooking the Atlantic Ocean. From fruit-stuffed orange French toast to saffron pasta sheets with eggplant, you know Chef Hubert des Marais has been here. See the chapter on Accommodations for information on staying at The Four Seasons Ocean Grand.

THE RESTAURANT
Four Seasons Ocean Grand Hotel
2800 S. Ocean Blvd.
$$$$ 582-2800

People talk about The Restaurant in somewhat hushed tones, not because the atmosphere is stuffy but because it takes the fine dining experience to a new level of primo seldom achieved. Noted dining critic and author Robert Tolf gives The Restaurant four stars for being an "Extraor-dinary Performer On All Fronts." Aside from Tolf, unpublished dining aficionados who roam from South Beach to Palm Beach say the Ocean Grand Restaurant is the ultimate.

Chef Hubert des Marais has a way with flavors, seasonings and textures, a gift he credits to his grandmother, who infused her grandson with a love of fresh ingredients and healthful combinations. Outside his kitchen is an herb garden where he also grows his own citrus, creating a tempting aroma that wafts throughout the Four Seasons courtyard. Des Marais favors an eclectic mix of Southern, Caribbean, Native American and South American cuisines. His followers are spoiled by the chef's previous successes at the Ritz-Carlton in Houston, Kiawah Island resort in South Carolina and Hawk's Cay Resort in the Florida Keys.

Favoring variety and unique flavorings, Des Marais gets raves over yucca-crusted oysters with caviar, grilled yellowfin tuna, wood-seared veal tenderloin, barbecued squab and sauces that will have you grabbing a culinary dictionary. The Restaurant is open only for dinner, in an artistically appointed setting of elegance — creamy linens complementing the damask, fresh flowers and hand-painted Oriental murals. Reservations are required.

TOOJAY'S
313 Royal Poinciana Way
$ 659-7232

This is one of 10 South Florida locations. See the Boca Raton listing in this chapter for details about this upscale deli-style eatery.

Photo: Four Seasons Ocean Grand Hotel

Enjoy a private balcony breakfast overlooking the Atlantic Ocean at one of the many area resort hotels.

Palm Beach Gardens

PANAMA HATTIE'S AND SQUID ROW
PGA Blvd. at the Intracoastal Bridge
$$-$$$ 627-1545

Panama Hattie's (a seafood and raw bar) and Squid Row (a casual restaurant) are a pair of good-time eateries that draw well among young professionals and young families.

The menus at both are heavy with seafood, but Panama Hattie's atmosphere tends to be a bit more formal, and the cuisine is a bit more continental. Squid Row offers many fried platters, sandwiches and finger foods.

Panama Hattie's happy hour is popular, even in the dog days of summer. Squid Row sizzles on Wednesday's weekly Goombay Art Fest at the docks from 5 to 10 PM, featuring live music, arts and crafts by South Florida artists and food and drink specials.

Both restaurants are open every day for lunch and dinner.

TOOJAY'S
4084 PGA Blvd.
$ 622-8131

This is one of 10 South Florida locations. See the Boca Raton listing in this chapter for details about this upscale deli-style eatery.

West Palm Beach

INDIA GARDEN
7504 S. Dixie Hwy.
$$-$$$ 586-9579

Curries, kebabs and Tandoori foods, cooked in clay ovens, are the specialties at India Garden. Folks who know the words "vegetarian" and "bland" need not be synonymous will also find a happy home here.

India Garden is open for lunch daily and for dinner everyday except Friday.

TOOJAY'S
2911 N. Military Tr.
$ 687-4584

This deli-style eatery is one of 10 regional TooJay's. The fare and the prices are excellent. See the Boca Raton listing for details.

Broward County

Fort Lauderdale

BY WORD OF MOUTH
3200 N.E. 12th Ave.
$$$$ (305) 564-3663

Here, in a hunter green building fronted by a green-and-white striped canopy, is a true Insiders' restaurant. This unassuming but fabulous place never advertises, hence the name, but its reputation keeps the seats filled every lunch and dinner.

There is no menu. Diners are shown the day's specialties and can make their selections after a presentation of the day's fare. Each day's selections contain several fish, fowl, beef, cheese, pasta and vegetarian entrees. A salad accompanies each entree. Appetizers and desserts are similarly available, and the selection is equally as impressive.

The food is outstanding, the presentation is superb and the service is as good as the best European restaurants, but not nearly as pretentious. The staff seems to enjoy its work, and the result is happy, satisfied diners.

Most publications feature the world:

Only one features your world:

Many newspapers and magazines concentrate on international events, the country's economy, national elections, major league sports, and so on. Then they advertise themselves as "local." Not us. Sure, we cover national and international news, but our focus is on stories that affect you more closely. Like local events, local politics, and sports news of local schools and teams. In short, when The News gives you the world, it's your real world. Call (407) 368-9400.

The Boca News.
Always a local point of view.

Photo: Tina Valant-Siebelts

One look at their smiles and there's no denying Kristen and Katie Tasca are happy to be on the beach at Spanish River Park in Boca.

Here's one hint: If the pesto-dried-tomato-mascarpone-cheese pate is among the appetizers during your visit, pounce. It's heavenly.

Open Monday through Friday for lunch; dinner is served Wednesday through Saturday. Reservations for dinner are required.

CANYON
1818 E. Sunrise Blvd.
$$-$$$ (305) 765-1950

Another new face on Fort Lauderdale's culinary scene, Canyon is tough to find even though it's on one of the city's main thoroughfares at its intersection with U.S. Highway 1. The adventurous (and maybe a little funky) Southwestern cuisine is a favorite, making this tiny restaurant much too good

to pass by. Along with the cuisine, Canyon's specialties are microbrewery beers (divided by color into blondes, brunettes and reds), 20 types of tequila and a wine list (divided into bubbles, pearls and rubies) to enthrall your taste buds.

The menu is divided into small plates, garden plates and main plates. Among the small plates, consider the lobster and avocado quesadillas or the Carpaccio of juniper-seared venison.

Among the main plates, let chile-dusted grilled lobster, braised hibiscus free-range chicken or brook trout with crabmeat salsa tempt you. For pasta devotees, the Indian ginger linguine is absolutely fabulous.

Canyon may be small but it's popular, making reservations a must.

It's open for dinner only, with late nights on Friday and Saturday.

CASABLANCA CAFE
Alhambra Ave. at U.S. Hwy. A1A
$$-$$$ (305) 764-3500

It took only days for word about this new restaurant to spread, but even if it means you need to wait for a table at this oceanside treat, consider giving it a try. It's worth the wait.

The menu reflects the strengths of the local cuisine, with Spanish and Cuban-inspired dishes, along with seafoods. Presentation of each course is superb. Some favorites include, for starters, the macadamia goat cheese salad, served on fresh mixed greens. The warm goat cheese is rolled in minced macadamia nuts, which takes the edge off the cheese and makes it simply mouth-watering. Another popular starter are the char-grilled vegetables. Pasta dishes? Say no more than Casablanca Fettuccine Au Rose. Cuban and Spanish-inspired main courses include the Steak Havana, Caribbean Paella and Sole Valencia .

The restaurant's building is as interesting as the menu. Originally called Jova House, it was designed by Francis Abreu for his grandfather, Juan Jacinto Jova, and built in 1927. Abreu, who designed the original building in Wilton Manors (also in Broward County) and Fort Lauderdale's Casino Pool, was a native of Cuba and used the Spanish-influenced designs of his homeland and the inspiration of Addison Mizner's work to guide him.

Casablanca Cafe is open daily for lunch and dinner.

ERNIE'S BAR-B-QUE AND LOUNGE
1843 S. Federal Hwy.
$ (305) 523-8636

Spicy conch chowder and homemade Bimini bread are the star attractions at this venerable Fort Lauderdale eatery. The walls are decorated with the management's homespun homilies, but diners pay little mind; they're too busy chowing down.

Barbecued pork, beef and chicken are available in a variety of ways, along with several Cajun-style selections. The homemade Key lime pie is a perfect complement.

Ernie's opens at 11 AM on Monday through Saturday and noon on Sunday and serves until. . . .

MAI-KAI
3599 N. Federal Hwy. (305) 563-3272
$$$ (800) 262-4524

Unique as a nightclub revue complete with a Polynesian village setting, and fairly unique as a continuous operation since 1956, Mai-Kai pleases with the aroma of its tempting dishes from the South Seas. Lauderdale tradition suggests you start with a Mystery Drink in the Molokai Bar, a saloon with more than 50 frosty, frothing ways to make you surrender to the island magic. Authentic cuisine is Cantonese, with some American selections too. Specialties are Peking duck, Lobster Bora Bora and numerous fresh seafood and grilled meat selections.

Dining rooms overlook waterfalls with tiki gods at their post. The entrance is across a wooden bridge lighted with tiki torches. Special packages include the Islander Express, which is appetizer, dinner and dessert plus the 45-minute floor show. Monday through Wednesday nights feature one show a night with two shows Thursday through Sunday. The floor shows — authentic Polynesian dancers performing sword routines and fire-throwing — carry a $7.95 cover charge. The atmosphere is contagious.

RIVERWALK BREWERY AND GRILL
111 S.W. Second Ave.
$-$$ *(305) 764-8448*

Just west of the railroad tracks in downtown Fort Lauderdale, in the shadow of the Broward County Governmental Center, is Riverwalk Brewery and Grill, producing tasty meals and six fabulous beers. The brewery area is glassed in so you can watch the brewmaster and his helpers at work. Each day, diners may choose from the Marlin Light, Riverwalk Red and Blackbeard's Gold varieties, plus a brewmaster's special, a fruit beer (don't pass up the raspberry if it's available) and a dark special.

The menu here is for hearty eaters; the Shaslik of Steer and New York strip are representative, but sandwiches and burgers are also available and are excellent. The service is casual, prompt and friendly.

The restaurant is open for lunch and dinner.

Pembroke Pines

THE ROASTED PEPPER
ITALIAN SEAFOOD AND GRILL
9893 Pines Blvd.   *(305) 450-8800*
$-$$

Let's say you're on your way to a ballgame at Joe Robbie Stadium and you're hungry but don't have a hankering for stadium food. The fast-food alternative isn't appealing, but the thought of dressing up for a full-course meal leaves you less than excited too; after all, you're already dressed for the ballgame.

Here's an alternative: a casual Italian restaurant with a light, pleasing menu that will satisfy your appetite but won't leave you so full that you can't snag an errant foul ball.

The Roasted Pepper's pasta specialties include Penne alla Areos (penne pasta with sun-dried tomatoes, diced chicken and sautéed fresh spinach) and Spaghettini Carlo Ponti (pasta strands with eggplant, zucchini, peas, tomatoes and onions).

Pizza fans, consider a gourmet pie, such as the Pesto Pizza, the White Pizza with three cheeses and dried tomatoes, or the Pizza alla Vodka, topped with mozzarella, prosciutto, peas, mushrooms and a vodka cream sauce. Salud!

Should you prefer a meat dish, try one of the two "heavy" entrees: the steak platter or the char-grilled Sausage Siciliano. The remainder of the meat dishes are lighter fare, featuring seafood, chicken and veal.

All entrees come with a house salad and freshly baked garlic rolls that melt in your mouth like cotton candy. It's worth coming here for the rolls alone, but all of the fare is excellent, and the service is pleasant, efficient and attentive.

The Roasted Pepper opens at 11:30 AM on weekdays and noon on weekends and stays open until about 10 PM.

Pompano Beach

OLD MUNCHEN
2209 E. Atlantic Blvd.
$$-$$$ 785-7565

Every day is an Oktoberfest at Old Munchen.

Luncheon specialties include cold sandwiches and platters and hot plates such as pork loin roast, potato pancakes and weiner schnitzel.

German specialty dinners are served with soup, salad, bread and a choice of spaetzle, potato or vegetables.

Old Munchen is open for lunch Monday through Friday and for dinner Monday through Saturday.

Quick-dining Spots

Alas, we are active, busy folks here. That sometimes means spending less time dining than we'd prefer. That doesn't mean, though, that we have to settle for swill-to-go. On the contrary, there are plenty of spots in the area for quality quick dining or take-out fare. Unlike full-service restaurants, however, most do not accept credit cards and, unless noted, that rule will apply for the following places.

Here are a few to share:

BW-3 GRILL & PUB
235 S. Federal Hwy.
Pompano Beach   (305) 785-6060
$

A trip to Buffalo, New York's, Anchor Bar, the shrine for chicken wings, isn't possible every time South Florida wing devotees get a hankering for wings slathered in spicy sauce, but a trip to bw-3 is no problem at all.

Wings and weck (sandwiches on special caraway-and-salt-topped Kaiser rolls) are the specialty here, and the atmosphere is far nicer than you'll see at most quick-dining restaurants.

There are interactive trivia games to play if you have a few minutes to spare.

bw-3 is open daily for lunch until real late.

South Floridians, as a rule, don't like much of anything from Buffalo. The football Bills routinely break the hearts of our beloved Dolphins, leaving a sour taste in our mouths. But the taste of Buffalo wings overcomes all petty rivalries, and bw-3's wings are among the best.

CAFE LA BOHEME
1118 Atlantic Ave.
Delray Beach   278-4899
$

A block or two from the hubbub at Atlantic Avenue and Highway A1A, tucked away in tiny Palm Plaza, is this gem of a sandwich shop, serving up Mediterranean specialties such as falafel, tabbouleh and babaghanouj and wonderful sandwich baskets.

There's limited seating inside, but plenty of tables on the patio.

Cafe la Boheme is open daily from 8 AM to 8 PM.

FRAN'S CHICKEN HAVEN
1925 N. Federal Hwy.
Boca Raton   395-0781
$

For more than 30 years, hungry Bocavians have flocked to Fran's, where Fran and Joe Gerace make luscious fried chicken, one basket at a time for the take-out crowd.

Whether you prefer all white, all dark, all wings, mixed, whatever, Fran's has a dinner to please you. Also available are two and three-piece snacks and chicken by the tub.

Fran's features Buffalo-style wings, fried seafood and homemade salads. Visit them for lunch and dinner Monday through Saturday and for dinner on Sunday.

NATHAN'S

21210-15 St. Andrews Blvd.
Boca Raton   347-0774
$

Nowhere is the frankfurter more revered than at Nathan's. Tube steak lovers flock here from all parts of South County to buy them and load theirs down with sauerkraut, fresh onions and mustard.

Nathan's is open from early lunch through dinner all week.

OFFERDAHL'S BAGEL GOURMET

10 E. Palmetto Park Rd.
Boca Raton   368-4088
$

Sports fans know the name Offerdahl well. John Offerdahl, a former All-Pro linebacker for the Miami Dolphins — who played with as much heart as talent — and his wife, Lynn, opened a tiny bagel shop in Weston, a West Broward community. Lynn loved making bagels for John because they were low in fat and great food for a football player who needed the carbohydrates but not the fat in his battle to stay at the proper playing weight. Folks flocked to the store from miles around, and the Offerdahls decided to add stores, first in Broward and now beyond the county borders.

Offerdahl's bagels are soft and chewy and come in a zillion flavors, including chocolate chip and blueberry. Of course there are always the old favorites, such as onion, garlic and salt. There are even seasonal favorites, such as pumpkin bagels in the fall. The perfect complement is cream cheese, and Offerdahl's adds spices and mix-ins, such as apple-cinnamon, walnut-raisin and garlic-herb. Other spreads, salads and jams are available as well.

If you'd like, sit down and enjoy a breakfast sandwich or a deli sandwich.

Offerdahl's is open early in the morning until mid to late afternoon all week long.

Pubs

Palm Beach County's next-door neighbor to the south, Broward County, is blessed with the largest population of British-born residents in the United States. Palm Beach County has more than a fair number of folks born under the Union Jack too.

All that means there's a great demand here for friendly places to sip a pint of your favorite ale, find a smiling face with a familiar accent, and buy decent pub grub, with names like ploughman's lunch, bubble 'n' squeak, Cornish pasty or bangers and mash. Even non-Brits can quickly develop an affinity for pubs. Here are some of the best in the area.

CALYPSO PUB AND RAW BAR

701 S. Cypress Rd.
Pompano Beach   *(305) 942-1633*
$-$$

The signs tell you the strip mall's name is Cypress Plaza, but the faded paint and boarded-up windows tell you the shopping center's best days are behind it . . . except at the cozy pub hidden behind the bougainvillea bush. You'll recognize it by the cars parked outside.

Calypso Pub blends a bit of Britain with a bounty from Barbados, and the result is a friendly place to bend an elbow and down a few chilled Red Stripes with friends or enjoy a sumptuous but reasonably priced meal.

The menu is filled with specialties from the Bahamas, Caribbean and West Indies, including Jamaican jerk chicken, a Jamaican fish specialty called Stamp & Go and excellent Bahamian conch salad. Be sure and try the pub's specialty, flying fish, which is flown in (that's not a pun!) three times a week from Trinidad. The delicate fillets are marinated in fresh lime juice and a peppery concoction, then deep fried. Whether you have them as an appetizer, a sandwich or as a main course, you'll find them spicy and scrumptious.

The sign outside tells visitors the pub's "hours of continuous enjoyment" are 11 AM to 10:30 PM Monday through Thursday, on Friday and Saturday, it's 11 AM to 11 PM and on Sunday, it's open from noon to 9:30 PM.

Overlook the external surroundings; Calypso Pub is a delight, mon.

IRISH COTTAGE PUB

2713 N. Federal Hwy.
Delray Beach   *272-2078*
$-$$ *No credit cards*

A little of the Emerald Isle in what was once a Delray Beach gas station? Aye!

Not only does the Irish Cottage offer authentic Irish fare, but also some fine Irish music to boot.

It's open from about 11 AM until the wee hours Monday through Saturday, and on Sunday it holds off opening until 2:30 PM.

LION & EAGLE

2401 N. Federal Highway
Boca Raton   *394-3190*
$-$$

As is tradition at better pubs in Britain and elsewhere in the world, you're only a stranger at Lion & Eagle once, and even then not for long.

This is a place where tradition reigns. There are daily newspapers from Great Britain so customers can follow their favorite soccer or cricket team's progress. There's a personable, friendly staff and excellent comfort food, including steak and kidney pie, Cornish pasty and Scotch pie.

Loosely translated to mean "crazy cook," Couco Pazzo can be your alibi the next time you need a "mental health day" away from home. The tiny Italian bistro at 915 Lake Avenue is well worth the trip and the time it takes to find it — across the street from historic Lake Worth City Hall.

Insiders' Tips

For midday sustenance, you can't beat the ploughman's lunch, a fresh green salad served with a dollop of Branston's pickle relish and the requisite pickled sour onion on top. It's accompanied by a substantial slice of cheese and fresh bread.

And, of course, there's special Sunday roasts: beef with Yorkshire pudding, pork with applesauce and lamb with mint sauce.

Lion & Eagle is open for lunch and dinner Monday to Friday and for dinner on Saturday and Sunday.

ROSE & CROWN PUB

3660-80 W. Commercial Blvd.
Fort Lauderdale   (305) 731-6245
$-$$

Rose & Crown pub has the requisite Tudor look, a cook from Scotland, eight varieties of imported beer and the loyal devotion of customers who return again and again for the house specialties: the roast beef special with Yorkshire pudding and fish and chips, served with mushy peas. The menu also includes several light dishes, cold platters and hot favorites, including steak and kidney pie, shepherd's pie or bangers and mash.

It's open 10 AM on Saturday, noon on Sundays, and stays open long enough to sample all eight of their beers several times — 'til 4 AM! (Take a cab home, laddie.)

ROYAL WINDSOR

2233 E. Atlantic Blvd.
Pompano Beach   (305) 781-1198
$-$$ No credit cards

It's a little light and airy to truly be considered a pub, but Royal Windsor has a bar and a sufficient number of British and domestic beers to make a good case for its authenticity.

What was once a fast food fish 'n' chips restaurant now urges its diners to take a seat, rest awhile and enjoy a much better class of British food. Menu specialties include fish, bangers, chicken, duck, prime rib, steak and kidney pie or shepherd's pie, all served with chips. Also available are the ploughman's lunch, fish sandwich with chips and stuffed, fresh hot potatoes "in the jacket." Side orders include Scotch egg and mushy peas.

Hours are Monday through Saturday. Lunch and dinner are served every day.

SHAKESPEARE'S PUB AND GRILL

1015 N.E. 26th St.
Wilton Manors   (305) 563-7833
$-$$

What was once a pizza joint in this Fort Lauderdale suburb was reborn as Shakespeare's in 1993. It's a cozy pub where one can quaff a pint with friends, play a game of darts, catch the latest FA games (soccer) on TV or simply curl up with a book. There is more than enough imported beer on tap and a menu that's filled with British favorites.

It's open Monday through Friday from dinner 'til late; Saturday and Sunday from lunch 'til late.

TEA AT LILY'S

3020 N. Federal Hwy.
Fort Lauderdale   (305) 565-1144
$-$$

If, instead of bangers and mash, your tastes run more toward scones, cucumber sandwiches and high tea, here's an oasis.

This adorable upstairs tea room serves lunch, and high tea Monday through Saturday.

Lunch offerings include a soup and quiche special daily as well as a daily salad and sandwich plate special. There's also a selection of European sandwiches. If you're looking for a light lunch, consider the cream tea, consisting of a pot of imported tea, scones with preserves and Devonshire cream.

Reservations are required for afternoon high tea, which includes a pot of imported tea, finger sandwiches, mini scones and pastries.

UGLY DUCKLING PUB

5903 N. Federal Hwy.
Boca Raton   997-5929
$-$$

The menu offers a sampler of lunch and dinner specialties from England, Ireland, Scotland and Wales. The entertainment offers musical variety as well, from jazz to soul and beyond.

Ugly Duckling Pub is open daily for lunch and dinner with a brunch on Saturday, and keeps late nights every night.

Sports Bars

They're a place to catch a cool brew and a hot game, a place to be with friends and relax. With the dose of camaraderie, they also offer a good dose of competition. They are, of course, sports bars, and sports-crazy South Florida is loaded with them.

"Sports bars" as a category is something of a misnomer. Many of them now feature full-service restaurants for folks who want a little more

than peanuts or a quick sandwich, but there's always a bar to belly up to. But they all offer a cozy feel, plenty of televisions and are filled with folks who love sports.

Here are some favorites:

PETE ROSE BALLPARK CAFE

8144 W. Glades Rd.
Boca Raton   488-7383
$

A visit here is as much a trip to a museum as to a restaurant, and your chances of running into baseball's all-time hits leader are good. Rose tapes his radio show here.

Among the hundreds of pieces of memorabilia on display is Rose's black Mizuno bat, with which he stroked hit No. 4,192, breaking Ty Cobb's total hits mark on September 11, 1985.

If you can drag yourself from the memorabilia and the kids from the game room, take time to sit down and enjoy a pleasant meal and a ball game. Booths are equipped with individual sets, and many larger sets are placed around the room.

The menu is divided into salads, sandwiches, burgers and entrees.

Though targeted at baseball fans, Pete Rose's Ballpark Cafe is a real all-around crowd-pleaser.

Hungry fans can drop by for lunch or dinner seven days a week.

SCOREBOARD RESTAURANT & SALOON

2090 W. Atlantic Ave.
Delray Beach   278-7077
$

Scoreboard, which makes its home at the eastern edge of the Congress Square shopping center, was among the first sports bars in western Delray.

And it's still one of the favorites. With its rich wooden appointments, carpeting and memorabilia, it radiates a warm, clubby feeling. Service is swift and friendly, and the patron is never made to feel rushed. One visit and you'll feel like a regular. Play darts or shoot some free throws if you want to unwind. Scoreboard offers typical sports bar fare, including appetizers and sandwiches; the homemade soups are delicious.

It's open from 11 AM 'til late every day from September through May.

SPECTATOR'S SPORTS CAFE
5850 Belvedere Rd.
West Palm Beach   *640-9100*
$

Spectator's serves as the 19th hole for thirsty golfers at the Golf and Sports Center of the Palm Beaches but also attracts plenty of local sports fans who enjoy the camaraderie and friendly service. The layout is open and airy, and, of course, there are plenty of televisions. The menu is light, featuring yummy custom burgers and sandwiches.

Spectator's Sports Cafe is open from 10 AM until late; the Sports Center closes around 10 or 11 PM, depending on the season.

SPORTS TICKET BAR AND GRILL
3499 W. Hillsboro Blvd.
Deerfield Beach   *(305) 698-6361*
$

The key word here is "ambitious." As in the ambitious furnishings, with a television at every table and larger televisions spread throughout. Then there's the ambitious menu, with dozens of items named after sports legends and teams, such as the Doctor J. (Philly-style cheesesteak sandwich), the Chris Evert (grilled ham and cheese) and the Jack Nicklaus (grilled, Manhattan-style corned beef).

The ambition at Sports Ticket is not unfulfilled. It's a fun place to visit and a great place to watch championship games (but be sure to arrive early; it fills quickly). If you're itching for action, play some pool or darts or sink a few free throws at the hoop. The food and service are pleasing, and chances are excellent you'll leave with a smile on your face.

Sports Ticket is located in the Shoppes at Deer Creek and is open daily from lunch until late.

Inside
Accommodations

Historically, Boca Raton's persona speaks from suspended disbelief massaged into fables and fact about one real hotel, The Cloister Inn of 1925. Three decades earlier, Palm Beach was a whistle stop in the 500-mile hotel culture of Henry Flagler, working its way toward becoming a resort destination for kings and queens of the day and others whose destiny was very much their own.

That precedent tended to shape later hotel development strictly toward the high-end, with several nods to the middle class in recent times. So there are accommodations for the less-wealthy who visit, and many incentives to sample the pinnacles of lodging during the off-season. Assume the most expensive rates will be between November and March, but it's best to inquire individually as to when each hotel adjusts its seasonal rates. Many, for instance, raise rates November 1 and again the week of Christmas.

Below are some favorites to acquaint you with area accommodations — from restored, historic castle-size properties to the contemporary luxury hotels and popular chains. They are listed by geographic area for your convenience. We welcome your comments and hope to include your own suggestions about places to stay in future editions of *The Insiders' Guide® to Boca Raton & The Palm Beaches.*

Each entry has a dollar code intended to serve as a general price guide. The designation is based on the cost of one night's lodging for two people during the winter (peak) season.

$50 and less	**$**
$51 to $100	**$$**
$101 to $150	**$$$**
$151 and more	**$$$$**

Unless otherwise noted, all accommodations accept at least MasterCard and Visa. Inquire when you make your reservation about which credit cards are accepted. Also, in the case of long-term stays, find out in advance what the accommodation's policies are regarding cancellations.

Here's wishing you a comfortable and pleasant stay.

Boca Raton

BEST WESTERN UNIVERSITY INN
2700 N. Federal Hwy.
$$ 395-5225

This is a good place to land, with complimentary van service to and from Palm Beach International and Fort Lauderdale International airports. The inn has 92 rooms, and prices include a continental breakfast served from 7 to 10 AM. In the off-season until December 15, the inn is an even better value. Adjacent Zuckerellos restaurant is a popular spot for moderately priced lunch and dinner. Amenities at the inn include a heated swimming pool, Jacuzzi and meeting rooms designed to accommodate up to 100 for seminars, banquets and social gatherings.

BOCA INN MOTEL

1801 N. Federal Hwy.
$ 395-7500

This inn can accommodate groups of 50 people in its exhibit space of 13,500 square feet. There are 50 guest rooms and a swimming pool, and the adjacent Punjab restaurant specializes in Indian cuisine. Inquire about extra-low summer rates.

BOCA RATON
MARRIOTT

5150 Town Center Cir.
$$$-$$$$ 392-4600

The hub of a 28-acre mixed-use destination of 30 upscale shops and boutiques and eight restaurants, the 12-story contemporary Marriott has 256 rooms, convention and banquet facilities with audiovisual equipment, a gift shop and in-house dining and entertainment at the 5150 Brasserie. Services include a concierge, car rental desk, self parking and valet service.

Recreational amenities include an outdoor swimming pool and a health club equipped with sauna, hydrotherapy pool and exercise room. Guests have complimentary use of the neighboring Bally's Scandinavian/Olympiad Health Club. Nearby are

golf and tennis, with the beaches and boating a few miles east.

The Shops at Boca Center, nee Crocker Center, enhance the hotel complex with fine merchandise, art galleries and salons. The Marriott provides transportation but also is within walking distance of Town Center mall, a regional shopping destination with department store anchors such as Bloomingdale's, Lord & Taylor, Saks Fifth Avenue, Burdines and Sears.

The hotel's fourth floor is designated nonsmoking. A concierge level has rooms with other upgraded services. Boca Raton Marriott is off Military Trail, west of I-95 and north of Palmetto Park Road.

BOCA RATON RESORT AND CLUB

501 E. Camino Real   395-3000
$$$$ (800) 327-0101

The term "hotel" in Boca Raton refers to Her, the one and only. The city has many fine establishments, marvelous places to stay, but the Hotel is the only incarnation of history, romance, legend and real life — with clean sheets that whisper and friendly ghosts who hum.

Our doyenne, and the inspiration for illustrator Thomas B. Allen's 1987 pastel "The Lady of Boca," she is a patron saint who knows how to cook.

Born in the imagination of Addison Mizner, and making her debut on February 26, 1926, the 100-room Ritz-Carlton Cloister Inn became the expanded private Boca Raton Club when Clarence Geist bought it in 1927. The hotel has

Photo: Delray CRA

The Colony Hotel is one of a myriad of first-rate accommodations in Palm Beach County.

hosted the rich, famous and well-connected, as you'll see in the chapters on History and Addison Mizner. A milestone in its elaborate past, current owners renamed her the Boca Raton Resort and Club in the mid-1980s.

Configured around 223 groomed acres perched along the west side of the Intracoastal Waterway, she continues to draw the world's most sophisticated travelers — people who can afford any accommodations and wouldn't stay anywhere else.

Guest room choices range from the original Mediterranean Revival-landmark Cloister and the Palm Court Club concierge-level; the contemporary 27-story Tower with ocean views; secluded Golf Villa apartments on the main golf course; and the Boca Beach Club, a sister property where a private half-mile stretch of ocean and beach cabanas complement the amenities package. Dozens of suites enhance a total of 963 rooms.

Room packages for three or seven nights include golf, tennis, health and fitness — maybe even romance.

Guests who like to hit the links will be pleased to know that the Resort and Club was rated one of America's top golf resorts by *Golf* magazine. Golfers can take advantage of two 18-hole championship courses, created by well-known designer Joe Lee, as well as the new Dave Pelz Short Game Golf School. If you'd rather pick up a racket than a club, revel in the fact that *World Tennis* magazine ranked the hotel among the top six tennis resorts in the country. Enjoy a game on one of 34 clay courts (open day and evening), participate in a clinic or take a private lesson from one of the resort's USPTA professionals.

Seven restaurants in the main hotel and four at the Beach Club comprise seemingly limitless dining selections.

Guest services include laundry and valet, room service, a concierge, a beauty salon and barber shop, valet parking, safe deposit boxes, a reading room and complimentary transportation between hotel properties and to the nearby shopping destinations Mizner Park and Royal Palm Plaza. A teak vintage motor yacht, *Mizner's Dream,* ferries passengers between the main hotel and the Beach Club. Retail treats include 10 boutiques and the Curzon art gallery.

Other amenities include Olympic-size swimming pools, a 23-slip marina, rental boats, watersports, fitness centers, biking, walking and jogging. Call for current rates, special packages and reservations.

BOCA TEECA LODGE
5800 N.W. Second Ave.
$$-$$$ *(800) 344-6995*

Daily, weekly and monthly accommodations are available at Boca Teeca Country Club (see our Retirement chapter), a condominium community in north Boca primarily popular with retirees. Forty-six rooms are available poolside. Amenities include access to the private golf course, free tennis, men's and women's exercise rooms, a large swimming pool (heated in the winter) and a recreation hall with pool table and Ping Pong. To reach Boca Teeca, take Yamato Road east of I-95 to N.W. Second Avenue (also Boca Raton Boulevard); turn left and go north; the guest lodge is on your right at the next traffic light.

COURTYARD BY MARRIOTT
2000 N.W. Executive Ct.
$$ *(800) 321-2211*

These hotels, designed with the business traveler in mind, adjust rates from weekday to weekend as well as seasonally. Holidays that fall on a weekday are therefore less expensive. The hotel has 152 rooms, including some that are handicapped accessible, 12 deluxe suites equipped with small refrigerators, a restaurant that serves breakfast and a lobby lounge open from 5 to 10 PM. A heated swimming pool and Jacuzzi offer guests a nice place to relax, and an on-site fitness room with Universal equipment and two exercise bikes is designed for those who like to stay in shape while traveling.

CROWN STERLING SUITES HOTEL
701 N.W. 53rd St.
$$$ *(800) 433-4600*

This four-story contemporary home-away-from-home has 182 suites, with hot cooked-to-order breakfast included. Conveniences include TV with remote and telephones in both rooms, a microwave oven, refrigerator and coffee maker. With 3200 square feet of meeting space accommodating 10 to 80 people, this facility is ideal for small to medium business conferences. There's an outdoor pool, and fitness-conscious guests are given complimentary passes to nearby Bally's Scandinavian/Olympiad Health Club.

DAYS INN OF BOCA RATON
2899 N. Federal Hwy.
$-$$ *395-7172*

Conveniently situated in central Boca, the inn, formerly an Econo Lodge, has 48 guest rooms and an outdoor swimming pool. Eateries within walking distance include a Denny's, the Boca Diner and Zuckerello's Restaurant.

EMBASSY SUITES
661 N.W. 53rd St.
$$$$ 994-8200

What an ace location! Of all the I-95 interchanges, exit 40 at Yamato Road is the easternmost point. Embassy Suites also hosts the city's Tri-Rail commuter station. The seven-story hotel has 263 suites, each outfitted with a separate bedroom, living room with sleeper sofa and work area, telephones and televisions in both rooms, a microwave oven, refrigerator and coffee maker. Guests receive a full, cooked-to-order breakfast and two-hour manager's reception daily.

The 80-seat Palm Theater or one of several conference hospitality suites are available for meetings and can be set up to accommodate special needs.

Dining and banquet facilities, an outdoor swimming pool and fitness center bring it all together for the busy traveler.

HOLIDAY INN
1950 Glades Rd.   368-5200
$$$ *(800) HOLIDAY*

Great access right at I-95 and two blocks from Town Center mall make the inn ideal for business travelers on the go. Accommodations include five levels of rooms and three levels of suites surrounding a sweeping expanse of landscaped courtyard, a large heated swimming pool, a whirlpool spa and a shallow wading pool. Dining in-house is lovely for breakfast, lunch or dinner, and several popular restaurants are within walking distance. Corporate meeting packages and wedding packages are available.

Make sure to visit the lively Bounty Lounge, where a galleon replica serves as one of several spots to merrily run aground.

HOLIDAY INN BOCA RATON WEST
8144 W. Glades Rd.   482-7070
$$$ *(800) HOLIDAY*

A hall of fame contender for value, this accommodation has the Pete Rose Ballpark Cafe, 97 guest rooms, meeting rooms for parties of 60, an outdoor heated swimming pool and super accessibility just west of Florida's Turnpike entrance. Hotel personnel can arrange limousine or bus transportation to Palm Beach, Fort Lauderdale and Boca Raton airports, area shopping centers, restaurants and other attractions. See the Restaurants chapter for details on the popular Pete Rose Ballpark Cafe and the owner's nationally syndicated radio show broadcast live from its sound booth.

Services include complimentary newspapers, free parking and safe deposit boxes. Call (800) 23-HOTEL for details on the inn's participation in Florida Mini-Vacation packages.

HOWARD JOHNSON MOTORLODGE
80 E. Camino Real
$$ 395-4545

The lodge's 53 guest rooms are walking distance to downtown, the Boca Raton Resort and Club, Addison's Restaurant, First Union Bank and Royal Palm Plaza. There's an on-site swimming pool. Take Palmetto Park Road east to Federal Highway and go south to Camino Real.

LA BOCA CASA BY THE OCEAN RESORT
265 N. Ocean Blvd.
$$ 392-0885

The timeshare resort has 19 furnished one-bedroom condominiums, occasionally available by the week. There's a swimming pool on the property, which is across Highway A1A from the ocean.

OCEAN LODGE
531 N. Ocean Blvd.
$$ 395-7772

Newly renovated this year, Ocean Lodge has 18 rooms — 14 with kitchens. Across from the beach and next to the Boca Raton Municipal Golf Course, the Lodge is five blocks north of Palmetto Park Road and a short drive from downtown, Mizner Park and Royal Palm Plaza. The Lodge has a heated swimming pool and shaded barbecue area, complimentary coffee service, maid service and a laundry room. Weekly and monthly packages are available.

PARAMOUNT HOTEL
2901 N. Federal Hwy.   395-6850
$$-$$$ *(800) 268-8998*

Formerly the Ramada Hotel, the Paramount is convenient for business travelers in need of meeting and catering facilities. There's a full-service restaurant and lounge, heated swimming pool and whirlpool spa. The hotel offers several rooms designed for disabled guests.

RADISSON BRIDGE
RESORT OF BOCA RATON
999 E. Camino Real
$$$-$$$$ 368-9500

Formerly The Bridge Hotel, the resort enjoys the same scrumptious views as the Boca Raton Resort and Club. Built 16 years ago by an affluent retired electrical contractor from New Jersey, the Bridge underwent a major redo of its 121 rooms in recent years. One early rumor described the unusual number of electrical outlets — said to be an idiosyncrasy of the original owner's taste for convenience. Others said he merely anticipated the future of legalized gambling and wanted to be ready to open a casino.

Well, gambling remains illegal, but almost anything else goes at the Bridge. It's great for a honeymoon, weekend getaway, a power lunch, bar or bat mitzvah celebrations, or Sunday brunch. The outdoor circular heated pool and sundeck are nestled close to the Intracoastal Waterway, literally in the shadow of the Inlet Bridge. Amenities include a separate health club and sauna for men and women, complimentary valet or self-parking, bicycle rentals and dockside rentals of Wave Runners and boats.

Carmen's Restaurant and Lounge at the Top of the Bridge has panoramic views of the city and serves one of Boca's best Sunday brunches. At Watercolors outdoor cafe (see our Restaurants chapter), one of only two Boca spots to dine on the Intracoastal, Bridge guests can share a meal or watch the world drift by as boats head to and from the inlet.

Business travelers especially appreciate the resort's executive meeting space for corporate seminars or conferencing. For worldwide reservations, call (800) 333-3333.

Photo:Four Seasons Ocean Grand Hotel

Pamper yourself in Palm Beach County's resort hotels.

RADISSON SUITE HOTEL BOCA RATON
7920 Glades Rd.
$$$ 483-3600

There's great accessibility here, with the hotel in the Arvida Parkway Center next door to Florida's Turnpike at Exit 75.

Shops, restaurants and sophisticated lakeside meeting facilities complement the Radisson's 200 suites. Each room has a microwave oven, coffee maker, mini-bar and private balcony. A hot cooked-to-order breakfast and complimentary two-hour cocktail reception are included.

Lakeside meeting facilities, including three meeting rooms in the hotel, a nearby 3,400-square-foot conference center and Pete's (neighboring restaurant) banquet room accommodate groups of up to 200 for business or social functions.

Whether you like to work out or just relax, the hotel offers a variety of recreational opportunities, including a heated outdoor pool and soothing whirlpool, an on-site fitness center

and a parcours lakeside jogging trail. Guests also enjoy privileges at nearby golf courses and country clubs, the use of a dine-around card good at Park of Commerce restaurants, and complimentary shuttle service within the Boca Raton area.

This hotel has received the Radisson President's Award six years running.

Use the reservations system at (800) 333-3333 to make the Radisson's acquaintance.

RESIDENCE INN BY MARRIOTT
525 N.W. 77th St.
$$ 994-3222

There are 120 guest suites at the Residence Inn, directly off I-95 at the Congress Avenue interchange north of Yamato Road. Two meeting rooms here can accommodate groups of 30. Amenities include a swimming pool, whirlpool spa, basketball court, gas barbecue grills, access to golf and tennis facilities and a health club.

RIVIERA APARTMENTS
424 N.E. Wavecrest Way
$ 391-5984

A small collection of 10 one- and two-bedroom apartments is available, though scarce, at Riviera, Highway A1A near the entrance to South Beach. Furnished one-bedroom units are available monthly. Two-bedroom apartments require a yearly lease, but at the time of this writing all units were occupied.

THE SHERATON INN-BOCA RATON
2000 N.W. 19th St.
$$$ 368-5252

A pond-skip from the Holiday Inn-Glades, the Sheraton is just west of I-95 and south of Glades Road at the corner of Sheraton Way. The 193-room, five-story hotel has full dining and live entertainment in the lounge on weekends.

Fax service, in-room data jacks for computers or fax machines, safety deposit boxes and same-day laundry or dry-cleaning service are also available.

A spacious, heated outdoor pool and a deck area are popular spots to relax. Or, play on one of the hotel's two tennis courts, work out in the on-site fitness center or utilize the facilities at the nearby Bally's Scandinavian/Olympiad Health Club. Golf privileges are available at several nearby clubs.

The business service center can accommodate banquets for up to 600 people.

For reservations, call (800) 325-3535.

THE SHORE EDGE MOTEL
425 N. Ocean Blvd.
$$ 395-4491

This cozy lodge is only 70 yards from the ocean and offers a choice of efficiencies and double rooms — when they're available. The Shore Edge has nine efficiencies with full kitchens and seven rooms with small refrigerators and microwave ovens. The manager serves coffee in the lobby, which you may carry to sip beside "the warmest pool" in the area. Weekly rates are available. Eighty percent of the business here is return and referral, so call ahead. Many guests stay a month or more during the winter.

Boynton Beach

ANN MARIE MOTEL
911 S. Federal Hwy.
$ 732-9283

The tiny vintage motel offers weekly and nightly rates on its 15 guest accommodations. Three are efficiencies with stove and dishes, and the other rooms also have refrigerators. Ann Marie is a ma-and-pa operation that offers conti-

Insiders' Tips

Hotel rates drop considerably after April and remain relatively low throughout the summer.

nental breakfast, bicycles for guests to borrow and a lending library. The 1952 building has been renovated, and each room has a 46-channel TV and a VCR. The Ann Marie Family Restaurant is next door, and the motel is AAA rated. Most rooms have double beds but you can ask for a king or queen. The motel is about two blocks from Ocean Avenue; the beach is about a mile east.

GOLDEN SANDS INN
520 S.E. 21st St.
$$ *732-6075*

There are 26 studio-size units available daily, weekly and monthly year round. All are equipped as efficiencies with sleeping quarters, full kitchens, cable TVs and telephones. There isn't a swimming pool, but the ocean is about a half-mile walk away. Golden Sands is also walking distance to Denny's, Arby's, Pizza Hut, Gentleman Jim's and Strebs restaurants. Golden Sands Inn is near downtown, three blocks south of Woolbright Road.

HOLIDAY INN CATALINA
1601 N. Congress Ave.
$$ *737-4600*

Catalina has all the convenience of a 150-room Holiday Inn plus proximity to one of only two Macy's in Palm Beach County. The motel has fine dining at Dominic's, which is open for breakfast, lunch and dinner. It's at Catalina Centre next to the Boynton Beach Mall — 150 fine shops and major department stores. The inn makes you feel welcome with complimentary newspapers, free parking, safe deposit boxes, a heated swimming pool and whirlpool spa. The beach is

only 3 miles away. Catalina offers corporate and group rates, family plans and golf packages. There's limousine and bus transportation by reservation to the Palm Beach and Fort Lauderdale international airports. To reach the Catalina, take the Boynton Beach Boulevard exit of I-95, go west to Congress Avenue and turn right.

HOLIDAY INN EXPRESS
480 W. Boynton Beach Blvd.
$ *734-9100*

The Express Inn is directly east and visible from I-95, about a 15-minute drive south of Palm Beach International Airport. There are 102 guest rooms, a swimming pool, complimentary breakfast and free local phone calls. In the evening, coffee is served in the lobby. Call for corporate rates and other discounts.

RELAX INN
222 N. Federal Hwy.
$ *732-4333*

A small establishment of 18 rooms, the Relax Inn is within walking distance of restaurants in downtown Boynton Beach. Weekly rates are available, as is a swimming pool.

SUN DECK MOTEL
6660 N. Ocean Blvd.
Ocean Ridge
$$-$$$ *732-2544*

This 17-unit resort accommodation has a five-day minimum stay and availability weekly and monthly for studio, one-bedroom and two-bedroom units. There is a heated swimming pool, free cable TV and local telephone service. Sun Deck is about 60 yards from the beach, only 25 yards from the Intracoastal Waterway and less than a mile north of the Banana Boat waterway cafe. To find the Sun Deck, take Boynton Beach Boulevard east to Federal Highway, one block south to Ocean Avenue, then east to Highway A1A and turn left.

Deerfield Beach

DAYS INN RESORT
1250 W. Hillsboro Blvd.
$$-$$$ (305) 427-2200
The 250-room inn includes 24 suites, a 24-hour restaurant, exercise room, meeting room, billiard and game room. A heated swimming pool and cocktail lounge complement the convenient Days Inn just south of Boca Raton.

DEERFIELD BEACH HILTON
100 Fairway Dr.
$$$$ (800) 624-3606
The 200-room hotel, owned by entertainer Merv Griffin, is easily accessible just east of I-95 at Hillsboro Boulevard. The location makes the Hilton convenient to Boca Raton restaurants and shopping, with the beaches a few minutes drive east. The Hilton also is positioned at the entrance to one of the area's busy commercial parks. Complimentary shuttle service is provided to area shopping, beaches and various attractions.

Breakfast, lunch and dinner are served daily in the hotel's Petal's restaurant, and for evening relaxation the Court of Palms lounge in the hotel lobby offers a variety of beverages. Weeknights, guests are treated to complimentary hors d'oeuvres, and

each morning, coffee is provided in the lobby.

Fitness enthusiasts can use the on-site workout room, featuring a Stairmaster and Universal equipment. For rest and relaxation, guests can swim in or sunbathe near the hotel's oversize heated pool.

For meetings, banquets or special occasions such as weddings, bar and bat mitzvahs and other celebrations, the Hilton offers 17,000 square feet of private space.

DEERFIELD BUCCANEER
120 N. Ocean Blvd.
$$$-$$$$ (305) 426-4672
A great value for a couple or foursome in town for a week or more, the Buccaneer has fully furnished one- and two-bedroom units with living rooms and kitchens. Amenities include a heated swimming pool, whirlpool spa, putting green and coin-operated laundry. The 38-unit Buccaneer is popular for its location near the beach, restaurants and nightlife in Boca Raton and points north and south.

Delray Beach

BERKSHIRE BY THE SEA
126 N. Ocean Blvd.
$$ 276-0901
Here you'll find 48 rooms; Berkshire is just north of fun central at 6 South, Boston's On The Beach and the Upper Deck restaurants.

BERMUDA INN OCEANFRONT
64 S. Ocean Blvd.
$$ 276-5288
A boutique-size property of 20 accommodations, the Bermuda Inn can

afford to boast that every room overlooks the ocean. There's a large heated swimming pool, and the inn is just a block from the unique, upscale shops, art galleries and nightlife along Atlantic Avenue. More than a dozen fine restaurants and the *Ramblin' Rose* dinner showboat are within walking distance. Smaller rooms have refrigerators, maid service is standard, and larger rooms also have microwave ovens, coffee pots and toasters. To find Bermuda Inn, exit I-95 at Atlantic Avenue and go east to Highway A1A; the inn is a block south past Boston's on The Beach.

BREAKERS ON THE OCEAN
1875 S. Ocean Blvd.
$$ 278-4501

Very reasonable rates make the Breakers quite attractive, especially with 22 apartments right on the ocean. There's a swimming pool, cabanas on the beach with chairs, free bottled water and ice, daily maid service and a complimentary continental breakfast. The Breakers is just south of Linton Boulevard and north of the exclusive Delray Beach Club.

BUDGET INN
2500 N. Federal Hwy.
$ 276-8961

A small 17-room establishment, the Budget Inn offers reasonably priced rooms and a swimming pool. It's convenient to I-95, about a mile south of Woolbright Road.

THE COLONY HOTEL
525 E. Atlantic Ave.
$$$$ 276-4123

If you call anytime between May 1 and New Year's Eve, the historic 1926 hotel is closed for the summer, thank you, in the tradition of a gracious bygone era. Owner Jestena Boughton reopens the sister property in Kennebunkport, Maine, when her Florida hotel buttons up for the off-season. You can make reservations at either property by calling (800) 552-2363. If you're reading this in time, call now to make reservations for The Colony's grand New Year's Eve bash, a black-tie gala to celebrate the city's Centennial. The Colony has 70 guest rooms, a dining room and a lounge in the lobby. The dining room serves breakfast and dinner during the winter, and lunch is offered at the Colony Cabana Club, 1801 S. Ocean Boulevard, a private beach club for hotel guests and members only.

CORAL SHORES
2500 N. Federal Hwy.
$ 276-8961

This demure accommodation has 17 guest rooms in northeast Delray, about equal distance between Atlantic Avenue and Woolbright Road. There's a swimming pool, and restaurants are nearby. From either exit of I-95, go east to U.S. Highway 1. Coral Shores is about 1.5 miles south of the Woolbright intersection.

COTE D'AZURE
2325 S. Ocean Blvd.
$-$$ 278-2646

The management has a selection of hotel rooms with kitchenettes and some larger apartments. On Highway A1A by the ocean, Cote D'Azure is south of Linton Boulevard.

DOVER HOUSE

110 S. Ocean Blvd.
$$$ 276-0309

Across from the Atlantic Ocean and walking distance to all the festivities on Atlantic Avenue, Dover House enjoys regular demand. There are 42 one-bedroom apartments with full kitchens, and you can take a dip in the on-site swimming pool. A two-night minimum stay is required in summer, and weekly rates are available. To reach Dover House, take Atlantic Avenue east to Highway A1A, turn right and proceed one block.

GROVE CONDOMINIUM
RENTAL APARTMENTS

30 Andrews Ave.   276-7729
$$-$$$

The Grove has 29 hotel rooms and fully-furnished apartments that are part of a rental pool, courtesy of the condo owners. Fully equipped units have microwave ovens, cable TVs, coin-operated laundry, direct-dial phones and access to a 15-by-40-foot heated swimming pool. All but the hotel rooms have kitchens.

The management offers hotel rooms, studios, one-bedroom and two-bedroom units. From November 1 to April 30, there's also a 5 percent discount for a one-month stay and a 10 percent discount for a two-month stay. Call for details.

From May 1 to October 31, the Grove is available daily, weekly and monthly, with a three-day minimum. To find The Grove, take the Atlantic Avenue exit of I-95 east to U.S. Highway 1 and go north eight blocks to George Bush Boulevard; head east until you reach Andrews Avenue, just past the Intracoastal Waterway.

HARBOR HOUSE

124 Marina Way
$$-$$$$ 276-4221

Perched right at the Intracoastal Waterway within a short walk to the beach, Harbor House has a premium location and 54 units. There are 25 rooms available on a daily, weekly or monthly basis and the rest are reserved for annual stays. There's a swimming pool, laundry area and shuffleboard courts. Harbor House is only one block south of Atlantic Avenue restaurants, nightlife, shops and art galleries.

HOLIDAY INN CAMINO REAL

1229 E. Atlantic Ave.   278-0882
$$$$ (800) HOLIDAY

The name throws people off since Camino Real is Boca's historic thoroughfare, but this Delray establishment certainly reflects the Mediterranean flavor and romance reminiscent of "the king's highway" era. The mid-rise structure features stucco, barrel tile roof, quarry tile flooring, wrought-iron grille work and lush landscaping.

Situated on the west side of Highway A1A on the city's gateway, the inn is a favorite spectator perch for offshore fireworks demonstrations. The 150 rooms have private balconies, small refrigerators and wet bars, not to mention ocean views and one of the top beaches. *South Florida Parenting* magazine calls Delray the "No. 1 beach in Palm Beach County," and *Travel Holiday* magazine says it's the "best swimming beach in the Southeast."

There's a heated outdoor swimming pool, a whirlpool and biking and walking paths. Beach activities include sailing, Jet Ski rentals, charter boat cruises and boat rentals.

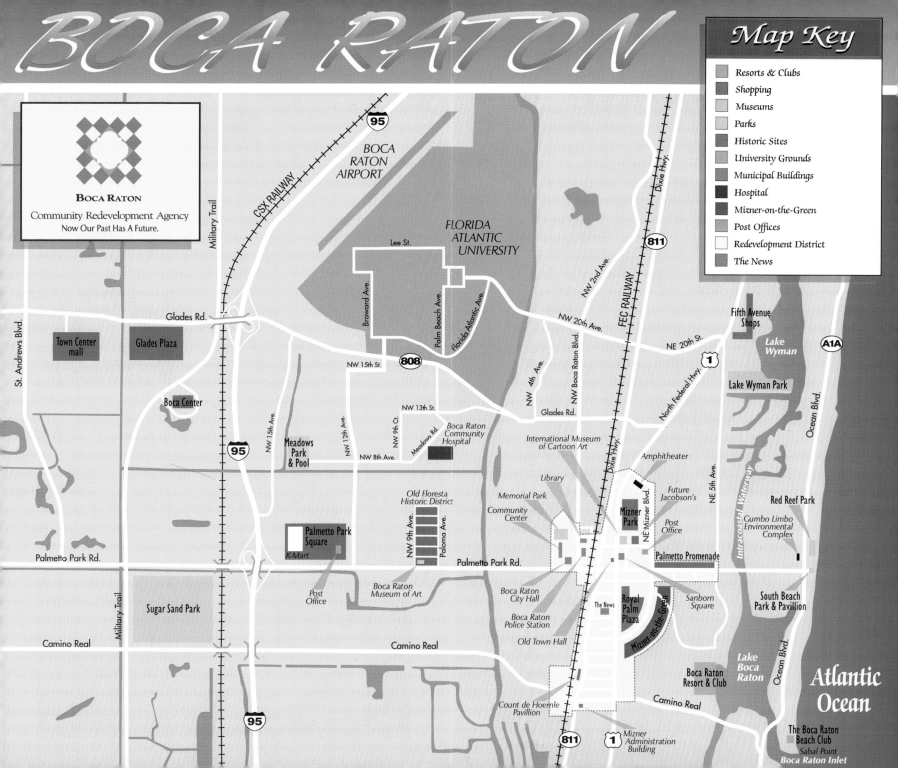

BOCA RATON

Map Key

- Resorts & Clubs
- Shopping
- Museums
- Parks
- Historic Sites
- University Grounds
- Municipal Buildings
- Hospital
- Mizner-on-the-Green
- Post Offices
- Redevelopment District
- The News

BOCA RATON
Community Redevelopment Agency
Now Our Past Has A Future.

BOCA RATON AIRPORT

FLORIDA ATLANTIC UNIVERSITY

CSX RAILWAY

FEC RAILWAY

Military Trail

St. Andrews Blvd.

Glades Rd.

Town Center mall

Glades Plaza

Boca Center

Lee St.

Broward Ave.

Palm Beach Ave.

Florida Atlantic Ave.

NW 15th St.

NW 13th St.

NW 15th Ave.

NW 12th Ave.

NW 9th Ct.

Meadows Rd.

NW 8th Ave.

NW 4th Ave.

NW 2nd Ave.

NW 20th Ave.

NW Boca Raton Blvd.

Dixie Hwy.

North Federal Hwy.

NE 20th St.

Fifth Avenue Shops

Lake Wyman

Lake Wyman Park

Red Reef Park

Meadows Park & Pool

Boca Raton Community Hospital

International Museum of Cartoon Art

Amphitheater

Library

Future Jacobson's

NE 5th Ave.

Gumbo Limbo Environmental Complex

Old Floresta Historic District

NW 9th Ave.

Paloma Ave.

Memorial Park

Community Center

Mizner Park

Post Office

NE Mizner Blvd.

Intracoastal Waterway

Palmetto Park Square

K-Mart

Palmetto Park Rd.

Palmetto Promenade

South Beach Park & Pavillion

Boca Raton Museum of Art

Post Office

Sugar Sand Park

Boca Raton City Hall

Boca Raton Police Station

The News

Royal Palm Plaza

Mizner-on-the-Green

Sanborn Square

Old Town Hall

Camino Real

Palmetto Park Rd.

Camino Real

Lake Boca Raton

Boca Raton Resort & Club

Ocean Blvd.

Atlantic Ocean

Count de Hoernle Pavillion

Mizner Administration Building

Camino Real

The Boca Raton Beach Club

Sabal Point

Boca Raton Inlet

State-of-the-Art Downtown

Photo by Phototastic

Photo by Phototastic

Photo by Robert Brantley

Boca Raton

CRA: Building a Better Downtown

Merchants are moving in. Medians and sidewalks are getting a new look. And businesses are planning to build new offices.

The Boca Raton Community Redevelopment Agency is making Downtown Boca Raton a premier spot in Palm Beach County through its projects to redevelop and rejuvenate the area.

Major results started appearing Jan. 1, 1991, with the opening of Mizner Park, a mixed-use development that is comprised of apartments, offices, restaurants, shops, an amphitheater and the International Museum of Cartoon Art.

Mizner Park and another mixed-use development, Mizner-on-the Green, are composed of an element that is one of the most important to the CRA - Downtown residences. As well as increasing the number of residential areas in the CRA district, the dwellings show that Downtown housing can be a success.

Businesses, as well as residences, are moving Downtown. As part of an extensive project that aims to revitalize

Photo by Sophie Brandstrom

the southern end of Downtown, a five-story office building is slated for the southeast corner of Palmetto Park Road and Federal Highway.

In addition to buildings, the CRA is concerned about Downtown beautification. It encourages Downtown beautification and improvement of drainage and landscaping sidewalks and medians. While improving drainage was one of the key objectives to improve Downtown, the most distinctive project may be beautification.

"It's the one thing that everyone can relate to and appreciate," says Jorge Camejo, CRA executive director.

Although sidewalks and medians along the north/south route of Federal Highway already have been transformed with landscaping and colored bricks, upgrades for the east/west East Palmetto Park Road will be the first geared to pedestrians.

The East Palmetto Park Road improvements include more colorful sidewalk bricks, light fixtures similar to those in Mizner Park, landscaped medians, buried power lines and tree-lined sidewalks.

BOCARATON

SHOPPING:
A Touch of a European Village

Landscaped sidewalks and medians; shops, apartments and offices linked by walkways; gourmet eateries to please the most discriminating palate; art galleries; and boutiques with the latest fashions.

If this conjures up the image of a European shopping village, you're not far off the mark. But you don't have to go to Europe, for this shopping village is in Downtown Boca Raton.

Downtown merchants offer the latest clothing styles; exquisite artwork; elegant furnishings; delectable baked goods; and even greeting cards, hardware and groceries.

Another drawing factor to Downtown is improvements along the shopping district's main artery, East Palmetto Park Road. Improvements will include landscaping and eventually a walkway that will connect Mizner Park and Royal Palm Plaza, two major shopping areas to the north and south of East Palmetto Park Road. In late 1996, Downtown will get a big addition: Jacobson's Department Store, which will be in Mizner Park.

Photo by Robert Brantley

Leisure activities year-round for everyone...

CITY OF BOCA RATON RECREATION SERVICES

- most extensive park system of any city in Palm Beach County
- athletic program encompassing all sports for all ages
- on-going personal enrichment classes at two community centers
- teen center for young adult activities
- 35 tennis courts for all ages and all stages of play
- community pool for instructional and recreational swimming
- 2.7 miles of protected beaches and award-winning beachfront parks
- over 200 acres of well-groomed golf courses for all levels of play
- complete library facilities showcasing over 137,000 books, records, videos, and other resource materials
- canoe and kayak rental opportunities in season
- shuffleboard complex for tournaments and team play
- unique environmental complex for all types of nature encounters at Gumbo Limbo Environmental Education Complex
- cultural programming at outside amphitheater in downtown Boca Raton
- various festivals, fairs, and special events scheduled throughout year

For information on recreational programming at its best...please call (407) 393-7806 or write...

**City of Boca Raton Recreation Services
201 W. Palmetto Road, Boca Raton, FL 33432**

Photo: Stephanie Murphy

The Boca Beach Club overlooks the Intracoastal Waterway and faces the ocean. Part of the Boca Raton Resort and Club, water taxi ferries guests between the two hotels.

A short walk along Atlantic Avenue takes you past exclusive shops and art galleries to the Intracoastal, where you'll want to check out the *Ramblin' Rose Riverboat.*

Holiday Inn offers meeting rooms for conferencing. Room packages include the Honeymoon Plan, Family Plan, Weekends and Weekdays.

Call (800) 23-HOTEL for details on the inn's participation in Florida Mini-Vacation packages.

HUNTINGDON RESORT
82 Gleason St.
$$-$$$ 278-1700

Huntingdon's 16 furnished apartments — studio, efficiency and one-bedroom units — are available daily, weekly and monthly. Amenities include a heated swimming pool, fully equipped kitchens, maid service and cable TV. Monthly rates include a 10 percent discount. Huntingdon Resort is near the beach on the last street before Highway A1A off Atlantic Avenue.

RIVIERA PALMS MOTEL
3960 N. Ocean Blvd.
$$ 276-3032

This side of the Mediterranean and across from the Atlantic Ocean, you have the Riviera Palms, with 17 units. There's a swimming pool but no in-house restaurant. To reach Riviera Palms, take the I-95 Woolbright Road exit east to Highway A1A and turn right.

THE SEAGATE HOTEL & BEACH CLUB
400 S. Ocean Blvd.
$$ 276-2421

The hotel has 70 guest accommodations, including studios, one-bedrooms and two-bedrooms with kitchenettes. Amenities include a restaurant, a private beach and heated freshwater and saltwater pools. The

Seagate is between Linton Boulevard and Atlantic Avenue on U.S. Highway A1A across from the ocean.

SPANISH RIVER RESORT
1111 E. Atlantic Ave.
$$ 276-7441

Right in the middle of all the excitement along Atlantic Avenue, the Resort has 72 guest rooms and is only a block from the beach and fine eateries such as 6 South, Boston's on The Beach and the Upper Deck restaurants (see our Restaurants chapter). Just west are other fine restaurants such as Ristorante Lunas and Bennardo's as well as the art galleries and unique shops on the Avenue. The Resort has an oversize swimming pool, two lighted tennis courts, a volleyball court and a basketball hoop. The in-house restaurant was closed for renovation at press time (August), but we expect it will reopen for business soon.

Fort Lauderdale

HOLIDAY INN HOTEL
& CONFERENCE CENTER
5100 S.R. 7 N.
$ (305) 739-4000

This property has 259 guest rooms and a large complex with 26 meeting rooms. It's about 15 miles from Fort Lauderdale International Airport in the Plantation area west of Fort Lauderdale.

MARRIOTT HARBOR BEACH
3030 Holiday Dr.
$$$$ (305) 525-4000

Celebrating its 10th anniversary, the Marriott recently completed an $8 million renovation which freshened 589 guest rooms, 35 suites, the lobby and the Oceanview restaurant. Lauderdale's premium beachfront hotel is on 16 secluded acres with five restaurants, water sports, tennis, a health club, and meeting and convention facilities.

Chaise lounges, beach chairs, showers and a wet bar make the hotel's 50 oceanfront cabanas in great demand. Guests have more than 1,000 feet of private beach to stroll or jog, and the free-form pool has a 12-foot cascading waterfall. For reservations, call (800) 222-6543.

RADISSON BAHIA MAR BEACH RESORT
801 Seabreeze Blvd.
$$$ (305) 764-2233

Known as the "Venice of America," with 300 miles of canals in addition to the Intracoastal and the ocean, Fort Lauderdale is the yacht capital of this hemisphere. Bahia Mar has stand-alone status among nauticos worldwide, so the Radisson enjoys a favorite-son berth any way you tack it.

Home of the Fort Lauderdale International Boat Show every fall, the Radisson is all the more worth the trip when gleaming hulls are tethered to the bollards at Bahia Mar.

Totally renovated this year, the Radisson has 295 all-new guest rooms with ocean or marina views, four restaurants, gift and specialty shops, an outdoor pool, tennis courts, a 350-slip marina, boat charters for fishing and sailing, and a dive school.

The Radisson has a covered walkway to the beach and easy access to Port Everglades cruising.

SHERATON YANKEE TRADER BEACH RESORT

321 N. Atlantic Blvd.
$$ *(305) 467-1111*

This vintage beach hotel has 465 guest rooms including 15 suites and nine different conference rooms. The property has a covered skyway across Highway A1A to the beach, a fitness center, 24-hour deli, tennis courts, in-room safes, a swimming pool, two restaurants and nightly entertainment.

Gulf Stream

GULFSTREAM MANOR

3901 N. Ocean Blvd.
$$ 272-6300

Delightful bargains are available several months a year in these apartment-type accommodations furnished like one-bedroom condominiums. Each unit includes a living room with sleeper sofa, dining area, total kitchen, bath and bedroom — so a one-bedroom unit can accommodate four guests. There aren't any elevators, so people should specify if they need a ground-floor unit. You'll find a washer and dryer and two televisions in each unit. Outside is a large swimming pool, whirlpool spa, shuffleboard court, gas barbecue grills and a nice gazebo and patio area overlooking the ocean and the Gulf Stream — a warm offshore current that originates in the Gulf of Mexico and travels slowly up the coast to merge with the North Atlantic Drift. The exclusive Town of Gulf Stream is named for the ocean phenomenon.

Units are available at a daily rate with a two-night minimum for one-sixth of weekly rates. Gulfstream Manor

is at the ocean, 1.3 miles south of Woolbright Road. It's two doors away from The Seahorse, which serves lunch and dinner during the winter season, and 2 miles north of restaurants and shops on Atlantic Avenue in Delray Beach. North on Ocean Avenue at the Intracoastal Waterway are Banana Boat waterway cafe and Two Georges seafood restaurant.

Highland Beach

HOLIDAY INN-HIGHLAND BEACH

2809 S. Ocean Blvd.   278-6241
$$$ *(800) 465-4329*

Directly on the ocean, just north of Boca Raton, this Holiday Inn has all the conventional hotel features plus oceanfront dining, beach cabanas and immediate access to a 15-mile jogging and biking path along Highway A1A. About 3 miles south is the entrance to fabulous Spanish River Park. The inn has a glorious swimming pool by the beach and a tiki bar for a sunset rendezvous. For reservations and current rates, call (800) 23-HOTEL. Call the same number for details on the inn's participation in Florida Mini-Vacation packages.

Jupiter

JUPITER BEACH RESORT

5 U.S. Hwy. A1A N.
$$$$ 746-2511

Formerly managed by the Hilton organization, the nine-story Jupiter Beach Resort has 190 guest rooms, fine and casual dining and beach activities including a children's program. Dallas-based Noble House Hotels & Resorts pur-

Photo: Cynthia Thuma

Sunbathers relax along the shoreline at Lake Worth's Municipal Beach.

chased the property a few years ago and now is spending $2.5 million to upgrade all guest rooms.

Choose from four-star dining at Sinclair's, more casual meals at The Cabana Club and sandwiches or snacks at The Sandbar by the swimming pool. There are tennis courts and Jet Skis for rent on the property.

To visit Jupiter Beach Resort, take I-95 Exit 59A and head east to the end of Indiantown Road, then north to Jupiter Beach Road at Highway A1A.

Lake Worth

ATLANTIS INN

331 Orange Tree Dr.
$$ *968-4000*

Affiliated with the semiprivate Atlantis Country Club, the Atlantis has 24 rooms available on a daily basis and special golf packages available year round. Besides golf, there's a swimming pool. To find Atlantis, take I-95 to Lantana Road, go west to Congress Avenue then north to Clubhouse Boulevard; turn left and drive to Orange Tree Drive.

GULFSTREAM HOTEL

1 Lake Ave.
$$ *586-9250*

Worth is the name of the town's namesake lake, and it's also the word many locals use to describe the trip just to see the bygone-era lobby of this 1921 jewel on the Intracoastal Waterway. Well, it's worth it. There are 121 guest rooms and 13 apartments. Rates include complimentary continental breakfast, and there's no extra charge for being only 10 minutes from the beach. Locals visit just to soak up the Roaring

Twenties atmosphere in the lobby. The lovely municipal golf course is two blocks away, and The Gulfstream has two swimming pools. In-season, the dining room is open for lunch and dinner seven days a week; in summer, the lounge doubles as a cafe.

For half a century, a Finnish family owned the hotel, which hosts an 18-piece Big Band orchestra on Wednesday nights during in-season. During the summer, there's live entertainment on Saturday nights after 9 PM — sometimes rhythm 'n' blues. Twice a month, The Gulfstream stages a murder-mystery dinner theater. Weddings are popular here year round.

HOLIDAY INN-TURNPIKE

7859 Lake Worth Rd.   *968-5000*
$$ *(800) 824-2545*

Convenient to anywhere in the Palm Beaches, the inn is right at Florida's Turnpike exit on Lake Worth Road. The motel has 114 guest rooms, three meeting rooms and exhibit space. There's a swimming pool as well as nearby golf and tennis.

IXORA MOTEL

722 N. Dixie Hwy.
$ *588-2101*

This small establishment is strictly for short stays. There are 19 rooms available at low daily rates. There's no swimming pool.

LAGO MAR MOTEL APARTMENTS

317 N. Federal Hwy.
$$ *585-4243*

The small complex has 14 units for rent year round. All units include one-bedroom and a kitchen. There's also a whirlpool spa.

Martinique Motor Lodge
801 S. Dixie Hwy.
$-$$ 585-2502

A total of 26 rooms, including one-bedroom apartments with kitchenettes, are available daily and weekly. There is a swimming pool too.

Palm Beach

The Brazilian Court
301 Australian Ave.
$$$$ 655-7740

Sunny and extravagantly romantic, the three-story Brazilian Court is a 1926 landmark renovated in 1986. A member of the Historical Hotels of America, it maintains exceptional quality to indulge the whims of the world's most sophisticated travelers.

A short walk from the beach, the hotel is a pebble-toss from Worth Avenue. Its vintage elegance transcends gentle though persistent efforts to coax the hotel into the 20th century. This Grand Heritage property offers 135 rooms. French doors from the dining room overlook a tropical flowering courtyard, and casual dining is set in the bistro. Dancing after dark is popular with guests and locals alike in Brazilian Court's Rio Lounge. For reservations outside Florida, call (800) 552-0335.

The Breakers
One South County Rd.
$$$$ 655-6611

A slice of another era awaits you at this historic oceanfront property listed on the National Register of Historic Places. Open year round, the Breakers hugs 140 acres of tropical landscape nudging the dunes about 6 miles from Palm Beach International Airport.

To celebrate its centennial throughout 1995, the Breakers is winding down from five years and $75 million devoted to refurbishing guest rooms, common areas, recreational amenities and service standards. The last phase of the facelift, scheduled for completion in November 1995, involves converting once-dormant space in the west wing into 60 additional guest rooms, for a total of 572. The area once housed servants in the entourage of hotel travelers. Also new is the Flagler Club, a concierge level with 28 luxury rooms.

A heady exercise in the opulence of founder Henry Morrison Flagler, the Breakers oozes Italian Renaissance with hand-painted ceilings, Venetian chandeliers and 15th-century tapestries. Originally the Palm Beach Inn and lost in a fire in 1903, the first Breakers also burned in 1925. A year later, the current design appeared as a nod to the Villa Medici in Rome.

Amenities include 36 holes of golf, 20 tennis courts, a half-mile of private beach, supervised children's activities, a full-service health club, a business conference center and world-class dining. Eight restaurants provide an assortment for every dining occasion. For reservations and current rate information, call (800) 833-3141.

The Colony Hotel
155 Hammon Ave.
$$$$ 655-5430

The quaint and stately Colony has 100 rooms including suites and villas and a meeting pavilion. Ideally located a block south of Worth Avenue and a block from the ocean, The

Colony has a swimming pool, two restaurants, tiki bar and Polo Lounge. Weekly discounts of 10 percent are available after seven days. To find The Colony, take Okeechobee Boulevard east to South County Road and turn right; turn right at the third traffic light, one block past Worth Avenue and behind Saks Fifth Avenue. For reservations, call (800) 521-5525.

FOUR SEASONS OCEAN GRAND
2800 S. Ocean Blvd.
$$$$ 582-2800

Six miles from Palm Beach International Airport, on six acres of incomparable oceanfront in the Town of Palm Beach, the Ocean Grand is one of the area's newest additions to the luxury resort genre. There are 210 guest rooms

including four two-bedroom hospitality suites, 38 deluxe oceanfront rooms and eight one-bedroom suites — each with a spacious terrace overlooking the Atlantic. All rooms have private balconies, large-screen TVs, VCRs and stereos, refrigerated private bars, in-room safes, full marble bathrooms, hair dryers . . . even bathroom scales and plush terry robes.

On the premises are a full-service beauty salon, gift shop, health spa and car rental service. The multilingual concierge staff is available seven days a week, and room service is offered 24 hours a day, seven days a week. The Ocean Grand is known among locals, too, as a primo dining destination — both in The Restaurant and The Ocean Bistro. Each is described in the chapter on Restaurants. In addition, the Ocean Grand has poolside bar and snack service and The Living Room, a luxurious lobby lounge serving cocktails in the afternoon and evenings, with piano music daily and a jazz trio to entertain on weekends.

Meeting planners will appreciate the conference and banquet area, with two ballrooms, meeting rooms, a formal boardroom and advanced audiovisual equipment.

There's the beach, a swimming pool and whirlpool spa, bicycle rentals, tennis courts, a pro shop, weight training and cardiovascular equipment, sauna and steam rooms, aerobics classes and the Kids Club. Beach-goers may rent cabanas and Hobie Cats, or may order other watersports equipment in advance. Guests have golf privileges at three area par 72 courses: Atlantis, Wycliffe and Emerald Dunes.

HOWARD JOHNSON HOTEL
2870 S. Ocean Blvd.
$$$ *582-2581*

Situated on the Intracoastal Waterway, the Hotel is across from the ocean and in the vicinity of the Four Seasons Ocean Grand and the Palm Beach Hilton. There's a swimming pool and a restaurant next door to the hotel. Take Southern Boulevard to Highway A1A and go south about 5 miles.

PALM BEACH HILTON OCEANFRONT RESORT
2842 S. Ocean Blvd.
$$$-$$$$ *586-6542*

Basking in the aura of its distinguished next door neighbor, the Four Seasons Ocean Grand, the Hilton has 134 guest rooms and meeting facilities, Sandcastles Restaurant and the Beachside Bar and Grill. The beach is private.

Amenities include two TVs in each unit (one in the bath), hair dryers, a heated pool, whirlpool and sauna, two tennis courts and watersports and beach rental equipment such as Wave Runners, Jet Skis, chaise lounges and more. The helpful staff can also arrange snorkeling and diving excursions.

To reach the Hilton, take the Lake Worth Road exit of Florida's Turnpike or I-95 and go east to Highway A1A, then turn south. From the Palm Beach airport, take Southern Boulevard east to Highway A1A, then go south for 5 miles.

PALM BEACH HOTEL
235 Sunrise Ave.
$$-$$$$ *655-4705*

Just a block from the beach and part of a condominium property, this 120-room hotel is within walking distance of eight fine restaurants in fabled Palm Beach. There's a swimming pool, bakery-deli and specials available for weekly, monthly and long-term, year-round stays. To reach the hotel, take Okeechobee Boulevard east to South County Road; turn left and go north past the intersection of Royal Poinciana Way. For reservations, call (800) 232-7256.

THE PLAZA INN
215 Brazilian Ave.
$$$$ *832-8666*

This European-style bed and breakfast is larger than most of that genre, with 50 rooms — each with a private bath — and two suites with sitting

Photo: Stephanie Murphy

The outdoor heated pool at the Radisson Bridge Resort of Boca Raton overlooks the Intracoastal Waterway.

rooms. Deluxe rooms are individually furnished, many with period furnishings, and room rates include a full breakfast. The Plaza has a heated swimming pool and whirlpool spa; it's walking distance to Worth Avenue shops and restaurants and only a block from the ocean. There are special seasonal packages with a one-month minimum stay. Reserve early for stays during the season, which is always booked well in advance. To reach The Plaza, take Okeechobee Boulevard east over Flagler Memorial Bridge and make a right onto South County Road; then turn right at Brazilian Avenue.

THE RITZ-CARLTON PALM BEACH
100 S. Ocean Blvd.
Manalapan
$$$$ *533-6000*

The six-story Mediterranean style resort has its own seven-acre slice of Palm Beach Island, a short ride from Palm Beach International Airport and minutes from Worth Avenue. The Ritz, with 270 guest rooms including king, double and oceanview suites, opened in 1991.

Putting on "the Ritz" got its challenge from the legendary Swiss shepherd Cesar Ritz, a 19th-century hospitality pioneer who set the European standard for luxury hotels. King Edward VII is credited with saying Ritz was "the hotelier of kings and the king of hoteliers."

A private elevator key takes guests to The Ritz Carlton Club, where perks include continental breakfast, afternoon tea and gourmet hors d'oeuvres with cocktails and beverages.

The Ritz has seven tennis courts, an outdoor pool with sun terrace and ocean boardwalk, outdoor cafe, specialty retail shops and a fitness center with spa.

Four restaurants and a business conference center make the Ritz a popular destination. You may call locally or dial the Ritz Carlton Hotel Company's reservation system, (800) 241-3333.

Palm Beach Gardens

COMFORT INN
11360 U.S. Hwy. 1
$-$$ *624-7186*

A continental breakfast is complimentary for guests of the inn. There's no restaurant but there is a health and fitness center. For reservations, call (800) 221-2222.

ECONOMY INN-INNS OF AMERICA
4123 Northlake Blvd.
$-$$ *626-4918*

Convenient to central and north Palm Beach County, the Economy Inn is in the process of changing its name to Inns of America. There are 96 guest rooms and a swimming pool, and the inn serves continental breakfast in the lobby. Economy Inn is northwest of Northlake Boulevard and I-95.

MACARTHUR'S HOLIDAY INN
4431 PGA Blvd.
$$-$$$ *622-2260*

The 280-room inn is named after John D. MacArthur, one of the county's most prominent entrepreneurs, landowners and philanthropists. The hotel has MacArthur's Vineyard Restaurant and a full-service cocktail lounge with nightly entertainment. To reach the inn, take I-95 to PGA Boulevard; it's directly west.

PALM BEACH GARDENS MARRIOTT
4000 RCA Blvd.
$$$ 622-8888

Demand for the 279-room Marriott is related to its proximity to golf resorts and The Gardens Mall. Most rooms are hotel-style; six suites are also available as well as 12,000 square feet of meeting space. The Marriott has a swimming pool, whirlpool spa, sauna and steam room. Guests have complimentary use of facilities at nearby Staying Alive Fitness Center. The 5,000-square-foot nightspot, Club Safari, is in the hotel as well as Sebastian's Grill restaurant. Within walking distance are a shopping center, movie theater and three restaurants. The Marriott is just east of I-95 off PGA Boulevard. Call (800) 228-9290 for reservations.

PGA NATIONAL RESORT AND SPA
400 Avenue of the Champions
$$$-$$$$ 627-2000

You may think it's all about golf, but PGA knows there may be tennis lovers and others in the family of a links lord. PGA has 339 guest rooms including 60 suites, plus 80 two-bedroom, two-bath cottages. There are 23 conference settings, a lounge and five restaurants. Recreational amenities include five championship golf courses, 19 tennis courts, five croquet lawns, a health and racquet club and a 26-acre lake with a man-made sandy beach. There are golf packages as well as special packages in the resort's full-service spa. Weekly and monthly rates are available. To visit, take the PGA Boulevard exit west of I-95 and watch for the signs.

Singer Island

DAYS INN OCEANFRONT RESORT
2700 Ocean Dr.
$$-$$$$ 848-8661

You can have the same location as pricier resorts and great value at this 165-room Days Inn on Singer Island. There's a swimming pool, whirlpool spa and tiki bar at the beach. Inside the inn is an International House of Pancakes. To reach Days Inn, take PGA Boulevard east to Highway A1A and head about 5 miles south.

ISLAND BEACH RESORT
3100 N. Ocean Dr.
$$-$$$ 848-6810

This property has 40 rooms currently available and 48 rooms under renovation, with availability estimated to be February 1996. Ask about the executive suites with king-size beds, Roman tubs, wet bars and kitchens. There's a swimming pool and the

Make it a point to get up early, go to the beach and watch the sun rise.

Insiders' Tips

four-star restaurant, The Chef's Touch. After the renovation, all rooms will be oceanfront. To reach the Island Beach Resort, take PGA Boulevard to Highway A1A and go south.

QUALITY RESORT
OF THE PALM BEACHES
3800 N. Ocean Dr.
$$$-$$$$ 848-5502

The oceanfront property has 126 rooms — some beachfront. All rooms have coffee makers, and other amenities include a swimming pool, whirlpool spa, a kids pool, sauna, putting green, natural coral reef for snorkeling, shuffleboard, volleyball, a jogging trail, lighted tennis, free parking, basic cable TV, an exercise room, meeting space, a poolside bar, cocktail lounge and restaurant, gift shop and beachside grill serving lunch. To reach the Quality Resort, take the PGA Boulevard exit of I-95 and go east to Highway A1A.

RADISSON RESORT
3200 N. Ocean Dr.   842-6171
$$-$$$$

The former Sheraton Ocean Inn changed its name as of August 1, 1995.

There are 202 rooms including suites, a swimming pool and two cocktail lounges.

To reach the Radisson Resort, take the Blue Heron Boulevard exit (Exit 55) of I-95 to Highway A1A and head north.

RUTLEDGE INN
3730 Ocean Dr.
$$ 842-6621

There are 60 units of motel rooms and efficiencies at the Rutledge, which is right on the beach at Singer Island.

The property has no restaurant but does have a swimming pool and tiki bar. To visit Rutledge Inn, take the Blue Heron Boulevard exit of I-95 to Highway A1A.

TAHITI ON THE OCEAN
3920 N. Ocean Dr.
$$-$$$ 848-9764

The atmosphere is strictly vacation-oriented on Singer Island and certainly at Tahiti, which has 52 guest rooms in a variety of sizes. This accommodation has two swimming pools, shuffleboard, a barbecue area, picnic tables, croquet and Ping Pong. It's on the beach and near hotel restaurants on Singer Island. To visit, take the I-95 exit at PGA Boulevard and go east until the road becomes Highway A1A; go south about 3 miles.

West Palm Beach

BEST WESTERN
1800 Palm Beach Lakes Blvd.
$$-$$$ 683-8810

The motel has 157 rooms, suites and efficiencies and is convenient to the Palm Beach Mall east of I-95. There's a swimming pool, discounts for golf and passes for Bally's health club. The Best Western provides van transportation within a 5-mile radius. Take the I-95 exit north of Okeechobee Boulevard and go east.

COURTYARD BY MARRIOTT
600 N. Point Pkwy.
$$ 640-9000

These hotels for business travelers adjust rates from weekday to weekend as well as seasonally. Holidays that fall on a weekday are therefore less expensive. The hotel has 149 rooms, a restaurant that serves breakfast and a lobby lounge open from 5 to 10 PM.

HAMPTON INN
1505 Belvedere Rd.
$$ 471-8700

Convenient to the Palm Beach International Airport, the inn has 136 guest rooms and serves a complimentary deluxe continental breakfast. There are meeting rooms and a swimming pool. Take the Belvedere Road exit of I-95 and go west to Hampton Inn.

HOLIDAY INN-INTERNATIONAL AIRPORT
1301 Belvedere Rd.
$$ 659-3880

The 200-room inn has meeting rooms, exhibit space, a swimming pool and health club. The property is directly north of the Palm Beach Airport.

OMNI WEST PALM BEACH
1601 Belvedere Rd.
$$$ 689-6400

This 220-room hotel has close proximity to Palm Beach International Airport and provides everything you'd expect from Omni accommodations, including meeting, banquet and exhibit space, a swimming pool, whirlpool spa, tennis court and a health club.

PALM BEACH AIRPORT HILTON
150 Australian Ave.
$$$ 684-9400

The 247-room Hilton has plenty of meeting and exhibit space, a swimming pool, health club, tennis, racquetball, a restaurant and nightclub.

RADISSON SUITE INN
1808 Australian Ave.
$$$$ 689-6888

The Radisson has 175 rooms in close proximity to Palm Beach International Airport. Amenities include a swimming pool, exercise room and meeting facilities.

RAMADA HOTEL CONFERENCE CENTER
630 Clearwater Dr.
$$ 833-1234

The hotel has 350 guest rooms and 14 suites, with more than a dozen meeting rooms for conferences. Amenities include a swimming pool, whirlpool spa, tennis courts and health club. Restaurants include the White Swan and the Key Cafe. Also, the Ramada has Cezanne, a local club that features jazz entertainers. The hotel is off Okeechobee Boulevard, east of I-95.

Photo: Mizner Park

Romantic evenings are de rigueur *in Palm Beach County.*

Inside
Nightlife

There was a time when sundown in Boca Raton came in two flavors: Suds at The Keg, standing on planks that held up the peanut shells, and champagne at the Top of the Tower, standing on ceremony. The Establishment removed The Keg, which always flirted with disapproval, and city shakers refined the rules so the Boca Raton Resort preached beyond the choir.

We who are bent on a good boogie have more choices today, including a broader range of fun for guests of the Boca Raton Resort and members of its exclusive Premier Club. The Keg fed a hungry bulldozer, but rest assured its soul is intact in pockets of tolerance up and down the coast.

Here, we suggest some nighttime pursuits, whether your bones lean toward dancing in the dark, cool jazz or hot rock, bubbling reggae, two-timing country or soulful rhythm and blues. The Gold Coast has the tunes and the times . . . plus comedy, billiards, TV sports hangouts, parimutuel wagering, offshore discos, dinner shows and the simple pleasure of a potion at sunset with your favorite someone. So listen up, for we've got the nightlife, we've got the boogie.

"South County"

Boca Raton

ACAPULCO GRILL
201 N.W. First Ave.   *394-5449*

The Acapulco Grill serves Mexican morsels with the option to picnic al fresco or sip Dos Equis at the bar while the kitchen wraps a skillet-prepared quesadilla or delectable fajitas. Different local bands play at 9 PM Sunday and 9:30 PM weeknights except Monday. Boss Mary Lamia used to sell advertising but has since traded her three-piece skirt for shorts and a T-shirt; owners have come and gone, but Mary remains the longest-running manager.

BOCA BILLIARDS
8221 Glades Rd.   *451-9200*

Boca Billiards is the million dollar-plus brainstorm of owner Sid Banner. Himself a nationally ranked billiard wizard, Banner in another life owns and operates Express Financial Mortgage. His dream come true is Boca Billiards, which offers a dozen pool tables, three billiard tables and snooker, all heated and imported from Scandinavia. It's a palace for the pure pool-player, set off Glades Road just west of Florida's Turnpike in Piccadilly Square. Beer and wine service is available, and happy hour runs from 1 to 7 PM. Sid shuts down about 2 AM or whenever the game is over.

THE BOUNTY LOUNGE
In the Holiday Inn I-95   368-5200

The ghost of a ship doubles as one of three bars surrounding the dance floor here. Sunday has been Big Band Night since the Dick Cully era; the music starts at 8:30 PM. Cully and his Big Band aren't always available, more's the pity . . . he's the sensational drummer described as the only stick man in the country capable of inheriting the Buddy Rich legacy. Watch the local papers for notices of where Cully is performing. Saturday is singles night at the Bounty, and a disc jockey plays dance music. The cover charge is $6.

CLUB BOCA
7000 W. Palmetto Park Rd.   368-3333

You'll find Club Boca on the lobby floor of Boca Bank Corporate Centre, a dramatic ziggurat-style Class-A office building at the intersection of W. Palmetto Park and Powerline roads. Open until 5 AM, the club has live music several nights and a DJ otherwise. The cover charge varies with the entertainment. Parents, this is where to look if the "kids" should have been home hours ago, are older than 21 or can fake it. The younger crowd may stare at you, but stay for a dance anyway.

CLUB NOTTE AT BOCA CENTER
5150 Town Center Cir.   393-1221

Club Notte opens at 6 PM Tuesday through Friday with dancing un-

til 2 AM. Saturday nights, anything goes from 6 PM until 5 AM. The club is in the middle of Boca Center adjacent to the Marriott Hotel on Military Trail, between Glades and Palmetto Park roads.

DIRTY MOE'S
395 N.E. Spanish River Blvd.   395-3513

This place was the mayor's raw bar, but that was two mayors ago. Sure, mayors come and go, but Dirty Moe's transcends and anchors a shopping center. Live entertainment, sometimes reggae or rock 'n' roll or Grateful Dead-like, happens Thursday through Sunday from 9:30 PM to 1:30 AM; there's no cover charge. As the spirit moves 'em, Moe's offers 50¢ beer or two-for-one Rum Runners — a fun-lover's potion you will hear about elsewhere so here's the recipe, give or take a thimble: 151 rum or Meyer's dark, blackberry brandy, creme de banana, Rose's lime juice and Grenadine. Lunch and dinner go on for hours too.

GOODFELLAS
One N. Ocean Blvd.   338-4242

Goodfellas offers cabaret entertainment Tuesday through Sunday. The restaurant serves Italian specialties for dinner and is open from 4:30 PM to 2 AM. Reservations are suggested.

JOSEPH'S RESTAURANT AND NIGHTCLUB
1499 W. Palmetto Park Rd.   391-9798

Joseph's is the current establishment in the International Plaza building just east of I-95. It was very popular as Ciro's Pomodora and usually finds favor with an upscale crowd wanting to dance. A live band plays Latin music on Wednesdays and '50s and '60s music on Thursdays.

MUSICANA SUPPER CLUB
2200 N.W. Boca Raton Blvd.   *361-9704*

True to its tag, "We sing for your supper," Musicana recruits dynamic young singers, dancers and musicians from around the United States who take the stage after waiting on your table. A successful concept in its 20th year, Musicana features original revues of popular standards and Broadway favorites. Open year round, Tuesday through Saturday programs begin with dinner at 6 PM followed by two shows; a similar schedule on Sunday begins at 4 PM. An evening at Musicana involves dancing too. Shows change themes every six weeks and include such programs as *A Salute to Andrew Lloyd Webber* and *Tin Pan Alley*. Menu selections include prime rib, Norwegian salmon, eggplant parmesan, New York strip, Chicken Hawaiian, Chick Au-Poivre, red snapper and scampi. Prices range from $21.95 to $29.95 and include a complete dinner and two shows.

PETE'S BOCA RATON
7940 Glades Rd.   *487-1600*

Pete's Boca Raton is equally popular as a restaurant and nightclub, so look for dining details in our Restaurants chapter. Owner Pete Boinis picked a tempting asymmetrical perch with window walls overlooking a scenic lake at the Arvida Parkway Center. The upscale, sophisticated hideaway/getaway wears an invisible scrawl in the air called "flaunt it" — good clothing, good cars, bold moves and cut-to-the-chase. A band plays backdrop to the *real* live entertainment — the patrons — who also dance. It's the place to be if being seen is your scene. With bars on four levels, it's also the place to rendezvous, enjoy the music and turn down the pace a notch at sundown. Valets have their hands full parking cars, so there must be copious throngs from both camps inside. Self-parking is okay too. Weekdays, Pete's draws professionals and the tennis set for Happy Hour drink specials and a buffet. Parkway Center also houses a Radisson hotel, the corporate headquarters of Arvida Corp., and numerous upscale shops, salons and galleries. Pete's is opposite the entrance to Florida's Turnpike.

POLLY ESTHER'S
99 S.E. First Ave.   *447-8955*

Polly Esther's is the new club that time didn't forget. New York has three such warps, two in Manhattan and a third on Long Island. The Florida Group of Polly Esther's opened here in June at the former Mizner Club. Take a déjà vu trip through the land of *Saturday Night Fever* and check out the authentic-looking dance floor, just like the one in the blockbuster movie. Enjoy a retro ride to the disco beat of the 1970s, with Hustle lessons on Thursdays and Donna Summer's "Last Dance" again and again. Owner Artie Lesavoy says he and partners Bob Watman and Tim Ouellette are scouting now for other Florida locations . . . possibly Coconut Grove, West Palm Beach, Fort Lauderdale, Fort Myers and Tampa.

There's a twisted tale going around about a human pretzel thing they do.

.. or is it really an exaggerated spinoff of Twister®? Game leader "Left Hand Blue" Lesavoy says let the spinner decide. The Boca establishment operates Tuesday through Saturday, with happy hour from 5 to 9 PM; Lesavoy expects to be open seven nights a week in-season. A disc jockey plays '70s dance music until 2 AM. Expect theme nights, Toga parties and John Travolta look-alike contests, backed up by ABBA, the Bee Gees and Gloria Gaynor. The 4,500-square-foot club has a game room including Pac-Man and other dawn-of-video-era favorites, a memorabilia wall and *Brady Bunch* shrine, board games, tabletop Pong and vestiges of *Playboy* magazine.

Lesavoy and company apparently started to get nostalgic for this particular decade about the time the '80s came to a close. So we had to ask: Is the five-year-old concept satire, tongue-in-cheek or a genuine longing to hug R2-D2? "All of the above," explains Lesavoy, whose ex-wife is the sister of Tom Cruise. The trend brings out costumers in platform shoes, bell bottoms and happy faces not unlike the neon one outside Polly Esther's. So have a nice day.

THE PORTERHOUSE BAR & GRILL
7050 W. Palmetto Park Rd.   391-6601

The Porterhouse draws people who work nights or just aren't ready to call it a night. Full dinners and a full bar until 5 AM? Yeah, the after-hours crowd always finds a club that starts to cook about the time other happy feet have tucked themselves in for the night. With the extended liquor license outside Boca city limits, Porterhouse is convenient for eastsiders and folks from the 'burbs, nosed into the north end of the Garden Shops of Boca on the west side of Powerline Road. On Wednesday and Thursday, the band plays Top 40; Friday and Saturday, it's jazz. Porterhouse opens at 4:30 PM seven days a week. Say hello to bartender and Rhode Islander Ricky Peters.

TAVERN IN THE GREENERY
301 Yamato Rd.   241-9214

This establishment decorates the atrium of classy Northern Trust Plaza. The bar draws suits and skirts from professional offices in the vicinity for Happy Hour and piano music from 6 to 8:30 PM. Lush plants and soft lights create a garden atmosphere in which to dine, and live music for dancing is performed Wednesday through Saturday starting at 8:30 PM. Lunch is served on weekdays. The Tavern is closed on Sunday.

THE UGLY DUCKLING
5903 N. Federal Hwy.   997-5929

The Ugly Duckling made quite a stir when its new owners decided it would be hatched at the precise site of the former, sacred and dearly departed Blarney Stone Pub. Well, dearies, we're in safe hands. Four nights a week, bands play a variety of soul, Motown and dance music. The Duckling is open from noon to 2 AM Monday through Friday, 10 AM to 2 AM Saturday and noon to midnight on Sunday.

THE WILDFLOWER
551 E. Palmetto Park Rd.   391-0000

The Wildflower received some overdue renovation this spring and

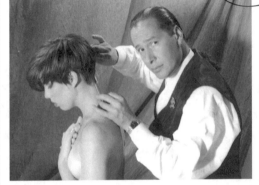
plans to reopen in 1996. A lot of history surrounds the city's first waterway cafe, so stay tuned for news on The Wildflower in the next edition of *The Insider's Guide® to Boca Raton & the Palm Beaches*.

Delray Beach

THE BACK ROOM
16 E. Atlantic Ave.   243-9110

The saxophone logo outside this place just seems to say "blues." Club owner John Yurt and house entertainers Junior Drinkwater and the Westside Blues Band deliver for a $6 cover charge. A telephone recording tells you which bands are on deck each week, from regional and local favorites to national contenders. Yurt and the Back Room crew frequently instigate jam sessions and shenanigans in the streets too, including special events during the Art and Jazz and Summer Nights on the Avenue festivals.

BOSTON'S ON THE BEACH
40 S. Ocean Blvd.   278-3364

Celebrating 16 years of overwhelming success where Atlantic Avenue meets the Atlantic Ocean, founder/owner Perry Don Francisco, a native of Beantown, expanded a few months ago to bring Boston's Upper Deck on line. Our Restaurants chapter provides details on fine dining in the new second-floor dining room and on the outdoor terrace, as well as Boston's regular groceries. Live music is performed seven days a week in-season and varies from classic rock 'n' roll to steel drum island-style. During the summer, Monday means reggae; other bands play Wednesday through Saturday. There's piano music on weekends at the Upper Deck until the dinner crowd heads downstairs to give the band their undivided attention. Don Francisco also has a 14-room hotel in the rear of Boston's, which sits across Highway A1A from the beach. Regulars from Boston visit all winter, and some have been known to shelve their car keys for the entire season.

Other Boca/Delray Options

You could spend a lost weekend just in the Downtown area, with other nightspots on the Avenue such as **Brody's South Pub & Lounge**, 1045 E. Atlantic Avenue, 278-5559; **Coaster's**, 777 E. Atlantic Avenue, 272-6004; **Elwood's Dixie BBQ**, 301 E. Atlantic Avenue, 272-7427; **6 South**, Ocean Boulevard, a SoBe-style (Miami's South Beach) addition just north of Boston's, 278-7878; the **Seacrest Room** at the Holiday Inn Camino Real, Highway A1A and Atlantic Avenue, 278-0882; and **Ristorante Lunas**, 777 E. Atlantic Avenue, 276-6379.

ERNY'S
1010 E. Atlantic Ave.   276-9191

Here you'll find piano music performed nightly except Sunday, and the Ted Knight Trio plays for your dancing pleasure on Friday. Owner Peggy Murphy hosts Erny's annual Jazz Fests during July and August (see our Festivals and Annual Events chapter). Special events are announced prior to each weekend.

MIAMI JOE'S CAFE
100 E. Linton Blvd.   274-9177

Miami Joe's is powdering its nose on the inside as we speak and getting over the sneezes from an outside facelift. This cafe opened in June 1995 as a combination neighborhood tavern and disco for dancing in the dark. The club serves lunch and dinner: A full menu is available until 1 AM.

The legendary, former Scoundrel's — more recently PJ's Hideaway — occupies the basement of an office building at Linton Boulevard and Dixie Highway, just south of the Delray Beach Mall. Lots of folks meet here for happy hour or to rendezvous before and after movies at the mall.

Construction to renovate the building's exterior around the elevator column was completed in August

1995, including some new walkways and an access ramp. New owner Joe Merlino, whose Miami area clubs included Pieces of Eight and Two Plus One, renovated the dance floor, upgraded the sound system, added a DJ booth and mirrored the lounge walls. Joe may bring in live music on occasion. His menu features island-style seafood, pastas, the tangy Steak from Hell and Miami Joe Shrimp.

THE ROD AND GUN CLUB
4285 W. Atlantic Ave.   *496-2150*

This club has live entertainment on weekends and two-for-one Happy Hour drink specials from 4 to 9 PM on weekdays. Gary Lane plays piano and sings Neil Diamond-like and Sinatra favorites on Fridays and Saturdays from 7 to 11 PM.

SCARLETT O'HARA'S
335 E. Linton Blvd.   *272-6239*

Scarlett O'Hara's has been back in the capable hands of Norman Briggs for the past year, and the boost in business likely reflects his experienced methods. A Dixieland band performs in-season on Tuesday, Friday and Saturday, and the American menu of prime rib, steaks and fish is served with Southern hospitality.

UGLY MUG
5065 W. Atlantic Ave.   *498-0634*

Ugly Mug has live bands after 10 PM on weekends. The club's 5 AM liquor license draws a democratic mix of night owls: yuppies, construction workers, farm workers, college students and those who cater to the rest of us earlier in the evening.

Boynton Beach

BANANA BOAT
739 E. Ocean Ave.   *732-9400*

Popular Banana Boat has multiplied to include locations in Broward and Palm Beach counties, and entertainment varies accordingly. The Boynton Beach saloon has a perch on the Intracoastal Waterway, and it's common for boaters to tie up and sample the seafood and suds. Sunday afternoons are usually punctuated with an island-style steel-drum band after 4 PM.

THE BACK ALLEY BAR & GRILLE
9770 S. Military Tr.   *738-4805*

The Back Alley is a four-year phenomenon perpetuated with the blessings of the neighborhood. There's a 5 AM license, but owner Sir Roland usually buttons up after 2 or 3 AM. Thursday is comedy night, and live bands perform Friday and Saturday from 10 PM.

Lantana

ABACO'S OYSTER BOAT
6186 S. Congress Ave.   *641-0373*

Abaco's offers live rock 'n' roll and rhythm and blues on weekends from 9:30 PM to 2 AM. Witness a jazz jam on Sundays from 7 to 11 PM.

Palm Beaches Area

COUNTRY NIGHTS
4833 Okeechobee Blvd.
West Palm Beach   *689-7625*

Country Nights features live entertainment from Nashville Tuesday through Sundays. Country karaoke is

THEATER

Movie Theaters

Nobody sees more flicks than the movie critics, so we asked a few cinema veterans which theaters are the most desirable among the 11 in South County.

The hands-down favorite is **AMC Mizner Park 8**, 300 N. Federal Highway, 395-3846. Talk about a primo setup: advanced sound system, multilevel concession operations, lobby layout with escalator to the upstairs, comfortable seats and adequate leg room.

Another new venue with a great lobby setup and congenial staff is the **Muvico Delray 10**, 1668 S. Federal Highway in the Delray Beach Mall, 272-2900. Renovation helped **The Movies at Town Center** in the mall, 21090 St. Andrews Boulevard, 395-0909. Best in the west is **Mission Bay Plaza 8**, Glades Road at State Road 7, 451-9011. **Shadowood Square**, 9889 Glades Road, has the most variety, frequently offering foreign and art films.

If you're looking for the theater closest to you, consider the following: **Delray Square**, 4809 W. Atlantic Avenue, 496-0884, and **Movies 5 of Delray**, 7421 W. Atlantic Avenue, 496-1004, both in Delray Beach; **Movies At Boynton**, 244 N. Congress Avenue, 736-5770, and **Cobb Boynton 8**, 2290 N. Congress Avenue, 734-0027, in Boynton Beach; and **Deerfield Cinema 5**, 2205 W. Hillsboro Boulevard, 428-0008, and **Deerfield Mall 8**, 3984 W. Hillsboro Boulevard, 429-3930, in Deerfield Beach.

Check the entertainment magazines of the daily newspapers each Friday for listings of new movies. *The News* provides an easy-to-read grid format of movie listings and theaters and a map daily and in the "Weekend" section.

Also be sure to plan an outing to see the world on a 40-foot screen at **Blockbuster's IMAX** theater at the Museum of Science and Discovery in Fort Lauderdale. Across from the Broward County Performing Arts Center, IMAX brings you unique video experiences such as footage from the space shuttle, the Rolling Stones in concert, fighting oil fires in Kuwait or global phenomena such as *Africa: Serengeti Plain*.

on tap from 10 PM to 1 AM Mondays, and free dance lessons are offered from 7 to 9 PM Monday through Friday.

JALAPEÑO HARRY'S
12794 W. Forest Hill Blvd.
Wellington   793-5445

This place is open from 11:30 AM to 3 AM seven days a week. Live bands play rock and country music on weekends. Folks come here for karaoke and line dancing as well.

JAZZ SHOWCASE
905 N. Dixie Hwy.
West Palm Beach   832-1200

Jazz Showcase presents live jazz from 10 PM Thursday through Saturday. Jorge Garcia's band, Athenas, plays Fridays.

E. R. BRADLEY'S SALOON
111 Bradley Pl.
Palm Beach   833-3520

E. R. Bradley's is open from 11 AM to 3 AM. There's music for dancing after 10 PM.

AU BAR

OK, we know some of you were wondering about this place, which garnered notoriety during William Kennedy Smith's trial. A bit of advice: Don't go. Why? It's closed.

TA-BOO
221 Worth Ave.
Palm Beach   835-3500

Yes, Ta-Boo has been open forever — anyone who remembers when it wasn't doesn't reveal their age. This veritable landmark is strategically positioned to accommodate all manner of agenda and offers piano music and dance music from 7:30 to 11 PM Mon-

day through Sunday. See dining details in our Restaurants chapter.

Broward County

Deerfield Beach

THE COVE
On the Intracoastal Waterway, just off
Hillsboro Blvd.   (305) 421-9272

Local bands play live music here Tuesday through Saturday nights, and a Jamaican steel band performs on Sunday afternoons. Boaters tie up for lunch, light meals and complete dinners as well as entertainment.

CRABBY JACK'S
1015 S. Federal Hwy.   (305) 429-3770

Crabby Jack's is a casual seafood haunt offering live music outside on the patio from 9 PM daily except Fridays. Inside is a DJ or karaoke. Food includes tasty ribs and such. Jack's is open 11:30 AM to 2 AM Sunday through Friday, until 3 AM on Saturday.

M.T. POCKETS ROCK & ROLL CAFE
100 N. Federal Hwy.   (305) 698-0383

M.T. Pockets offers room to spread out, with a dance floor, a trio of bars and a stage area for the disc jockey's shenanigans and a showcase of music from the '50s through the '90s. Live music happens Thursday through Saturday.

P.G. DOOGIE'S
1025 E. Hillsboro Blvd.
at U.S. 1   (305) 428-6438

You can chill out at Doogie's seven days a week, 11 AM to 2 AM. Jazz is the password, with regional trios and bands cranking up from 4:30 PM "to whenever." You won't go hungry here, with choices of sandwiches, ribs and seafood.

Pompano Beach

FISHERMAN'S WHARF
222 Pompano Beach Blvd.   (305) 941-5522

This restaurant and lounge is perched pierside on the ocean. Live bands play nightly. Sunday's sounds wax "reggaesque," and blues and jazz are performed on Mondays.

Fort Lauderdale

BAJA BEACH CLUB
3200 N. Federal Hwy.   (305) 561-2432

This club takes a California approach: Ladies drink free seven days a week from 5 to 9 PM in the sports bar-daiquiri bar-restaurant, where light fare is served, including burgers, chicken sandwiches and salads. A DJ spins tunes nightly from 9 PM until 2 AM — 3 AM on Saturdays — for "the world's largest dance party, with surfing bartenders, dancing waitresses and a whole lotta craziness."

Baja Beach Club also performs this trick at 3015 Grand Avenue in Coconut Grove, (305) 445-0278. If you're heading south, calls for the rules of the house in the Grove. Baja also boogies up north in Orlando.

CHEERS
Dixie Hwy.
and Cypress Creek Rd.   (305) 771-6337

Cheers wears its colors — blues — and offers music specials from 10:30 PM weeknights. Two bands play from 9 PM on Friday and Satur-

day, and the kitchen serves until 4 AM. This is a relaxing hangout for dart competitions.

COMIC STRIP
1432 N. Federal Hwy.   (305) 565-8887

Comic Strip has shows at 9:30 PM Tuesday through Thursday and Sunday; 10 PM Friday; and 7, 9:15 and 11:30 PM on Saturday. If you're lucky, you'll hit a night when Max Dolcelli is on deck. A guest on HBO and in comedy clubs throughout the country and a regular entertainer on one of the top cruise ship lines combing the Caribbean, Max often footnotes his kitschy profundities with the question, "Or am I the only one?" He's bright, outrageous and well worth the drive.

MAI-KAI
3599 N. Federal Hwy.   (305) 563-3272

Mai-Kai is the kind of tourist trap most folks are happy to fall into. A Lauderdale tradition for decades, Mai-Kai recreates the Pacific Islands with authentic and elaborate Polynesian dancers and musicians. Dining is authentic too, but you can start slowly in the lounge with the Mystery Drink and some succulent appetizers. The atmosphere is contagious. Two shows are performed nightly for a $7.95 cover charge.

MUSICIAN'S EXCHANGE CAFE
729 W. Sunrise Blvd.   (305) 764-1912

This cafe hosts local acts on Wednesdays and local and national performers Thursdays through Saturdays. You can get down upstairs to the sounds of jazz, rock, reggae and rhythm and blues. Two shows usu-

An intimate and elegant lobby lounge, The Living Room at Four Seasons Ocean Grand serves cocktails afternoons and evenings.

ally happen on Friday and Saturday, one at 8:30 or 9 PM and another at 10 or 11 PM. Cover charges range from $5 to $15 or more. A recorded message gives the schedule two weeks in advance, including show times and prices.

O'HARA'S PUB
722 E. Las Olas Blvd.   (305) 524-1764

O'Hara's is a must-see and go-hear, especially if be-turbaned Dr. Lonnie Smith graces the keyboard. Jazz is the operative word seven nights a week, from 9 PM to 1:30 AM. Wednesday night is time for the blues, and every other Sunday is a Big Band bonanza from 2:30 to 6:30 PM. O'Hara's serves sandwiches, pizza and salads from 11 AM. Plans call for adding Cajun treats to the menu for Fall '95.

SEPTEMBER'S
2975 N. Federal Hwy.   (305) 563-4331

September's features an eight-piece show band from 9 PM to 2 AM Tuesday through Sunday. There's piano music Wednesday through Saturday in the dining room.

SQUEEZE
2 S. New River Dr.   (305) 522-2151

Squeeze is not your average club — go and see for yourself. Dancers compete for the spotlight with all manner of fringe accoutrements attached to the ceiling and walls. Local bands contribute to the progressive niche. Squeeze is open from 9 PM to 2 AM nightly except Saturday, when it stays open until 3 AM.

Photo: Marc Vaughn

A courtyard leads from the shops at Boca's Town Center to the Marriott.

Inside
Shopping

Satisfying the caliber of sophisticated consumer, the Gold Coast attracts imposes a serious challenge on most tourist destinations. Fortunately for Insiders born to shop or well-taught to spend, the vicinity is home to a treasure trove of marketplaces.

Your cash, credit cards and travelers checks are welcome at regional indoor and outdoor malls, neighborhood centers, smaller plazas, large anchors, specialty shops and intimate boutiques.

Area malls are described further along in this chapter.

Three Jewels

MIZNER PARK

407 Plaza Real
Between U.S. Hwy. I and N.E. Mizner Blvd.
Boca Raton 362-0606

Many newcomers get acquainted with Boca Raton at Mizner Park, a shopping destination unique in the Southeast United States. (Please see also our Mizner Park chapter for additional information and insight.) Its concept — a 30-acre mixed-use urban village — might remind visitors of Boston's Fanuel Hall or Baltimore's Harbor Place.

It's an all-day or all-evening, self-contained hangout geared for fun — people-watching and celebrity-gazing;

having a snack or full gourmet meal; browsing through books, music and artwork; taking in a movie in the fancy octa-plex, multilevel AMC cinema; or enjoying a champagne picnic and outdoor concert under the stars at the Mizner Park Amphitheater.

The diversified mix of stores will make you itchy to buy. The look and feel of this place says money, fashion and instant gratification, but the thrifty don't have to go home empty-handed. If you're waiting for the airline to retrieve your luggage from Boca Grande, stop by Bass Clothing for some basic, moderately priced weekend wear. Forget the passé bags and visit Bolufé Leatherware for new luggage or a leather jacket that squeaks respectfully in the presence of a Harley. Even if they didn't misplace your threads, make a beeline to Jodan for the most exciting shoes — exotic-skin boots, Reeboks from the boutique line, Frankie & Baby sequined flats or Stuart Weitzman pumps. The family-owned business started by Joan Gilbert and her late husband has great accessories too, from hats and belts to unusual specialty clothing that helps you indulge those whims essential to stress management.

Still curious about the Bruno Magli footwear featured in a certain Los Angeles criminal trial? Check out Madison Avenue Shoes for men. They also carry Rockport, which as far as we know are innocent.

If you're determined to spend money, try the Versace jeans imported for Punch. And if you go looking for Jeannie's On The Park from past years, they've moved south, back to Royal Palm Plaza.

Adjacent to the city center on the east side of Federal Highway, Mizner Park is home to an upscale bookstore, Liberties Fine Books & Music (see this chapter's section on Bookstores and Newsstands), with its own cappuccino den. It's also home to the folks who live above some of the stores, since upper-level rental apartments and townhomes complement the commercial marketplace. Envisioned as an elite stage set with books, music and art, Mizner Park treats shoppers, visitors and residents to shaded promenades, gazebos and fountains.

Buying or browsing can be a day and night occupation, starting with the aforementioned Liberties Fine Books & Music; Steve's, Heidi's and David's ice cream shop; coffee specialties at Gourmet Experience; women's apparel at Made In France, Mieka, Suzi Saint Tropez and Deborah James; sportswear and specialty wear at Fitigues, Arlene, Kiwi, Chico's, Dillan Isle Clothing Co., Swim 'n Sport and Dock Square Clothiers; Visual Eyes; Stepping Out Shoes; second-generation Altier Jewelers, Illusion Gems and Ice Jewelry; gifts at N.Y. Floral Co. and Israeli imported gift items at Ahava; curiosities at Celebrations; artwork at Masterpiece Gallery, Addison Gallery, Christy Taylor Galleries, Marcus Animation Gallery and L'Atelier D'Art; Chenzo & Co. full-

service beauty salon. Eateries include the Bavarian Colony and Mozzarella's. You can also read about Max's Grille, Baci and Bistro L'Europe in our chapter on Restaurants.

NationsBank, with a location here, has acquired Intercontinental Bank, which earlier bought Boca Bank. And you even can shop for a luxury residence at Limited Edition International Realty.

Open since 1991, Mizner Park is a necklace around a Spanish-flavor courtyard with fountains, tiled walkways and crisp landscaping. One-way traffic moves counterclockwise along two-lane Plaza Real. Under construction opposite Liberties is the International Museum of Cartoon Art, described in the chapter on Arts and Culture.

Mizner Park parking is complimentary and convenient — either on-street, valet or in one of the covered parking garages. To visit, exit I-95 at Palmetto Park Road, go east to Federal Highway and turn north. Call for more information.

ROYAL PALM PLAZA

300 S. Federal Hwy.
Between U.S. Hwy. 1 and S.E. Mizner Blvd.
Boca Raton 395-1222

About two blocks south of Palmetto Park Road, this open-air Spanish-style center has 80 specialty shops opening onto quaint landscaped courtyards, arched porticos, decorative tile accents and the refreshing whisper of fountains.

The doyenne of existing shopping centers in Boca Raton, "The Pink Plaza" has been drawing discerning shoppers for more than 30 years.

Royal Palm Plaza is home to fine, exclusive merchandise; an eclectic restaurant mix, including Mido's Japanese Restaurant (see our Restaurants chapter), Intermezzo Cafe, Food Amongst the Arts, Cyrano's, La Viola's and Sapori; and cultural tenants such as the Little Palm Theatre, Boca Ballet Theatre and Jan McArt's Royal Palm Dinner Theater; interior designers, art galleries and studios.

Apparel shops offer resort wear, designer clothing, career dressing, lingerie, beach and sportswear — even threads for nuptials. Artwork, gifts, tuxedos and power ties — Royal Palm Plaza offers diverse shopping opportunities.

Notable shops include Maus and Hoffman, Harold Grant's and La Fererra's (upscale men's and ladies' clothing); Patchington's (fine ladies' clothing); Gattle's (bed and bath); Crystal Bowl (fine crystal); Hoffman's Chocolates; Donald Laser and Hall of Frames (artwork); and Jubilee (gourmet grocery).

Access is along Federal Highway between Palmetto Park Road and Camino Real as well as Mizner Boulevard to the east. Plentiful parking is scattered throughout the plaza and the merchants association provides free trolley service to Mizner Park and other downtown locations.

WORTH AVENUE
Palm Beach

Worth Avenue is famous even without the backdrop of Palm Beach, but island legends don't hurt sales at Tiffany & Company, Cartier, Louis Vuitton, Gucci, Charles Jourdan, Martha's, Polo Ralph Lauren, Uomo-Erre, Calvin Klein, Chanel, Escada, Salvatore Ferragamo, Daniel Foxx, Marisa's, Lacoste Boutique or Van Cleef & Arpels. Travelers who frequent Rodeo Drive, Bond Street or Madison Avenue easily can make do on the Avenue.

Once a tourist trap known as Alligator Joe's, Worth was the whim of Palm Beach dream merchants Paris Singer and Addison Mizner. Singer's money and Mizner's vision replaced the reptile farm with shops and apartments along the narrow Avenue. Via Mizner and Via Parigi were the first enclaves to include residential quarters on the upper floors of the fabled street later called "The Mink Mile." Shops date to the 1920s, with many of the existing buildings Mizner originals and most of the famous tenants well-positioned for decades.

Besides the individual array of rarified merchants is the two-story open-air Esplanade at 150 Worth Avenue. Anchored with Saks Fifth Avenue, Esplanade has 48 shops, salons and restaurants and a parking garage.

Worth Avenue also is headquarters for magazine publisher Jim Sheeran of *Palm Beach Society*, the arbiter of island glitterati from his perch at No. 240.

There's convenient on-street one-hour parking, metered parking one block north on Peruvian Avenue, and valet parking off Hibiscus Avenue. To reach Worth Avenue, take the Okeechobee Boulevard exit of I-95 and go east past Flagler Drive and over Memorial Bridge to Palm Beach; turn right onto South County Road for a half-mile to the entrance.

"Downtown" Destinations

Boca Raton

The area between Royal Palm and Mizner Park and the east-west corridor has some delightful stores, including **Etoile**, 359 E. Palmetto Park Road, with a second location at Boca Center, 5250 Town Center Circle.

Store traffic relies on finding European designs such as Karl Lagerfeld, Sonia Rykiel or Giorgio Armani — especially veterans of Rodeo Drive who also are spoiled with the emerging wave of Japanese designers throughout Los Angeles catering to the film and costume industries.

Look Great, 771 E. Palmetto Park Road, is three operations in one: Cosmetics, European Day Spa, and Headquarters for Hair. Definitely the pampered zone, this is a feel-good, look-great opportunity for a facial, spa treatments, hair coloring and treating, style makeovers . . . the works.

Force-E, 877 E. Palmetto Park Road, is a force to be reckoned with, for sure. Multiple locations in South Florida specialize in everything the diver needs for snorkeling and scuba excursions. They carry a limited selection of moderately priced swimwear and T-shirts. Force-E also arranges all levels of boat trips and snorkeling expeditions, even arranging your dive in exotic ports such as Belize, Cozumel and the Great Barrier Reef in Australia. It's open seven days, with additional stores at 7166 Beracasa Way, Boca Raton; 660 Linton Boulevard, Delray Beach; 1399 N. Military Trail, West Palm Beach; 11911 U.S. Highway 1, North Palm Beach; 2160 W. Oakland Park Boulevard, Oakland Park; and 5550 N.W. 51st Avenue, Coconut Creek.

If you're really looking for adventure, **TNT Swimwear**, 146 S. Federal Highway, offers custom bikinis. A custom suit can be ready within 20 minutes of the final fit. Patterns are kept on file, so you can call in an or-

der and pick it up a half-hour later. TNT offers exercise and workout wear too.

If you need a sarong for that designer maillot, try **Doreen's Swimwear**, 347 E. Palmetto Park Road.

If your curls get hopelessly tangled in the wind, go see **Carlos di Carlos**, 193 E. Palmetto Park Road for a new hairdo. If Carlos is busy, consider time out at **Albee's Boca Beach Market & Grill** at Palmetto Park Road and Highway A1A. Albee's is an excellent vantage point for sizing up your next stop. A cappuccino, a newspaper, something from the deli, and you're back in the spending game.

By now, you've undoubtedly remembered a gift you need to buy, and

Brown's Bountiful Baskets is nearby at 98 S. Federal Highway. Pick the basket, the ribbons and the goodies that go in it, and you'll be proud of the attractive end results.

GLADES PLAZA
2200 Glades Rd.   *391-5964*

This open-air configuration has 51 stores in pods arranged in quadrants, with color-coded designations and readily available brochures showing where stores are. Two popular destinations are **Barbara Katz** for spectacular designer clothes and **Dolly Duz** for shoes such as Charles Jourdan and Cole Haan, a Donna Karan handbag and fashion accessories. Shoe selection is good, even for those tiny tots.

Visit the **Coffee Roaster Cafe & Market**, for outrageous breakfast goodies and gift items. The aroma of croissants, bagels and danish is irresistible. For a lunch stop there's **Mario's of Boca**, which you can read more about in our Restaurants chapter.

FIFTH AVENUE SHOPS
2108 N. Federal Hwy. 392-0555

The center is a mile north of Glades Road on the east side of Federal Highway. Visit **Best Wishes**, which has several other South Florida stores, for custom jewelry and terrific gifts. Then, walk over to **Angelica's Attic**. Quaint and merry, the Attic wafts with the aroma of potpourri which complements the live birds singing in cages and the music in the background. Speaking of wings, angels are plentiful, with lots of unique floral arrangements, antique accessories and more.

You'll also find a **Publix Supermarket**, a 24-hour **Eckerd Drugs**, **Hit Or Miss** discount women's apparel, **Peking Chinese Restaurant** and **Andover Reed** men's clothing and tailor shop, to name just a few.

THE POLO CLUB SHOPPES
5030 Champion Blvd. 997-2002

The center is named for the adjacent upscale country club, just north of Clint Moore Road off Military Trail. Two of our favorite shops here are **Shari's Place**, a women's clothier reflecting both European and American designers, and the **Polo Club Book Shoppe**.

PLAZA REAL
Clint Moore and
Powerline Rds. 241-7401

Here, you can accomplish one-stop shopping for those last-minute items on the way from work or running away from home: *The New York Times*, a bottle of Dom Perignon, fresh-cut roses and frozen yogurt. It's also the place to fill 'er up and kick back while the "Touchless" system washes your ride.

THE SHOPS AT BOCA CENTER
Military Tr. between
Palmetto Park and Glades Rds.
Boca Raton *No central phone*

The complex draws shoppers from throughout the region and guests at its centerpiece **Marriott Hotel**. You can spend the day browsing the 28-acre contemporary complex, trying on a Sonia Rykiel outfit, vegging for an hour's massage and facial at **John DeMederios**, lunching at **Uncle Tai's**, popping into **Chico's** for a cool cotton, studying food gadgets or the olive oils at **Williams-Sonoma**, selecting a matte at **Fastframe**, then head-

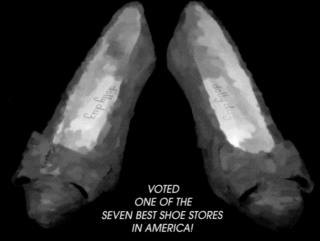

Dorjon

AVEDA
THE ART AND SCIENCE
OF PURE FLOWER AND PLANT ESSENCES

Images by Aveda

Hair • Nails
Skin Care
Cosmetics

392-3555

Palms Plaza Boca Raton

ing back to **Etoile** to actually buy the Rykiel outfit.

Children and the young at heart will be happy to know there's even a designer **McDonald's**.

To reach The Shops at Boca Center, take I-95 to Palmetto Park Road and exit west; turn right on Military Trail and head north to the intersection of Town Center Circle.

Assorted other Boca area neighborhood centers include **Oaks Plaza** near Florida Atlantic University, the **Shoppes at the Sanctuary** between Spanish River Boulevard and Yamato Road on Federal Highway, and **Del Mar Shopping Village** at Powerline and Palmetto Park roads.

Delray Beach

ATLANTIC AVENUE

The gateway to Delray Beach is center stage for a marketing master plan that blends the merchandising of its shops, galleries and restaurants into the seamless image of civic pride, social responsibility and progressive attention to infrastructure. Culture and history are the ribbon on the package, and people are buying it.

The Avenue redecorated itself in recent years to showcase more than 150 tenants, including apparel and gift boutiques, art galleries, restaurants, professionals, service businesses, the Chamber of Commerce and six government entities. Customers enjoy on-site parking and the streetscape of brick sidewalks, nostalgia street lamps and sidewalk cafes where an alfresco pause makes it easy to organize today's shopping list.

The **Elegant Trunk**, 1051 E. Atlantic Avenue, specializes in unusual gifts, table tops and other home accessories. One Insider did all her holiday shopping there one year. Elegant Trunk makes it possible to pick out an item you'd be proud to give for a modest $25.

Gloria Waldman's **Artcetera**, 640 E. Atlantic Avenue, is a good example of the Avenue's colony of art galleries. Waldman's gallery specializes in large, eclectic pieces — ancient and contemporary — and matches collectors with artists and interior designers. The sculptures of Esther Wertheimer are among her permanent exhibition.

Waldman's colleagues, Daniel and Carole Lynn, offer **Forms ... A Southwest Gallery**, 415 E. Atlantic Avenue. They showcase artists of that geographic genre in every medium imaginable, from woven-fiber to sculpture, pottery, masks and hand-painted furniture. From Santa Fe to Sedona, Taos and Phoenix come relics, drums, symbols and artifacts.

In clothing, there's **Mark, Fore & Strike, The Trouser Shop, Nina Raynor** and **Courtyard Boutique**, to name a few. **Kemp's Shoes** recently moved to 1004 E. Atlantic Avenue, after two decades as the footwear institution of Royal Palm Plaza.

In Chocolate offers an extensive selection of fine sweets: chocolate-covered cornflakes, orange- and chocolate-frosted pecans or a half-gallon of dipped popcorn, golf balls, pigskins and caramel crunch bars, to name a few possibilities. (See our sidebar in this chapter for more delicious details.)

The Avenue offers jewelers, salons, office supplies, furniture, appliances, printing, quaint hotels, a spirits nook, bicycle shop, camera shops and the hometown newspaper. Our Business chapter covers more about Delray's renaissance over the past decade.

While you're discovering Delray's shopping haunts, don't overlook the **Indoor Flea Market**, 5283 W. Atlantic Avenue. More than 150 vendors display affordable name merchandise Wednesday through Sunday.

Malls

TOWN CENTER AT BOCA RATON
Glades Rd. at St. Andrews Blvd.
Boca Raton   *368-6000*

Town Center is the "inner city" of a shopping megalopolis just west of I-95. In the "suburbs," there's Glades Plaza (with dozens of one-of-a kind-shops and the **Wholly Harvest Market and Cafe** and **Hooters**) to the northeast and Boca Village Square (with Roadhouse Grill and a variety of shops and eateries) to the southwest.

Town Center's anchor stores are **Bloomingdale's**, **Saks Fifth Avenue**, **Mervyn's**, **Sears**, **Burdines** and **Lord & Taylor** and more than 100 specialty shops.

The mall is the home to the lone **Caswell and Massey** store in South Florida, for folks who can't live without the fine soaps, perfumes and toiletries made by the venerable apothecary.

The food court is a bustling place that's a popular meeting spot for young and old alike.

Town Center is open from 10 AM to 9 PM Monday through Saturday and noon to 6 PM on Sunday.

THE GARDENS OF THE PALM BEACHES
PGA Blvd., between I-95 and U.S. Hwy. 1
Palm Beach Gardens   *775-7750*

Take a deep breath as you walk through the glass doors into The Gardens; it's a breathtaking place. First, the statistics: 185 specialty stores plus restaurants and cafes for a chance to get off your feet and enjoy a breve at **Cafe Cappuccino**, a čuppa at **Marianne's Tea Room** or something cold and delightful, such as a glass of champagne and caviar on toast points at **Petrossian Rendez-vous Cafe** at Bloomingdale's.

Built on two levels, The Gardens is anchored by **Bloomingdale's**, **Burdines**, **Macy's**, **Saks Fifth Avenue** and **Sears**, and is filled with interesting, upscale shops. There's a pretty good mix of shops, with a special accent on clothiers and shoe stores.

The last word on The Gardens also is about shoes: Wear comfortable ones when you visit. This is one huge place.

The mall is open Monday through Saturday from 10 AM to 9 PM and on Sundays, from noon to 6 PM. Sears opens at 11 AM on Sundays.

POMPANO SQUARE
Federal Hwy. at Copans Rd.
Pompano Beach   *(305) 943-4683*

Literally and figuratively, the old Pompano Fashion Square is in the pink again as Pompano Square. The new-look mall has taken on a tropical theme and a face lift, now sporting pastel pinks and greens.

The mall is anchored by **Mervyn's**, **Sears**, **JCPenney** and **Burdines**, and has more than 100 specialty stores. One that draws considerable interest is **This End Up**, which produces casual furniture from packing crates.

There are a few restaurants and cafes on the lower level, and the upstairs **Sundeck Food Court** which offers many quick dining selections.

Pompano Square is open Monday through Saturday from 10 AM to 9 PM and on Sunday from noon to 5:30 PM.

THE FASHION MALL AT PLANTATION
University Dr., just north of Broward Blvd.
Plantation (305) 370-1884

With three levels of shopping, just like layers of a cake, The Fashion Mall at Plantation is quite a treat. With more than 100 specialty stores and anchors **Lord & Taylor** and **Macy's**, the mall also plays host to a **Sheraton Suites Hotel**.

As the name suggests, fashion stores are big here, but there's plenty for everyone, including a **Williams-Sonoma**, for fine cooks.

The food court is substantial, but if your sweet tooth kicks up and you're not hungry enough to stop for a meal, make a stop at the **Candy Barrel**, featuring hundreds of old-fashioned candies.

The mall is open Monday through Saturday from 10 AM to 9 PM and on Sundays from noon to 6 PM.

FESTIVAL FLEA MARKET
Sample Rd. at Florida's Tnpk.
Pompano Beach (305) 979-4555

Bargain hunters from Boca Raton and environs need not drive far to find fabulous values here. More than 600 vendors offer their wares in the 400,000-square-foot building that also includes a games area for the young and young at heart, a food court and an eight-screen Fox theater.

The mall is open Wednesday through Friday from 9:30 AM to 5 PM and on Saturday and Sunday from 9:30 AM to 6 PM.

BAYSIDE MARKETPLACE
Biscayne Blvd. at N.E. Third St.
Miami (305) 577-3344

You might think Miami is a bit far to drive for a mall, but Bayside is special — a collection of more than 100 upscale shops and more than 30 tony cafes, bistros, restaurants and eateries that reflect the international flavor of the Big Orange. Its setting is alongside Bayfront Park at Miami's old Pier 5.

Around 4:30 PM weekdays, the stream of downtown office workers heads to Bayside to unwind with friends before embarking on the drive home on I-95. It's the perfect place to decompress, too, with its waterfront promenade and panorama of Biscayne Bay. There's an excellent choice of entertainment, too, from salsa to a different beat at the **Hard Rock Cafe**.

Many Insiders love Burdines because it stands behind its merchandise. Of course, for style-conscious fashion hounds, that might mean they end up wearing something somebody else returned.

Insiders' Tips

Bayside stores are open from 10 AM to 10 PM Monday through Thursday, 10 AM to 11 PM Friday and Saturday and 11 AM to 9 PM on Sunday. Hours are extended at restaurants, outdoor cafes and bars.

DELRAY BEACH MALL
Linton Blvd. at Federal Hwy.
Delray Beach   272-1781

Not too long ago, Delray Beach Mall was suffering, but like much of the city around it, it has been resuscitated and is prospering in its new life.

The mall is anchored by **Marshalls** and **Byrons** and is now home to a **Muvico 10** theater complex and a **Roadhouse Grill** steakhouse. Also on the property are a **Publix** supermarket, **Eckerd** pharmacy, **Clothestime** and **Morrison's Cafeteria.**

The mall is open Monday through Saturday from 10 AM to 9 PM and on Sundays from noon to 5 PM.

BOYNTON BEACH MALL
Congress Ave. at Old Boynton Rd.
Boynton Beach   736-7900

With five anchor stores and 140 specialty shops, Boynton Beach Mall is pretty sizeable on its own, but add a slew of others from the Boynton Beach Promenade and some from the eastern edge of the mall grounds, and you've got a retail community.

The mall's anchor stores are **Macy's, Sears, Burdines, JCPenney** and **Mervyn's.** For the hungry, there's a large food court, **Morrison's Cafeteria** and **Ruby Tuesday.**

On the periphery, there are plenty more shopping opportunities at **Toys 'R' Us, OfficeMax, Boston Proper,**

the **Mark, Fore & Strike Outlet Store, Visionworks** and **Barnes & Noble Booksellers.**

The mall is open 10 AM to 9 PM Monday through Saturday and 11 AM to 6 PM on Sunday.

PALM BEACH MALL
I-95 at Palm Beach Lakes Blvd.
West Palm Beach   683-9186

Palm Beach Mall is one of the oldest malls in the county and still hums with activity at the crossroads of Central Palm Beach.

The mall is anchored by **Burdines, JCPenney, Lord & Taylor, Mervyn's** and **Sears.** There are 125 specialty stores and a food court.

Hours are 10 AM to 9 PM Monday through Saturday, noon to 5:30 PM on Sundays.

THE GALLERIA
Sunrise Blvd. at Bayview Dr.
Fort Lauderdale   (305) 564-1015

The Galleria, which grew from the site of the Sunrise Shopping Center, bills itself as "world class shopping," and there's more than just a ring of truth to it. It's Broward County's foremost high-end mall and attracts a significant number of foreign shoppers and, of course, local folks and domestic tourists.

The anchor stores at this dazzling, split-level mall are **Neiman-Marcus, Dillard's, Burdines, Lord & Taylor** and **Saks Fifth Avenue.** A huge **Pearle Vision** store is on the lower level beneath Saks Fifth Avenue, and there are about 150 specialty stores, with a strong emphasis on fashion, housewares and sporting goods. The downstairs food court offers great variety, and there are

Palm Beach County is a shopper's paradise.

restaurants and spots to stop and nibble scattered throughout.

The Galleria is open Monday through Saturday from 10 AM to 9 PM and from noon to 5:30 PM on Sunday.

SAWGRASS MILLS

12801 W. Sunrise Blvd.
Sunrise (305) 846-2350

With more than 200 stores, seven anchor stores and an 18-plex theater complex, Sawgrass Mills, which opened in 1990, already is one of the world's largest outlet malls, but plans call for this behemoth to grow even more formidable.

Plans released in June 1995 call for the addition of a new shopping wing to add three more outlets: **Neiman-Marcus, Mikasa** china and **Service Merchandise,** that add to existing anchors **Target, Burlington Coat Factory, Marshalls, Spiegel, Waccamaw** and **Bed, Bath & Beyond.** Add to that an IMAX theater, a concert hall and **Hockeyland,** a two-rink ice-skating mecca.

The present mall offers two international food courts, three restaurants, automated teller machines and a currency exchange.

Mall hours are Monday through Saturday from 10 AM to 9:30 PM and 11 AM to 6 PM on Sundays.

CORAL SQUARE MALL

Atlantic Blvd. at University Dr.
Coral Springs (305) 755-5550

It has billed itself as "The City in the Country," but Coral Springs, in far northwestern Broward County, has grown into quite a shopping haven, and its brightest jewel is Coral Square, anchored by **Sears, Mervyn's, JCPenney** and **Burdines**.

Outside the mall, on its western border along University Drive is the **Coral Square Promenade,** crammed with more shops, restaurants and nightspots.

Think of the intersection of Atlantic and University as the literary crossroads of southeastern Florida, because a quarter-million or so books are on sale here. **B. Dalton** and

Waldenbooks in Coral Square were here first, followed by Barnes & Noble, on the southeastern corner of the intersection, recently joined by Borders Books & Music on the northwestern corner. (See the Bookstores and Newsstands section in this chapter for additional listings.)

Mall hours are 10 AM to 9 PM Monday through Saturday and 11 AM to 6 PM on Sunday.

PLAZA DEL MAR

E. Ocean Ave. at U.S. Hwy. A1A
Manalapan   586-6447

Plaza del Mar is an open-air shopping center, home of the Lois Pope Theatre and more than 40 upscale shops and boutiques such as Patchington, Native Sun, Stepping Out and Mark, Fore & Strike.

OAKBROOK SQUARE

PGA Blvd. at N. Federal Hwy.
Palm Beach Gardens   626-3880

Anchored on its north end by Jacobson's and on the south by Publix, Oakbrook Square is also home to 40 shops and boutiques set around an open-air patio.

PROSPERITY CENTRE

PGA Blvd. at Prosperity Farms Rd.
Palm Beach Gardens   624-9165

Among the major tenants in this open-air shopping center are Barnes & Noble Booksellers, Homelife, T.J. Maxx and Office Depot.

CROSS-COUNTY MALL

Okeechobee Rd. at Military Tr.
West Palm Beach   683-8884

This central Palm Beach County mall is home to Kmart, OfficeMax,

Fashion Bug and the AMC Cross County 8 Theatres, among others.

ESPLANADE SHOPS

Worth Ave. at S. County Rd.
Palm Beach   833-0868

It's not one of the county's bigger malls, but it certainly is one of its most prestigious. Tenants at this double-decker patio mall include Saks Fifth Avenue, Georgette Klinger, Krizia, The Purple Turtle, Liz Claiborne, Calvin Klein and Polo Ralph Lauren.

Supercenters

There are two supercenters in southeastern Florida that deserve notice. What are supercenters, you ask? Well, Gulliver might call them Brobdingnagian shopping centers, filled with megastores such as Incredible Universe, Builders Square II and OfficeMax.

DELRAY CROSSING

Linton Blvd. and I-95 N.
Delray Beach   274-0013

Shoppers come here for stores such as Circuit City, Builders Square II, Famous Footwear, Sportsman's Paradise, Target, Ross and The Linen Store.

OAKWOOD PLAZA

Stirling Rd. and I-95 N.
Hollywood   No central phone

The major stores here are Incredible Universe, OfficeMax, PETsMART, MacFrugal's, Kmart, Just for Feet, Builders Square II, Service Merchandise, Marshalls, Famous Footwear and the biggest Barnes & Noble Booksellers in the

Boca Burger Company:
Where's the Beef?

Max Shondor's Boca Burger Company, 1660 N.E. 12th Terrace, Fort Lauderdale, (305) 524-1977, produces soy-based, meatless burgers in three flavors that are making news lately because of high-profile customers such as President Clinton and because the product has achieved significant crossover status. Not just for health food nuts, Boca Burgers are known for taste, and texture, and a fast-assimilating protein that gives a long-term high-energy boost. They're high-fiber, low-calorie and popular enough to be carried in Publix, Winn-Dixie, Hyde Park, Xtra, Wholly Harvest, Albertson's, Sabatino's and King's. Or you can order one at The News Cafe on Ocean Drive, South Beach.

Boca Burgers began in Boca Raton, but Shondor moved to Fort Lauderdale in 1995 to expand his production operation to meet demand among distributors in all 50 states: national and regional chains plus private labels for fast-food restaurants at Disney World, Pritikin and La Costa spas — a chain in Hawaii, Puerto Rico, Bermuda and throughout the Caribbean.

Shondor offers three flavors: Vegan, the original with "absolutely no fat" or animal products; Chef Max's favorite, 98 percent fat-free with a bit of Cheddar cheese; and Hint of Fresh Garlic, 99 percent fat-free with a bit of Mozzarella. The White House, which ordered about 8,000 Boca Burgers in the past year, used to call here directly. Shondor says they now deal with a distributor in Maryland.

The company has about 13,000 square feet to produce current demand of about 12 million burgers. Shondor says people who are trying to modify their diets discover his product through word of mouth.

"They'll switch if they like something as well or better than meat. I have a customer who's a doctor who thanks me for no longer having to go for fast-food burgers. Now he wants to know what I can do about lobster and steak . . ."

Boca Burgers come four to a box. Shondor says it takes about five minutes to prepare them from frozen to ready: Just put them in a skillet, crust the outside, simmer a few minutes, add the bun and your favorite condiments. There are directions for microwave, skillet or barbecue. He says he's proud to have won 38 tasting contests, and he loves the articles about Boca Burgers that have appeared in *Penthouse*, *The Washington Post* and *The New York Times*.

area, complete with a coffee bar that serves Starbucks coffee specialties.

Citrus Groves

The days of hearing Anita Bryant gush "A day without orange juice is like a day without sunshine" are long gone, but the link between the Sunshine State and citrus fruit is inextricable.

Many people underestimate our state's value in agriculture, but

Florida can hold its weight with the big boys. It's not just our three outstanding college football teams who vie for No. 1 every year — Florida is No. 1 in agricultural production in the Southeast, No. 8 overall in the nation. And at the top of the state's leading agricultural counties is Palm Beach County. In 1992, for example, Palm Beach County reaped $1.2 billion, nearly three times more than the No. 2 county.

In terms of citrus production, no other state even comes close to the Sunshine State. Florida produces 70 percent of the country's citrus supply. Ninety-three percent of all oranges grown in Florida are processed for orange juice. Central Florida is the widest point in the state's citrus belt, but excellent citrus fruit is available in South Florida, and visitors here always seem to want to pay a visit to the groves. Even for longtime Floridians, a visit to a grove can be lots of fun. There's much to learn, and the sampling is excellent.

BOB ROTH'S NEW RIVER GROVES
5660 Griffin Rd.
Davie   *(305) 581-8630*

A wide variety of citrus products and farm-grown vegetables is available here along with a dizzying array of Florida food specialties. (How about a jar of seagrape jelly for that favorite aunt?) New River Groves specializes in shipping citrus and stone crabs around the globe.

New River Groves is open daily from 8 AM to 6 PM.

FLAMINGO GARDENS
3750 Flamingo Rd.
Davie   *(305) 476-6013*

Flamingo Gardens is much more than just an orange grove. In addition to its processing, shipping and retail activities, a number of educational activities are offered, many involving agricultural topics. Call before you visit to see what's happening on the monthly calendar of activities.

Flamingo Gardens is open daily from 9 AM to 5 PM.

BLOOD'S HAMMOCK GROVES

4549 Linton Blvd.
Delray Beach 498-3400

Since the 1940s, folks have been streaming to Blood's for fresh citrus products. The neat-as-a-bandbox sales facility is also home to a plant boutique, where visitors can purchase flowers, ornamentals and fresh herbs, decorative pots and other gardening items.

Blood's is open Mondays through Saturdays November through April from 8:30 AM to 5 PM. See also our Attractions chapter for more information.

KNOLLWOOD GROVES

8053 Lawrence Rd.
Boynton Beach 734-4800

This 30-acre grove is as much an educational entity as a working grove. Want to learn about the citrus industry? Take the fruit tram then tour the plant. Visit the Hallpatee Seminole Indian Village to add to your knowledge of Florida's indigenous people and their fascinating culture.

The grove is open daily 9 AM to 5:30 PM throughout they year but is closed on Sundays from June through September.

PALM BEACH GROVES

7149 Lawrence Rd.
Lantana 965-6699

The tram tour teaches how citrus trees are grown, maintained and har-

vested. The packinghouse tour teaches how the fruit is graded and packed for shipping. Stroll through the gardens to learn more about other exotic fruit grown in this climate and soil and take all the pictures you wish.

A gift shop, juice bar, ice cream parlor, plant shop and country store are all on the premises.

Palm Beach Groves is open daily from October through May.

Bakeries

OK, we're old-fashioned. We loved the days when bakeries were small shops, filled with great smells and even better tastes.

We have our share of supermarket bakeries, but we also have many of the other kind too. Here are a few:

LUND'S DANISH BAKERY

1402 Boynton Beach Blvd.
Boynton Beach 737-8500

Scandinavian pastries and fresh breads are tops here. Stop by in the morning when the aroma is intoxicating.

POLAR BAKERY

130 S. Third St.
Lantana 582-5844

Mmmmmm. Polar Bakery, like Lund's, specializes in Scandinavian and American baked goods, and the pastries are sooooo good.

ROSELLA'S BAKERY AND DELICATESSEN
630 N.E. Eighth St.
Delray Beach   276-6847

Rosella's pastries, including cookies, mini French pastries, pecan rolls and even doughnuts, are all baked on site. So are the sourdough rye and other specialty breads.

UNION BAKERY
2111 N. Dixie Hwy.
Lake Worth   586-6962

Smooth, creamy flan, rich, delicious tres leches and numerous other traditional Cuban baked goods are here to tempt you daily. Also available is a limited supply of sandwiches, including one of the best medianoches in Palm Beach County.

NAPOLEON PASTRIES
6618 S. Dixie Hwy.
West Palm Beach   588-6295

Classic European baked goods and some traditional Hispanic desserts are offered at this friendly, family shop.

Bookstores

Partially it's because Palm Beach countians are well educated and tend to read more. They tend to be global-minded citizens with a desire to keep informed. Partially, too, it's because this area is filled with folks who have a vital *need* to stay in close touch with the rest of the world because of family or business interests elsewhere. Whatever the reason, Boca Raton, the Palm Beaches and the nearby communities have an abundance of good bookstores and newsstands.

For starters, nearly every major mall contains a B. Dalton Booksellers or Waldenbooks, and many malls contain both. Barnes & Noble's freestanding stores are popping up near major shopping areas, and other chains and independent stores are holding strong.

Boca Raton

BOOK STOP
8903 Glades Rd.   479-2114

Book Stop contains thousands of titles covering hundreds of topics and is a favorite destination for browsers, bibliophiles and magazine readers, all of whom love the abundant selection. Its strengths are children's literature and books for computer enthusiasts.

B. DALTON BOOKSELLERS
Town Center
6000 W. Glades Rd.   391-5512

B. Dalton emphasizes what's hot in the book world. This national chain's shops are favorite haunts for folks who enjoy bestsellers and romance novels as well as for fanciers of books on tape and literary puzzles and games. Each store also offers a well-rounded selection of magazines.

LIBERTIES FINE BOOKS AND MUSIC
Mizner Park
309 Plaza Real   368-1300

Liberties is a favorite place for book lovers, night owls and insomniacs. Liberties Cafe serves coffee 'til closing and offers an interesting mix of entertainment in the evenings. The bookstore is open from 9 AM to midnight Sunday through Thursday and 9 AM to 1 AM on Friday and Saturday. The cafe opens an hour before the bookstore and closes when the bookstore does.

The selection of books is tremendous, and the sales staff at Liberties is

This Mediterranean Revival tower beckons to shoppers at Royal Palm Plaza in downtown Boca Raton.

helpful, knowledgeable and friendly. There are plenty of leather wingback chairs for you to curl up in to check out the books you intend to buy, an excellent, extensive children's section and hundreds of book signings and literary discussions annually. Among the authors who have participated in book signings include local favorites and authors of worldwide renown, from John Grisham to former president Jimmy Carter.

BRENTANO'S
Town Center
6000 W. Glades Rd.   392-8848

Brentano's is a good place to find the hot new titles before they reach the bestseller list. The hardcover fiction and nonfiction sections at the front of each store offer a selection of titles far beyond those on the *New York Times'* list. Proceed further into the store and you'll find a well-balanced selection of books, audio books and magazines covering a variety of topics.

Boynton Beach

BARNES & NOBLE BOOKSELLERS
1895 N. Congress Ave.   364-9611

This is a good place to find popular novels, including a hefty selection of bestsellers. You'll also find romance novels, magazines, audio books and literary-related games and novelties.

Coral Springs

BARNES & NOBLE BOOKSELLERS
645 University Dr.   (305) 753-6650

This national chain offers a wide selection of bestsellers, romance novels, books on tape and magazines.

BORDERS BOOKS & MUSIC
700 University Dr.   (305) 340-3307

A new player on the South Florida literary front, Borders pleases its customers in many ways, with more than 100,000 books on hand, tons of CDs, dozens of newspapers and its coffeehouse. Author appearances, lectures and book signings are all part of the program here.

B. Dalton Booksellers

Coral Square Mall
Atlantic Blvd. at University Dr.   *(305) 752-5003*

What's big in the world of popular literature? You'll find the answer to this question at B. Dalton, where you'll also find magazines, audio books and literary games.

Waldenbooks

Coral Square Mall
Atlantic Blvd. at University Dr.   *(305) 755-6107*

A treasure trove for fiction fans, Waldenbooks stocks a full selection of paperbacks to please mystery, suspense, Western and romance novel readers. You'll also find the latest in new fiction and nonfiction titles as well as magazines and comic books.

Delray Beach

Delray Mall Bookstore

1644 S. Federal Hwy.   *272-6666*

The store made a minor move a while back, down a few yards and across the mall floor. But with its move, the Delray Mall Bookstore has been able to add a greeting card section and lots of new books.

Hand's

325 E. Atlantic Ave.   *276-4194*

Hand's is a bit of many things — an office supply store, a card shop, art supply store and an eclectic bookstore. It has been open since 1934 and is an institution downtown.

Shining Through

430 E. Atlantic Ave.   *276-8559*

Shining Through boasts of being an alternative book and gift store. For folks who are working on spiritual enlightenment and empowerment, the books here are downright indispensable.

Levenger

420 Commerce Dr.
Delray Beach   *276-2436*

This is not a bookstore per se, but as America's purveyor of "Tools for Serious Readers," Levenger is a place the literary-minded need to visit. Be sure and sign up for the mailing list because that will get you advance notice of special events and weekend sales, which offer incredible values.

Levenger sells readers' aids such as magnifying glasses, leather bookmarks, book covers and other leather goods, furniture for the library or study and fine writing implements. Everything Levenger sells is heirloom quality, but prices are reasonable. If reading is a delight to you, a stop at Levenger is a must.

Hollywood

Barnes & Noble Booksellers

Oakwood Plaza
4170 Oakwood Blvd.   *(305) 923-1738*

All the Barnes & Noble stores in South Florida are stocked with a fabulous selection of books and magazines, but this one also offers a cafe, featuring Starbucks Coffee creations, granitas, pastries and a modest but pleasing selection of gourmet sandwiches.

Lake Worth

JEANI'S SECRETS
4469 S. Congress Ave.   *642-3255*

Billing itself as a place of "privileged information and harmless indulgences," Jeani's is the place where New Age thinkers flock to buy books and gifts.

Palm Beach

CLASSIC BOOKSHOP
310 S. County Rd.   655-2485, 655-0938

This tiny bookshop is crammed with the latest titles, an excellent collection of books about Florida and an incredibly helpful sales staff.

DOUBLEDAY BOOK SHOP
228 Worth Ave.   *655-0736*

You'll find piles of books from the floorboards to the ceiling at this cozy shop, including the hottest bestsellers and lots more excellent reading.

THE CLASSICAL MUSIC & BOOK STORE
215 Royal Poinciana Way   *659-6700*

Like Classic Bookshop, this is a small bookstore with character and a friendly staff that knows and loves books.

Palm Beach Gardens

BARNES & NOBLE BOOKSELLERS
Prosperity Centre
2480 PGA Blvd.   *627-2828*

This relative newcomer on the Palm Beach County scene has be-

come an instant hit. Along with a mind-boggling selection of books and magazines, Barnes & Noble sponsors a variety of special events including lectures, workshops and author book signings. Be sure to browse the bargain books; you'll often find unexpected esoteric titles.

BRENTANO'S
The Gardens of the Palm Beaches
3101 PGA Blvd.   *624-0117*

Whether you seek up-and-coming titles in hardcover fiction and nonfiction or paperbacks and magazines covering a broad range of topics, Brentano's has a selection to satisfy book lovers. You'll also find a good selection of audio books here.

RAND MCNALLY
The Gardens of the Palm Beaches
3101 PGA Blvd.   *775-7602*

Rand McNally is a bookstore and shop for folks on the go. You'll find a wide selection of travel books and maps along with accessories, bags and even some luggage.

WALDENBOOKS
The Gardens of the Palm Beaches
3101 PGA Blvd.   *775-1604*

Waldenbooks offers a variety of titles representing a variety of genres: romance, Western, mystery and suspense, to name a few. You'll also find copious magazines and comic books.

Browse for an airplane or a sportscar, as many professional athletes do, at The Toy Store Collection Group on Sunrise Boulevard in Fort Lauderdale east of U.S. Highway 1.

Insiders' Tips

Pompano Beach

B. DALTON BOOKSELLERS
Pompano Square
Federal Hwy. at Copans Rd.   (305) 943-5930
You'll find a wide selection of popular titles here, including bestsellers, romances, audio books and magazines.

WALDENBOOKS
Pompano Square
Federal Hwy. at Copans Rd.   (305) 946-9168
10 N. Federal Hwy.   (305) 782-4858
Waldenbooks offers a huge selection of paperbacks, including the latest in fiction and nonfiction titles and magazines.

Sunrise

BOOKS-A-MILLION
Sawgrass Mills Mall
12801 W. Sunrise Blvd.   (305) 846-7093
If you're planning a visit to this monster mall, be sure and stop here. You'll find the place is adequately named. Thousands of books, from bestsellers to discounts, are on sale here.

West Palm Beach

WALDENBOOKS
Palm Beach Mall
I-95 and Palm Beach Lakes Blvd.   683-2807
Whether you crave fiction, nonfiction, magazines or pop culture publications — including comic books — Waldenbooks has a selection to satisfy your literary appetite.

Newsstands

Readers come in all shapes and sizes. So does reading material. And while some folks prefer the hardbound vari-ety, others opt for something they can roll or fold under an arm.

If you're in the hunt for a selection of newspapers, magazines, comic books and the like, then you need to check out the following venues.

In Boca Raton, peruse the selection at **Dee's Candy 'n News**, 23014 Sandalfoot Plaza Drive; **Gateways Newsstand**, 500 Town Center, 6000 W. Glades Road; and **NewShack**, 1375 W. Palmetto Park Road.

If you're in Delray Beach, stop by **Delray News and Tobacco Center**, 429 E. Atlantic Avenue.

You'll find **Century News & Tobacco** at 1818 W. Hillsboro Boulevard in Deerfield Beach.

And in Lake Worth there's **Main Street News**, 608 Lake Avenue. You'll also find Main Street News at 255 Royal Poinciana Way in Palm Beach.

Home Interiors

If you're looking for furnishings, floor coverings or appointments and accessories for your abode, Palm Beach and Broward counties have a multitude of home interior stores to explore. We've listed a handful of options — some time-honored, some unique — to help you on your way.

If you're interested in checking out the large furniture chains, such as City Furniture, Levitz and Rooms To Go, rest assured you'll find them in convenient locations throughout both counties as well.

ARCADE ANTIQUES
824 Lake Ave.
Lake Worth   533-7273
Looking for an Indian blanket, some Venetian glass, an old-fashioned clock,

Whisper Sweet Somethings . . .

Need something sweet? Better yet, chocolate, decadent and with primo presentation? You are in luck at In Chocolate, 402 E. Atlantic Avenue, Delray Beach, where proprietor Nancy Goldberg refines the notion of confectionery niceties.

The mission began long-distance: A Pensacola attorney called with a quest. A damsel was visiting South Florida on business and he wanted to surprise her in a meaningful way — chocolate-covered strawberries delivered to her hotel. Several candy experts offer the hand-dipped delicacy, but most say it can't be done in May when the berries are shy.

Clearly, the fellow needed an Insider — Nancy Goldberg — who made a special trip to her secret farmer's market, where premium strawberries perk up when they hear her voice.

Nancy dipped the fruit in her best chocolate, dressed an ebony platter with a white doily and purple sash, and sent the masterpiece, with a *billet doux*, by private courier to the lady's hotel in Fort Lauderdale. The cost, including delivery, was $30. The attorney says it was a bargain.

mirrors and rare collectibles? Arcade Antiques has them all and much more: Lalique crystal, Rookwood rare pottery, Tiffany glass, oak furniture, period furniture, wicker, toys, wrought-iron patio dressing, fishing tackle, chandeliers, cut crystal and those one-of-a-kind items decorators crave.

Arcade Antiques is open from 10 AM to 5 PM seven days a week; noon to 5 PM on Sundays during July and August.

BLUM'S PORCH AND PATIO SHOP
2980 N. Federal Hwy.
Boca Raton   *395-5400*

Fort Lauderdale-based Casual Furnishings Group acquired one of the Blum's affiliates but kept the time-honored name. The emphasis is on furniture and accessories for less-formal living spaces — indoors and outdoors. That includes mobile pieces, in case you want to rearrange the family room for a big holiday feast or take larger pieces outside for an evening on the terrace.

BROWN'S FURNITURE AND DESIGNS
4501 N. Federal Hwy.
Boca Raton   *368-2703*

Steve and Dana Brown's family-owned business is a household word in many popular South Florida communities. Their design team has decorated model homes at Gleneagles, The Polo Club - Boca Raton, Woodfield Country Club, Broken Sound and Wycliffe, to name a few. A design studio that happens to sell furniture, Brown's buys directly from manufacturers, so prices are competitive. The store has been at this location since 1975.

CLASSIC INTERIORS
2980 N. Federal Hwy.
Boca Raton   *395-5212*

For more than 30 years, Peter and Teena Blum operated the landmark

Blum's of Boca home furnishings and interior design organization, which blossomed from one store to a chain of six. Now retired, the Blums sold their store to Classic Interiors, which retained the same location and the same customer service philosophy: to provide a design staff to consult on one item or on furniture and accessories for an entire residence — from an accent lamp to a complete master bedroom suite.

CLOSET DESIGN GROUP

1000 Clint Moore Rd.
Boca Raton 241-1445

Closet Design Group has a showroom and manufacturing plant for its custom closets and hardwood shelving. Custom tops (Corian, mica and lacquer finishes), bathroom vanities and other storage products are all completely adjustable and designed to provide 30 percent more hanging space than comparable products. Also check out Closet Design Group's location at 2800 U.S. Highway 1 N. in the Fran Murphy Building in Juno Beach.

CRAIGE'S FURNITURE-INTERIORS

111 E. Atlantic Ave.
Delray Beach 276-5781

A mainstay on the Avenue since 1946, Craige's has more than 25,000 square feet of showroom space filled with furnishings, floor coverings and accessories. Inventory includes furniture from Baker, Milling Road, Sherrill, Century, Whitecraft, Weiman, Hekman, Lane, Pearson and others.

ELITE FINE ART

9982 Glades Rd.
Boca Raton 852-5903

Eli and Joseph Benaim, owners of Elite Fine Art, are pretty confident

their picture-framing studio has endless variety that is both affordable and high-quality. So confident in fact, that if you don't find the frame you're looking for at Elite, maybe the painting is at fault.

A small studio that also is an art gallery, Elite carries artwork that other galleries don't, just to cover their niche. They have plenty of sources for ordering what you don't see in the studio, and pride themselves on being a small operation with creative solutions and unique finished products.

Metals, woods, antique finishes, beveled mirrors, mica finishes or 22-karat gold — Elite Fine Art puts your artwork in the framing of your choice, usually within a week. Elite Fine Art is at Westwind Mall near Home Depot, at U.S. 441 across from Mission Bay.

ORIENTAL FURNITURE WAREHOUSE

60 S. Federal Hwy.
Boca Raton 394-0656

Think Far East for lacquered chests, hand-painted Shoji screens, porcelain vases, lamps and distinctive bedroom and dining-room furniture.

PAST PERFECT
CONSIGNMENT SHOWROOM

99 N.E. Mizner Blvd.
Boca Raton 338-5656

The operative words here are "deeply discounted prices" on upscale, name-brand home furnishings, accessories and antiques. Many are decorators' mistakes. Lines include Saporiti, Henredon, Lexington,

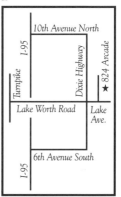
Drexel, Thomasville, Baker and more.

ROYAL PALM INTERIORS
7608 N.W. Sixth Ave.
Boca Raton　　　　　*997-9678*

Experts say kitchens and baths — "those juicy wet rooms" — are what consumers get most lathered up about when they're house-shopping. Certainly, Madison Avenue has proven sudsability sells, and builders have learned from years of home shows that visitors will stand transfixed, eyes glazing over, at demonstrations of the latest plums in plumbing fixtures.

Royal Palm Interiors is a Boca Raton company with 10 years experience in designing and manufacturing fairy-tale kitchens and spectacular splashes. Owners Ken Malsky and Jerry Rowland

have moved their team of designers from their original space off Holland Drive to 6,000 square feet in the Boca Park of Commerce, at I-95 and the Congress Avenue interchange.

The firm has a large referral business, both from builders and satisfied homeowners they've worked with over the years. And if they have to try something brand new to conjure up those dream rooms, so be it.

Royal Palm caters to the high-end market, which doesn't always mean the most expensive appliances or cabinetry. The company promotes itself as offering affordable fine cabinetry, from concept to completion. If you don't see what you want in their showroom or a catalog, they'll do a custom design and manufacture it.

Special Events Services

Throwing a big party or looking for gifts for a big occasion? The following companies provide unique services and are good places to start to help you plan virtually any major celebration or special event.

DALSIMER OF BOCA RATON INC.

21000 Boca Rio Rd.
Boca Raton   *483-2600*
Inside the Boca Raton Resort
501 E. Camino Real
Boca Raton   *392-4501*

Dalsimer is a standard in the destination and event industry, both nationally and internationally, offering creative attention to scenic, floral and lighting effects, theme party production, special occasions and corporate events.

The Dalsimer Group originated in Long Island, New York, in 1918, and has been regarded as a leading special-event company since the mid-1900s. Dalsimer has a regional corporate headquarters in Boca Raton, serving clients throughout the Southeast, the Caribbean Basin and South America. Additional South Florida locations include Coral Gables and The Eden Roc Resort on Miami Beach.

Services include event planning, custom floral and theme decor, atmospheric and theatrical lighting, linens and table appointments, set and stage design, audio visual, scenery production, destination management, ground transportation, meeting planning, music, entertainment, fireworks, boating, sports and recreation activities, gifts, favors and mementos.

Dalsimer's handles weddings, corporate events and conventions, fundraisers for numerous large, nonprofit and charitable organizations ... from a fashion show to a large carnival ... and bar and bat mitzvahs, handling every detail from table tops to lighting, balloons, invitations and video recordings, custom T-shirts and just about any memento you need.

I.J. BENNETT LTD.

940 Clint Moore Rd.
Boca Raton   *241-8689*

Owned by Roz Adenbaum and modeled after an earlier business, Lincoln Manor Gift Service, which Adenbaum had for many years in Englewood Cliffs, New Jersey (outside Manhattan), I.J. Bennett creates unique gifts for corporate events, specialty promotions, product announcements and major marketing campaigns.

Coordinating successful and lasting first impressions, I.J. Bennett draws from a wide variety of products and resources to accomplish creative and innovative themes.

Adenbaum's experience is vast; she has performed gift assembly ser-

Photo: Delray Beach Community Redevelopment Agency

Shoppers on Atlantic Avenue in Delray Beach have a variety of stores from which to choose offering clothing, art and furniture.

vices for major public relations firms such as Hill and Knowles, Burson-Marsteller, Ogilvey and Mather, Ketchum and many others. Past corporate clients include Ralph Lauren, Yves St. Laurent, Best Foods, Lipton Tea, Nike, *Mirabella* magazine and *Woman's Day*.

Stationery, specialty invitations and high-end gifts are a few of the items available at I.J. Bennett, where a staff of four gives each order strictly kid-glove treatment.

Explains Adenbaum, "This is not about shrink-wrap. We order unusual, high-quality merchandise and we package gifts with expensive ribbons and finishes. I go to all the trade shows, fancy foods, for instance, and shop extensively out of the area to make sure we have a selection to satisfy any request."

And don't be shy to ask for assistance if you don't have anything particular in mind; chances are, Roz Adenbaum has the answer, even if you don't know what you're looking for.

Major Supermarkets

Large chains with plenty of regional locations include Publix Supermarkets, Winn-Dixie and Albertson's.

A Fortune 500 company based in Lakeland, **Publix** has food markets, bakeries and deli operations. Some of its new and larger locations have a pharmacy and most have floral nooks. The company is aggressive with expansion, occasionally building the centers it anchors if a suitable developer isn't ready.

Publix will deliver, and our Insider friend who's disabled and doesn't drive a car says they're very helpful about scouting the store for what she wants before she asks a friend to go get it.

Winn-Dixie, a public company based in Jacksonville, has an equal monopoly on number of locations and maintains an edge on price. Of the two chains, Publix tends to dominate the marketplace in the Boca area, with more new stores and better maintenance on old ones. Buyers who favor Winn-Dixie overlook the lag in upgrading existing stores.

Albertson's is also a public company based in Boise, Idaho. The chain offers competitive pricing and the advantage of pharmacies and liquor stores adjacent to the market. Besides food, Albertson's offers video rental, photo finishing, a bakery, fresh seafood and lottery tickets.

PriceCostco is a members' market that caters to people who own businesses and those who belong to certain credit unions. The store is great for bulk buying of food, housewares, pet supplies, soft drinks, beer and wine. You can also buy office equipment, furniture, electronics, cameras, jewelry, tires and auto parts, tools and even specimen trees and plants. Cigarettes, gasp, are wholesale prices for companies that resell them.

Whenever you're in Broward County, consider a road trip to **Xtra Super Food Center**, Oakland Park Boulevard and U.S. Highway 441. Xtra is owned by publicly traded Pueblo International. It's an experience just to visit the mega-store's produce area, where you'll need a dictionary to spell every exotic vegetable, root and spice you see.

The following are some dots on Palm Beach County's grocery store landscape:

ALBERTSON'S

20409 S.R. 7, Boca Raton
4801 Linton Blvd., Delray Beach
3701 W. Hillsboro Blvd., Deerfield Beach
1901 N. Military Tr., West Palm
3950 Northlake Blvd., Lake Park
4481 Lake Worth Rd., Lake Worth

PUBLIX

21230 St. Andrews Blvd., Boca Raton
1968 N.E. Fifth Ave., Boca Raton
7060 W. Palmetto Park Rd., Boca Raton
22973 U.S. Hwy. 441, Boca Raton
5050 Champion Blvd., Boca Raton
7431 N. Federal Hwy., Boca Raton
9846 Glades Rd., Boca Raton
3003 Yamato Rd., Boca Raton
3740 W. Hillsboro Blvd., Deerfield Beach
1538 S. Federal Hwy., Delray Beach
4771 W. Atlantic Ave., Delray Beach
7375 W. Atlantic Ave., Delray Beach
314 N.E. Second Ave., Delray Beach
4753 N. Congress Ave., Boynton Beach
133 N. Congress Ave., Boynton Beach
3775 Woolbright Rd., Boynton Beach
501 S.E. 18th Ave., Boynton Beach
4966 Le Chalet Rd., Boynton Beach
820 Southern Blvd., Lake Worth
926 S. Military Tr., Lake Worth
1910 Lake Worth Rd., Lake Worth
265 Sunset Ave., Palm Beach
10566 U.S. Hwy. 1, Palm Beach Gardens

WINN-DIXIE

7024 Beracasa Way, Boca Raton
648 Glades Rd., Boca Raton
499 N.E. Spanish River Blvd., Boca Raton
23072 Sandalfoot Plaza Dr., Boca Raton
19595 S. R. 7, Boca Raton
291 W. Camino Real, Boca Raton
11411 W. Palmetto Park Rd., Boca Raton
13801 N. Congress Ave., Delray Beach
3155 S. Federal Hwy., Delray Beach
1565 S. Congress Ave., Delray Beach
334 N. Congress Ave., Boynton Beach
3609 S. Federal Hwy., Boynton Beach
9840 S. Military Tr., Boynton Beach
3131 Forest Hill Blvd., Lantana
6128 S. Congress Ave., Lantana

Additional Food Markets

Additional Boca area food markets include **Jubilee** at Royal Palm Plaza, site of the former Woolley's Emporium, an upscale full-service operation with specialty items, imported chocolates, a bakery, gourmet meals for takeout and a deli.

This fountain welcomes shoppers to Royal Palm Plaza in downtown Boca Raton.

King's Deli, 1900 Military Trail in Boca Raton, between Palmetto Park and Glades roads, offers an Italian bakery, imported cheeses, fresh fish, fresh meat and a huge selection of produce. It's a complete grocery store, much larger than a deli, and very popular. **Sabatino's Gourmet Market & Catering**, 8177 Glades Road, is the place to shop for food or to buy it already cooked.

Howard's Market & Deli, 6060 S.W. 18th Street, offers fine merchandise in an intimate neighborhood setting: a selection of imported beer, wines, farmer's market-quality produce, cooked pasta and other delectables ready to go.

Health Food Specialists

The following shops offer products for folks who adhere to or are in part interested in a wholistic lifestyle.

WHOLLY HARVEST MARKET & CAFE
2200 Glades Rd.
Boca Raton 392-5100
Wholly Harvest stocks a selection of vitamins, fresh produce and other groceries and offers seafood, poultry and deli favorites. The cafe offers on-site service as well as take-out.

WHOLE EARTH FOODS
7098 Beracasa Way
Boca Raton 394-9438
Whole Earth Foods offers all-natural foods including organically grown produce, a full selection of vitamins and deli products. There is also a cafe on the premises.

Photo: Michelle Lord

Children can get into the swing of things in South County.

Inside
Kidstuff

Originally, the Palm Beaches were developed as a wintertime respite for chilled-to-the-bone patricians who often brought their children and grandchildren with them to enjoy the mild winters. More than a century later, Boca Raton and the Palm Beaches are still captivating children's interest with activities that are educational, cultural and just plain fun. Here are 10 suggestions:

SPORTS

Sports of all sorts, such as football, basketball, baseball and softball, for youths and teens are offered throughout Palm Beach County. See our Participant Sports chapter for more complete listings.

BOCA RATON/DELRAY BEACH COMMUNITY EDUCATION CONNECTION

High schools:

Atlantic	243-1250
Boca Raton	338-1420
Olympic Heights	852-6905
Spanish River	241-2205

Middle schools:

Boca Raton	338-1479

Elementary schools:

J.C. Mitchell	338-1469
Verde	241-2283
Loggers' Run	241-2283

This organization offers a variety of day and after-school programs for children. The courses come from two programs: Early Childhood Educa-

tion, a day-care program for children 3 to 5 years of age, and Children's Academic Enhancement, for students in grades 1 through 5. The enhancement program offers sports programs, music, reading, math, languages, computer skills and more. Summer camp programs also are available. Call for details.

CHILDREN'S SCIENCE EXPLORIUM
Royal Palm Plaza, Ste. 15
131 S.E. Mizner Blvd.
Boca Raton   395-8401

More than 25 hands-on science exhibits, 10 computers and a 180-gallon aquarium filled with denizens of the deep await inquiring young minds of preschool age to grade 5 at the Explorium. Exhibits include Dino-Mite, Space Invaders, How We Grow and Stormy Weather. The Explorium also works with Scout programs and presents Sunday workshops on rocketry, robotics and other special topics. Program prices vary.

BOCA RATON CHILDREN'S MUSEUM
498 Crawford Blvd.   368-6875

Follow the giant footsteps outside the 1912 cracker-style house, the city's oldest wooden structure, and learn about South Florida's indigenous plants. When you've finished, step inside and let your child learn about local history, folklore and crafts. Hits with the kids are the mini market and mini bank, where they can shop and bank and gain hands-on knowledge about how our economy works.

The annual Kidsfest! is a favorite among city children. Puppetry, arts, crafts and special events are all part of the fun.

About 60,000 guests visit the museum annually. Hours are Tuesday through Saturday from noon to 4 PM. Admission is $1 for children, and a $1 donation is suggested for adults.

DREHER PARK ZOO
1301 Summit Blvd.
West Palm Beach   547-WILD

Dreher Park's animal census tops 500 inhabitants representing 128 species. Take a boat trip through the park and see these marvelous creatures in natural settings. A nature trail and picnic and petting areas are provided.

The zoo is open 9 AM to 5 PM daily. Admission is $5.50 for adults, $5 for seniors 60 and older, and $4 for children 3 to 12. Children younger than 3 are admitted free.

Plan a whole day for your visit so you can also take in the South Florida Science Museum (see next listing). Also see our Attractions chapter.

SOUTH FLORIDA SCIENCE MUSEUM
4801 Dreher Tr. N.
West Palm Beach   832-1988

Think of this museum, nestled just behind the Dreher Park Zoo, as a scientific smorgasbord. Available are exhibits on natural and physical science, a planetarium and observatory.

Museum hours are 10 AM to 5 PM daily except Friday, when it is open from 10 AM to 10 PM. Admission is $5 for adults, $4.50 for seniors older than 62 and $2 for children 4 to 12.

Photo: Sophie Brandstrom

A young citizen checks out a police dog.

Children younger than 4 are admitted free. The planetarium show costs an extra $1.75; the laser show is $2.

BUEHLER PLANETARIUM
Broward Community College, Central Campus
3501 S.W. Davie Rd.
Davie   (305) 475-6680

The planetarium's Saturday and Sunday afternoon presentations, such as "Larry Cat in Space," delight young audiences, while teens learn about astronomy as they rock to the beat of Pink Floyd, Pearl Jam and others at midnight shows on Friday and Saturday evenings. The planetarium also offers special science exploration programs. Prices and showtimes vary, so call for details.

MUSEUM OF DISCOVERY AND SCIENCE
401 S.W. Second St.
Fort Lauderdale   (305) 467-6637

If you can drag your child past the huge Great Gravity Clock outside (adults become pretty slack-jawed watching it too), a cornucopia of adventures in science awaits. Children can travel through the human body, a living coral reef, space and more. The Blockbuster IMAX Theater presents nature, science and documentary films seven days a week. Call (305) 463-4629 for IMAX information.

The museum is open from 10 AM to 5 PM Monday through Friday, 10 AM to 8:30 PM on Saturday and noon to 5 PM on Sunday. Museum admission is $6 for adults, $5 for children 3 to 12 and seniors 65 and older. IMAX

Boca Raton Recreation Services cosponsors youth sports leagues that run nearly year-round, including football, basketball, soccer, baseball and softball.

Insiders' Tips

Theater admission is $5 for adults and $4 for children and seniors. Also available is a combination museum-movie pass at $8 for adults and $7 for children and seniors.

MORIKAMI MUSEUM
AND JAPANESE GARDENS
4000 Morikami Park Rd.
Delray Beach   *495-0233*

Children and their parents receive hands-on experience learning Japanese decorative crafts such as origami, toy- and mask-making and the art of bonsai through the museum's Saturday Family Programs. Sessions cost $4 per participant. (See the Attractions chapter for additional information.)

BOOMER'S FAMILY RECREATION CENTER
3100 Airport Rd.
Boca Raton   *347-1888*

Fill your wallet and prepare for a rollicking time at this Australian-theme fun park. Activities include a huge game room, roller rink, bumper boats, indoor playground, miniature raceway and two 18-hole miniature golf courses.

PHOTOGRAPHY BY MARYBETH
338 S.E. Second St.
Deerfield Beach   *426-2562*

Professional photographer Marybeth Hamberger specializes in group and individual portraits as well as candids of children and families.

Marybeth sets her cap and her shutter speed to record the freckles . . . the grins . . . the dimples . . . the days of Tooth Fairies, first haircuts, first communions, bar mitzvahs . . . you get the picture.

RAPIDS WATER PARK
6566 N. Military Tr.
West Palm Beach   *842-8756*

Here's a cool spot for those hot summer days!

Rapids has everything to keep you and your children in the swim. The complex contains a wave machine and man-made beach, rapids and water slides. There also are other areas for your children to clomp, romp and splash, always under the watchful eyes of trained lifeguards. Also part of the complex is an 18-hole miniature golf

Of all the celebrities who live in Boca Raton, you're the one we feature most.

True, many of the rich and famous live here. And true, we do stories on them when they're making news. But the headlines in our paper are mostly about you, your family and your neighbors. We thrive on events like graduations, weddings, Bar Mitzvahs, new business openings, birth announcements, write-ups of your kid's ball team, our town's society and much more. To sum up, in a local paper like The News, the celebrities we celebrate are you.

Call (407) 368-9400.

The Boca News.
Always a local point of view.

Photo: Palm Beach County Convention and Visitors Bureau

Children and adults enjoy 47 miles of sandy beaches.

course, picnic areas and two self-service snack bars.

Between Memorial Day and Labor Day, the park is open daily from 10 AM to dusk, weather permitting.

In the spring and fall the park is open on weekends and holidays.

The cost is $14.95 per person per day.

Inside
Attractions

Yes, South Florida is a wonderful place to live. And why not, with so many fascinating attractions, many right in our own backyards. But it's also a wonderful place to visit and explore. From the wild and natural to the educational, historical, entertaining and delicious, Palm Beach County has something to attract everyone.

Places to See in South Florida

Palm Beach County

FLORIDA HISTORY CENTER
Burt Reynolds Park
805 U.S. 1 N.
Jupiter   747-6639

There's much to learn about the land and the early people in Florida history at the big red lighthouse that's a landmark in northern Palm Beach County. The Florida History Center Jupiter Lighthouse and Dubois Pioneer Home, all located in close proximity, combine a rich historical resource and a fine recreational opportunity.

The Florida History Center is open Tuesday through Friday from 10 AM to 5 PM and 1 to 5 PM on Saturday and Sunday. The lighthouse is open Sunday through Wednesday from 10 AM to 4 PM and the Dubois house is open from 1 to 4 PM.

Bring a picnic basket, sunscreen and swim suits and make a day of it in beautiful Jupiter. Admission is $4 for adults, $3 for seniors and $2 for kids.

DREHER PARK ZOO
1301 Summit Blvd.
West Palm Beach   547-9453

More than 500 animal species, many endangered, roam Dreher Park's 25 acres, including the Florida panther.

A paved nature trail allows visitors to enjoy the native flora and fauna up close and personal. The park also has a boardwalk trail.

Small animals are the highlight of the children's zoo.

The zoo is open from 9 AM to 5 PM daily, rain or shine. The cost for adults (13 and older) is $5.50. Adults 60 and older are $5, and children 3 to 12 are $4.

LION COUNTRY SAFARI
On Southern Blvd., 15 miles west of I-95
West Palm Beach   793-1084

Forty or so years ago, Boca Raton was home to a wild-animal park known as Africa USA. Today, modern homes and swimming pools dot the area where lions, tigers and other exotic animals once roamed. But you still have an excellent chance to see animals from the veldt and plain up close without the expense of an African safari.

Lion Country's 500-acre preserve plays host to about 1,000 animal species. Animals are on display in what was the nation's first drive-through cageless zoo in 1967. Each section is themed, and the animals are matched to the themed areas accordingly. Among the creatures here are giraffes, zebras, ostriches, water buffaloes, chimpanzees and more.

The chimpanzee habitat is among Lion Country's top exhibits and has been recognized by the Jane Goodall Institute. It is one of 16 nationwide ChimpanZoo sites, where chimpanzee behavior is studied. The chimp islands are surrounded by moats, and visitors can observe the primates while taking the drive-around loop.

After cruising the loop, stop at the park's Safari World, which has more animal exhibits and a nursery.

There's a campground for those who enjoy roughing it; there's also miniature golf as well as plenty of other creature comforts.

Lion Country Safari is open daily from 9:30 AM to 5:30 PM. The cost is $13.95 for adults, $9.95 for children ages 3 to 15.

WHITEHALL — THE HENRY MORRISON FLAGLER MUSEUM
Cocoanut Row at Whitehall Way
Palm Beach   *655-2833*
Henry Flagler, the Standard Oil magnate and visionary, had a dream of building a railroad that went all the way to the sea. The Florida East Coast Railway did eventually reach Key West, if only for a while, but the construction of the railway line also served to establish Palm Beach and several other scenic Florida coastal towns as resorts.

Flagler built Whitehall in Palm Beach in 1901 as a gift for his wife. The building has been restored to its original opulence and gives visitors a glance of Palm Beach during its golden era. Whitehall is listed on the National Register of Historic Places, and the museum complex also features Flagler's fully restored personal railroad car, dubbed "The Rambler."

The Henry Morrison Flagler Museum is open Tuesday through Saturday from 10 AM to 5 PM and on Sundays from noon to 5 PM. Admission is $7 per person.

BLOOD'S HAMMOCK GROVES
4549 Linton Blvd.
Delray Beach   *498-3400*
Things get really juicy in South County come November — that's when orange season starts. And visiting Blood's Hammock Groves is as much a treat for the eyes as it is for the taste buds and tummy when the lush, tropical 110-acre citrus grove is abloom. Colorful flowers line the pathways within the groves, which have been in South Florida and operated by three generations of the Blood family since 1949. (For more information about South Florida's citrus groves, including Blood's, see "Citrus Groves" in our Shopping chapter.)

At Blood's, visitors can see how the most-pampered fruit in Florida is harvested, polished and selected by hand. If you develop a yearning for citrus during your visit, don't worry . . . you can buy numerous varieties of fruit, includ-

ing honey tangerines and pomelos (Chinese grapefruit). If you want some produce and can't take it with you, or if you have a gift-giving occasion coming up, Blood's will be happy to arrange shipping throughout the United States and the Canadian provinces of Ontario and Quebec.

Admission is free, and Blood's hours are 8:30 AM to 5 PM. But remember, the groves are open only from November through April. To reach Blood's, head west 2 miles off I-95 at the Linton Boulevard exit in Delray Beach.

MORIKAMI MUSEUM AND JAPANESE GARDENS

4000 Morikami Park Rd.
Delray Beach   495-0233

This framework for the intricate simplicities of Japanese culture offers an alluring backdrop for several high-attendance festivals (see our Festivals and Special Events chapter).

George Morikami donated 200 acres of land to Palm Beach County, for establishment of a park dedicated to Japanese culture. The park and gardens offer a tempting destination during these annual festivals, and have a way of making even "ordinary" days into special events.

Revel in the excitement of Japanese performers, a feast of ethnic foods, the street fairs, arts and crafts displays — all set in a tranquil oasis of pine forests, nature trails and lakes. The Morikami Museum and Japanese Gardens offer an authentic taste of Japan in the tropics.

PALM BEACH PHOTOGRAPHIC MUSEUM AND WORKSHOPS

71 S.E. Second Ave.
Delray Beach   *391-7557*

This nonprofit learning center is devoted to education, preservation and promotion of traditional and state-of-the-art photography and cutting-edge digital imaging. Leading mentors is various disciplines supplement a formidable year-round matrix of educational programs for photographers, graphic designers, art directors, educators, artists and serious amateurs.

Founded in 1987 by Fatima and Art NeJame, Palm Beach Photographic Museum and Workshops is located in an 11,000-square-foot property with 2,500 square feet set aside for its Museum of Photography, plus two digital imaging classrooms, expanded darkrooms, a large studio and classroom, and a 2,000-square-foot camera store.

Palm Beach Photographic Workshops is a member of the Palm Beach County Cultural Council. Call for information on the weekly lecture and workshop schedule or to register for FotoFusion '96 (see our Festivals and Annual Events chapter).

BURT REYNOLDS RANCH STUDIOS

16133 Jupiter Farms Rd.
Jupiter   *746-0393*

Sets from Reynolds' films *B.L. Stryker* and *Smokey and the Bandit* are here, along with the black Trans Am made famous in the latter production. Areas of interest to children include a petting zoo and an exotic animals display.

Daily hours are 10 AM to 5 PM. Admission is $10 for adults, $8 seniors and $5 for children 6 to 12.

BOCA RATON OLD TOWN HALL

71 N. Federal Hwy.
Boca Raton   *395-6766*

The most celebrated architect in Boca Raton's history undoubtedly is Addison Mizner, and it is Mizner who drew the original plans for Old Town Hall. The design that was constructed, however, was a modification of Mizner's, drawn by William Alsmeyer.

Old Town Hall is home to the Boca Raton Historical Society and is often the site of photographic and art shows, historical exhibits, slide presentations and tours. A gift shop is on the premises, and meeting rooms are available for rent to organizations.

Old Town Hall is open Monday through Friday from 10 AM to 4 PM. Admission is free.

CLUETT MEMORIAL GARDENS

Episcopal Church of Bethesda-by-the-Sea
141 S. County Rd.
Palm Beach   *655-4554*

This is an attraction unlike any other we've encountered. It is a stately, majestic formal garden — planted with biancospini, bougainvillea, bottlebrushes and more — located at one of the county's most venerable, historic churches. For a bit of respite in our hectic county, a moment's peace and sanctuary and a place to reflect, meditate and feel closer to one's maker, there is no finer place in the Palm Beaches.

The gardens are open 8 AM to 5 PM daily. Admission is free.

Broward County

INTERNATIONAL
SWIMMING HALL OF FAME
1 Hall of Fame Dr.
Fort Lauderdale *(305) 462-6536*

Originally opened in 1965, the Hall of Fame and its attached aquatic complex have recently undergone a splashy $13 million overhaul; the distinctive new wave-motif facade looks simply marvelous.

Inside the 10,000-square-foot exhibition hall, museum and art gallery, the world's greatest swimmers, divers, synchronized swimmers and water polo players and their coaches are honored. The complex also contains an extensive aquatics library, theater and meeting room.

The museum is open seven days a week from 9 AM to 5 PM. The cost of admission is $5 per family, $3 for adults and students, $1 for seniors and military.

On most days, the pool is also open to the public. Its usual operating hours are 6 AM to 4 PM. Monday and Friday evenings offer an additional session from 6 to 8 PM.

Photo: Blood's Hammock Groves

Folks enjoy the scenic beauty and serenity as well as the citrus products at Blood's Hammock Groves.

THE DEERFIELD BEACH
INTERNATIONAL FISHING PIER
200 N. Ocean Blvd.
Deerfield Beach   *(305) 426-9206*

For a small fee, visitors can walk out on the pier to watch anglers catch barracuda, blowfish, bonefish, bonitos, mackerel, snapper and snook, to name a few species. It's also a good place to view the ocean and beach from another perspective. And you know that if fish are around, pelicans and gulls are flying by to check out the catches. It costs $1 to walk on the pier. If you are 12 and older, and want to fish, it will cost you $3; if you are 11 or younger, you'll pay $2.

BUTTERFLY WORLD
Tradewinds Park South
3600 W. Sample Rd.
Coconut Creek   *(305) 977-4400*

A galaxy of 2,000 butterflies of all colors and sizes flutter by in this enchanting place that children love. In fact, almost a quarter-million people visit here each year. As tempting as it is, leave your net at home.

The park is open Monday through Friday from 9 AM to 5 PM and 1 to 5 PM on Sundays. Tickets cost $9.95 for adults, $5 for children ages 4 to 12. No tickets are sold after 4 PM.

Dade County

If you're thinking Miami's attractions are out of reach in a daytrip from Palm Beach County, think again — the places we note here are typically a one- or two-hour drive away, depending on where in Palm Beach County you're coming from.

HISTORICAL MUSEUM
OF SOUTHERN FLORIDA
Metro-Dade Cultural Center
101 W. Flagler St.
Miami   *(305) 375-1492*

Southern Florida isn't particularly revered as an historical treasure-trove, but it truly is one, and this fascinating museum helps demonstrate and explain why.

Recapture the sights, sounds and smells of Florida in its bygone days — the cigar factories in Key West and Ybor City, Miami Beach's Art Deco District during the Roaring '20s and even prehistoric Tequesta settlements.

The museum is open daily except Thanksgiving, Christmas and New Year's Day from 10 AM to 5 PM Monday through Wednesday, Friday and Saturday. Thursday hours are from 10 AM to 9 PM and Sunday, noon to 5 PM. The cost is $4 for adults, $2 for children ages 6 to 12.

PARROT JUNGLE AND GARDENS
11000 S.W. 57th Ave.
Miami   *(305) 666-7834*

You'll swear South Florida has gone to the birds upon visiting the famed Parrot Jungle. From flashy pink flamingos to vivid macaws and thousands of others, the winged wonders of the world are here.

As you drive south for your visit, note the terrain and surroundings. Much of this area, decimated by Hurricane Andrew in 1992, has regrown and repaired nicely, although some scars remain.

The park is open daily from 9:30 AM to 6 PM. The cost for adults is $12.95 plus tax. Children ages 3 to 12

Photo: Tom Fagan - Phototastic

Deerfield's beach and pier welcome the gentle waves of the blue Atlantic.

are $7.95, and adults 65 and older are $9.95.

MIAMI SEAQUARIUM
4400 Rickenbacker Cswy.
Miami   *(305) 361-5705*

The Seaquarium is probably southeastern Florida's best-known tourist attraction and is the home of Flipper and Lolita, the Killer Whale. What many folks don't know is that the Seaquarium also serves as a refuge and R&R haven for injured marine mammals.

The walk-through marine displays are simply stunning. The colorful reef fish look iridescent as they dart by; the sharks, with dark, unblinking eyes, show why they are the predators of the deep. The alligators and crocodiles are throwbacks to prehistoric reptiles.

The Seaquarium is open from 9:30 AM to 6 PM daily. Admission cost is $18.95 plus tax for adults, $13.95 plus tax for children ages 3 to 9.

VIZCAYA
3251 S. Miami Ave.
Miami   *(305) 250-9133*

Built in 1916, Vizcaya, an Italian Renaissance-Baroque country home, was the winter home of Chicago industrialist James Deering. Operated now by the Metro-Dade Park and Recreation Department, Vizcaya is often the reception site for visiting dig-

nitaries, among them Pope John Paul II, President George Bush and Queen Elizabeth II.

Restored to its original opulence and superbly maintained, Vizcaya is an artistic and educational resource. Its gardens, overlooking Biscayne Bay, are a wonderful spot for quiet reflection.

If you're here the third week in March, stop by Vizcaya for the Italian Renaissance Festival.

Be sure to bring your photographic memory to Vizcaya — the use of cameras within the house is prohibited.

Vizcaya is open daily except Christmas from 9:30 AM to 4:30 PM. The admission cost for adults is $10; children ages 6 to 12 are $5.

METROZOO
12400 S.W. 152nd St. (Coral Reef Dr.)
Miami   *(305) 251-0400*

This cageless zoo lets animals roam in settings that are similar to their natural habitats. Among the animals that come from the continents of Africa, Asia and Europe are chimpanzees, orangutans, elephants, antelope, Siamese crocodiles and even rare white Bengal tigers. The wildest thing to hit the zoo, however, wasn't the animals, it was Hurricane Andrew in 1992. But the zoo is bouncing back and continuing to heal daily from that bruising. For visitors who like to take a rest while still watching the zoo's

Insiders' Tips

Sign up at Gumbo Limbo Environmental Complex to watch sea turtles lay eggs. A couple of months later, you can watch the hatchlings head out to sea.

Photo: The Hemingway Home and Museum

The Hemingway House, the Key West manor of Nobel Prize-winning author Ernest Hemingway, has been preserved as it was when Hemingway wrote many of his literary classics here. Six-toed cats, descendants of Hemingway's famous felines, still roam the lush, tropical grounds.

wildlife, animals shows are presented three times a day. The zoo is open daily, 10:30 AM to 5:30 PM. Admission is $6 for adults and $3 for children ages 3 through 12.

MONKEY JUNGLE

14805 S.W. 216th St.
Miami   (305) 235-1611

If you're in the mood for monkey business, Monkey Jungle is the place to be. More than 30 species of primates roam in enclosures that simulate their natural habitats, while the humans watch enclosed in a walkway.

The park is open daily from 9:30 AM to 5 PM. Admission is $10.50 for adults; $9.50 for folks 65 and older and active military personnel, and $5.35 for children ages 4 through 12.

Photo: City of Boca Raton Recreation Services

Special events scheduled throughout the year and organized by Boca Raton Recreation Services include fishing tournaments, wheelchair tennis play and many, many opportunities for recreation and fun.

Inside
Festivals and Annual Events

Boca Raton, Delray Beach and their environs came by their party-town reputations honestly. And with the variety of cultures represented throughout Palm Beach County, there are festivals on a regular basis.

Our climate allows us to celebrate throughout the year, but you'll note that most of our festivals run in the winter months and early spring. That's because these are the most pleasant months to be outside for visitors and exhibitors alike.

Basic survival at most outdoor gatherings in these parts means wearing comfortable shoes, loose cottons, hat or visor, sunglasses and sunscreen.

Bring an appetite, your happy feet and extra time to kick back for terrific tunes and tempting treats. Enjoy the myriad annual happenings whose organizers have you in mind.

Following are some of the major ones in the area listed by month.

January

ART DECO WEEKEND
Along Ocean Dr. in the Art Deco District
Miami Beach   (305) 672-2014

Art deco, the funky, geometric style popular in the 1920s and '30s, is alive and well in Miami Beach's Art Deco District, where many old hotels and homes built in that style have been restored to their past glory.

The festival is a street party featuring a sidewalk art show, entertainment, food and tours of the District.

PALM BEACH SHAKESPEARE FESTIVAL
Contact: Kermit Christman
353 U.S. Hwy. 1 S., Suite F-103
Jupiter   575-7336

This Jupiter-based educational theater organization produces the Bard's treasures and new works. In 1995, for instance, festival founder Kermit Christman produced *The Vanished People*, a historic drama based on shipwrecked Quaker Jonathan Dickinson. The new play, with choreography by Demetrius Klein, interpreted the journal Dickinson penned after he reached Philadelphia in 1696.

MUCKSTEPPERS REUNION
Pioneer Park
Belle Glade   996-2161

To many of us, the rich, dark earth that nurtures the vegetables we eat is simply black gold. To folks who live in the area, it's simply called "the muck."

The Mucksteppers Reunion is a storytellers' conference and festival aimed at keeping alive the tradition of oral history as practiced by those who toiled in the muck.

Call for information about admission costs and location.

SOUTH FLORIDA FAIR

South Florida Fairgrounds
Southern Blvd., 7 miles west of I-95
West Palm Beach   *793-0333*

The South Florida Fair fills the month's calendar with a bewildering number of displays, contests, exhibits and entertainment. So if your tastes run from dirt bike supercross racing, car shows and antique shows to livestock and other expositions, concerts and American Indian culture, chances are you'll have plenty to keep you busy.

For the children, there are the ever-popular Midway rides, special programs, educational exhibits and contests, games and loads of sticky cotton candy and candied apples to be consumed.

JAPANESE NEW YEAR

Morikami Museum and Japanese Gardens
4000 Morikami Park Rd.
Delray Beach   *495-0233*

Oshogatsu, the Japanese New Year, is January 6. Traditional household decorations set the theme for *Hatsugama*, the first tea ceremony of the New Year. Visitors learn to make *mochitsuki*, or traditional rice cakes. Games include *Hanetsuki*, similar to badminton, and *Fuki Warai*, sort of like "pin the tail on the donkey." There are demonstrations in calligraphy and *Nengajo,* the making of greeting cards. Call for details.

PALM BEACH INVITATIONAL INTERNATIONAL PIANO COMPETITION

P.O. Box 3094
Palm Beach 33480   *833-8817*

In 1996, this three-day competition in late January marks the 10th anniversary of this prestigious event (see also our Arts and Culture chapter). The winner earns $15,000 and the chance to perform at Lincoln Center in New York. Tickets are $20 for one performance and $5 for each additional performance. Piano Competition Guild members pay $15.

Several months prior to the competition, the Guild presents weekly Sunday Salon and Living Room Concerts at the Four Seasons Ocean Grand Hotel, 2800 S. Ocean Boulevard, Palm Beach. Sunday programs running through February begin at 4 PM, and tickets are $20. Call for more information.

February

ARTIGRAS AT THE GARDENS

PGA Blvd., between I-95 and U.S. I
Palm Beach Gardens   *775-7750*

This annual event, put on by the Northern Palm Beaches Chamber of Commerce, celebrated its 10th anniversary in 1995. Hundreds of booths are set up adjacent to The Gardens of the Palm Beaches megamall.

Arts, crafts, food and New Orleans-style music are set up on the mall's east side. An Artful Decade, the promoter, has seen ArtiGras' attendance grow from a few hundred folks to the more than 55,000 who took part in the '95 event's three-day celebration. Tickets are $3 ($2 in advance), and proceeds benefit the chamber's pledge to Palm Beach County schools.

BookFest of the Palm Beaches
Old School Square
Delray Beach   731-0398

BookFest moved to Delray Beach for its 1995 event, and the sixth annual literary free-for-all promises to be even bigger and better in mid-February. Old School Square hosts the event, and the addition of a major new sponsor won't hurt, especially since Levenger, America's purveyors of "Tools for Serious Readers," is the exponential toy store for bookworms. Insiders, ye of the dog-eared potboilers and Churchill lamps, will want to look up Levenger in the chapters on Business and Shopping long before BookFest '96.

BookFest expects to draw attendance of more than 20,000, especially with the related "Authors on the Avenue" dimension added this year. The Delray Beach Joint Venture coordinated a series of book signings with merchants, art galleries and restaurants hosting author receptions on Atlantic Avenue. People wander from book exhibits and nearby lectures to meet authors — shopping and browsing along the way.

BookFest showcases mystery writers, children's book authors, first novelists, storytelling — almost any genre — Zen, art, rare or common, bestseller and never-seller.

Theatrical performances at the Old School Square stage are part of the action, thanks to the Palm Beach Shakespeare Festival (see this chapter's listing for more information).

The Palm Beach County Library Association coordinates BookFest.

Delray Beach Winter Championships
Delray Beach Tennis Center
200 W. Atlantic Ave.   243-7360

Formerly the Virginia Slims of Florida tennis bonanza, this tournament takes the Tennis Center by storm in late February through early March (see also our Spectator Sports chapter). The stadium has been called the best-built tennis center in the United States. Since Palm Beach County kicked in funds to expand permanent seating to 8,500, the tennis stadium also is a much in-demand stage for top-name entertainment.

FotoFusion '96 International
71 S.E. Second Ave.
Delray Beach   391-7557

Calling all shutterbugs! This first-ever photo event " . . . where creativity and technology meet . . . " takes place in late January through early February in downtown Delray Beach. Your host will be Palm Beach Photographic Museum and Workshops (see our Attractions chapter).

FotoFusion '96 is a five-day forum and fair expected to draw more than 2,000 attendees who work or play in photography and digital imaging. Major sponsors are Kodak and Canon USA. The format is seminars, workshops, round-table discussions, lectures, portfolio reviews, social events, a technology showcase, photography exhibitions at downtown art galleries, book signings, an information exchange — even a famous photography auction. Social activities include a Fusion Schmooze and an awards gala and dinner.

Call to register for FotoFusion '96.

GREEK FESTIVAL

St. Mark Greek Orthodox Church
2100 Yamato Rd.
Boca Raton   *994-4822*

This festival is Greek to everyone . . . but everyone is clued into what's going on. St. Mark Greek Orthodox Church opens its doors to one and all for a celebration of Greek religion and culture that is also a big fund-raising event for the church.

Traditionally held in the spring, the festival includes music and dance, boutiques, arts and crafts and, of course, food. On the menu, festival-goers will find gyro sandwiches, spinach pie and much more.

ART AND JAZZ ON THE AVENUE

Atlantic Ave., Delray Beach
Contact: Delray Beach Joint Venture   *279-1381*

Join 30,000 of your closest friends and other fun-seekers for casual, intimate gatherings. At these Thursday night street parties you'll find (and hear) tunes on every block.

Expect spirited live entertainment, from jazz to blues to reggae and rock 'n' roll. Mimes, flame-swallowers, clowns and such mingle with live-wire personalities, puppies on leashes and politicians on the loose. Many art galleries host new exhibitions; open houses at various establishments and special to-dos at restaurants are regular features. And there's always a contest!

Usually scheduled quarterly, Art and Jazz lasts from 5 PM to midnight, with free trolley rides along the avenue from Highway A1A to west of Swinton Avenue. Scheduled dates are in early and late February.

HATSUME FAIR

Morikami Museum and Japanese Gardens
4000 Morikami Park Rd.
Delray Beach   *495-0233*

Hatsume Fair takes place in late February, when the Japanese celebrate the first "bud" of the year. The park's largest folk festival attracts about 20,000 visitors for a weekend of *taiko* drums, exotic music and dance, *bonsai* demonstrations, arts, crafts, food and drinks. Call for details.

IRISH FEST

Bubier Park
Las Olas Blvd. at Andrews Ave.
Fort Lauderdale   *(305) 525-5500*

During this three-day festival, everyone's Irish.

Traditional fare from Ireland and the British Isles is featured, and there's plenty of strong Irish beer to wash it all down.

Cultural programs and exhibitions, Irish dance and folklore are all part of the show. So, too, are an astonishing number of vendors selling all things Irish.

FLORIDA RENAISSANCE FESTIVAL

Snyder Park
3299 S.W. Fourth Ave.
Fort Lauderdale   *(305) 468-1585*

The days of knights, wizards and fair ladies come alive again. Dramatic, musical and visual arts of the era, jousts and more are part of this popular event. Admission is $9.50 for adults and $5 for children 12 and younger.

Crowds gather at SunFest along Flagler Drive. A yacht club lies in the background.

March

BOYNTON BEACH G.A.L.A.
Ocean Ave. and Boynton Beach Blvd. area
Boynton Beach   375-6235

Boynton Beach celebrates the 15th anniversary of its "Great American Love Affair" in '96. G.A.L.A. goes all out with art, live music on multiple stages and open-air family activities over a three-day period.

Centralized downtown east of Seacrest Boulevard, G.A.L.A. has a homespun marketplace, games and rides for kids, picnic area, beer garden, exhibitors' row for businesses and cultural groups, and more than 250 artists on display. They compete for merit and cash awards in several categories: watercolor, ceramics, oil, acrylics, drawing and graphics, photography, jewelry, sculpture, mixed media and crafts. Boynton's largest outdoor family festival also showcases a youth art exhibit. Call for schedule information.

MEET ME DOWNTOWN
Downtown Boca Raton   395-4433

This event celebrates its 14th year in 1996 as Boca Raton's largest arts and entertainment festival. Events spill all through downtown, with more than 400 arts and crafts booths sprinkled around Mizner Park. Entertainment will dominate the Amphitheater stage, while the weekend fills with strolling acts such as jugglers, mimes, stilt walkers and a Banjo-mobile.

The event benefits the Golden Bell Foundation, an education initiative founded by the Greater Boca Raton Chamber of Commerce. More than 150,000 people turn out for the spring weekend fair. Food vendors, art and craft exhibits and entertainment help the Chamber of Commerce raise money for education; schools received more than $30,000 from Meet Me Downtown '95. The three-day '96 event is scheduled for early March.

For information on exhibitors, call festival director Lois Niesen.

ST. PATRICK'S DAY PARADE
229 E. Atlantic Ave.
Delray Beach   278-4130

Everyone is Irish on this day. And the Irish line Atlantic Avenue in downtown Delray Beach to watch the parade pass and revel in their new-found Irishness. Held the Saturday before St. Patrick's Day and sponsored by Powers Lounge, the parade will have its 28th running in 1996.

The first year, parade founder and Powers Lounge owner Maury Powers was the only person marching in the parade. Now, floats and bands from as far as West Palm Beach and Fort Lauderdale won't let the parade go by without them. Local merchants build floats, local residents donate time, clowns perform, antique cars cruise the Avenue and retailers set up booths along the parade route.

Powers organizes the event every year, starting the preparations in October. Money from advertisements appearing in the parade program pays police and other expenses. And whatever money is left over from all the revelry is donated to charity.

LAS OLAS ART FESTIVAL
Bubier Park
Las Olas Blvd. at Andrews Ave.
Fort Lauderdale   (305) 525-5500

More than a quarter-century old, the Las Olas Art Festival is one of South Florida's best-loved sidewalk art shows. On the weekend this event takes place, Fort Lauderdale's downtown area becomes virtually impassible because of the number of participating artists and the tidal waves of pedestrian traffic. If you plan to go, get there early and wear comfortable walking shoes.

HIGHLAND GAMES
Crandon Park
Key Biscayne   (305) 792-8017

Even if watching brawny men in kilts try to toss the telephone-pole-like caber doesn't interest you, this festival offers plenty to amaze and amuse. In addition to the athletic events, the Highland Games also offer bagpipe-playing and Scottish dance competitions.

There also are plenty of vendors peddling Scottish mementos and foodstuffs.

The festival food runs from the sublime (bangers and mash and other typical festival fare) to the uncommon such as haggis (sheep or calf victuals mixed with oatmeal and boiled within the animal's stomach). There's plenty of porter and stout, plus soft drinks too.

LATIN FEST
Dreher Park, near the zoo
1301 Summit Blvd.
West Palm Beach   835-4913

Latin Fest is a tri-annual family-oriented event celebrating the Hispanic culture, including music, food and fun for all. Sponsored and organized by Miguel Lavin, publisher of *El Latino Semanal* (see our Media chapter), this late March festival features bands from Puerto Rico, the Dominican Republic and New York. Major costs are covered by underwriting, and proceeds from refreshment sales are donated to Hispanic Human Resources.

Admission is free.

Latin Fest also takes place in June and October.

April

DELRAY AFFAIR
Various locations along Atlantic Ave.   278-0424

A dalliance with Downtown, this event began as the farm community's show-and-tell — with the pawing of ripe melons and the bare throats of flowers, specifically "the ocean city's" global gladiolas. It dates to 1962, always reheats the week after Easter, and admission is free. More than 250,000 visitors browse Atlantic Avenue and parallel side streets from the Intracoastal Waterway to Swinton Avenue.

Artists and craft exhibitors — regional, national and international — work throughout the year to produce the trademark freshness Delray expects for its one and only Affair. Food vendors spice up the three days with world-famous conch fritters, 'gator bites, other local delicacies and more conventional temptations. Dozens of music and dance ensembles turn multiple stages and many street corners into a running serenade.

Delray Affair now includes a business expo and something for every age group, with a midway of rides and games just for the wee ones. The fair is especially pedestrian-friendly and safe, with motor traffic closed on Atlantic Avenue and convenient park-and-ride shuttle service.

The Southeast Tourism Society gives Delray Affair thumbs up as one of the Top 20 festivals with the ability to rekindle the public's passion time and time again. "Same time next year" is mid-April.

The Delray Beach Chamber of Commerce is the sponsor, but Ignatz, an Aztec persona in pottery, is the event's real alter ego. To inquire about exhibiting, write Ignatz at the Delray Beach Chamber of Commerce, 64 S.E. Fifth Avenue, Delray Beach 33483; include color slides or photos and a description of the artwork, product or service you want to display. A committee will choose exhibitors about two months prior to the event.

PALM BEACH INVITATIONAL INTERNATIONAL PIANO COMPETITION
P.O. Box 3094
Palm Beach 33480   833-8817

This early April 1996 competition features some of the world's most accomplished pianists. See the January listing for more details.

BLACK GOLD JUBILEE
Belle Glade Marina
Belle Glade   996-2745

Held during the third weekend of the month at the end of the annual harvest, the festival combines a blessing of the soil and a means of recognizing the agricultural workers who labor in "America's Salad Bowl."

Jubilee events include sports contests such as volleyball, tennis, golf and a road race. There also is a street festival with booths, crafts, entertainments and, of course, fireworks in the evening.

CONCH REPUBLIC INDEPENDENCE CELEBRATION

The Keys   (305) 296-0213

This series of events commemorates the Keys' mock secession from the United States in 1982. Events in Key West include a water fight, bed race and parade. Traditionally, this celebration has been held only in Key West, but organizers say they hope to add events in the "Northernmost Territories" (anything north of the Stock Island Bridge in Key West), for the 1996 event.

May

SUNFEST

Flagler Dr. at the Intracoastal Waterway
West Palm Beach   659-5992

Held in early May, SunFest is five days of hot reggae, cool jazz, sultry blues plus rock 'n' roll, country, pop, oldies and Top-40 music drawing more than 300,000 folks downtown; there's something to tantalize almost every musical taste.

But SunFest is more than just great music performed by national headliners, such as Harry Connick Jr., Ray Charles and Nestor Torres, and favorite local artists. There are fireworks displays, juried art and crafts shows, games and amusements for the children and,

of course, loads of food and drinks. This extravaganza of the arts is set against the backdrop of Flagler Drive's big bend and its panoramic view of the Intracoastal and Palm Beach beyond.

A baker's dozen years ago, it began with music, oozing with jazz, big names and emerging talents, and over time dappled the Drive with food delicacies from hundreds of vendors, powerboat racing and water-ski exhibitions, kite flying, dance performances, a juried art show, midway carnival, crafts marketplace, games, fireworks, and a nightly laser light and sound show projected onto a multi-story screen.

Four stages and three gates shape the stream of traffic toward the waterfront from Lakeview Avenue north to Banyan Street. There are bus shuttle service, reasonable prices for parking, special events at nearby downtown merchants, and a new wrinkle this year: a "kissing booth" set up by the Clerk of Courts for folks who decide to tie the knot at SunFest. One-day passes have been $12 with a three-day sweep for $25 — no sweat since cosponsor NationsBank sets up a mobile ATM on-site. Advance tickets are available at lower prices, so call in advance for details.

Headliners for the '95 event included B. B. King, Roberta Flack, Fleetwood Mac and Ramsay Lewis, and Jimmy Buffett jumped on stage for an impromptu jam with Savana.

The atmosphere is festive and fun. The air crackles with excitement and energy. This is one of the most popular festivals in Palm Beach County. Don't miss it.

Photo: Stephanie Murphy

SunFest `95 crowds loved Savana and were pleasantly surprised when Jimmy Buffett jumped onstage impromptu.

SEAFARE

Jupiter Park Lighthouse
U.S. I, north of the Jupiter Federal Bridge
Jupiter

This annual frolic the weekend before Memorial Day cuts to the chase: bounty from the sea, fun and entertainment. Set for mid-May 1996, as Sunday morning gets down, Seafare unfolds at Jupiter Park Lighthouse, the 1860 beacon that shines for 18 miles along the Gold Coast.

More than 14,000 seafood lovers attended the '95 festival, played out at the base of the landmark lighthouse. For information, call the Florida History Center and Museum, 747-6639.

CAJUN ZYDECO CRAWFISH FESTIVAL

Mills Pond Park
Fort Lauderdale   (305) 761-5813

If Zydeco or Cajun music, the boogie from the bayou, sets your heart racing and your feet tapping, this is the place for you at one of South Florida's newer festivals.

Supplementing the musicians and groups from the heart of Cajun Country in Louisiana is a constant supply of steaming hot Cajun crawfish, icy-cold Hurricanes and other lip-smacking specialties.

There are booths and games for the children, arts and crafts and community displays for everyone. And, of course, there's a Mardi Gras-style parade.

June

GOOMBAY FESTIVAL

Grand Ave. at Main St.
Coconut Grove   (305) 539-3000

Originally a cultural festival saluting the influence of Bahamian settlers in South Florida, the Goombay Festival has grown to reflect Miami's cultural diversity.

Stroll along Grand Avenue and take in the sights, sounds and scents of the Grove. Don't pass up the chance to sample *arepas* (a Central American corn and cheese pastry), tart and tangy mango salad made with green mangos and vinegar, or Bahamian specialties such as conch fritters, conch salad or chick peas and rice. You can even buy gyros or souvlaki here.

The Nassau Police Band from New Providence Island in the Bahamas usually entertains throughout, wearing their traditional red-and-white parade uniforms. There also is plenty of other entertainment, including Latin music and junkanoos, who don traditional Bahamian costumes of bright crepe with outlandish colorful hats and make merry music with drums, horns, whistles and other hand-made percussion instruments.

LATIN FEST

Dreher Park, near the zoo
1301 Summit Blvd.
West Palm Beach   *835-4913*

This celebration of Hispanic culture in mid to late June features Latin music and traditional ethnic food. The Father's Day 1995 event drew more than 5,000 people.

Admission is free at this tri-annual festival. See the March listing of Latin Fest for more information.

July

HEMINGWAY DAYS FESTIVAL

Key West   *(305) 294-4440*

The literary colony's most famed resident is commemorated with a short story contest, look-alike contest, literary symposia and many other activities.

18TH ANNUAL
ROOTS CULTURAL FESTIVAL

Pompey Park Recreation Center
1101 Martin Luther King Blvd.
Delray Beach   *276-2099*

Always strong as an expression of black pride, the Annual Roots Cultural Festival continues to show unmistakable progress as a tribute to knowledge, competitive excellence and celebration of heritage.

Once a momentary salute — part of one day to honor the beauty of being black — the All-America City Roots Cultural Festival has expanded to a month-long institution that teaches and reaches far beyond Delray's black community.

One of the longest-established consecutive community celebrations in Palm Beach County, Roots Festival traditionally gets under way with a church dedication ceremony. Christ Missionary Baptist Church again hosted 1995's kickoff festivities.

Highlights include academic contests, athletic tournaments, a parade and flag ceremony plus assorted musical entertainment. With selected events that showcase black culture in a positive way, the Festival is headquartered at Pompey Park. Presented each year by Roots Cultural Festival Inc., a nonprofit corporation, the event is officially sanctioned by the City of Delray Beach and the State of Florida.

"All of South Florida benefits by this annual event . . . which celebrates the black experience in meaningful ways," explains Marjorie Ferrer of the Delray Beach Joint Venture. "This area is home to American blacks as well as others who have relocated from Caribbean islands featuring predominantly black societies. The elements of their common heritage should be appreciated by people of all racial and ethnic backgrounds who live in the region we all share."

The Roots Festival Committee chairman is Tommy Stevens. Festivities often have an annual theme to direct the efforts of youth, especially in the academic contests. In recent years, themes have reflected the community's awareness of the need for a grass-roots response to urban issues such as street crime. Festival events this year include racquetball, basketball, bowling, softball, golf and tennis tournaments, Gospel Fest, Phi Beta Sigma Sweetheart Dance, an oratorical contest, an essay contest and spelling bee, a math contest, Youth on Parade, the Coronation of Festival Royalty, Jammin' at the Theater, Festival Parade, a flag raising ceremony, Jazz in the Park and a talent show, a prayer breakfast, a health fair, Youth Explosion, a step show, All-day Festival in the Park and All-day Gospel Festivities.

SOULFEST

Phil Foster Park
Riviera Beach   *842-7146*

The 1995 SoulFest marked the first time the event was held in summer. In previous years, SoulFest coincided with Black History Month in February.

Held at Phil Foster Park under the Blue Heron Bridge, the three-day late July/early August event combines arts and crafts, entertainment and plenty of good food. Aside from being just plain fun, the focus here is on educational awareness of black history and the black cultural heritage. Headline entertainment takes the stage every night. The Suncoast Chamber of Commerce sponsors SoulFest, which drew 18,000 attendees in 1995. Admission is $7 for adults, and seniors and children younger than 12 get in free.

SUMMER NIGHTS ON THE AVENUE

E. Atlantic Ave.
Delray Beach
Contact: Delray Beach Joint Venture   279-1381

This year marks the second annual Summer Nights schedule of events, resembling in spirit the Art and Jazz street festivals held quarterly. Businesses take turns hosting block party-style events every other weekend, with a section of the city's gateway cordoned off for dancing. Events this year go through early September.

Summer Nights is coordinated by the Delray Beach Joint Venture, which coordinates everything from table and chair setup to sponsors, vendors who sell refreshments and crowd-friendly police patrolling on bicycles.

ERNY'S ANNUAL SUMMER JAZZ FESTIVAL

1010 E. Atlantic Ave.
Delray Beach   *276-9191*

No cover. No minimum. Just great jazz every weekend for a month at Erny's, the family-owned supper club east of the Intracoastal Waterway. From Bourbon Street to Harlem nights and every musical memory in between, Erny's pulls out all the stops but never stops delivering on its reliable menu and unforgettable entertainment. If you missed Erny's in our Nightlife chapter, they're popular for lunch and dinner, serving consistently fine American food that's not terribly expensive.

During July, the festival finale coincides with the aforementioned Summer Nights on the Avenue.

ART AND JAZZ ON THE AVENUE
Atlantic Ave., Delray Beach
Contact: Delray Beach Joint Venture   279-1381

The Thursday night street parties heat up the early July evening.

Live music from jazz to blues to reggae and rock 'n' roll and other entertainment is on tap. (See the February listing for details.)

August

BOCA FESTIVAL DAYS
Various locations
Boca Raton   395-4433

Boca Festival Days heats up every summer, with the whole month of August devoted to a feather-flying flamingo strut of a recreation festival. You need roller skates, a calendar and maybe a compass to keep up with dozens of events scattered around town.

Voted one of the Top 20 events by the Southeast Tourism Society for the past six years, Boca Festival Days also raises money for local nonprofit organizations.

Folks wash dogs, exhibit art, compete in an underwater photography contest, fly kites, play polo, play music, hunt treasure, sculpt sand, fish and cut bait. Fashion shows, antique cars, softball and gymnastics are a few of events that have kept Boca Festival Days a hot ticket for the past 18 years.

August isn't long enough for all the activities, so the annual Wine & All That Jazz kicks off in late July. The ceremonial sipping takes place in the romantic chambers of the Boca Raton Resort and Club and usually benefits Hospice by the Sea.

BOCA EXPO
(PART OF FESTIVAL DAYS)
Florida Atlantic University Gymnasium
Off Glades Rd., just east of I-95
Boca Raton   395-4433

The Greater Boca Raton Chamber of Commerce's annual business trade fair is a major highlight of Boca Festival Days in mid-August.

More than 20,000 attend the show over three days, with contests, prize drawings, plenty of giveaways, free demonstrations and aromas from the outdoor food court wafting over the grounds.

If you're new to the area, Boca Expo is ideal for checking out local merchants, service organizations and even cultural groups.

Businesses offer free seminars and advice, so it's easy to get acquainted in a casual, friendly atmosphere. Expo is a bargain: Advance tickets are free and $1 at the door. To find out what's in store for Boca Expo '96, write Boca Festival Days Committee, 1800 N. Dixie Highway, Boca Raton 33432. For a rundown on individual events, call 395-4433.

BON FESTIVAL

Morikami Museum and Japanese Gardens
4000 Morikami Park Rd.
Delray Beach   495-0233

Bon Festival is Japan's most important summer celebration, and the Morikami's condensed version is among its most popular. This event is usually held in mid-August.

Obon is a déjà vu of sorts, a time when ancestral spirits get down with the living for some serious fun. The occasion pays tribute to one's quality of life, owed largely to friendly ghosts who prepared the way. The day starts gently with *Ocha* or the tea ceremony and *Ikebana* demonstrations of flower arranging; then things crank up with *Bon odori* folk dancing and the resonant thunder of *Taiko* drums — which you may recall from the movie *Rising Sun*.

At twilight is *Toro Nagashi*, when lanterns are set adrift on the pond, and *Hanabi Taikai*, a fireworks display to light the way for spirits homeward-bound. Highlights of *Obon* include *Ennichi*, a street fair with games, shopping, food and beer gardens, museum exhibits and the nature walk.

Thousands of visitors take in the Bon Festival each year. Admission is $5 for adults, $3 for members and $1 for children from 6 to 18. Parking is complimentary, and there is a shuttle bus for convenience.

SUMMER NIGHTS ON THE AVENUE

E. Atlantic Ave.
Delray Beach
Contact: Delray Beach Joint Venture   279-1381

Events in '95 included a street party at Elwood's Dixie BBQ in the 300 block of E. Atlantic Avenue, a concert at Veteran's Park on the Intracoastal Waterway, a POG tournament and, in September, a Labor Day weekend beach party on Ocean Boulevard at Atlantic Avenue. Call Delray Beach Joint Venture for information about the '96 event.

September

SOCIETY OF CHILDREN'S BOOK WRITERS AND ILLUSTRATORS LITERARY CONFERENCE

2158 Portland Ave., Wellington
Contact: Barbara Casey   798-4824

The Florida chapter of this literary and visual art association gathers each fall for this conference for "anyone who is interested in children's literature." The event features guest speakers as well as professional writers, editors, publishers and illustrators. The conference includes manuscript evaluations for interested attendees. "Learning" is the key, according to regional advisor Barbara Casey, who invited Boyds Mill Press editors Stephanie Gordon Tessler and Judy Enderle (both of whom are also children's book authors) to attend the

---

1995 event. Call Barbara Casey or the Palm Beach County Library System, 731-0398, for more information.

CLEMATIS BY NIGHT

Clematis St.
West Palm Beach   659-8004

The Downtown Development Authority sponsors this concert series on Thursday nights from 5 to 8 PM. Downtown streets are closed to traffic, and regional bands thrill crowds with the sounds of rock 'n' roll, jazz, reggae, country . . . you name it. Although a year-round event, the region's relatively light amount of September events makes Clematis By Night a natural choice for this month's itinerary. This event is free to the public.

October

OKTOBERFEST

American German Club picnic grounds
Lantana   967-6464

You'll do the Chicken Dance until your hips ache at this rollicking annual festival. The mood is relentlessly upbeat, and the participants couldn't be more blissful. The only sour thing you'll see is sauerkraut, and there's plenty of that.

The festival runs during two weekends of the month, giving you plenty of time to don your dirndls or lederhosen, sample all the traditional German fare and libations and polka 'til you drop.

Because the festival is so wildly popular, shuttle service is available from John Prince Park in nearby Lake Worth.

DIWALI — FESTIVAL OF LIGHTS

Morikami Museum and Japanese Gardens
4000 Morikami Park Rd.
Delray Beach   492-0233

Another of South Florida's young festivals, this one is sponsored by the Association of Indians in America and provides an excellent glimpse of Asian Indian tradition. Participants can learn about many facets of Indian life, including ayurvedic medicine, a traditional Hindu method of healing that utilizes herbs, oils and other natural substances.

The arts and crafts of India are well-represented. Demonstrations by puppeteers, wood carvers and metal smiths, as well as traditional activities such as henna hand painting, sari draping and folk dances are offered throughout the day.

Enjoy curry of all types, tandoori chicken and many of the other spicy and sweet specialties.

Parking at the festival site is scarce. Free shuttle bus service is available from Spanish River High School, 5100 Jog Road, Boca Raton.

Insiders' Tips

Check out Boca Raton's annual holiday parade along Federal Highway in early December, featuring floats decorated by local organizations, youth entertainment and live music.

LATIN FEST

Dreher Park, near the zoo
1301 Summit Blvd.
West Palm Beach 835-4913

Featuring bands from Puerto Rico, the Dominican Republic and New York as well as traditional ethnic food, Latin Fest in late October coincides with Hispanic Heritage Month.

Admission is free. See the March listing for details about this cultural celebration.

CENTENNIAL CELEBRATION IN DELRAY BEACH

Various locations around town
Delray Beach

Delray's 100th birthday continues with the city's annual Heritage Month and features music, art, history, food and sports events. This celebration coincides with Florida's sesquicentennial and runs throughout the entire month of October.

ART AND JAZZ ON THE AVENUE

Atlantic Ave., Delray Beach
Contact: Delray Beach Joint Venture 273-1381

Live music and other entertainment feed the senses at this late October event. (See the February listing for details.)

FANTASY FEST

Key West (305) 296-1817

Fantasy Fest is a miniature Mardi Gras where just about anything goes. About 60,000 people converge on Key West for the 10-day event. The theme for the 1995 event is "Tinseltown Dreams ... Lights, Camera, Fantasy!" Scheduled events include the crowning event, Twilight Fantasy Parade, Goombay Celebration and King and Queen's Coronation Ball, Fantasy

Yacht Race, Masked Monday, Masked Madness and Headdress Ball, Pet Masquerade and Parade, the Two Wheelers in Paradise Bicycle and Moped Costume Contest, a street fair on Duvall Street and the Duvall Street Promenade.

November

JAPANESE CULTURE DAYS

Morikami Park and Japanese Gardens
4000 Morikami Park Rd.
Delray Beach 495-0233

Bunka No Hi, or Japanese Culture Days, are held to honor traditional arts such as *ikebana, haiku* poetry, and *shakuhachi* (bamboo flute) and *koto* music. *Bonsai,* classical dance, lectures, performances, workshops and demonstrations make up the schedule. Call for details.

FRONTIER FAMILY DAYS

Royal Palm Polo Grounds
Jog and Clint Moore Rds. 395-1183

This three-day professional rodeo at Royal Palm Polo grounds is an annual fund-raiser to benefit the George Snow Scholarship Fund. Our Philanthropy chapter tells more about the late George Snow, a prominent real estate developer, builder and former school teacher.

Major corporate sponsors, professional cowboys and an exciting, well-rounded program draw thousands for the rodeo. Frontier Family Days always the first weekend of November.

Events on opening day highlight old-Florida frontier life, including the Media/Sponsor Barrel Race. Folks from regional newspapers and radio and TV stations will compete with representatives of sponsors for a real barrel of fun that earns prizes. The Cowboy Ball follows, including country music by Hot Walker Band, a barbecue dinner, line-dancing and square-dancing lessons, a bonfire and hayrides. New for '95 are live and silent auctions for fine jewelry, trip packages, celebrity contributions, sports collector merchandise and much more. Tickets for the ball are limited to 500, and admission is $25.

On Saturday and Sunday, the rodeo opens at noon with professional riders from Five Star Rodeo competing in sporting events for points toward national titles. Live country music and line-dancing, great barbecue, a carnival midway, a chili corral, a kids' stage with continuous entertainment and an arts and crafts show are a few of the family activities on deck.

Advance rodeo tickets are $8 for adults and $4 for children younger than 12. They're available at all Publix supermarkets in Boca Raton and Delray Beach, as well as NationsBank centers throughout Palm Beach County. Special VIP seating for Saturday and Sunday performances is available through the George Snow Scholarship Fund.

ARMENIAN FESTIVAL
St. David Armenian Church
2300 Yamato Rd.
Boca Raton 994-2335

Food preparation for this festival — traditionally held the weekend before Thanksgiving — usually starts in summer. Members of the congregation stock their freezers with Armenian delicacies.

St. David, built in the late 1980s, has about 250 year-round members

and another 200 during the winter season. But don't let that lead you to believe this festival doesn't attract a myriad of visitors. Nonmembers flock to this festival to sample such treats as boorma, bakhlava, and kadeyif pastries, which are filled with raisins and nuts. In addition to food, festival-goers can get a taste of Armenian culture.

Call the church for details.

HARVEST FEST
Downtown Delray Beach 278-0424

This cultural showcase, featuring the agricultural heritage of Delray Beach, combines arts and crafts with a farmers' market, children's petting zoo, live entertainment and an all-around street fest. Harvest Fest is sponsored by the Delray Beach Chamber of Commerce. This event happens in mid-November and admission is free. Call for details.

WESTFEST
At the Village Hall grounds
Royal Palm Beach Blvd. and Okeechobee Rd.
Royal Palm Beach (800) 790-2364

Pull on those boots, strap on your chaps and head to Royal Palm Beach, friends, for Westfest, a dancin' and ridin' and ropin' good time, held early in the month each year.

American Indian and Western crafts, dancing and equestrian events are just part of the fun.

JEWISH COMMUNITY FESTIVAL OF ARTS, BOOKS AND CULTURE
Adolph and Rose Levis JCC
9801 Donna Klein Blvd.
Boca Raton 852-3241

This annual, two-week-long event hosts leading Jewish literary personalities, and a book fair showcases con-

Morikami Museum and Japanese Gardens is the site of numerous festivals and special events.

temporary and classical Jewish authors. For information, call Zinman Hall Box Office at the listed number.

GRASSY WATERS FESTIVAL

On the lakefront, just off of Southern Blvd.
Pahokee   924-5579

November's first Saturday is set aside for this annual festival named for Pai-hai-o-kee, the Indian word for "grassy waters," which eventually was shortened simply to Pahokee.

The Grassy Waters Festival is a community event that emphasizes the importance of the family. The day's activities include games, entertainment, a food festival and an automobile show. Call for details.

CENTENNIAL CELEBRATION IN DELRAY BEACH

Old School Square
Delray Beach

Delray's 100th birthday party continues. Events include lighting a 100-foot holiday tree in late November.

December

PALM BEACH ROUND TABLE

230 Royal Palm Way, Ste. 202
Palm Beach 33480   655-5266

The Palm Beach Round Table dates to the 1932 season, when Dr. and Mrs. Alexander M. Hadden of New York spent the winter at The Breakers Hotel. Round Table is the doyenne of Florida-based forums on world affairs. Modeled after the illusive ideal of King Arthur, the Haddens' cadre of intellectuals dined and socialized to examine diverse notions of the day. Internationalists parried with patriots, who determined early on the Round Table's charter: "To help in strengthening the principles of American democracy as a way of life."

Elder statesman Frank Wright steered the organization from 1962 until 1994, when Ben Starling III assumed the post of executive director.

With sellout memberships the norm, Round Table has moved its

Photo: Stephanie Murphy

stage to Kravis Center, where programs take place in the Eunice and Julian Cohen Pavilion, an 11,000-square-foot hospitality hall with banquet and catering facilities. Starling expects to release the 1995-96 schedule in October. The 1995 event begins in December and continues through May 1996. For information on membership or specific speakers, write or call the Round Table.

VIRGINIA SLIMS
LEGENDS TENNIS TOURNAMENT
Delray Beach Tennis Stadium
200 W. Atlantic Ave.
Delray Beach   491-7115

This tournament, held in early December, is part of the city's centennial. Events focus on women on the tennis court and in concert. The final stop in a 1995 tour featuring the lineup of a dozen greats includes Chris Evert and Martina Navratilova. Instead of prize money, a major portion of the revenue goes toward AIDS research.

HOLIDAYS, SOUTH FLORIDA-STYLE
Atlantic Intracoastal Waterway
Various cities

This annual event means boat parades along the Intracoastal Waterway in every major city. Every size craft from dinghy to yacht looks festive when dressed to the nines in twinkling lights and Christmas decorations. People gather along the banks of waterway homes to view the procession. Bridges are kept open, so the key factor is to decide before 6 PM whether you want to watch from the east or west side of the waterway. For 1995, Boca Raton's boat parade is set

for mid-December; Delray's is in early December.

SILVER AND GOLD (PARADE)
Along Federal Hwy.
Boca Raton

Boca's 25th annual downtown holiday parade is scheduled for early December. A tree lighting ceremony takes place in late November at City Hall.

CENTENNIAL CELEBRATION
IN DELRAY BEACH

A handful of events round out Delray's Centennial Celebration:

JINGLE BELL RUN

Giddyup, jingle-bell runners, pick up your feet in early December! This event is sponsored by the American Heart Association. Call Marjorie Ferrer at the Greater Delray Beach Chamber of Commerce, 278-0424, for details.

ATLANTIC AVENUE PARADE

Where else would you expect to find this parade but on Atlantic Avenue? The festivities happen in early December.

LIGHT UP DELRAY
Various locations throughout Delray Beach

Neighborhoods dress it up for the holidays in mid-December.

BREAKFAST WITH SANTA

Santa takes time out of his busy schedule to share a morning meal on two dates in mid-December. Call Marjorie Ferrer at the Greater Delray Beach Chamber of Commerce, 278-0424, for details about the event's location and scheduled dates.

NEW YEAR'S EVE PARTY

Colony Hotel
525 E. Atlantic Ave.
Delray Beach   *276-4123*

This black-tie affair on December 31 rings in the new year and rings out Delray's yearlong Centennial Celebration.

Photo: Delray Beach Community Redevelopment Agency

Delray's Atlantic Avenue beach.

Inside
Our Beautiful Beaches

The delicate ribbon of sand that rings most of this state has a magnetic effect on tourists and residents alike. Our beaches, scented with salt spray, suntan lotion and the aroma of meat grilling over charcoal fires, are captivating places. In South Florida, life is truly a beach.

Palm Beach County's beaches are excellent in general, and Boca Raton's (2 miles of beaches) and Jupiter's beaches in particular are superb.

Our beaches are governed by a variety of authorities: several municipalities, the county and the state. Most of Palm Beach County's beachfront or beach-access parks permit free entry and parking, and the town of Jupiter allows beachside parking without charge and even provides a few free beach-access parking lots. As for the remainder of the beaches in Palm Beach County, you'll need to shell out some cash for the chance to frolic among the seashells.

Some communities, such as Lantana, Lake Worth and Palm Beach, provide metered lots for beach-goers. You can pay for several hours of parking at each, but be sure to bring plenty of quarters.

Communities such as Boca Raton and Boynton Beach, and state-operated areas such as John D. MacArthur Beach State Park, charge an entry fee for vehicles.

The entry fees at some of Boca Raton's beachside parks dampen some folks' enthusiasm, but as you reach into your wallet, consider what you're getting: off-road parking, grills, playgrounds, restrooms and other amenities such as nature trails and picnic shelters.

Beach Permits

If you live inside Boca city limits, the Greater Boca Raton Beach Tax District or Palm Beach County, you can buy an annual permit for parking privileges at various beachside parks in Boca Raton: **Red Reef Park**, **South Beach Park** and **Spanish River Park**. The permits are good for the fiscal year, so it's best to buy them in September. The parks are free for pedestrians and bicyclists.

Although it might seem confusing, the following information outlines the beach permit procedures and guidelines. This information is for fiscal year 1994-95 (the only information available at press time). Be aware that rates and other details may change for the 1995-96 fiscal year.

Procedures and Guidelines

You must prove residency by showing a tax bill, phone bill, electric bill, water deposit receipt, rental or lease agreement, driver's license or voter's registration card. You also must show documents on the vehicle, including car registration regardless of state or country, car title, bill of sale or lease agreement with your name on it. If it's a company car, you need to show a business card or employer's letter stating the car is assigned to you.

Permits are on sale at the Boca Raton Community Center, 150 N.W. Crawford Boulevard, one block west of City Hall and north of Palmetto Park Road; or at the James A. Rutherford Community Center at Patch Reef Park, 2000 N.W. 51st Street, just west of Military Trail. The centers are open 8 AM to 10 PM weekdays and 8 AM to 5 PM on Saturdays. Also, on weekends, permits are on sale at the Park Ranger Station at Spanish River.

Fees for beach permits are $24.25 for Boca Raton residents, who have privileges at South Beach, Red Reef and Spanish River parks. Residents within the Greater Boca Raton Beach Tax District pay $24.25 for South Beach and Red Reef access, plus half the daily rate at Spanish River Park. For an annual fee of $40.15, residents may access all three parks. County residents may buy permits for South Beach only for $24.25.

If you are a nonresident, thus ineligible for permits, daily parking rates at Red Reef Park are $8 on weekdays and $10 on weekends and holidays; South Beach, $7 on weekdays and $9 on weekends and holidays; and Spanish River Park, $8 on weekdays and $10 on weekends and holidays. Metered spaces fill up quickly in-season,

so remember what they say about the early bird.... And though it varies by community, you can often feed the meter enough to satisfy its appetite for many hours. For example, the meters at Deerfield Beach cost 25¢ for 15 minutes and can take up to four hours worth of quarters ($4).

Please note that you may not possess or consume alcohol on municipal or county beaches, nor are pets allowed.

If beach permit information and its caveats are still confusing, and you'd like to ask specific questions, call the Boca Raton Community Center at 393-7806. The folks there more than likely can help you.

Beach Wheelchairs

Both Delray Beach and Boca Raton have special chairs to make the beach more accessible for the physically challenged. The chair can be pushed through the sand to the water's edge. In Delray, the chair is available from 9 AM to 5 PM at the lifeguard stand on the beach nearest Atlantic Avenue and U.S. Highway A1A. The chair has a two-hour limit and is available on a first-come, first-served basis. Use of the chair is free, but users must sign a waiver and provide proper identification. In Boca, the chair is available at Tower 19 at Spanish River Park from 10 AM to 4 PM. The user's companion must submit a valid driver's license as a deposit for the chair.

Photo: Heather Selwitz

Catamarans line the shore in Delray Beach.

Palm Beach County's Beaches

Here are the best municipal and county beaches Palm Beach County has to offer:

RED REEF PARK

1400 N. Ocean Blvd.
Boca Raton

The 67-acre city-owned beach park has lifeguards on duty from 9 AM to 5 PM daily. It features a children's play area, picnic facilities, boardwalk and barbecue grills and is adjacent to the city-owned Red Reef Executive Golf Course (see our Golf chapter).

The park is open 8 AM to 10 PM daily.

SPANISH RIVER PARK

3100 N. Ocean Blvd., just south of Spanish River Blvd.
Boca Raton

This huge city-owned park, which spreads from the beach west to the Intracoastal Waterway, features 1,850 feet of beach frontage and beach volleyball courts on the east side of Highway A1A. The western sector is densely covered with native vegetation and crisscrossed with nature trails. There are plenty of picnic tables and grills and five covered shelters that are ideal for birthday parties and company picnics. The children will enjoy the 40-foot, two-level observation tower.

The park is open 8 AM to sunset daily.

SOUTH BEACH

U.S. Hwy. A1A and Palmetto Park Rd.
Boca Raton

Although you won't find the facilities available at other Boca Raton-owned beach parks, this city-owned park is noted for its pavilion. There's also a large parking area.

South Beach is open daily from 8 AM until sunset.

DELRAY BEACH PUBLIC BEACH

Ocean Blvd. at Atlantic Ave.
Delray Beach

One of the county's liveliest beaches, this 7,000-foot strip of sand bustles with activity. If you tire of swimming, sunning or playing volleyball in the sand, simply cross Highway A1A and pick up a burger and quaff a tall, cold one at one of the many hotels or restaurants that cater to the beach crowd. Metered roadside parking is available on Highway A1A.

The beach is open from 9 AM until 5 PM, and lifeguards are on duty throughout that time.

DEERFIELD BEACH MUNICIPAL BEACH
U.S. Hwy. A1A at the pier
Deerfield Beach

This city-owned beach has 5,700 feet of frontage — the entire length of the Deerfield Beach city limits. The facilities and "amenities" are vast: grills and picnic tables at the covered pavilion, restrooms, tiki huts along the beach, cabana service and a popular fishing pier. North of the pier is the "active" area where folks can play Frisbee or paddle ball, surf or get a pickup game going at the volleyball nets.

The beach is open from 7 AM to 11 PM, and lifeguards are on duty from 9 AM to 5 PM. Metered parking is available.

LAKE WORTH MUNICIPAL BEACH AND BARTON PARK
Lake Ave. at U.S. Hwy. A1A
Lake Worth

If you saw the film *Body Heat*, you have gotten a glimpse of Lake Worth and its city-owned beach, which offers more activities in one area than any other in the county.

For starters, there's 1,200 feet of beach frontage, a favorite of local surfers who ride the waves near the pier. Cabanas are available for rent, as are fixed observation telescopes.

The pier is a bargain. Plunk down $2 for each adult or $1 for each child younger than 12 and you can fish all day. Spectators are welcome too; admission is 50¢.

Across the street is the Barton Park tot lot and a quiet seagrape-shaded picnic area. Next door is the Lake Worth Municipal Pool, where you can take a dip for just $2 for adults, $1 for children and seniors.

Adjoining the Lake Worth complex is Palm Beach County's Richard G. Kreusler Memorial Park, open from 8 AM to 8 PM daily, which provides an additional 450 feet of beach frontage, restrooms and additional parking.

Lifeguards are on duty at both areas from 9 AM to 5 PM.

Metered lots are available at both area, but use the Kreusler Park meters if you can. Meters cost 25¢ for 20 minutes; the Lake Worth Municipal lot charges 25¢ for 15 minutes.

OCEAN INLET PARK AND BEACH
9600 N. Ocean Blvd.
Ocean Ridge   964-4420

South Lake Worth Inlet, a popular fishing spot, serves as backdrop

---

Insiders' Tips

Oil spilled from tankers out at sea sometimes washes ashore and mingles with the sand, causing tarballs that stain bare feet. Try a few dabs of nail polish remover to wipe the stains away.

for this popular county-owned park and beach area, open from 8 AM until sundown. The park offers an observation tower, marina, snack bar, grills and picnic tables and restrooms. The beach is guarded daily from 9 AM to 5:20 PM. Admission is free.

BOYNTON BEACH MUNICIPAL BEACH AND OCEANFRONT PARK

U.S. Hwy. A1A, just north of Ocean Ave.
Boynton Beach   737-4507

In addition to a beautiful stretch of beach, the area includes a playground, picnic tables, grills and pavilions, snack bar, showers and restrooms.

Lifeguards are on duty from 8 AM to 5 PM.

The daily admission fee is $5 per car from May 1 to November 15, $10 for the remainder of the year.

TOWN OF LANTANA PUBLIC BEACH

U.S. Hwy. A1A at E. Ocean Ave.
Lantana

Lantana's municipal beach, wedged alongside the giant Ritz-Carlton Hotel, is a small, diverse beach with much to offer. In addition to its ocean frontage, there is a volleyball court, children's playground, grills and picnic tables scattered beneath the seagrape trees on the shore. Restrooms and showers also are available on site.

The Dune Deck Cafe enables you to eat breakfast and lunch to the sounds of waves breaking on the shore. A supply shop offers beach toys, postcards, reading materials, suntan products and other sundries.

The beach is open from an hour before sunrise to an hour after sunset daily; lifeguards are on duty from 9 AM to 5 PM daily.

Parking is metered and costs 25¢ for 20 minutes.

PALM BEACH MUNICIPAL BEACH

U.S. Hwy. A1A, between Royal Palm Way and Gulf Stream Rd.
Palm Beach

If swimming's not your thing, Palm Beach's city-owned beach promenade may be. The walkway, which runs along Highway A1A from Gulf Stream Road at the beach's northern boundary to Royal Palm Way at the south, helps keep the sand out of your shoes but allows the ocean sounds and smells to fully permeate your senses. If you'd like to stop and watch, there is an observation deck at Chilean Avenue.

The beach is monitored by lifeguards. Parallel parking is available

Surfers and snorkelers have special areas set aside for them on Boca Raton's beaches. The recommended snorkeling area is at the south end of Red Reef Park. Areas designated for surfing are located at the north end of Spanish River Park, the south end of South Beach and the south end of Red Reef Park.

Insiders' Tips

Sunburn!

If you saw the film *Grumpy Old Men*, you might recall the scene where Ann-Margret walks into the small-town apothecary and creates a stir when she asks the pharmacist about a special shipment from California. Her comment on the aroma of fresh Tea Tree Oil soaking into your pores seems to have a melting effect on Jack Lemmon and Walter Matthau.

It also has a soothing effect on sun blisters, which is good to know when you're trying to keep your carcass from becoming a big one.

If you've priced Tea Tree Oil, you know the Australian healing agent can be expensive in concentrated form.

We suggest you try Tea Tree Burn Relief from Caribbean Pacific, an Orlando-based manufacturer of natural eco-safe skin-care products. Ingredients include aloe vera gel, eucalyptus, amigel, a patented plant extract, a natural emulsifier, vitamins A, D and E, potassium and sorbate.

Tea Tree Burn Relief is available by mail order for $10 plus 7 percent sales tax and $4 shipping; call (800) 432-6723.

Caribbean Pacific also manufactures assorted skin enhancing lotions and a series of natural sunscreens with NAYAD® plant extract.

on Highway A1A. Meters cost 25¢ per 15 minutes.

RIVIERA BEACH MUNICIPAL BEACH
N. Ocean Dr. at Beach Ct.
Riviera Beach

The beach and the Ocean Mall across the street work together to provide a Coney Island-like atmosphere with restaurants, bars and beach and bikini shops.

The wide beach area allows for a dozen or so beach volleyball courts west of the sand dunes and the beach and lifeguard stand on the east side.

The beach is open from sunrise to sunset daily. Metered parking is available on the roadway between the volleyball courts and Ocean Mall and behind the mall. Meters cost 25¢ for 15 minutes.

JOHN D. MACARTHUR BEACH STATE PARK
10900 U.S. Hwy. A1A
North Palm Beach   624-6950

One of Florida's most beautiful beach and wildlife sanctuaries is MacArthur Beach State Park, which occupies the barrier island covering much of the northern part of Singer Island.

In addition to its glorious beach, the park also contains 225 acres of preserved land and 535 acres of submerged land, much of it covered with mangrove plants that provide a home in their complex root structure for fish and marine life. The park operates an interpretive center, nature trail, fishing and swimming areas, picnic area, showers and restrooms.

Atlantic sea turtles nest here from May through August, and the

Photo: Delray Community Redevelopment Agency

Delray's Atlantic Avenue Beach.

park offers ranger walks to search for the gentle reptiles. If you inadvertently happen upon a nest, do not disturb it in any way. Rather, notify a park ranger about its location — he or she will have a sure-fire destination for the ranger walks, and the nest can be protected and preserved.

The park is open from 8 AM to sundown daily. Firearms are not permitted in the park, and glass containers are not permitted on beach areas. Lifeguard service is not provided.

Admission is $3.25 per vehicle (with up to eight occupants).

JUNO BEACH PARK
14775 U.S. Hwy. A1A
Juno Beach

Open 8 AM to sunset daily, Juno Beach Park provides plenty of beach parking, covered picnic tables, restrooms, phones and a small playground.

Lifeguards monitor the beach from 9 AM to 5:20 PM daily.

Jupiter

A drive to Jupiter from the Boca Raton area takes about an hour, but the beaches there are unlike any others in the county. Pack a picnic lunch and spend a breezy day checking out Jupiter's windswept beaches, curious flora and dramatic rock formations. Blowing Rocks Park on Jupiter Island is a favorite place for surf anglers; Carlin, Coral Cove and Jupiter Beach parks all cater to swimmers. But be aware: Not all beaches are protected by lifeguards.

JUPITER BEACH PARK
1375 Jupiter Beach Rd.
Jupiter

A beautiful county park at the Jupiter Inlet, Jupiter Beach Park offers guarded beaches, a jetty, picnic pavilions and picnic tables, a children's play area and restrooms. It's open from 8 AM until sunset daily, except for inlet fishing.

Lifeguards are on duty daily from 9 AM to 5:20 PM.

CORAL COVE PARK

19450 S. R. 707
Tequesta

A jewel on windswept Jupiter Island, Coral Cove Park is a county-owned area which offers a guarded beach, children's play area, promenade and restrooms.

Lifeguards are on duty daily from 9 AM to 5:20 PM.

CARLIN PARK

400 U.S. Hwy. A1A S.
Jupiter

Many folks first heard of Carlin Park because it's a popular site for high school cross-country races, but this huge county park is also a wonderful oceanfront retreat.

In addition to the guarded beach, the park offers baseball diamonds, football/soccer fields, a parcours, tennis courts, snack bar, picnic areas and restrooms.

Lifeguards are on duty daily from 9 AM to 5:20 PM.

DUBOIS PARK AND MUSEUM

19705 Dubois Rd.
Jupiter   747-6639

Visitors to Dubois Park receive a historic bonus on Sundays at the beach. That's where you can tour the 1896 Dubois House Museum, furnished in turn-of-the-century pioneer style. The museum is operated by the Loxahatchee Histori-cal Society. Admission is free, but donations are appreciated.

The museum is open from 1 to 4 PM Sundays, except holidays.

Dubois Park, a county facility, also provides a guarded ocean beach, picnic tables, pavilions and restrooms.

Lifeguards are on duty daily from 9 AM to 5:20 PM from Memorial Day until Labor Day only.

Ocean Swimming Hazards

With all the sand, sea and other alluring diversions here, swimmers may be distracted and drop their usual caution, sometimes with disastrous results. No matter how good a swimmer you are, only swim at beaches protected by lifeguards. When you venture out into the water, do so with a buddy and heed the lifeguards' advice. As placid and inviting as the Atlantic seems on its surface, there are perils lurking below: rip tides that seemingly spring up from nowhere, jellyfish, sea lice (see this chapter's sidebar) and the Portuguese man-o-war drifting by for an unannounced visit. Stop by the lifeguard stand before you stake out your spot on the sand and see if special conditions exist that merit your attention.

Sea Lice

The euphemistic and environmentally correct name for the summertime scourge suffered by beach swimmers in southeastern Florida is Ocean Swimmers' Eruption (a.k.a. Sea Bathers' Eruption), but the alias by which the malady is better known is simply . . . sea lice.

Sea lice are from the sea but aren't lice, even though the nasty red welts they leave make affected swimmers feel pretty lousy. They are larvae of the thimble jellyfish, an innocuous-looking creature about the size of a thumbnail. Through the middle of May to the beginning of July, give or take a week or two, the tiny jellyfish is at the point of its developmental phase when its larvae are released. The larvae float freely until they come in contact with a surface to which they can anchor, such as Sargasso grass (which we usually simply call seaweed), live coral, live sponge or soft, tender swimmers. As long as the host remains submerged, there is no problem. The larvae nestles into a dark crevice, often where the swimmer's suit and skin meet, and continues its developmental cycle.

When the swimmer leaves the water and the larvae begin to dry in the air, they release their toxin. It is from that tiny bit of knowledge that you may gain the greatest advantage. Shower immediately upon leaving the water, remove your swimsuit and change into clean, dry clothes as quickly as possible. Many South Florida beaches have only outdoor showers, making swimsuit removal an impractical proposition. So during these months it is recommended that you confine your swimming to pools. If you *must* swim in the ocean, take to the water only at beaches where there's a bathhouse or showers and changing rooms nearby.

Among insistent ocean swimmers who find they have fallen victim to sea lice, some find the liquid antacid or weak ammonia solution used on man-o-war stings are helpful. Some treat them like chigger bites, with a shot of hair spray or by dabbing clear nail polish on the spot. Others swear by a solution of vinegar and tap water. Most, however, find absolutely nothing prevents or gives relief against sea lice.

Those who have allergies or experience unusually strong reactions to insect stings are emphatically urged to call on one of our local dermatologists for advice before heading to the beach during this time. The doctor may prescribe a cortisone-based ointment to use on the welts or advise against taking the plunge. Otherwise, call the local beach patrol office to see if there have been sea lice reported; find out which beaches are affected and ask for recommendations.

Despite knowing the odds, comprehending the risks and understanding how uncomfortable sea lice can be, some foolhardy folks insist on swimming or surfing during this time of year. The resulting nasty red welts, they'll tell you, are their red (and bumpy) badges of courage.

You be the judge.

Helpful Numbers

Boca Raton:
Marine Safety headquarters, 393-7820;
Ocean, beach and weather conditions recording, 393-7989.

Boynton Beach:
Beach conditions recording, 734-7989.

Delray Beach:
Beach Patrol headquarters, 243-7352;
Beach conditions recording, 27-BEACH.

Deerfield Beach:
Lifeguard headquarters, (305) 480-4412;
Beach and ocean conditions report, (305) 480-4413.

Palm Beach County:
Beach Safety headquarters, 966-6629;
Beach conditions recording, 624-0065, for the northern part of the county; 276-3990, for beaches in the southern half.

Man-o-wars

Man-o-wars are especially hazardous, especially in November through April when the blue bubble-like pests are most abundant and more swimmers are in the water. If you see one, stay away; its tentacles extend well beyond the bubble and cause an exceptionally painful sting, which can have grave consequences for people who have allergic reactions. Even a beached man-o-war is unsafe to touch.

Notify a lifeguard immediately about any man-o-war stings. He or she will probably apply a weak vinegar solution to the area. Some folks swear by liquid antacid or unseasoned meat tenderizer to relieve the pain. The tenderizer contains papain, a pineapple enzyme, which counteracts the sting. Don't rub the sting area, as this releases more toxin into your skin.

Rip Tides

A rip tide is formed when strong currents whip through sandbar troughs on the ocean floor, creating a frothy river of water that runs perpendicular to the shoreline.

When caught in a rip tide, most swimmers' first reaction is usually to fight the tide and make for shore, straight in against the tide. Unfortunately, that reaction can prove fatal. Tarzan couldn't outswim a rip tide, and neither can you. The so-

Photo: Stephanie Murphy

Boaters reach the Atlantic Ocean via the Boca Raton Inlet.

lution is to keep your cool and swim with the tide until it releases you. Then you can easily swim parallel to shore, and let the natural action of the waves assist you back in.

Lifeguards often can point out danger spots for rip tides and at some beaches fly special warning flags when rip tides are occurring.

Photo: City of Boca Raton Recreation Services

*Boca Raton's Recreation Services organize wheelchair tennis play
and many other events.*

Inside
Parks

Think of our parks and recreation system as a four-layer cake, with layers representing national, state, county and city parks. Then think of yourself as an honored party guest.

City and county parks address the community's needs for recreational facilities for active sports. These places are where you'll find lots of tennis courts, jogging trails and softball diamonds.

State and national parks reflect Floridians' love of the wilderness, our respect for the environment and our need to preserve and manage natural resources for future generations.

National Parks

EVERGLADES NATIONAL PARK
Main Entrance: U.S. Highway 9336
10 miles southwest of Homestead,
35 miles south of Miami   (305) 247-6211

Three visitor centers dot the behemoth, 1.4 million-acre park that sprawls across Dade, Monroe and Collier counties: at the park headquarters at the main entrance; at Shark Valley, just off U.S. 41 west of Miami; and at the Flamingo Visitor Center at the tip of the state and touching Florida Bay.

The main entrance visitor center is the recommended entry point. It's a considerable drive to get there from points in Palm Beach County, but the reward is considerable as well. The center has an introductory film, park information, activity schedules and a shop that stocks insect repellent, film and other necessities. Call (305) 247-6211.

Shark Valley, the northeast entrance to the park, is just east of the Miccosukee Indian Village. The valley gets its name from the Shark River, which flows through the glades. Its 15-mile paved loop road cuts through a sawgrass prairie and draws many bikers and hikers. Tackle the trail on a bike, and it will take you 2½ hours to get through; on foot, it takes seven hours. If you can't bring your bike, don't worry — you can rent one there. For those less inclined to rough it, a narrated tram tour winds its way through the trail. One of the tram's stops is at a 50-foot-high observation tower. Other activities here include fishing and boating. And don't forget your binoculars and high-powered camera lens, especially if you are bird watching. Shark Valley's phone number is (305) 221-8776.

Flamingo is 38 miles southwest of the main entrance. In the middle of one of the largest mangrove forests in the world, it offers guided walks, bike paths, canoe trips and tram tours. Plus, sightseeing cruises leave from the marina daily during the winter season. Call

(305) 253-2241. If you plan a trip to the Keys, a side trip to the Everglades is a natural.

ARTHUR R. MARSHALL
LOXAHATCHEE
NATIONAL WILDLIFE REFUGE
U.S. 441, north of Atlantic Ave.
Delray Beach   734-8303

This national park is more than an angler's paradise. It's also a nature lover's paradise, and one that is very close to home — about a 20-minute drive from Boca Raton. Reclaimed land that was reflooded into marshland, Loxahatchee features a boardwalk trail through a cypress swamp and marsh trails.

This area is among the best in Florida for birdwatching. In addition to the usual herons, egrets, ibises, limpkins, pileated woodpeckers and red-winged blackbirds, birders can see the occasional great-horned owl nesting high in a cypress, migratory waterfowl, wood storks and the rare Everglades kite.

Other wildlife includes raccoons, white-tailed deer, turtles, bobcats and, of course, alligators — big and small — and sometimes on the same paths that humans take. Go over the levee at the far west end of the road and you'll find boat ramps and the canoe trail. Be sure to take along binoculars, a camera with a strong lens and insect repellent.

State Parks

JONATHAN DICKINSON STATE PARK
16450 S.E. Federal Hwy.
Hobe Sound   546-2771

In 1696, Jonathan Dickinson, a Quaker merchant, ran his mercantile ship aground off the coast of Hobe Sound. He, his crew and family abandoned the wrecked vessel and made the perilous journey up the coast to the nearest inhabited city — St. Augustine. His journals provided much of the early information available in the "civilized" world about the wilds of southeastern Florida.

Today, the 11,500-acre park commemorates Dickinson and his contributions. The park's entrance is on U.S. 1 at Hobe Sound, and the park stretches west to the Loxahatchee River.

During World War II, the area that is now part of the park was Camp Murphy, home of the Southern Signal Corps School. Nearly 7,000 troops were trained and housed there. Two of the wartime Army buildings remain on the camp site. After the war, the land was turned over to the state, which opened it as a park in 1950.

The park offers boating, canoeing, fishing, camping and excellent hiking and walking trails. Cabins are available for rent, but be sure to call well in advance. Canoes are available for rent as well.

Jonathan Dickinson State Park is one of Florida's many natural areas where you can get up close and personal with alligators. Leave them alone and don't feed them, and they'll leave you alone.

The park is open daily from 8 AM to sundown. Admission is $3.25 per vehicle (with up to eight occupants).

JOHN D. MACARTHUR BEACH STATE PARK

10900 U.S. Hwy. A1A
North Palm Beach   *624-6950*

One of Florida's most beautiful beach and wildlife sanctuaries is MacArthur Beach State Park, which occupies the barrier island covering much of the northern part of Singer Island.

The park covers 760 acres (225 acres of preserved land and 535 acres submerged), much of it covered with mangroves that provide a home for fish and marine life in the plants' complex root structures. The park operates an interpretive center, nature trail, fishing and swimming areas, picnic area, showers and restrooms.

Atlantic sea turtles nest here from May through August, and the park offers ranger walks to search for the gentle reptiles. If you inadvertently happen upon a nest, do not disturb it in any way. Rather, notify a park ranger about its location so the nest can be protected and preserved.

The park is open from 8 AM to sundown daily. Firearms and alcohol are not permitted in the park.

Admission is $3.25 per vehicle (with up to eight occupants). For beach information, see this park's listing in our Beaches chapter.

County Parks

Palm Beach County

CALOOSA PARK

1300 S.W. 35 Ave.
Boynton Beach   *964-4420*

Here's a place that hums with youth and adult league action. This park is jammed with baseball and softball diamonds, soccer/football fields and basketball courts. It also features a small fishing pond, bike paths, a parcours, racquetball, handball and tennis courts. Concession stands, restrooms, picnic tables and grills are also available.

LAKE IDA PARK

2929 Lake Ida Rd.
Delray Beach   *(407) 964-4420*

South County water-skiers call this home. The park is divided into south and west sections. In the south portion, you'll find the lake plus picnic areas and restrooms. The western section houses the Delray Beach Playhouse, 272-1281, and a children's playground.

JOHN PRINCE PARK

2580 Lake Worth Rd.
Lake Worth   *964-4420*

A favorite staging area for road races and high school cross country meets, John Prince Park is tucked around Lake Osborne and provides a wide range of recreational activities including fishing, boating, camping, golf and baseball training areas, nature trails, tennis, softball and bike paths.

HOWARD PARK

901 Lake Ave., West Palm Beach
Senior Center: 835-7055
Tennis Center: 659-1239

Seniors can enjoy lawn bowling, shuffleboard and other active pursuits at this park just west of I-95 near Parker Avenue and Okeechobee Boulevard. Other facilities include tennis and basketball courts and softball and multipurpose fields. A senior center, picnic areas and restrooms are also available.

LOGGERHEAD PARK

14200 U.S. Hwy. 1
Juno Beach

This park is a hub of athletic and environmental activities. Facilities include a nature trail and scenic overlook, four lighted hard-surface tennis courts, a gameroom, restrooms, a snack bar and picnic shelters with grills.

Loggerhead Park is open daily from sunrise to sunset and is home to the Marinelife Center of Juno Beach, 627-8280.

OKEEHEELEE PARK
AND NATURE CENTER

7715 Forest Hill Blvd.
West Palm Beach   964-4420

The western reaches of the county seems an unlikely place to hold water-ski competitions, but national-caliber contests are routine here.

Other facilities include baseball and softball diamonds, a BMX (bicycle) track and football/soccer fields.

The Okeeheelee Nature Center offers classes, workshops and exhibits touting the area's environment and conservation.

PHIL FOSTER PARK

900 E. Blue Heron Blvd.
Lake Worth

Dangle a line or launch your boat from this watery wonderland at the Lake Worth Inlet.

The county park provides a guarded beach, children's playground, fishing area, docking slips, a boat ramp and small boat rentals, picnic areas and restrooms.

Lifeguards are on duty from 9 AM to 5:20 PM daily. Admission is free.

SANDALFOOT COVE PARK

2220 N.W. 57th Ave.
Boca Raton

In the evenings on weekdays and on weekends, this park teems with youth league sports action. Facilities include two lighted baseball diamonds, a soccer/football field, a children's playground, a concession stand, restrooms and a public phone.

The park is open daily from 8 AM to 11 PM.

VETERAN'S PARK WEST BOCA

9400 W. Palmetto Park Rd.
Boca Raton

A favorite destination for active sports enthusiasts, Veteran's Park's facilities include four lighted hard-surface tennis courts, two lighted basketball courts, a soccer/football field, a children's playground, a picnic area with grills and a walking path. Restrooms, public phones and a community center are also on the premises.

Families and folks of all ages enjoy relaxing canoe trips on Palm Beach County's waterways.

Photo: Palm Beach County Convention and Visitors Bureau

The park is open daily from sunrise to sunset.

City Parks

Boca Raton

MEMORIAL PARK

150 Crawford Blvd.   *393-7806*

This downtown park is the hub of Boca Raton's sports community. The city recreation department's administrative offices are in the Community Center, on the west side of the City Hall. On the east side of park property is the newly refurbished Memorial Park Tennis Center, 393-7978, which provides a world-class facility, offers a full slate of group and individual lessons and a junior training program. The center also sponsors several teams in the Palm Beach County Women's League.

Memorial Park is also equipped with diamonds for baseball and softball, a football/soccer field, basketball court, children's playground, shuffleboard center (call 393-7818), and the Mainstream Teen Center, (368-4099), where youths ages 12 to 18 can socialize and enjoy games in a safe environment.

PATCH REEF PARK

2000 N.W. 51 St.   *997-0791*

A collaborative effort between Boca Raton and the Greater Boca Raton Beach Tax District, Boca Raton's sprawling showplace park provides a 17-court tennis center, soccer/football fields, a softball and baseball complex, a playground and the James A. Rutherford Community Center, which offers an array of courses from martial arts to dance, cooking, freelance writing and other personal-enrichment topics.

JAMES A. RUTHERFORD PARK

600 N.E. 24 St.   *393-7845*

Virtually hidden behind the Fifth Avenue Shops on Federal Highway, this park is the city's best-kept secret. Stroll the boardwalk through the cocoplums, mangroves, gumbo limbo trees and other indigenous vegetation and feel your tension slip away.

Kayaks and canoes may be rented for a leisurely sojourn along the watercraft trail.

Drop by and you'll agree: This little park is a gem. It's open Friday through Monday and on holidays throughout the year. Hours of operation depend on tide and weather conditions. Call before you visit.

GUMBO LIMBO
ENVIRONMENTAL COMPLEX

1801 N. Ocean Blvd.   *338-1473*

As with Patch Reef Park, Boca Raton and the Greater Boca Raton Tax District collaborated on this project with the assistance of the Palm Beach County School Board and Florida Atlantic University.

The complex is a collection of classrooms, laboratories and other facilities used as an educational resource for teaching about the environment. Through exhibits and guided and self-guided programs, community members can expand their knowledge about South Florida's native flora and fauna. Make sure to stop by the outdoor tanks to watch the sea turtles swimming.

The complex is open 9 AM to 4 PM Monday through Saturday and noon to 4 PM on Sunday.

There is no admission charge, but donations are accepted.

Delray Beach

VETERANS PARK

802 N.E. First St.   *243-7351*

A recent face lift gave this popular park new life. Situated on the west bank of the Intracoastal Waterway, the park's highlights are its contemporary children's playground, built by 2,000 volunteer workers over five days in November 1993, the city's 16-lane shuffleboard complex and a seven-rink lawn bowling center.

Travel to the park by car or boat. It's open Monday through Friday from 8:30 AM to 4:30 PM. On Saturdays during the winter, it's open from 8:30 AM to 3:30 PM, and in the summer, it closes at 11:30 AM. Sunday hours are 1 to 4 PM throughout the year.

POMPEY PARK

1101 N.W. Second St.   *243-7356*

The action inside the community center and outside on the field is intense throughout the year. Inside, there's an auditorium and stage, kitchen, game rooms and a basketball court where the U.S. Olympic women's basketball team stopped to train on their way to a tournament in South America.

Outdoors are the ball fields that host recreation-league games and the

Photo: City of Boca Raton Recreation Services

Meadows Park Pool, staffed by certified instructors, offers a year-round variety of recreational and instructional programs for infants through senior citizens.

Delray Braves semipro baseball team. There are also tennis and racquetball courts, basketball and volleyball courts, a swimming pool and a children's playground.

Lake Worth

NORTHWEST PARK AND BALLFIELDS
900 22nd Ave. N.　　　*533-7359*

This is a hub of baseball and softball action in Lake Worth, with one field each for the city's T-ball, Pinto, Mustang, Colt, Pony and Lassie leagues.

BRYANT PARK
BANDSHELL AND BOAT RAMP
Corner of Golfview and Lake Ave.　585-2357

A lovely spot alongside the Intracoastal, Bryant Park provides a concert bandshell with stage area, public-address system, seating for about 500 and restrooms. Other park features are

a parcours, horseshoe pits and a boat ramp with four launching slips.

OSBORNE COMMUNITY CENTER
1699 Wingfield St.　　　*533-7363*

The Joint Community Center, Head Start program and the Community Action Council all call the Osborne Center home and it also serves as an adult education site, but the surrounding acreage is one of Lake Worth's hottest recreational spots as well. The center includes four basketball courts, a lighted softball diamond, two tennis courts, a playground and picnic facilities.

Lantana

LANTANA MUNICIPAL PARK
Iris St. at Dixie Hwy.　　　*582-9094*

This small downtown park packs lots of activities into a small space. The park contains a multipurpose recre-

A Walk on the Wild Side

Your friends cautioned you about Florida's wildlife, no doubt: mosquitoes the size of hummingbirds, palmetto bugs bigger than Chihuahuas, chameleons that look like iguanas; alligators that can bite a person in two.

In truth, our mosquitoes are disgustingly normal in size and mosquito season, thanks to modern spraying programs, isn't what it used to be. Palmetto bugs are disgusting, but not nearly as big as their reputation and not as common as legend spinners would have you believe. The Palm Beaches have chameleons in two sizes: itty bitty and small. Both sizes are scared to death of humans and run like thieves whenever they see us. Many folks actually allow a chameleon or two into their homes because they are great insect-control devices. They especially love those mosquitoes.

But, yes, we have alligators here and, yes, these small-brained reptilian throwbacks to the Stone Age are ugly as sin but can run like the devil. But mostly, they want to lie around in the water, occasionally bask in the sun and not mess with you (hint: you don't want to mess with them either). If you insist, they'll get nasty. And, yes, they can be fatal.

Many of Florida's state, national and county parks have alligator populations. Do not expect them to saunter by your picnic table and clean off the scraps. They won't leave their watery habitats; but don't bring scraps to feed them. They're very effective hunters and can forage for themselves, thank you.

Always heed alligator warning signs. And, finally, when boating or canoeing in alligator-infested water, don't advertise yourself as an hors d'oeuvre. Keep your fingers, hands and feet out of the water. It's tempting to dangle some fingers in the cool water, but your phalanges are just bait to a hungry gator.

ation building, four hard-surface tennis courts, four shuffleboard courts and a barbecue area with picnic tables.

The tennis courts are open daily from 7 AM to 10:30 PM. Admission is free.

LANTANA BICENTENNIAL PARK
E. Ocean Ave.
At the Intracoastal Waterway   582-9094

Here's a great place to cool off, stroll and enjoy a scenic overlook of the Intracoastal. The park provides a short nature trail and a promenade along the waterway. Picnic tables and a youth playground are provided as well.

Lake Park

LAKE SHORE PARK
Foresteria Dr. and Federal Hwy.

A beautiful little city park, Lake Shore Park maximizes its exposure with a promenade along the Intracoastal. The park also includes six hard-surface tennis courts and a pro shop, four shuffleboard courts, parcours, a small multipurpose recre-

Photo: Visual Dynamics/Jefrey Toll

*The Sports, Health & Fitness Center at the Athletic Club of Boca Raton has a
7,500-square-foot complete facility with state-of-the-art
cardiovascular equipment.*

ation building, a playground and restrooms.

Palm Beach Gardens

PALM BEACH GARDENS MUNICIPAL COMPLEX

10500 Military Tr.   *775-8270*

Well known as a young, vibrant city, Palm Beach Gardens' Municipal Complex provides facilities for the community's active lifestyle.

The complex contains seven baseball/softball fields, a soccer field, six lighted hard-surface tennis courts and a pro shop, four horseshoe courts, a playground and six shuffleboard courts.

PALM BEACH GARDENS MUNICIPAL POOL

4404 Burns Rd.   *775-8270*

In addition to the pool, this park, located just south of the Municipal Complex, maintains a parcours with red clay jogging surface and the multipurpose community center.

Riviera Beach

NEWCOMB RECREATION HALL AND MARINA

13th St. E. at Grandview Pl.

The city marina and an all-purpose recreation building are just part of the facilities available at this center.

An Australian pine-shaded picnic area, two picnic pavilions and picnic tables and grills are provided. An outdoor beach-style volleyball court is provided.

The center is open daily from 7 AM to 10 PM. Admission is free.

West Palm Beach

LAKE LYTAL PARK

3645 Gun Club Rd.   *964-4420*

Many central Palm Beach County sports leagues make their home here. You'll find everything from underwater hockey teams to the famed Lake Lytal Lassies Softball League.

Facilities include an Olympic-size pool, baseball and softball diamonds, football and soccer fields, racquetball and handball courts, playground, restrooms, snack bars and picnic facilities.

Inside
Boating

With the beautiful Atlantic Ocean to the east and the Intracoastal Waterway to the west, South Florida's Gold Coast is a great place for boating of any kind. From powerboats and sailboats to canoes and fishing vessels, if it floats, you'll probably find it in Palm Beach County.

The Atlantic Ocean is the perfect spot for sailing, fishing and cruising for pleasure, while water skiers enjoy Lake Ida in Delray Beach and Lake Osborne in John Prince Park in Lake Worth. Canoeing is popular at James A. Rutherford Park in Boca Raton and in the Loxahatchee River at Jonathan Dickinson State Park in Hobe Sound. Pleasure boaters also enjoy cruising along the Intracoastal Waterway.

Inlets

The ocean is easily accessible through the Hillsboro, Boca Raton, Boynton Beach, Lake Worth and Jupiter inlets. The Hillsboro Inlet, an important base for party boat anglers, connects with the Hillsboro River and the Intracoastal Waterway. The inlet light sits atop an octagonal cone-shaped tower that rises 136 feet above the water. Standing on the beach on the north side of the inlet, the light tower houses a radio beacon. The channel is maintained privately with buoys, lights and a day beacon for guidance. Its entrance is also marked by protective jetties. Rocky reefs extend northward and southward of the channel entrance lights. Popular fishing areas extend about 1 to 2 miles offshore between the inlet and Port Everglades in Fort Lauderdale.

Pleasure boaters, divers and anglers also utilize the Boca Raton, Boynton Beach and Lake Worth inlets. The Port of Palm Beach is a deepwater port a little more than a mile west of the entrance to the Lake Worth Inlet. The port is primarily used as a cargo and commerce harbor and is marked by a 30-foot entrance with lights and buoys. A reef with scattered rock formations extends about 300 yards eastward of Peanut Island. Two fish havens are situated less than a mile and about 1.5 miles from the north side of the entrance. Another popular fishing spot lies 1.5 miles off the south entrance. (See our Fishing chapter for information about license requirements, tackle and the species you might encounter.)

To the north, the Jupiter Inlet light stands 146 feet above the water atop a 105-foot red brick tower on the north side of the inlet. A radio beacon is about 100 yards east of the light. The entrance of the inlet leads north to Jupiter Sound, west to the Loxahatchee River and south to Lake

Worth Creek. Private day beacons mark the entrance that includes a short stone jetty on the north side and a steel barricade to the south.

The Jupiter, Boynton and Boca inlets are reported to be three of the most hazardous in the area, so boaters are encouraged to be aware of traffic and sandbar and tidal conditions when approaching the ocean through them.

Charters and Cruises

For those who prefer to leave the driving to someone else, there are a number of charter opportunities throughout Palm Beach County. The type of charter vessel will depend on your needs and activities and the number of people in your party. There are boats available for fishing, snorkeling, diving, parties and just cruising the waterways. And, if you want to get out on the water and be behind the helm, you can rent just about any type of boat that floats.

Following are some of our favorite rental and charter companies:

Boat and Water Scooter Rentals

BEACH WATER SPORTS INC.
3109 E. Atlantic Blvd.
Pompano Beach   (305) 946-2601
Beach Water Sports offers Jet Ski and Wave Runner rentals, ocean trips and group discounts. Local residents are eligible for discounts too. Rates are $35 a half-hour, $55 an hour.

BOCA BOAT RENTALS
999 E. Camino Real, Boca Raton   394-9094
Located at the Radisson Bridge Resort, Boca Boat Rentals is stocked with Yamahas, Sea-Doos, Scarabs and Four Winns. Equipment can be rented by the hour, with group discounts, and the vessels can be taken on the ocean, which is accessible through the nearby Boca Raton Inlet. Rates start at $139 for two hours; $199 for four hours; and $299 for eight hours. For rentals taken at 9 AM, $15 is taken off the bill.

BOYNTON BEACH BOAT RENTALS INC.
551 N.W. 14th Ave.,
Boynton Beach   735-2149
Whether boaters want to cruise around South Florida waters, fish, ski or dive, they can choose the appropriate craft here. The boats are touted as safe and easy to operate, plus ocean use is permitted. Boynton Beach Boat Rentals Inc. does not require patrons to possess a license. Rates are $159 for three hours; $169 for a half-day; and $250 for a whole day.

CLUB NAUTICO
743 N.E. First Ave., Boynton Beach 738-1988
1755 S.E. Third Court, The Cove Marina
Deerfield Beach   (305) 421-4628
Club Nautico has two of its more than 70 worldwide locations in Boynton Beach and Deerfield Beach. Its fleet, which can be taken on the ocean, includes 20- to 30-foot powerboats, Yamaha Wave Runners and Scarabs. Fishing and ski equipment are available too. Club Nautico does not require boating licenses and offers insurance. Rates range from $99 to $699, depending on whether or not you are a Club Nautico member, what type of vessel you rent and the length of time that the vessel is rented.

Photo: Stephanie Murphy

Yachts bob in Lake Worth. Palm Beach landmarks dot the background.

EAGLE BOAT RENTALS
7848 S. Federal Hwy.
Hypoluxo (800) 713-0233

Eagle's rental boat stock includes 19- to 24-foot boats, including fishing boats and speed boats. If you want to fish but don't have the equipment, rods are available here too. For a 19-foot Capri to ski or cruise the Intracoastal Waterway and carry seven people, expect to pay $179 for a half-day (two four-hour windows are available — 8 AM to noon and 1 to 5 PM) and $249 for a full day, 9 AM to 5 PM.

INTRACOASTAL JET SKI RENTAL
2280 N. Federal Hwy.,
Boynton Beach 735-0612

Rental equipment here includes Wave Runners and Sea-Doos — great for taking advantage of the miles of riding area on the Intracoastal Waterway. Rates for single-seaters are $35

a half-hour and $55 an hour. For larger craft, the rates are $45 a half-hour and $64 an hour.

Boating Charters

AHOY MARINE AND CHARTERS
3004 N.E. Fifth Ter.
Fort Lauderdale (800) 653-4049

Here you have a choice of what to do out on the water — either charter a boat and captain for the day, or take matters into your own hands and learn how to pilot the boat yourself. Ahoy's 30- to 65-foot sailing yachts will go to the Bahamas, Florida Keys or Dry Tortugas. If you learn while you sail, you can work toward earning sailing certification. Rates are $350 for a day with a boat and captain; if you are learning to sail, it's $325 each for the first two levels.

AIR AND SEA CHARTERS
490 E. Palmetto Park Rd., Ste. 330
Boca Raton   368-3566

Air and Sea offers luxury charters on a 55-foot catamaran. Enjoy Intracoastal trips, dinner and cocktail cruises, full- and half-day charters, sunset champagne sails, and fishing, cruising and snorkeling trips. The catamaran sails from The Cove in Deerfield Beach on Sundays for a two-hour cruise. It's $30 per person and includes beer, wine, soft drinks and snacks.

If speed is your passion, Air and Sea's 800 horsepower offshore race boat is sure to give you a thrill with speeds up to 80 mph. The boat is available for half-hour ($50 per person) and hour ($80 per person) rentals, with a two-person minimum. The boat can carry six passengers. And for those who like to sit and sail in the lap of luxury, Air and Sea's 45-foot sailing yacht comes with a captain and fuel, but not food and beverages. It costs $275 for two hours; $395 for four hours; and $650 for a full day.

INTERNATIONAL YACHT MANAGEMENT AND VACATION SPECIALISTS
962 Tropic Blvd., Delray Beach   278-9729

International Yacht offers a 44-foot sail boat for half-day and full-day sails. Trips will take you through the Boca Raton Inlet and off the Boca Raton shoreline. Sometimes, it comes back to its port by sailing through the Hillsboro Inlet and north in the Intracoastal, giving passengers a close-up view of the homes lining the waterway. When you sail, be sure to bring food and beverages. International Yacht also brokers other boats with uses that range from parties to fishing. The half-day sail lasts four hours and costs $300 for the boat for up to six passengers; the price goes up to $450 for the eight-hour, full-day sail.

WINDRIDGE YACHT CHARTERS
501 E. Camino Real, Boca Raton   368-6114

Windridge's fleet is prepared to carry groups for special occasions. The fleet includes *Windridge*, which at 100 feet is meant for exclusive parties and carries up to 12 passengers; *Lady Windridge*, which at 170 feet can hold 100 to 150 passengers; the 142-foot *Kathleen W*, which holds 50 to 150 passengers; and the 131-foot *Isis II*, which carries 15 to 150 passengers. Rates are $80 to $150 per person for these four-hour luxury yacht charters.

Luxury Cruises

And if a first-class trip to a faraway place is what you're looking for, South Florida is one of the cruise capitals of the world. With a number of luxury ships representing the various commercial cruise lines that arrive and

Hurricane Preparedness

Boat owners should develop a plan of action to secure their vessels in marinas or remove them from threatened areas prior to the hurricane season, that runs from June 1 through November 30. All records, including insurance policies, a recent photo of the vessel, boat registration, equipment inventory, marina lease agreement or storage area and telephone numbers of appropriate authorities should be consolidated. Make an inventory both of items removed and those left on board the vessel. When a hurricane is approaching, remove all moveable equipment such as canvas, sails, dinghies, radios and cushions. Lash down everything that cannot be removed, such as tillers, wheels and booms. Make sure the electrical system is cut off, and remove the battery to eliminate the risk of fire or other damage.

depart the Port of Miami and Port Everglades in Fort Lauderdale every week, the possibilities are almost endless. Both ports are just a short drive from the Palm Beaches. (See our Daycations chapter for information about South Florida's day-cruise options.)

Rules, Regulations and Recommendations

Federal law requires that every person on a vessel, powered or nonpowered, have a personal flotation device that is properly fitted, in good condition and meets U.S. Coast Guard guidelines.

Children 13 and younger must wear their life vests while on vessels. Children older than 13 and adults must have a life vest on the deck of the boat at all times. All boats 16 feet or more in length, excluding canoes and kayaks, must also have one throwable device on board. All boats must carry a marine-approved fire extinguisher as well.

Boating Etiquette

*When approaching a vessel head-on, pass to the right of it.

*Vessels approaching from the right have the right of way.

*Manually powered and sailing vessels have the right of way over powered vessels.

*All boats must have a 360-degree white running light on at night as well as bow lights — red on the port side and green on the starboard side.

*When the red light is on, it means yield; when green is on, it means right of way; and when red and green are on, it means pass on the right.

Navigation Signals

*One short blast (one second) will show an intention to direct the course of a vessel to its own starboard (right).

*Two short blasts will show intention to direct the course of a vessel to its own port (left).

*Three short blasts will indicate the vessel's engines are going astern (in reverse).

*Five or more short and rapid blasts is a danger signal used when the other vessel's intentions are not understood or the other vessel's indicated course is dangerous.

*Prolonged blast (4-6 seconds) will indicate situations of restricted visibility or maneuverability.

Marine Radio Licenses

A valid FCC ship station license for the radio transceiver on your boat is required before you use your radio. All marine radio equipment, including hand-held units, must be licensed.

Recommended Safety Equipment

The following list has been compiled courtesy of the U.S. Coast Guard:

*VHF radio   *Chart and compass
*Visual distress signals   *Boat hook
*Spare anchor   *Spare propeller
*Heaving line   *Mooring line
*First aid kit   *Food and water
*Flashlight   *Binoculars
*Mirror   *Spare batteries
*Searchlight   *Marine hardware
*Sun protection   *Extra clothing
*Tool kit   *Alternate propulsion (paddles)

*Ring buoy   *Fuel tanks and spare fuel
*Whistle or horn
*Dewatering device (pump or bailer)

The Coast Guard offers boating safety and seamanship classes. For information call (800) 336-2628. The Pompano Beach Power Squadron also provides safe boating courses. Call (305) 782-7277. For additional information, call the Boating Safety Hotline at (800) 368-5647.

Licensing and Registration

Florida law requires that all motorized vessels be titled and registered. The annual registration renewal period begins June 1. Registering a new vessel requires a manufacturer's certificate of origin completed by the dealer, a bill of sale, sales tax equal to 6 percent of the vessel's purchase price and the presence of all registered owners to sign an application for title. Registering a used vessel requires a title certificate, a bill of sale, sales tax and the presence of all registered owners. Call the tax collector's office at 930-7922 for more information.

Loxahatchee River Adventures

A great way to see the natural vegetation and wildlife of the area is to travel to Jonathan Dickinson State Park and take a two-hour boat tour along the beautiful Loxahatchee River on the 44-passenger

Insiders' Tips

Never remain on a boat during severe weather.

A passenger-laden catamaran cruises the Intracoastal Waterway.

Loxahatchee Queen II. A park-trained, Coast Guard-licensed captain relates the history and discusses the wildlife of the river as you watch from the comfort and safety of your own individual armchair. Typically seen along the tour are alligators and the West Indian Manatee, and frequently seen are various types of bird and animal life such as bald eagles, raccoons and a variety of other species. For those who would like to go it alone, canoe rentals are available at the park. For information, call (800) 746-1466.

Public Boat Launches

SILVER PALM PARK BOAT RAMP
600 E. Palmetto Park Rd.
Boca Raton

BOAT CLUB PARK
U.S. Hwy. 1 and N.E. 21st St.
Boynton Beach

KNOWLES PARK
U.S. Hwy. 1 and S.E. 10th St.
Delray Beach

BURT REYNOLDS PARK
800 U.S. Hwy. 1 N.
Jupiter

BRYANT PARK
Golfview and Lake Aves.
Lake Worth

LANTANA PUBLIC BOAT RAMP
E. Ocean Ave.
Lantana

PHIL FOSTER MEMORIAL PARK
900 E. Blue Heron Blvd.
Riviera Beach

CURRIE PARK
23rd St. and Flagler Dr.
West Palm Beach

Other Useful Numbers

The following numbers may be helpful if you need advice or information about boating safety, activities, rules and regulations in the Greater Palm Beach County region.

Florida Marine Patrol	624-6935
Palm Beach County Parks & Recreation Department	966-6600
Boca Raton Recreation Services	393-7811
U.S. Coast Guard Auxiliary Station (Boca Raton)	391-3600
U.S. Coast Guard Station (Lake Worth)	844-5030

Inside
Fishing

Finding a place to wet a line in Florida is easy. After all, this is the Peninsula State and a fishing mecca for catching both freshwater and saltwater species. But because of the state's efforts to responsibly manage our marine resources and protect our natural habitats, Florida has a maze of laws governing fishing. As a result, it might at first seem easier to get a law degree than a fishing license. Really, it's not that difficult.

The **Florida Game and Fresh Water Fish Commission** (FGFWFC) regulates hunting on public land and freshwater fishing. The FGFWFC is headquartered in the Ferris Bryant Building, 620 S. Meridian Street, Tallahassee, (904) 488-1960. The local office for Palm Beach County is the Everglades Region, at 551 N. Military Trail, West Palm Beach, 640-6100.

The **Florida Marine Patrol** (FMP) is the law enforcement division for the Department of Environmental Protection, which oversees saltwater fishing activities. The DEP's headquarters are in the Marjory Stoneman Douglas Building, 3900 Commonwealth Boulevard, Tallahassee, (904) 488-7326. Palm Beach County is in the FMP's District 10. District headquarters are located at 13000 Marcinski Road, Jupiter, 624-

6935. Don't be shy about asking any of these folks for help; they're used to it. You'll find them friendly and willing to assist.

Fishing Licenses

If you plan to fish in Florida, plan on buying a license unless you fall into any of the following categories. You are exempt from license requirements if:

1. You are a Florida resident who is certified as totally and permanently disabled. (Your county tax collector will issue you a permanent saltwater license.) You are considered a resident for licensing purposes as soon as you establish a permanent address within the state or if you have lived in the state continuously for six months or longer.

2. You are younger than 16 or are a resident older than 65.

3. You are a resident and member of the Armed Forces on leave for 30 days or less and not stationed within the state.

4. You are fishing from a boat that has a valid saltwater license, from a private pier in saltwater that has a valid license, or in a private freshwater pond of more than 20 acres whose owner has a valid license. (Most party boats, charters, piers and private ponds are licensed, but it's your responsibility to make sure you're covered.) Pri-

vate ponds of less than 20 acres do not require a license.

5. You are a resident fishing in your home county in fresh water using a cane pole or hand lines without a reel and using live or natural bait.

6. You have been accepted by the Department of Health and Rehabilitative Services to receive developmental services or have been ordered by the court to an HRS rehabilitative program involving training in aquatic resources.

This list of exemptions is representative, not all-inclusive. The best idea is to check at the county tax collector's office or the tackle shop where you buy your license; they'll make sure you get a perfect fit.

Saltwater License Options

RESIDENT
10-day license/$10
One-year/$12
Five-year/$60

NON-RESIDENT
Three-day/$5
Seven-day/$15
One-year/$30

Freshwater License Options

RESIDENT
Series CO (One year, hunting and fishing)/$22
Series RF (One year, fishing only)/$12
Series SP (One year, sportsman's license)$66

NON-RESIDENT
Series NF (One year, fishing only)/$30
Series SF-7 (One week, fishing only)/$15

County tax collectors add a $1.50 fee per license, and tackle shops may tack on an additional 50¢.

Lifetime License Options

Residents also may purchase lifetime saltwater fishing and sportsman's licenses, both exceptional bargains.

The **lifetime saltwater license** allows the holder to engage in saltwater fishing as well as lawfully harvest snook and crawfish. The **sportsman's license** allows the holder to engage in freshwater and saltwater fishing as well as hunting and related activities permitted by the following additional stamps: management area, turkey, muzzle-loading gun, Florida waterfowl, archery, snook and crawfish.

Funds from the sale of these licenses are used for marine enhancement, research and law enforcement activities.

Lifetime Licenses

Cost Requirements by Age:

Age	Saltwater	Sportsman
0-4 years	$125	$400
5-12	$225	$700
13-63	$300	$1000
64 or older	none	$12

Once you've finally waded through the red tape and small print and have your rod, reel and tackle box in one hand and a bucket of bait in the other, it's time to get down to business.

Freshwater Fishing

The best fishing spots in Palm Beach County are at Lake Okeechobee's 748 square miles of fish-

Photo: Cynthia Thuma

The Pahokee Marina and Pier is a popular place for anglers to seek out delicious Okeechobee catfish.

ing heaven, the Arthur R. Marshall Loxahatchee National Wildlife Refuge area and along U.S. Highway 27, which runs through the western part of the county. Other anglers prefer Lake Ida in Delray Beach, Lake Osborne in Lake Worth and Lake Catherine in Palm Beach Gardens. Several excellent fish camps in and near Palm Beach County provide boat launching ramps, marine fuel, dock space, bait and tackle shops and other amenities, including a priceless commodity: good advice.

ARTHUR R. MARSHALL LOXAHATCHEE NATIONAL WILDLIFE REFUGE
Lox Rd., 6 miles west of Hwy. 441

The facilities are rather Spartan here, but this is a favorite boat-launching spot, and it's not uncommon to have to wait in line to use a ramp. Airboat rides are available; snacks, film and alligator souvenirs are also sold.

PAHOKEE MARINA AND PIER
171 N. Lake Ave., Pahokee   924-7600

Fish from the pier or the public marina, or rent a boat here. A campground and a bait and tackle shop are on the premises as well.

BELLE GLADE MARINA CAMPGROUND
110 Southwest Ave. E.
Belle Glade   996-6332

This complex is on Lake Okeechobee's Torry Island. It offers 350 campsites, eight boat ramps, a miniature golf course, restrooms, picnic tables and grills. Bait and tackle shops are nearby.

ROLAND MARTIN'S MARINA
920 E. Delmonte Ave.
Clewiston   (813) 983-8930

Clewiston is nestled along the southwest edge of Lake Okeechobee just west of the Palm Beach County line in Hendry County. Roland Martin's hosts numerous bass tournaments; the Bassmasters hang out here.

Fishing Guide Services

If you're not comfortable renting a boat and taking on Lake Okeechobee (the country's biggest freshwater lake) or any other sizeable fishin' hole by yourself, consider hiring a guide service. Here are two:

LAKE OKEECHOBEE GUIDE ASSOCIATION
3235 U.S. Hwy. 441., Ste. A
Okeechobee   (813) 763-2248

INSTRUCTIONAL BASS GUIDE SERVICE
1309 N.W. 16th St., Lot 37
Belle Glade   996-7204

Freshwater Inhabitants

The species you're most likely to encounter include several varieties of bass, bluegill, warmouth, Oscars, shellcrackers, catfish, crappie and

Insiders' Tips

The Loxahatchee Recreation Area, west of Boca Raton, is an angler's paradise.

Photo: PBC CVB

Two young anglers share some "reel" time together.

grass carp. The bass and panfish (such as the shellcrackers, crappie and warmouth) have specific bag and length limits and may be affected by regional, management area or local regulations. The grass carp may not be harvested anywhere in the state. If you hook one, release it unharmed.

Anglers use a variety of baits to attract freshwater prey. Oscars and crappie favor minnows and small artificial lures. Bluegill and bream tend to like natural baits such as nightcrawlers and crickets. (Panfish are most abundant March through September.) Bass are persnickety; try your luck with shiners, artificial worms, spinnerbaits and crankbaits. (Bass are most abundant September through March.)

Catfish, which are scavengers, enjoy chicken livers, cheese balls, dough balls or small chunks of cut hot dog. Catfish don't fight like bass or some of the scrappy non-edibles caught in freshwater, but they're fine eating. Nothing beats a "mess" of Okeechobee catfish served with steaming portions of grits and collard greens. And serving catfish without hushpuppies is simply unthinkable.

Saltwater Fishing

The size of the challenge rises in salt water, but so does the cost of participation. To be sure, there are some excellent fish to be caught from land or pier. Tarpon and snook, which live in brackish bays, tidal pools and estuaries, are two examples. Pier fishing is fun, but trophy-size fish are rarely caught there.

In the Gulf Stream

To fish where the action is, you'll need a boat, but because Palm Beach County lies close to the Gulf Stream, anglers don't have to venture 10 to 20 miles offshore. That means party boat anglers can reel in some big catches only a mile or two from land. Check with dockmasters at local marinas to see which boats are bringing in the biggest and best catches and book your boats accordingly.

Billfish are the most-prized catches here. Sailfish fishing is at its height in December and January.

Blue marlin are most abundant from March through July, and white marlin catches peak in January. Other prized sportfish include dolphin (May through August), cobia (January and February), bluefish (April and May) and King mackerel (November through February).

In-shore and On-shore

If you're fishing from a pier, live or cut shrimp and cut squid are commonly used baits. If you're fishing from a party or chartered boat, check ahead to make sure your bait is provided.

A real key to fishing success in fresh and salt water is seeking out expert advice. Tackle shops and dockmasters are excellent sources of information. If their customers are successful finding fish, their businesses will be successful too.

In the Surf

Surf fishing is a popular pastime for many South Florida anglers.

When you head for your nearest bait and tackle store for supplies and to ask about the hotspots on our shores, make sure your saltwater fishing license is valid and be aware of the prevailing local laws.

Once you've got your spot selected and know the rules, it's time to buy bait, tackle and other gear. Start with the rod. You'll need a surf rod, long spinning rod or a bait-casting rod with a sturdy reel. You'll also need a rod holder for each rod, to keep it secure in the sand. Your reels should be equipped with 20- to 30-pound monofilament line.

Your bait choices are many, including: live shrimp, cut bait, small bait fish (such as pilchards), squid or mullet.

You'll want to use a heavy lead sinker of at least four to five ounces, depending upon the strength of the line you are using and related weather and water conditions (strength of wind and tide). Use the sinker with one of several types of prepared rigs that work well in the surf, including a bottom-drop or slider rig.

Once the hooks are baited and in the water, open up your beach chair,

Photo: PBC CVB

Boating and fishing in the easily-accessible Gulf Stream waters are popular pastimes.

relax and wait; surf fishing is a great time for contemplation and reflection, but keep an eye on your rod tips for strikes. What will take your bait? Just about anything you can catch from a pier can be caught from the beach including pompano, bluefish, snook, snappers and jacks.

Tackle Shops

No fisherman worth his salt is going to tell you where his secret spots are; you'll need to find yours by trial and error. But folks new to the area don't even know where to start looking. Fine places to start are at tackle shops. There you can not only get some tips on spots and technique, but you'll be able to learn what lures, leaders, baits and other equipment work best. And while you're there, you can stock up on gear. Tackle shops also sell Florida fresh and saltwater licenses and supplemental stamps to upgrade those licenses.

Here are some excellent places to start:

KLEISER'S
125 Datura St.
West Palm Beach   *659-2321*

When they're not out plying their favorite pastime, fly fishing enthusiasts flock to Kleiser's for feathers, clamps, line and other accoutrements plus bountiful, friendly advice.

TUPPEN'S
1002 N. Dixie Hwy.
Lake Worth   *582-9012*

From bobbers to boats, Tuppen's excels as a complete marine and tackle store. If what you're plying has fins, scales and swims in salt water, Tuppens can help you track it down and reel it in.

CAPT. JOHN'S BAIT & TACKLE
312 E. Ocean Ave.
Lantana   *588-7612*

Whether you plan to fish from the seawall at Sportsman's Park or Bicentennial Park, ply the Intracoastal or head to the ocean, Capt. John's has the bait, tackle and advice you'll need.

Other good bets include:

SAWGRASS BAIT & TACKLE
7660 S.R. 7 N.
Pompano Beach   (305) 421-5904

WALKER'S BAIT & TACKLE
209 W. Hillsboro Blvd.
Deerfield Beach   (305) 426-2061

7 SEAS BAIT & TACKLE
1308 N.W. Second Ave.
Boca Raton   392-4772

CUSTOM ROD & GUN
1835 N.E. 25th St.
Lighthouse Point   (305) 781-5600

POMPANO BEACH BAIT & TACKLE
1542 N. Federal Hwy.
Pompano Beach   781-6105

Inside
Participant Sports

Folks in Palm Beach County love to watch high-quality competitive athletics but, much like a popular athletic shoe manufacturer suggests, would rather "just do it" themselves when it comes to sports. We've got miles of fairways on golf courses here (which we've detailed in our Golf chapter), tons of clay on tennis courts and baseball diamonds and miles of grass on soccer and other playing fields; nonetheless, it seems the myriad courts, diamonds and fields are always busy.

We wake up in the morning and see joggers running on the roadways outside our windows — and we see more again in the evening. These folks are getting the "max" out of the fabulous South Florida climate and the numerous athletic opportunities it affords. If that's your wish too, here are some places to turn to fulfill your sports needs.

Sports Leagues

For adults and children in Palm Beach County, there are plenty of opportunities to compete in league play.

First, here is a list of numbers in the Boca Raton area to try for specific sports leagues.

Baseball

American Legion	394-7534
Babe Ruth	551-5741
Boca Raton Little League	241-8644

Basketball

Boca Hoops (youth basketball)	395-7372

Football

Boca Jets (youth tackle football)	499-5182
City of Boca Raton Flag Football	367-7001

Roller Hockey

City of Boca Raton Roller Hockey	367-7001

Soccer

Soccer Association of Boca Raton	
Recreation league	368-3070
Competitive league	241-5107

Softball

Boca Raton Youth Softball Association	361-8477
City of Boca Raton Adult softball leagues	997-0791

General Information

Youth Sports Hotline	393-7806
(Dial 3 for updated information)	

For folks living outside the city of Boca Raton or the Greater Boca Raton Beach Tax District limits, call the Palm Beach County Parks and Recreation Department's South District Office at 964-4420. The county operates adult softball leagues and can help you get in contact with youth leagues that play on county-owned parks, such as the Southwest Area Recreation Association, which offers baseball, softball, soccer and flag football leagues for youths in unincorporated areas west of Boca Raton.

In Delray Beach, the best way to get linked up with a team is through the city's Parks and Recreation Department. For information on adult team programs, call 243-7264. For youth programs, call 243-7256.

Other Individual and Organized Options

Beach Volleyball

Beach volleyball is rapidly growing in popularity, from the novice to the pro level. Deerfield Beach plays host to an annual women's pro tournament, and amateur tournaments are held up and down the coast nearly every weekend. Some of the best spots to pick up a game are at these beaches:

DEERFIELD BEACH MUNICIPAL BEACH
U.S. Hwy. A1A at the pier
Deerfield Beach

DELRAY BEACH PUBLIC BEACH
Ocean Blvd. at Atlantic Ave.
Delray Beach

TOWN OF LANTANA PUBLIC BEACH
U.S. Hwy. A1A at E. Ocean Ave.
Lantana

RIVIERA BEACH MUNICIPAL BEACH
N. Ocean Dr. at Beach Ct.
Riviera Beach

Follow Blue Heron Drive east to Singer Island to reach the beach. The volleyball courts are located between the dunes and the Ocean Mall shopping area.

Bowling

Palm Beach County's tenpin enthusiasts have multiple options to satisfy their urges at bowling centers, with copious lanes and amenities including automatic scoring, billiard rooms, pinball and electronic games, clean restrooms, snack bars, lounges, nurseries and pro shops — all the trimmings. Some are even open 24 hours.

CALUSA LANES
3185 S. Main St.
Belle Glade   996-3330

DON CARTER'S ALL-STAR LANES
350 Maplewood Dr.
Jupiter   743-9200

6591 S. Military Tr.
Lake Worth   968-7000

21046 Commercial Tr.
Boca Raton   368-2177

FAIR LANES PALM SPRINGS
3451 Congress Ave.
Lake Worth   968-0600

FAIR LANES BOYNTON BEACH
1190 W. Boynton Beach Blvd.
Boynton Beach   734-1500

Water, Water Everywhere

The ideal, of course, would be water, water everywhere and nary a drop you can't drink. After all, the abundant water-oriented lifestyle is one of the things that draws visitors to South Florida and tempts them to move here. Local government closely monitors water quality in the municipal supply to homes and businesses, but the process of treating and "massaging" water in swimming pools is left up to personal preference.

The conventional method of doctoring the pool with chemicals such as chlorine has had stiff competition in recent years from refined processes of electronic ionization. The method is gaining popularity as an alternative water disinfectant for indoor and outdoor swimming pools, whirlpool spas, fountains, decorative ponds and cooling towers.

Electronic ionization eliminates a broad spectrum of microorganisms, including bacteria, viruses, algae, fungi and yeast. This is especially practical in our tropical climate, since potentially harmful organisms thrive in warm water environments.

Superior Aqua Products, 2755 S. Federal Highway, Suite 15, Boynton Beach, offers an electronic system that provides long-term stable disinfecting residual action — still effective even when pumps, filters and circulation systems are temporarily inactive.

Electronic water treatment is desirable for odor-free swimming with no irritation to the eyes or skin. The nontoxic process is not affected by heat or sunlight, and is designed to prolong the life of equipment such as pumps and filters.

The Superior Aqua system of products is cost-effective, environmentally safe and user friendly. Superior's products also have the approval of Underwriters Laboratories for end-user safety. Superior Aqua packages are priced according to the size and water depth of the pool. Installations become cost-effective by eliminating the majority of monthly chemical applications and maintenance. East to install and maintain, Superior Aqua Products takes the worry and the chlorine out of water treatment. For information on banks that are willing to finance the cost at very reasonable terms, call 736-8355.

LANTANA LANES
200 N. Third St.
Lantana   585-7934

RIVIERA LANES
1715 Broadway
Riviera Beach   848-6631

VISTA BOWLING CENTER
2101 Vista Pkwy.
West Palm Beach   683-5200

Canoeing and Kayaking

JAMES A. RUTHERFORD PARK
600 N.E. 24th St.
Boca Raton   393-7845

This is Boca Raton's best-kept secret. Nestled behind the Fifth Avenue Shops on Federal Highway is Rutherford Park, named after the city's longtime recreation director. Here, a boardwalk nature trail winds through a tangle of mangroves along the Intracoastal Waterway. A watercraft trail and canoe and kayak rentals are available as well.

The park is open Friday through Monday only, and you'll need to call ahead to find out the hours of operation, as they vary depending on the tides and weather conditions.

Drag Racing

MOROSO MOTORSPORTS PARK
17097 Beeline Hwy.
West Palm Beach   622-1400

You don't have to be a pro to enjoy the thrills of auto or motorcycle racing. Moroso's Operation Street Legal gives those folks who have a need for speed a safe, legal environment to exercise their lead feet on a 1/8-mile drag strip.

If you've got a valid driver's licence, a street-legal car or motorcycle and $10, the race is on. Entry fee for spectators is $8. Call for race dates.

Fitness Centers

The ever-growing interest in personal fitness is nothing new in Palm Beach County. Private centers have sprung up and now compete with many of the national players on the scene. We've included a sampling of each.

MICHAEL'S BODY SCENES
AEROBICS AND FITNESS CENTER
5994 S.W. 18th St.
Boca Raton   750-7945

BALLY'S TOTAL FITNESS
21069 Military Tr.   368-6441
Boca Raton   (800) 695-8111

501 Village Blvd.   683-5800
West Palm Beach   (800) 695-8111

GOLD'S GYM
5700 N. Federal Hwy.
Boca Raton   997-5464

ATHLETIC CLUB OF BOCA RATON
1499 Yamato Rd.
Boca Raton   241-5088

THE ATHLETICS CENTER
AT BOCA POINTE COUNTRY CLUB
22971 Via de Sonrisa del Norte
Boca Raton   394-3455

PALM BEACH GYM
AND FITNESS CENTER
Linton International Plaza
660 Linton Blvd.
Delray Beach   278-7111

Gymnastics

Every four years, interest in gymnastics surges dramatically. That's largely due to its increased exposure via the Olympic Games. But there is year-round interest in the sport in many areas, and the Boca Raton area's seems to be particularly strong. The following clubs do a fine job developing young gymnasts.

AMERICAN GYMNASTICS
6500 W. Rogers Cir.
Boca Raton   998-9797

CATS GYMNASTICS, INC.
6451 E. Rogers Cir.
Boca Raton   997-7411

Horseback Riding

THE RIDING SCHOOL AT PALM BEACH POLO AND COUNTRY CLUB
12221 S. Shore Blvd.
Wellington 791-3424

Private and group lessons are available. Participants need not be PBPCC members to join in the fun.

Lawn Bowling

VETERAN'S MEMORIAL PARK
801 N.E. First St.
Delray Beach 243-7351

Delray Beach's seven bowling greens are home to a friendly, enthusiastic group of bowlers, most of whom grew up under the Union Jack. They love to share their sport with newcomers. The game is fun but frustrating, and learning the vagaries of the bowl's bias is a lot tougher than it looks.

Veteran's Park is open Monday through Friday from 8:30 AM to 4:30 PM. On Saturdays, it's open from 8:30 AM to 3:30 PM in the winter, 8:30 AM to 11:30 AM in the summer. On Sundays, it's open from 1 to 4 PM.

Paintball

PAINTBALL CITY
2300 W. Copans Rd. #2
Pompano Beach (305) 752-5218

Remember when you played cops 'n' robbers and war games as a child? The action sport of paintball transforms these children's games into adult fantasy competition for millions annually. This is not simulated warfare; each competitor is armed with a carbon dioxide-powered weapon that shoots gelatin-covered blobs of paint. Get hit on exposed skin and the paintball will cause a welt, but once you're properly armed and protected, getting splattered doesn't hurt and the game's a blast. It's easy to get hooked.

Plan to pay about $50 for admission, semiautomatic weapon, starter CO_2 and protective gear rental. Paintballs cost about $7 per round of

100. If you're a newbie, you'll be pretty tired out after an hour or two. Experienced players can play all day.

Paintball City offers play indoors or on outdoor fields, with excellent heavy local terrain. It's open Wednesday, Thursday and Friday evenings from 6 to 9 PM, Saturday and Sundays from 9 AM to 6 PM.

Running

South Florida has many excellent running clubs, and the subsequent three are among them. Contact them to link up with other runners at your level for training runs, fun runs and competitions, which are numerous here.

BOCA RATON ROAD RUNNERS
P.O. Box 810820
Boca Raton 33481   487-0605

FLORIDA ATHLETIC CLUB
3250 Lakeview Blvd.
Delray Beach   499-3370

PALM BEACH RUNNERS
P.O. Box 8205
West Palm Beach 33407   689-2648

Shuffleboard

MUNICIPAL SHUFFLEBOARD COMPLEX
N.W. Crawford Blvd.
At the north end of Memorial Park
Boca Raton   393-7818

Learn to play shuffleboard through classes offered here, or compete as a member of the complex's club. Annual dues are $5.

The courts are open May through September from 12:30 to 4:45 PM and 7 to 10 PM Monday through Saturday. From October through April, the courts are open by request.

VETERAN'S MEMORIAL PARK
801 N.E. First St.
Delray Beach   243-7250

The 16 courts here were renovated as part of the park's recent overhaul, making Veteran's Park into an urban showplace.

Courts are open Monday through Friday from 8:30 AM to 4:30 PM, on Saturdays from 8:30 AM to 3:30 PM in the winter and 8:30 to 11:30 AM in the summer, and from 1 to 4 PM on Sundays.

Swimming

If you prefer to get your strokes in at a pool instead of the beach, there are several excellent public facilities to access. See our Beaches chapter for information about ocean access.

MEADOWS PARK POOL
1300 N.W. Eighth St.
Boca Raton   393-7851

The pool is open to the public from noon to 5:45 PM daily. Specialized classes are offered on Monday through Saturday from 10 AM to noon and include water aerobics,

---

Insiders' Tips

For safety's sake, mark your location with a diving flag when scuba diving off Palm Beach County's coastline.

Palm Beach County has more than 145 golf courses.

Swim and Stay Fit classes and lessons for beginners. A Saturday morning learn-to-swim program for youths is also available, and the facility also offers lifeguard classes.

The Boca Raton Masters Swim Team, for swimmers ages 19 and older, calls Meadows Park Pool its home.

POMPEY PARK POOL
1101 N.W. Second St.
Delray Beach 243-7356

Pompey Park Pool was being refurbished and enlarged to Olympic size at press time. Call to keep tabs on its progress.

AQUA CREST POOL
2503 Seacrest Blvd.
Delray Beach 278-7104

Located on the campus of Atlantic High School, Aqua Crest Pool is one of several pools owned and operated by the Palm Beach County Parks and Recreation Department.

Hours of operation are 10 AM to 6 PM Tuesday through Saturday and noon to 6 PM on Sunday.

Tennis

Finding a tennis court in the Boca Raton area is as easy as stepping from a boat and finding water. Most high schools, many middle schools and city parks have tennis and racquetball courts available. At the costlier end of the spectrum, there are many excellent private facilities, many of them part of country clubs. In the middle, there are several municipal tennis complexes and a few private tennis centers that offer excellent values for practice, play and competition.

MEMORIAL PARK TENNIS CENTER
271 N.W. Boca Raton Blvd.
Boca Raton 393-7978

With five clay courts and four hard courts open for play seven days a week, this friendly downtown tennis center gets a lot of use. Lessons and group classes are available, and the center also offers a mixed doubles round robin league and a Women's B evening league, sponsors a team in the Palm Beach County Women's League and is a hotbed of summer youth tennis activities. Throw in a few tournaments here and there and you'll understand why calling in court reservations is a must.

The complex is open Monday through Saturday from 7:30 AM to 10 PM and Sunday from 7:30 AM to 7 PM.

PATCH REEF PARK TENNIS CENTER
2000 Yamato Rd.
Boca Raton 997-0881

Patch Reef Park Tennis Center boasts 17 lighted hard courts and a world-class pro shop with many of the amenities of private clubs, yet it's set in a busy public park.

There's a full schedule of clinics, classes, leagues and lessons available, and the center often hosts national-caliber events.

The complex is open Monday through Saturday from 7:30 AM to 10 PM and from 7:30 AM to 6 PM on Sunday.

CITY OF
DELRAY BEACH TENNIS CENTER
201 W. Atlantic Ave.
Delray Beach 243-7360

Officially completed in January 1994, the center wowed the United States Tennis Association so completely, they named it the 1993 New Facility of the Year.

The complex is the heart of tennis activity in Delray Beach and also home to the Delray Beach Winter Championships women's professional tournament (see also our Festivals and Annual Events chapter) that draws the likes of Steffi Graf, Aranxta Sanchez Vicario, Gabriela Sabatini and other tennis luminaries.

Fourteen clay courts and five hard courts fill the grounds, along with a two-level clubhouse that many private facilities would yearn for, plus a pro shop, dressing rooms and indoor lounge.

As with Boca Raton's public facilities, Delray Beach's center stays humming with lessons, clinics, classes, leagues and tournaments.

The complex is open daily from 8 AM to 9:30 PM.

SEGUSO-BASSETT
TENNIS TRAINING CENTER
10333 Diego Dr. S.
Boca Raton 488-2001

Where Greg Louganis and other world-class swimmers and divers once trained at the Mission Bay Aquatic Center, world-class tennis players now hone their strokes at the Seguso-Bassett Tennis Training Center, overseen by a pair of world-class pros, Carling Bassett and husband Robert Seguso.

Insiders' Tips

Red Reef Park in Boca Raton is a popular spot for snorkeling.

Photo: City of Boca Raton Recreation Services

Tennis enthusiasts are offered clinics and lessons at several public facilities in locations throughout Boca Raton.

The center offers 32 courts, representing six types of playing surfaces. The highlight is the Grand Slam Stadium, comprised of four courts with Grand Slam surfaces of red clay, green clay, grass and hard court.

The complex also offers ample training facilities, an Olympic-size pool, aerobics studio, training track and video analysis center.

Special training programs are available, ranging from half-day to weeklong.

Trap and Skeet Shooting

PALM BEACH TRAP & SKEET CLUB
2950 Pierson Rd.
West Palm Beach   793-8787

The 100-acre layout offers skeet, trap and sporting clays fields and hops, with activity on the weekends including nationally sanctioned tournaments.

Walking

Most of the runners clubs listed earlier welcome race-walkers, and most of the road races in the area feature walking divisions.

But for those who walk for their health, several area malls offer mall-walkers clubs or open the malls early for walkers to pursue their activity in a safe, climate-controlled environment.

Palm Beach Mall, 683-9186, in association with Humana Hospital offers a mall-walkers club as part of a wellness program that meets at 9 AM weekdays.

The North Broward Hospital District coordinates mall-walkers clubs at the following three malls.

Coral Square Mall, (305) 755-5550, is the home of Club Tread. Meetings for blood pressure screenings are the second Tuesday of the month from 10 to 11 AM in the Center Court area.

The **Pompano Square**, (305) 943-4683, Mallwalking Club meets the first Wednesday of each month at the Sundeck Food Court at 9 AM.

S.T.A.R. Walkers at the **Galleria**, (305) 564-1015, meet the first Tuesday of each month in the Palm Court at 8:30 AM.

The mall-walkers at **Sawgrass Mills**, (305) 846-2350, are truly ambitious. The mall is open to the mall-walkers Monday through Friday at 8 AM. Club members can register Monday mornings.

The following malls open their doors early and welcome walkers:

Boynton Beach Mall, 736-7900, opens its doors at 9 AM (an hour earlier than opening time) on Monday through Saturday for walkers.

Town Center, 368-6000, in Boca Raton opens its main doors at 8 AM to mall-walkers, except on Sundays.

Water Skiing

LAKE IDA PARK
2929 Lake Ida Rd.
Delray Beach   964-4420

On a beautiful sunny day, Lake Ida is the place to be if you're a water skier, whether a novice or in the pro ranks. This county park maintains a boat ramp, practice slalom course and a trick course. Lake Ida sometimes hosts competitions as well.

OKEEHEELEE PARK
7715 Forest Hill Blvd.
West Palm Beach   964-4420

Site of the 1995 Nationals, Lake Okeeheelee is a popular venue for championship competition. The Ski Club of the Palm Beaches works with the county to maintain a slalom course, tricks course and a jump course.

Inside
Golf

As home to the PGA of America, the National Golf Foundation, the Florida Golf Council and more than 100 golf courses, Palm Beach County certainly qualifies as golf heaven.

But news in the kingdom isn't all good. The bad news? Even if you're an avid golfer, you're not going to be able to play some of these courses. That's partly because there are so many of them, but mostly because so many are private.

Now the good news: You're hardly left with the dregs. There are some excellent municipal courses that charge modest greens fees and still offer golfers a challenge. There also are some daily-fee courses that rival the most picturesque and strategically demanding private ones.

And if that's not enough, there's golf-goofy neighbor Broward County, which is crammed with courses; and if you're willing to drive a little farther, Dade, St. Lucie and Martin counties offer some excellent opportunities.

What does it cost to play at these courses? Generally, greens fees range from around $10 to as much as $100 per round. Each course bases its fees on the date and time of day — some courses have as many as three price changes daily. The costliest time is early morning, just after the greens have been cut; the cheapest is usually after 2 PM.

A huge bargain for golfers is the American Lung Association's Lung Card, which allows golfers unlimited free greens fees or discounted rates from May through November at more than 400 Florida courses and 160 courses in Alabama, Georgia and Mississippi. The card is valid at 34 courses in Palm Beach County, 30 in Broward. Other participating Florida courses are in Indian River, Martin, Dade, Monroe, Osceola and St. Lucie counties.

Golfers must pay for their carts and may play any time during the day on weekdays and after 1 PM on weekends.

Golf cards cost $25 each, but if you purchase three cards, the fourth is free.

Call the American Lung Association at 659-7644 for more information.

Because of the growing interest in fitness, walking the round is gaining renewed popularity. (The American Lung Association would likely endorse this option.) Some courses prohibit this option, however, as it characteristically slows down play. If you wish, ask about walking your round when you arrange a tee time.

While there are plenty of courses to choose from, we'll concentrate on those where any golfer can pay and play. The first three courses presented here opened in 1990, clearly a vintage year for golf courses in South Florida. We'll start our course review with an eye-popper.

Regulation Courses

Palm Beach County

EMERALD DUNES
2100 Emerald Dunes Dr.
West Palm Beach   684-GOLF

Just west of Florida's Turnpike, off Okeechobee Boulevard, springs a golfing oasis, designed by Tom Fazio. It offers the yin of a lush and magnificent golfing environment and the yang of a challenging par 72 course measuring 7006 yards from the championship tees and 4676 yards from the women's tees, with three intermediate sets of tees.

BINKS FOREST
400 Binks Dr.
Wellington   795-0028

Designed by Johnny Miller, Binks Forest already has played gracious host to the Sazale Classic, a pro team event. The course is beautifully set amidst indigenous pine and palmetto.

The par 72 course measures 7065 yards off the championship tees, 5599 yards off the women's red tees.

POLO TRACE GOLF & TENNIS CLUB
13401 Hagen Ranch Rd.
Delray Beach   495-5301

Course designer Karl Litton and tour player Joey Sindelar collaborated on this Scottish-style links course that uses the natural terrain to its full advantage.

The par 72 course measures 7096 yards off the championship tees, 5314 yards off the women's tees.

BOCA RATON MUNICIPAL COURSE
8111 Golf Course Rd.
Boca Raton   483-6100

One of several courses operated by the Boca Raton Parks and Recreation Department, the Muni, designed by Charles Ankrom, is a golfers' favorite. The regulation course is 18 holes, par 72. The course plays 6953 yards off the men's blue tees and 5306 yards off the women's red tees. Also available is a par 30 executive course that plays 1877 yards from the blue tees, 1628 yards off the red.

SOUTHWINDS GOLF COURSE
19557 Lyons Rd.
Boca Raton   483-1305

This county-run course is a shortish par 70 rimmed by numerous lateral water hazards. It plays 5643 yards off the men's blue tees, 4327 yards off the women's red tees.

DELRAY BEACH GOLF COURSE
2200 Highland Ave.
Delray Beach   243-7380

Not too many years ago, Delray Beach's public course was looking pretty shabby; now it's one of the hottest golfing spots in town. With the opening of the new clubhouse, the transformation is complete.

The historic course, designed by Donald Ross and opened in 1923, is a relatively short par 72, measuring 6657 yards from the men's blue tees and 5265 yards off the women's red tees.

Photo: Palm Beach County Convention and Visitors Bureau

Palm Beach County's myriad golf courses challenge golfers of all ability levels.

BOYNTON BEACH
MUNICIPAL GOLF COURSE
8020 Jog Rd.
Boynton Beach 969-2201

Opened in 1984, Boynton Beach's Bruce Devlin-Robert VonHagge course is a delight. The course is built as three nine-hole courses. If you're playing 18 holes, you'll play the 3272-yard white course and the 3044-yard red layout. If you're out for a short nine, you'll play the 2018-yard blue course.

Water comes into play on numerous holes, and there's enough sand on this course to fill a beach.

The clubhouse, with its wooden exterior, seems as though it was transplanted from an Adirondack logging camp. It houses the snack bar, pro shop and restrooms.

SHERWOOD PARK GOLF CLUB
170 Sherwood Forest Dr.
Delray Beach 499-3559

Sherwood Forest is home to this short but cozy course tucked into a western Delray neighborhood and is one of several delightful smaller courses that dot Delray Beach. It's a great place to play if you want to leave your woods at home and give the long irons a thorough workout. The par 62 course plays 3733 yards off the blue tees; 3304 yards off the red.

DOUG FORD'S LACUNA
GOLF & COUNTRY CLUB
6400 Lacuna Blvd.
Lake Worth 433-3006

The tour legend's 18-hole, par 71 layout offers a nice challenge, tempting the golfer with nine amiable holes to start with, nine longer and narrower ones on the back. The course measures 6428 yards off the blue tees and 5119 yards off the red.

Be sure to stop in the pro shop and check out Ford's memorabilia on display. Ford is often on site and may serve as your guide!

THE VILLAGE GOLF CLUB
122 Country Club Dr.
Royal Palm Beach   *793-1400*

Designed by Mark Mahannah and opened in 1968, the par 72, 7000-yard Village course is both a test of golfing skill and a lesson in science. This scenic course is located 5 miles west of Florida's Turnpike and gives golfers the chance to observe and appreciate native species of flora and fauna up close while enjoying a round on this challenging layout.

Also offered at the golf center is an extra-long, 280-yard driving range for John Daly-like hitters.

LAKE WORTH MUNICIPAL GOLF CLUB
1 Seventh Ave. N.
Lake Worth   *533-7364*

Nestled alongside the Intracoastal and rimmed by venerable, gnarled Australian pines, Lake Worth's municipal course is a delight to play. The layout is a nice mix of par 3s, 4s and 5s, making up a par 70 course, 5744 yards off the back tees, 5423 off the front.

LONE PINE GOLF COURSE
6251 N. Military Tr.
West Palm Beach   *842-0480*

A pine-studded, par 62 course comprised of par 3 and par 4 holes, totaling 4120 yards off the back tees, 3795 from the front.

The course also provides a lighted driving range if you want to give your woods an extra good workout.

NORTH PALM BEACH COUNTRY CLUB
940 U.S. Hwy. 1
North Palm Beach   *626-4344*

A formidable, challenging course with water in play on 11 of the course's 18 holes, North Palm Beach's par 72 municipal course measures 6275 yards from the blue tees, 5055 from the red.

Broward County

ARROWHEAD GOLF AND SPORTS CLUB
8201 S.W. 24th St.
Davie   *(305) 475-8200*

Arrowhead is a bustling, popular course, thanks in no small part to former owner Earl Morrall, a former mayor of Davie, but better known as quarterback of the Miami Dolphins during their 1972 perfect season. Even now, Morrall frequents The Perfect Season, the club's appropriately named restaurant/sports bar. Newspaper cover pages depicting the Dolphins' memorable, record-setting campaign decorate the walls.

Insiders' Tips

Call the course you intend to play a few days in advance so you can learn how far in advance you can reserve a tee time, what the course's policies are on carts versus walking, and if there's a dress code.

Arrowhead's par 71 course plays longer than it looks. The course is 6506 yards off the aqua tees and 5025 yards off the orange. If you feel the need to ask about the unique tee-marker colors . . . you haven't been paying attention.

CAROLINA CHAMPIONSHIP PUBLIC GOLF
3011 Rock Island Rd.
Margate   (305) 753-4000

Not far from the Palm Beach County line in northwestern Broward County, Carolina is a pleasant course to play because it is maintained to the same exacting standards as a private club. The par 71 Karl Litton layout plays 6550 yards off the blue tees, 4978 yards off the red.

The course tends to play longer than it looks, and there are water hazards to trap the unwary. A word of caution: The course is built over ancient coral deposits which tend to turn bad bounces into horrible ones.

The pro shop here is one of the best in the area, and the restaurant is excellent.

CONTINENTAL GOLF CLUB OF CORAL SPRINGS
9001 W. Sample Rd.
Coral Springs   (305) 752-2140

Formerly known as Broken Woods Country Club, Continental now welcomes the public onto its par 69 course that measures 5659 yards off the men's blue tees and 4874 off the women's red tees.

The course is a mix of par 3s and 4s, with three 5s thrown in, including the one-two punch of the 474-yard 12th hole followed by the 542-yard 13th.

CYPRESS CREEK COUNTRY CLUB
9400 N. Military Tr.
Boynton Beach   732-4202

Cypress Creek offers a nice mix of par 3, 4 and 5 holes to provide a well-balanced challenge. Water frequently comes into play.

The course measures 6808 yards off the championship tees, 5425 yards off the women's red tees.

DEER CREEK GOLF CLUB
2801 Country Club Blvd.
Deerfield Beach   (305) 421-5550

Like Carolina, Deer Creek is a popular Broward County course situated near the Palm Beach County line. Deer Creek is a former host of the LPGA Whirlpool Championships. The recently redesigned par 72 course plays 6732 yards off the blue tees and 5303 yards off the red.

ROLLING HILLS RESORT
3501 W. Rolling Hills Cir.
Davie   (305) 475-3010

Should you get to play a round here — thousands of golfers do every year — and the course seems eerily familiar, it's not *déjà vu*: Rolling Hills was transformed into Bushwood Country Club for the movie *Caddyshack*. You can even buy Bushwood memorabilia in the pro shop.

The layout features the 18-hole, par 72 Oaks course, that plays 6905 yards off the blue tees and 5630 yards off the red. There's also the nine-hole University course, a par 36 layout that plays 3357 yards from the blue tees, 2794 yards off the red.

ORANGEBROOK GOLF COURSE

400 Entrada Dr.
Hollywood   *(305) 967-GOLF*

Here's a set of courses with history. The first 18-hole course, designed by Ralph Young, a friend of city founder Joseph Young, was completed in 1937 and hosted the Hollywood Open that same year, an event that drew golfing luminaries such as Sam Snead, Byron Helson and Ben Hogan.

A second course was added later, and Orangebrook remains one of the most heavily played municipal courses in the country. In the late 1980s, the courses underwent significant renovation and upgrading that even Hurricane Andrew couldn't destroy.

For more than 50 years, Orangebrook has been home to the Women's Invitational Four-Ball, the crowning event on the Orange Blossom Trail series of world-class women's amateur tournaments. Past competitors include Babe Didrikson Zaharias, Louise Suggs and many current LPGA players.

Orangebrook's East Course is par 72, 6848 yards of the blue tees, 5645 off the red. The West Course is 6476 yards off the blue tees, 5699 off the red.

CITY OF
POMPANO BEACH GOLF COURSE

1101 N. Federal Hwy.
Pompano Beach   *(305) 786-4141*

Nothing fishy about it. Pompano Beach, the city named after the elusive sportfish, is proud home to two challenging courses and a newly renovated clubhouse, pro shop and restaurant.

The VonHagge-Devlin courses include the par 72 Pines layout — 6886 yards from the gold tees, 5748 from the red — and the par 71 Palms course — 6336 yards off the gold tees, 5397 from the red.

Dade County

DORAL COUNTRY CLUB

4400 N.W. 87th Ave.
Miami   *(305) 592-2000*

Watching Doral's PGA tournament on TV, you'd never dream the resort is merely an oasis in northwest Miami's congested industrial area. But an oasis it is.

The club offers five 18-hole courses and a nine-hole executive course, but the layout that gets the most attention is the famed, cantankerous Blue Monster, on which the PGA's Doral-Ryder Open is played. It's a par 72 challenge that plays 6939 yards off the championship tees and 5786 yards off the red.

Dick Wilson designed the course with water on every hole, the reason behind the course's nickname, and conditions are extra-nasty during the spring when the winds kick up.

Robert VonHagge designed the other Doral courses, and each offers plenty of challenges. The par 72 Silver course is links-style with lots of lakes; it plays 6801 yards off the championship tees. The Gold course, also a links-style layout, is a mite easier at par 70, 6279 yards. The par 71 Red course, measuring 6400 yards, features copious sand and water. The White course is a par 72 layout covering 6208 tree-rimmed yards, but its wide fairways make it the most forgiving of the bunch.

THE LINKS AT KEY BISCAYNE
6700 Crandon Blvd.
Key Biscayne   *(305) 361-9139*

The Links, a county-run course, plays gracious host to Miami's annual PGA Seniors event. The course is set on beautiful Biscayne Bay, a visual diversion that makes it tough to keep your mind on your game.

The par 72 course plays 7070 yards off the championship tees and 5690 yards off the women's tees.

Eighteen-hole Short Courses

LAKEVIEW GOLF CLUB
1200 Dover Rd.
Delray Beach   *498-5486*

A friendly neighborhood course with a family atmosphere, par 60 Lakeview is a mix of par 3s and 4s, measuring a cozy 2969 yards off the back tees and 2765 off the front. At publication time, the City of Delray Beach was moving ahead to buy Lakeview.

Executive/Nine-hole Courses

Palm Beach County

BOCA RATON
EXECUTIVE COUNTRY CLUB
7601 E. Country Club Blvd.
Boca Raton   *997-9410*

Nestled in northern Boca Raton, just west of the FEC tracks, Boca Raton Executive Country Club is a cozy little course that enjoys a loyal local following. The course measures 3202 yards off the men's tees and 2689 off the women's and features water on all but a few holes.

Also available is a lighted driving range, open until 10 PM nightly, for those who want to work the kinks out of their swings.

JUPITER DUNES GOLF CLUB
401 U.S. Hwy. A1A N.
Jupiter
746-6654

"The Little Monster" is how this par 54 executive course bills itself — and with good reason. Located near the ocean, the breezes affect the ball's flight, and the course is studded with water hazards galore, sand and dense foliage.

The course measures 1926 yards off the back tees, 1576 off the front.

RED REEF EXECUTIVE GOLF COURSE
1111 U.S. Hwy. A1A N.
Boca Raton   *391-5014*

This is a delightful course if you want to get in a quick nine holes. The wind at the rolling, oceanside course makes your round all the more challenging.

The course is par 32, 1253 yards.

Broward County

ECO GOLF CLUB
1451 Taft St.
Hollywood   *(305) 922-8755*

This is a nine-hole, city-owned

Are you hitting the ball longer here in South Florida? Quite possibly. Many South Florida courses are built on a thin layer of sand covering a layer of coral rock; this gives the ball a greater amount of roll. On hotter days, you'll find the ball goes farther still.

Insiders' Tips

course with teeth. Unlike courses that bite you with a murderous finishing hole, Eco's 518-yard fourth hole packs the wallop. The remaining holes are a nice blend of three par 4s and five par 3s, and there's plenty of water to contend with.

In all, the par 32 course measures 2259 yards off the back tees, 1893 off the front tees. This course is no cream puff; bring your woods.

PALM LAKES GOLF COURSE
7590 W. Atlantic Blvd.
Margate   (305) 979-9446

Palm Lakes' nine holes are clustered around two large lakes, putting water into play on every hole, but especially so on four holes: the 127-yard 2nd hole, the 128-yard 7th, the 114-yard 8th and the backbreaking 301-yard finishing hole.

The par 28 course measures 1220 yards off the men's tees, 1047 off the women's.

SUNSET GOLF CLUB
2727 Johnson St.
Hollywood   (305) 923-2008

Like Delray Beach, Hollywood is a golf-crazy city with several delightful smaller courses sprinkled around town — cozy layouts that weren't built as part of a housing development. Sunset, a nine-hole course designed by Robert S. Lawrence, is one of Hollywood's gems.

The par 35 course measures out at 2799 yards from the yellow tees and 2543 yards from the red. Water comes into play on seven holes, and the course is densely landscaped and rimmed with towering Australian pines.

Par 3s/Pitch 'n' Putts

GOLF AND SPORTS CENTER OF THE PALM BEACHES
5850 Belvedere Rd.
West Palm Beach   640-9100

This little, lighted par 3 course is one of the few you can walk on and play; if there's a wait, bide your time on the driving range or putting green. The par 54 course measures 2344 yards for the men and 1889 yards for the women.

THE PINES AT DIVOTS GOLF CENTER
16169 Southern Blvd.
Loxahatchee   790-5270

This course is aptly named and a fun way to get a quick workout on your short game. Constructed around a young pine forest, the nine-hole, par 27 Pines course measures 1164 yards from the back tees — holes range from 72 to 192 yards — and 892 yards from the front.

THE LINKS AT JOHN PRINCE
4754 S. Congress Ave.
Lake Worth   642-7596

Bring only a short iron or two and your putter to play this tiny course at John Prince Park; the nine holes range from 44 to 94 yards. This par 27 layout measures 611 yards, and water touches every hole.

BOGEY'S DRIVING RANGE AND PAR 3
5400 S. University Dr.
Davie   (305) 434-3566

Bring your 9-iron and a putter, play three rounds through this six-hole layout of 46 to 76 yards . . . and you've played 18 holes. It's a nice workout with friends or if you simply must get in a few holes but have lim-

Photo: Tom Fagan - Phototastic

World-famous Deer Creek Golf Club in Deerfield Beach.

ited time. If you need to pull out the woods and wail on the ball, try the driving range next door.

Miniature Golf Courses

BOCA GOLF
3500 Airport Rd.
Boca Raton   *338-5008*

Here's an idea so good it's unbelievable: What about creating a miniature golf course of real grass? That way putting fans have a ball and serious golfers can work on their putting game on grass.

"Most people don't believe us when we say [the course has] real greens with real grass," a Boca Golf employee notes. "It gets pretty addicting."

That it does. Holes No. 10, 14 and 15 are nightmares, particularly No. 15, with three palmetto trees crowding the approach, leaving players only three tiny ribbons of grass to aim for.

The holes measure 60 to 160 feet, and you're likely a world-class putter if you can make par (43) here.

Boca Golf is open daily from 8:30 AM to 10 PM. The cost for miniature golf is $8 for adults, but $5 specials are routinely offered. The cost for children is $3.

BOOMER'S
3100 Airport Rd.
Boca Raton   *347-1888*

Boomer's two miniature golf courses are frequently jammed with children and their parents, teenagers and friends enjoying the sunshine, fresh air, camaraderie and the chance to enjoy some gentle competition.

The two courses — Koala Pass and Outback — are of the new-fashioned adventure variety, complete with caves and waterfalls and streams gushing about.

The miniature golf courses at Boomer's are open from 10 AM to 11 PM Sunday through Thursday and 10 AM to 1 AM Friday and Saturday. The cost is $4 per round.

GOLF AND SPORTS CLUB
OF THE PALM BEACHES
5850 Belvedere Rd.
West Palm Beach   *683-4544*

This is an old course, but has undergone extensive renovation recently and is fun to play. It's also one heck of a challenge. Six of the holes are par 3; this might seem ludicrous for miniature golf, but it's entirely merited here.

The course is open daily from 8 AM to 10 PM. The cost per round is $3.25 for adults, $2.50 for children.

JOHN PRINCE
CHAMPIONSHIP MINI GOLF COURSE
4754 S. Congress Ave.
Lake Worth   *642-7596*

This is another refurbished older course built in the traditional style, with quick, true greens and some formidable challenges.

If you want to keep swinging after you've finished the miniature golf course, consider heading over to the batting cages — you get 12 swings per $1 token. Also available are a driving range and a nine-hole "mini executive" golf course.

The complex is open daily from 9 AM to 10 PM. The cost is $3.25 for adults, $2.75 for children.

DIVOTS GOLF CENTER
16169 Southern Blvd.
Loxahatchee   *790-5270*

If you grew up in the 1950s, when miniature golf was the rage and most courses were marked by the obligatory white mini-buildings with red roofs, this course will provide a heady dose of nostalgia.

It's open daily from 8 AM to 9 PM, and the cost is $3 for adults and $1.50 for children younger than 12.

WHIRLY BALL SKATE & PUTT
9130 S.R. 84
Davie   *(305) 452-2800*

One 18-hole, indoor course is part of this recreation center that includes Whirly Ball, roller skating, Laser Storm and arcade games.

The miniature golf course is open noon to 11 PM daily and costs $2.50 per round.

BLOCKBUSTER GOLF & GAMES
151 N.W. 136th Ave.
Sunrise   *(305) 846-7650*

Two 18-hole adventure mini-golf courses are part of this mini theme park. The cost per round is $5 for adults, $4 for children younger than 9.

Other parts of the park are an 80-tee driving range, 17 baseball/softball batting cages, the Adventure Lagoon bumper boats and the Games Arena — with diversions such as pinball and virtual reality games.

The center is open daily from 10 AM to midnight.

Insiders' Tips

Greens fees are most reasonable during the summer months, when most Insiders play.

GRAND PRIX GOLF-O-RAMA
1801 N.W. First St.
Dania   (305) 921-2416

There are five (count 'em!) meticulously landscaped and maintained 18-hole miniature golf courses here — 90 holes to putter around on. The courses are a nice cross between the traditional skill and the contemporary adventure layouts. The layout is dotted with sphinxes, Victorian houses, waterfalls . . . and, yes, even a few obligatory windmills.

If you get pooped out putting, you might consider a visit to the other parts of the park — the 24-hour arcade, the Skycoaster, NASKART racing and a multi-station batting cage.

Grand Prix's mini-golf courses are open from 10 AM to 11 PM daily. The cost is $4.75 per round for adults, $3.75 for children.

BROADWALK MINIATURE GOLF
1100 N. Broadwalk
Hollywood   (305) 927-7888

The nautical theme on this 18-hole beachside layout could hardly be more appropriate. The course is dotted with coconut palms, ocean buoys, lifeguard stands and the like.

Although new, this course was built with traditional-style, fast-as-lightning felt greens. It's a fun place for children and anyone who enjoys walking — a stroll down the Broadwalk after playing a round is a delightful way to unwind.

Broadwalk Mini Golf is open from 9 AM to midnight daily. The cost is $3.75 per round.

CLOVERLEAF MINIATURE GOLF
150 N.W. 167th St.
North Miami Beach   (305) 947-1211

Cloverleaf is one of South Florida's veteran courses and still a toughie for folks who think they're master putters. No. 4 on this 18-hole layout features a frustrating double turn that's as tough as any hole in coastal Florida. A subtle rise on No. 9 makes an otherwise easy hole a monster. Nine holes are par 3 and one is par 4.

The course is open daily from 10:30 AM to 11 PM. A round costs $3 for adults and $2.25 for children younger than 14.

TRADEWINDS PARK
3600 W. Sample Rd.
Coconut Creek   (305) 968-3880

QUIET WATERS PARK
6601 N. Powerline Rd.
Deerfield Beach   (305) 360-1315

Each park's 18-hole, traditional-style course is open daily from 10 AM to 4 PM and costs $1.75 per round.

Entry to the parks is free on weekdays, $1 per person on weekends and holidays. Admission for children younger than 5 is free.

Polo matches at Royal Palm Polo Sports Club in Boca Raton are jam-packed with action.

Inside
South Florida
Spectator Sports

In the beginning—as far as South Florida sports fans are concerned — there were the Miami Dolphins. The year was 1965 and the advent of the National Football League's aqua and orange franchise signaled the area's ascent from a mere tropical paradise to something far more exciting.

More than two decades later, the Dolphins were followed in 1988 by the National Basketball Association's Miami Heat and their spanking-new home in Miami Arena. Along came Major League Baseball's Florida Marlins in the spring of 1993, and later that fall the National Hockey League's Florida Panthers took to the ice.

Add to these high-profile teams a handful of professional golf and tennis events, beach volleyball and the world's best in more obscure sports such as polo and croquet. There's also outstanding college sports competition, from the University of Miami — whose Hurricanes football team is always in the hunt for an NCAA title — to Lynn University of Boca Raton, whose Knights men's and women's soccer teams are consistently among the top teams in the National Association for Intercollegiate Athletics (NAIA).

Put it all together, and South Florida is arguably one of the best all-around spectator sports areas in the country. So pull on your sneakers and a comfortable shirt and shorts and let's get busy.

While some of these venues are not in the immediate Palm Beach County area, the action you'll see is certainly worth the drive out of town.

Football

National Football League

MIAMI DOLPHINS
Joe Robbie Stadium
2269 N.W. 199th St.
Miami   (305) 452-7000

In 1965, a Minnesota lawyer named Joe Robbie and his partner, entertainer Danny Thomas, anted up $7.5 million for an American Football League franchise that would play its games in Miami's Orange Bowl. With its first draft picks, the team chose Kentucky quarterback Rick Norton and Illinois running back Jim Grabowski. Early in 1966, the Dolphins selected George Wilson as their first head coach; in August of that year, the franchise opened its first training camp at St. Petersburg Beach. A month later, the Dolphins moved camp to St. Andrews School in Boca Raton.

Like most expansion teams, the Dolphins struggled the first few years, but the arrival of Don Shula in 1970 signaled the beginning of an era of increasing success. The Shula-led Dolphins reached the playoffs for the first time that year, and in 1971 the Dolphins advanced to their first Super Bowl, where they fell 24-3 to the Dallas Cowboys.

In 1972, the Dolphins were back at the Super Bowl, capping an undefeated year with a 14-7 victory over the Washington Redskins. To this day, the Dolphins are the only team in NFL history that can claim a perfect season. Just for good measure, the Dolphins also won the Super Bowl in 1973, topping the Minnesota Vikings 24-7.

The Dolphins have made it to the Super Bowl two other times, losing 27-17 to the Redskins in 1983 and falling 38-16 to the San Francisco 49ers in 1985.

Now, every game the Dolphins win drives Shula's record as the NFL's winningest coach a bit higher. Five Dolphins have been elected to pro football's Hall of Fame: quarterback Bob Griese, whose No. 12 jersey is the only number retired by the team; guard Larry Little, a Miami native; center Jim Langer; wide receiver Paul Warfield; and fullback Larry Csonka.

Hard-core Dolphins fans love their team but aren't quite as vehement in showing it as, say, Redskins, Bears or 49ers fans. Still, their love for the aqua and orange runs deep if quietly. With marquee quarterback Dan Marino recovered from some career-threatening injuries, the Dolphins' future again seems bright.

Dolphins tickets are $33 to $40 per game.

Parking at the stadium for Dolphins games is expensive ($15) and scarce. A few private lots nearby offer parking, but wear your hiking shoes if you plan to exercise (literally) this option. One viable alternative is Tri-Rail. An $8 ticket permits you to depart from Tri-Rail stops in West Palm Beach, Lake Worth, Boynton Beach, Boca Raton, Deerfield Beach, Pompano Beach and Fort Lauderdale and travel to the Golden Gables station. From there, board a shuttle bus to Joe Robbie Stadium (call it JRS — everybody else does). The ticket also includes shuttle bus service back to the station and the Tri-Rail ride back to your original departure point.

Call (800) TRI-RAIL for more information.

The Dolphins' practice facility is in Davie, at 7500 SW 30th Court, on the western edge of Nova Southeastern University. Spectators are welcome to watch the team practice, but call ahead at (305) 452-7000 to find out the practice schedule for the day.

Arena Football League

MIAMI HOOTERS

Miami Arena
721 N.W. First Ave.
Miami   (800) 289-4587

For folks who can't get enough gridiron gratification, there are the Hooters, Miami's entry in the Arena Football League (that's indoor football, for all you folks who don't speak sports). Catch this ear-splitting, rock 'n' roll, razzle-dazzle version of the game at the 15,008-seat Miami Arena. Actually, arena football is a lot of fun; there's never

Photo: Michelle Lord

Florida Atlantic University athlete Amy Stokes awaits some action at first base.

a dull moment on the field. Purists may grumble at the kickoff screens, the smaller field and other modifications, but the supercharged atmosphere should win them over.

The season runs May through August. Tickets cost $7.50 to $50.

Baseball

Major League Baseball

FLORIDA MARLINS

Joe Robbie Stadium
2269 N.W. 199th St.
Miami   *(305) 626-7400*

April 5, 1993, is a day that will live forever in South Florida baseball fans' minds. On that sunny afternoon, Charlie Hough threw a knuckleball past the Los Angeles Dodgers' leadoff hitter and officially made South Florida a major-league baseball community.

The Marlins are building their team behind stalwart younger players. Even if Team Teal doesn't reach the playoffs for a while — a common dilemma for new franchises — fans appreciate the team's commitment to building a top-notch club.

To make Joe Robbie Stadium more family-friendly, owner Wayne Huizenga's crew added an interactive games area and other innovations to make a day at the ballpark attractive to more than just dyed-in-the-wool fans. Since the arrival of Huizenga, the stadium has taken on a more festive air, with ethnic food and specialty beverage stands, an adventure playground for the kids, and baseball skills and video games for the young and the young at heart.

The 1995 season marked the opening of JRS Sports Town, a 40,000-square-foot tent located at Gate G in the parking lot. It features 10 interactive games such as 50-yard quarterback challenge, Dolphins Sumo Wrestling, Panthers Slap Shot, Marlins Speed

Pitch and the ever-popular Pop-A-Shot. There are also plenty of concessions stands, two bars and live music. JRS Sports Town is open before Marlins and Dolphins games.

Parking is abundantly available at Joe Robbie Stadium and costs $5. Marlins tickets cost $4 to $30.

Spring Training

It appears Palm Beach County will remain the spring training home of the Atlanta Braves and the Montreal Expos, and as soon as their new training headquarters in Jupiter are complete, they'll leave their old home at West Palm Beach's Municipal Stadium for their new digs. Expos officials say that move is at least two years away, and the team's single-A farm team also will move to Jupiter.

For information on the Braves, call 683-6100. For Expos information, call 684-6801.

Other major league teams training in southeastern Florida include the New York Mets, Los Angeles Dodgers and Florida Marlins. The Boston Red Sox are contemplating a spring move to Fort Lauderdale, replacing the New York Yankees, who had trained there for many years.

The New York Mets and their single-A farm team, the St. Lucie Mets, play at Thomas J. White Stadium, 525 N.W. Peacock Boulevard, Port St. Lucie, 871-2100.

The Los Angeles Dodgers and their Florida State League squad,

the Vero Beach Dodgers, play at Dodgertown, 4001 26th Street, Vero Beach, 569-4900.

The Florida Marlins and the single-A Brevard County Manatees' spring training home is the Carl Barger Training Complex and Space Coast Stadium, 5800 Stadium Drive, Melbourne, 633-9200. The Marlins' single-A team, the Manatees, also play home games at Space Coast Stadium.

Basketball

National Basketball Association

MIAMI HEAT

Miami Arena
721 N.W. First Ave.
Miami (305) 577-4328

Standout center Rony Seikaly is gone, but the Heat is still getting better by degrees, so to speak. Ownership concerns that once affected the team have abated, and the fan base remains steady and the team remains popular. You can tell who's hot in Miami by who's getting the court-side seats, from golfer Ray Floyd to 2 Live Crew rapper Luther Campbell.

The NBA's regular season runs from November to April, with playoffs following. Tickets are $10.50 to $30, and parking near the Arena is scarce and expensive. A good alternative is taking one of the park-and-ride services to the game. There's a Metrorail station across the street from the Arena entrance.

Charlie Hustle

(By Vin Mannix)

Has it been almost 10 years since Pete Rose broke Ty Cobb's Major League career hit record? And eight years since he played in his last Major League game?

It seems like last week that the crewcutted Rose mowed down catcher Ray Fosse for the winning run in the 1970 All-Star game.

Where has time flown on 54-year-old Pete Rose?

"Let me tell you something," said the guy who was known as "Charlie Hustle," as air time drew near for his radio show from the Pete Rose Ballpark Cafe. "I've got kids who work here, they come up to me and say, 'Wow, [are] those records all yours? You did all that stuff. I didn't know that.'

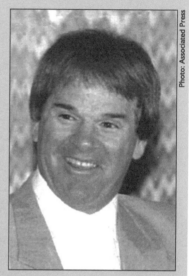

Pete Rose

They look at me like I'm dead. Then I've got my customers, kids 12, 13, 14 and up. They think I'm Pete Rose hit king. Kids younger than that think I'm Pete Rose the man with all the video games."

Rose chuckled in his radio booth, overlooking the happy-hour crowd at his club that opened in west Boca Raton in December 1992. He's at the restaurant everyday, mixing with his patrons when he's not doing his radio show Monday through Friday on the Florida Sportsfan Network. Located on Glades Road just west of Florida's Turnpike, the Pete Rose Ballpark Cafe is a spacious 12,000 square feet, with seating for 500, two bars, 65 television sets and 66 video games.

"As long as you're known for something. . . ," said Rose, who has lived in Boca Raton for five years with his wife, Carol; son, Tyler, 10; and daughter, Cara, 5. "Maybe when they get older, they'll catch on to who I was."

Although banned from baseball in 1989 for gambling, and having served an 18-month prison stretch in 1990-91 for income tax evasion, Rose is biding his time to apply for reinstatement to the game, then winning a place in the Hall of Fame.

"Baseball has to get its house in order first, but I can wait. I have to believe that every day that goes by in my life is another day in the plus column. I was told I had to reconfigure my life, and I did. No more gambling, no more hanging with undesirables. I'm a good man, a good husband, a good businessman. I do positive things in the community."

Rose is involved extensively with charity work for Cystic Fibrosis and the American Cancer Society in South County. He also is known to drop in at former Yankee Bucky Dent's Baseball School and give impromptu help to campers.

"There are other people who have been given two, three, four chances and more in baseball," he said. "Why not Pete Rose?"

Good question. Decorating the foyer of the restaurant is an impressive array of awards — World Series rings, MVP trophies, Gold Gloves, to name a few — that give ample testimony of his achievement. But what truly sets him apart from today's players are the records that he holds as the all-time Major League or National League leader in 19 categories.

Did you know that over the course of 24 years in "the bigs" — 18 with Cincinnati, five with Philadelphia, one with Montreal — Rose played at least 500 games apiece at first base, second, third, left field and right field? That is only one mark of his durability and consistency, as well as his renowned competitive drive. Among the other records:

- Most career hits: 4,256
- Most games played: 3,562
- Most seasons of 200 or more hits: 10
- Most seasons with 150 or more games: 17
- Most years played (National League): 24
- Most career runs (NL): 2,165
- Longest consecutive game hitting streak (NL modern): 44.

The record of which Rose is proudest?

"I played in more winning games than anybody else in the history of baseball — 1,972. That's gotta qualify me as the biggest winner in this country. Baseball players play more games than any other sport. I always tried to do three things: hit, score runs and win games. It's very important to win."

Yet, it was a loss that stands out as Rose's favorite World Series memory. It was Game 6 of the 1975 World Series, the 7-6 thriller won by the Red Sox on catcher Carlton Fisk's dramatic leadoff homer in the bottom of the 12th inning.

"I came up to bat in the top of the 11th and told Fisk that win or lose, this game had to be the greatest game ever," Rose recalled. "Well, the SOB had so much fun, he ended it next inning."

Of course, the Reds came back to win Game 7 and the World Series.

Photo: Palm Beach County Convention and Visitors Bureau

Spectators enjoy polo action from December through April.

Continental Basketball League

FLORIDA BEACHDOGS

West Palm Beach Auditorium
1610 Palm Beach Lakes Blvd.
West Palm Beach 683-6012

Beginning in November 1995, the Florida Beachdogs hope to make the West Palm Beach Auditorium feel like one big doghouse to visiting teams. The Beachdogs are the former Rapid City (S.D.) Thrillers, one of the league's most successful franchises, that had announced their intention to move to West Palm Beach on July 18, 1995.

The team will play 28 home games on its 56-game schedule at the 5,500-seat auditorium. Call for ticket or other information.

Hockey

National Hockey League

FLORIDA PANTHERS

Miami Arena
721 N.W. First Ave.
Miami (800) GO PANTH

When the temperature's 85 and the beach is inviting, hockey might seem like a tough sell. But it's not.

The Florida Panthers made a splashy National Hockey League debut in 1993 and quickly became the darlings of the South Florida sports scene. It didn't hurt either that the team set the points record for first-year expansion teams and missed the playoffs by a single point in a stretch race.

Be sure to bring a sweater to the Arena; even though the action on the ice is sizzling, the temperature can be a little on the chilly side. Game tickets range from $8 to $100.

Sunshine Hockey League

WEST PALM BEACH BLAZE
West Palm Beach Auditorium
1610 Palm Beach Lakes Blvd.
West Palm Beach   *640-9544*

The Blaze is the southernmost team in the Sunshine Hockey League and has formed a winning tradition during its tenure in West Palm Beach. The crowds at the 5,500-seat arena are loud, appreciative and knowledgeable.

The Blaze's season runs from November to March. Tickets are $6.50 to $12.50.

Parimutuels

Harness Racing

POMPANO HARNESS TRACK
1800 S.W. Third St.
Pompano Beach   *(305) 972-2000*

Pompano Harness Track, built in 1964, has hosted more Breeders Crown races than any other harness track in the United States.

The track is open every month but September and schedules a racing card for Mondays, Wednesdays, Fridays and Saturdays, although days and hours may vary. Call in advance for details.

Grandstand admission is $1; clubhouse admission is $2.

Jai-Alai

DANIA JAI-ALAI
310 E. Dania Beach Blvd.
Dania   *(305) 920-1511*

The sport of the Basques is popular among bettors in South Florida. Jai-Alai is akin to handball, but competitors throw rock-hard balls — called *pelotas* — adding speed and spin with a *cesta* — a long, hand-woven basket strapped to the throwing hand.

Post times are 7:15 PM Tuesday, Thursday, Friday and Saturday, with matinees on Tuesday, Thursday and Saturday at noon and on Sunday at 1 PM. General admission is $1; seating is $1.50. After 7 PM, parking is 75¢.

Greyhound Racing

PALM BEACH KENNEL CLUB
Belvedere Rd. at Congress Ave.
West Palm Beach   *(407) 683-2222*

If you decide to enjoy a day of greyhound racing, don't blink at the start of the race or you'll miss it. These canines are incredible athletes.

Matinees are Monday, Wednesday, Thursday and Saturday at 12:30 PM and Sunday at 1 PM. Evening sessions are Wednesday and Saturday at 7:30 PM.

General admission is 50¢; terrace seating is $1.

Insiders' Tips

Pack a tailgate picnic and watch Sunday polo matches at the Royal Palm Polo Sports Club from January through April.

Photo: Florida Atlantic University Relations

An NCAA Division I school, Florida Atlantic University fields teams in nine sports. The women's basketball team is especially strong.

Thoroughbred Racing

GULFSTREAM PARK
901 S. Federal Hwy.
Hallandale (305) 454-7000

Gulfstream Park, which last played host to the Breeders' Cup in 1992, is the world's winter home of horse racing. The run for the orchids — The Florida Derby — held in April, is the track's annual showcase event. Other high-profile races include the Donn Handicap and the Pan-American Handicap.

The track is open January through April and races are run every day but Tuesday. Post time is 1 PM.

Grandstand admission is $3; clubhouse is $5. Admission prices include parking and a program.

Golf

While we've listed only professional tour events in this chapter, see our separate Golf chapter for information about some of South Florida's most prominent pay-to-play courses, including some of those listed here.

PGA Tour Events

ROYAL CARIBBEAN CLASSIC
The Links of Key Biscayne
6700 Crandon Blvd.
Key Biscayne (305) 365-0365

This is one of two PGA Seniors events in South Florida and is held in late January to early February. The Links is a county-owned course on lovely Key Biscayne, which also is the site of the Crandon Park beaches. The atmosphere here is casual and cordial; the pros often talk with members of the gallery after they've completed their rounds.

DORAL-RYDER OPEN
Doral Country Club
4400 N.W. 87th Ave.
Miami (305) 477-4653

Doral is an oasis in the industrial sprawl of western Miami. Its famed Blue Monster course turns treacherous when the wind kicks up. The PGA's annual Doral-Ryder Open is held in late February to early March, and its past winners represent many of golf's greatest names.

THE HONDA CLASSIC
Heron Bay Country Club
(No address at publication time.)
Coral Springs (305) 346-4000

The PGA's Honda Classic plans to return to a new Coral Springs home in 1996 after a stint at Weston Hills in western Broward County. Before then, the tournament had been played at Coral Springs's Tournament Players Club. Construction of Heron Bay, which will sprawl across northern Coral Springs and the neighboring community of Parkland, may be completed in time for the March 1996 event.

Insiders' Tips

Arrive early, especially on holiday weekends, if you plan to picnic at any of Boca Raton's beach barbecue spots.

Photo: Palm Beach County Convention and Visitors Bureau

Pick your favorite greyhound at the Palm Beach Kennel Club.

The annual tournament is held in early to mid-March. Weekly passes are your only option and cost $30 each.

PGA SENIORS CHAMPIONSHIP
PGA National Golf Club
1000 Avenue of Champions
Palm Beach Gardens   *622-4653*

The Champions Course at PGA National provides a fitting test for the golfers, and fans provide appreciative galleries for some of golf's greatest legends. The tournament is played in mid-April.

Tennis

Pro Tour Events

DELRAY BEACH WINTER CHAMPIONSHIPS
Delray Beach Tennis Center
201 Atlantic Ave.
Delray Beach   *(305) 491-7115*

After a childhood in Key Biscayne and adolescence at The Polo Club in Boca Raton, the fully mature Delray Beach Winter Championships, formerly known as the Virginia Slims of Florida, has settled in at the reconstructed Delray Beach Tennis Center, where tennis fans greet the late February/early March event with warmth and enthusiasm. And why not? Many of the pros have competed in this area as juniors, and a few live nearby. Famous competitors include Gabriella Sabatini, Aranxta Sanchez and Steffi Graf, who has a home at the aforementioned Polo Club.

The players love it because they can thaw out, play for a very attractive purse and get ready for the Lipton International Players Championships in front of appreciative fans.

LIPTON INTERNATIONAL TENNIS CHAMPIONSHIPS

International Tennis Center
7300 Crandon Blvd.
Key Biscayne   (305) 446-2200

Designed originally as a "Wintertime Wimbledon," the Lipton has found a more spring-like home on the calendar in mid-March, and, after stops in Delray Beach and Boca Raton, it also has found a permanent home at the Metro Dade County-owned tennis center on Key Biscayne. The Lipton brings together the top male and female players such as Andre Agassi, Boris Becker, Mary Jo Fernandez and Steffi Graf for a sizzling event that seems to break attendance records yearly.

Polo

Major Tournament Venues

ROYAL PALM POLO SPORTS CLUB

6300 Old Clint Moore Rd.
Boca Raton   994-1876

Come winter, many of the world's notable polo players come to South Florida for its temperate climate, great training and playing facilities and fat prize purses.

Royal Palm Polo operates its Hartman League for medium- and low-goal players and the high-goal Sunshine League in January and February. After league play concludes, the big-money tournaments begin, high-

lighted by the $100,000 International Gold Cup in March.

You'll see spectators of all shapes, sizes and sorts at the Sunday afternoon matches: Oklahoma cowboys with crust on their boots sucking down beers and watching the action, young families clad in Duck Heads and Dockers swigging Vichy, and society dowagers sipping champagne make for a curious collaboration of onlookers. The play is superb, the atmosphere is casual, and everyone has fun.

General admission is $6; box seats are $15.

PALM BEACH POLO AND COUNTRY CLUB

13198 Forest Hill Blvd.   (407) 793-1440
West Palm Beach   (800) 327-4204

Prince Charles has played here. So has Sylvester Stallone. So, too, have most of the world's 10-goal players, the highest achievement in polo.

Not simply content with offering just great polo, Palm Beach Polo provides great — and varied — game-day entertainment of other sorts, with concerts, exhibitions and other special events. Almost as much fun is peoplewatching (Is that the Maharajah of Jaipur? And over there, Ivana Trump?) and here, tailgating is elevated to an art form. It's a great Sunday afternoon of fun.

Insiders' Tips

Boca Raton's parks offer great recreational opportunities — playgrounds, ballfields, basketball and tennis courts and children's classes — at little or no cost.

Chris Evert
(By Lisa Goddard)

Chris Evert is known the world over as one of the greatest tennis players in the history of the game. Recently inducted by unanimous vote to the International Tennis Hall of Fame, the 40-year-old retired champion calls Boca Raton home much of the year. When not on the road working as an NBC broadcaster or playing in a tennis exhibition, Evert, her husband, former Olympic skier Andy Mill, and their two young sons, Alexander and Nicholas, divide their time between homes at the Polo Club Boca Raton and in Aspen, Colorado. A native of Fort Lauderdale, Evert won three high school individual state titles at St. Thomas Aquinas High School and catapulted into the national spotlight in 1970 when, at age 15, she beat the then-No. 1 player in the world, Margaret Court, in an exhibition match. The next year, Evert made it to the semifinals of her first U.S. Open, and the following year she reached the semifinals of her first Wimbledon. In 1974 she became the youngest person to rank No. 1 since Maureen Connolly Brinker in 1953 and also garnered a 55-match win streak. Over the next 18 years, Evert — "Chrissie" to millions of fans — won 157 singles titles, among them 18 Grand Slams that included seven French Opens, three Wimbledons, six U.S. Opens and two Australian Opens. Evert retired after losing in the quarterfinals to Zina Garrison in the U.S. Open in 1989 and began providing tennis commentary for NBC the next year. For the past five years, Evert has hosted the Chris Evert/Ellesse Pro-Celebrity Tennis Classic at the Boca Raton Resort and Club to benefit the fight against drug abuse and child neglect in South Florida.

Photo: Michelle Lord

Chris Evert plays in the 1994 Chris Evert/Ellesse Pro-Celebrity Classic Tournament. Evert owns a home in Boca Raton.

Play begins right after Christmas and runs through April. Highlights of the season include the United States Polo Association's Rolex Gold Cup and the $100,000 World Cup.

General admission is $6.

College Sports

UNIVERSITY OF MIAMI
#1 Hurricane Dr.
Coral Gables   *(800) GO CANES*

It seems that each year at season's end the Hurricanes are vying for the final No. 1 football ranking. But don't think of 'Canes sports as one-dimensional: UM's athletic program is a well-rounded winner. A slew of former Hurricane hardballers are in the major leagues, and the UM baseball squad always seems to be playing for a berth in the College World Series. The women's basketball team has comfortably become one of the better programs in the Big East conference. And other sports, such as tennis, golf, swimming and crew, are traditionally strong at the University of Miami.

Call the UM athletic ticket office toll-free for information and schedules.

FLORIDA ATLANTIC UNIVERSITY
Glades Rd. at I-95
Boca Raton   *367-3710*

Like the University of Miami, FAU is a NCAA Division I school; unlike the 'Canes, FAU does not field a football team. The school does, however, have a vigorous athletic program offering 15 intercollegiate sports and is a member of the Trans America Athletic Conference.

The blue and gray Owls compete in men's baseball, women's softball and volleyball, and men's and women's swimming, tennis, golf, basketball, soccer and cross-country.

LYNN UNIVERSITY
Military Tr. at Potomac Rd.
Boca Raton   *994-0770*

Lynn University, affiliated with the NAIA and NCAA Division II , offers a well-rounded program, but is best known for the strength of its men's and women's soccer teams, which are annual staples at the NAIA national championships. In 1993, for example, the soccer Knights had a stretch of 965 minutes (nearly 11 games!) in which the men's team was not scored upon.

National titles earned by Lynn in 1995 include NAIA National Championships in women's golf and women's tennis (its second). Other recent titles include individual tennis titles in 1992, an individual women's golf title in 1993, and an individual men's golf title in 1994.

Photo: Palm Beach County Convention and Visitors Bureau

Palm Beach County's beaches offer a serene destination for respite and reflection.

DON'T BLINK

FLORIDA PANTHERS

FOR TICKETS CALL
1-800-GO PANTH

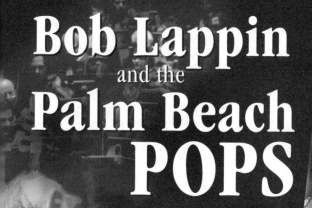

Inside
Arts and Culture

The visual and performing arts form connective tissue in Palm Beach County, a melting-pot of cultural heritages, ethnic diversity, musical tastes, arts education and audience experience.

We match and rival the most sophisticated international capitals when it comes to world-class names on the marquee and top-flight excellence on stage. We pride ourselves also on emerging cultural offerings developed from loyal community support and plenty of homegrown talent that also turns heads in faraway places.

Here, we buy culture, nurture it, fight over it and for it — whether the genre is professional, community, collegiate, student or showcase level. Competition among the players was hot even before two new major venues began presenting world-class talent and entertainment on their own stages. The Raymond F. Kravis Center for the Performing Arts in West Palm Beach imploded the playing field in November 1992, just a year after Fort Lauderdale audiences welcomed the Broward Center for the Performing Arts. Major arts companies rotate productions on both stages. Look for details on various venues at the end of this section.

Kravis Center for the Performing Arts

As Kravis Center readied its inaugural season, *South Florida Business Journal* dubbed it "The Best Special Use/Public Deal of the Year" in the annual real estate contest cosponsored by Ernst & Young. The fact that a $55 million performing arts center opened virtually debt-free tells a lot about our public and private commitment to the arts: Private gifts totalled more than $40 million, including donations from corporations, businesses, foundations and individuals. The state, the county and the city of West Palm Beach made up the difference.

Dominating the million-dollar club of private donors is the late Raymond F. Kravis, an oilman from Oklahoma and longtime winter resident of Palm Beach whose friends kicked in another $6 million in his honor. The geologist died a year after Kravis Center opened.

Another big name is Alex Dreyfoos, owner of WPEC-TV Channel 12 and Photo Electronics Co., both in West Palm Beach. An inventor and congenial optimist who relocated his company here in the 1970s, Dreyfoos found it frustrating to lose top executives unwilling to move to a "cultural wasteland." Convinced the area's eco-

The Crest Theater at Old School Square in Delray Beach was the theater for Delray High School.

nomic future depended on balancing a vibrant business climate with an attractive quality of life in order to lure corporate execs here, he spearheaded the Palm Beach Council of the Arts in 1978, developing and promoting the arts countywide. Dreyfoos and those who joined his cause spent 14 years propelling people and events toward a world-class facility of multipurpose venues for presenting any show the planet could unearth.

On opening night, November 28, 1992, the pinch-me show afforded a glimpse of the great names and faces Kravis Center patrons can expect for years to come: emcee Burt Reynolds, the Florida Philharmonic Orchestra, opera divas Roberta Peters and Leontyne Price, violinist Isaac Stern, Broadway star Faith Prince, comedienne Lily Tomlin, singing legend Ella Fitzgerald and The Alvin Ailey American Dance Theater.

Drama at Every Turn

Toronto architect Eberhard H. Zeidler created the Kravis Center to raise eyebrows. The formidable Modernist structure draws on European influences to anchor the raft of competing styles imposed on Florida's face in the past century. Copper roofing crowns a tiered rotunda topping the multilevel windowed walls of the lobby and the audience chamber. Twin 35-foot metal finials punctuate corners of the stage tower — the whole perched on the highest ground in West Palm Beach. Robert Metzger Interiors of New York collaborated with the designer for an interior Moderne motif dominated by rose, green, gold and beige.

The Alexander W. Dreyfoos Jr. Hall, with 2,189 seats and three balcony levels, proves the finer points of fine arts theater design, achieving intimacy and a proximity to performers

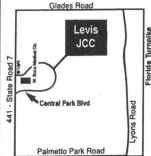

Where to find hundreds of bargains is classified information.

Read our classified columns for an exclusive and endless variety of the best buys in town. To name a few, you'll find everything from cars, homes and bicycles to jobs, cameras, handymen, lawyers and garage sales. What's more, in many cases, you can even negotiate with the seller for an even better price. In short, if it's worth looking for, look for it in The News first.

Call (407) 368-9400.

BOCA RATON
THE NEWS

The Boca News.
Always a local point of view.

astounding for an area of 90,000 square feet. Only 100 feet separate the farthest point from Florida's largest stage, which measures 150-by-65 feet with 100 feet of fly-in space. A palette of claret accented with gold is pure theater below the hall's engulfing chandelier and ceiling mural of pretend-night-sky.

The Marshall E. Rinker Sr. Playhouse is a 300-seat "black box" theater, rehearsal hall and performance facility for small productions and arts education programs. Adjacent is the Eunice and Julian Cohen Pavilion, an 11,000-square-foot hospitality hall with banquet and catering facilities. Outdoors is the Michael and Andrew Gosman Amphitheatre with seating for 2,300.

Developers Henry Rolfs and David Paladino donated the 5.4-acre site for Kravis Center. The city of West Palm Beach owns and operates the five-level, 1,100-car parking garage on its west flank. In addition, valet parking for performances costs $8 and involves only a moderate wait.

Palm Beach County Cultural Council

The umbrella organization Dreyfoos founded was forerunner for the Palm Beach County Cultural Council, which advises the county commission on cultural development and has a contract to administer some of its tourist development funds. Offices are at 1555 Palm Beach Lakes Boulevard, Suite 900, West Palm Beach. For information, call 471-2901 or 930-2787.

If you arrive at Palm Beach International Airport, you'll see the Council's presence in more than 50 permanent works of art and rotating exhibits of individual artists. The Council stages dozens of music and dance performances at a special stage in the airport and manages a cultural information kiosk near the baggage claim area.

The nonprofit agency draws support from the Florida Division of Cultural Affairs, the National Endowment for the Arts (NEA), the John D. and Catherine T. MacArthur Foundation, numerous corporations and private individuals. The largest private local cultural agency in Florida, the Council has a $1.3 million budget and allocates more than $2 million a year in cultural grants throughout the county. Its 2,000 members include individuals, artists, cultural organizations, foundations and businesses.

President/CEO Will Ray took charge in 1982, shortly before the campaign supporting a local option tax — or "bed-tax" — on hotel, motel and short-term apartment rentals to provide revenue for grants to local cultural groups. By 1991, when the Council estimated the annual impact of cultural events at $70 million, the NEA and the MacArthur Foundation agreed to pay for a long-range cultural plan for Palm Beach County, which the county's board of commissioners included in its comprehensive plan.

Based on studies of cultural facilities — current and proposed — audience surveys and focus groups, Palm Beach County claimed the title

"Florida's Cultural Capital." Ray says the designation also reflects the volume of money the county attracts from corporations, individuals and government agencies.

Humor Saved the Day

"In these studies, we found that [Palm Beach County] met the qualifications to be a true cultural center in four cases out of five," Ray said. "We have a major performing arts center, a major collecting and exhibiting museum, a rapidly improving zoo, a science museum, historical museums, a regional symphony, a regional ballet company, as well as outstanding programs of classical music and dance at Kravis Center and Florida Atlantic University. We had the 'infrastructure' — the means to satisfy once visitors are here — but we lacked one element, a stand-alone attraction that is one-of-a-kind . . . unique enough to compel people to travel here."

Boca Raton provided the missing link: The International Museum of Cartoon Art is under way at Mizner Park. The museum will be the only one of its kind in the world dedicated to collecting, preserving, exhibiting and interpreting all genres of cartoon art. For details on this museum, see the Museums and Galleries section of this chapter.

Other new attractions that cement our claim as "Florida's Cultural Capital" include the Palm Beach International Film Festival and the recently expanded annual BookFest at Old School Square in Delray Beach. The following is a taste of what you can expect on stage in the next several months.

Cultural and Performing Arts Organizations

BALLET FLORIDA
500 Fern St.
West Palm Beach   Box Office: 659-2000

Palm Beach County is justifiably proud of its own professional regional ballet company, with artistic director Marie Hale. The company performs at Kravis Center and at the Eissey Theatre of Palm Beach Community College in Palm Beach Gardens.

Starry Night, choreographed by William Soleau, is the 1995 season opener. Hale's rendition of *The Nutcracker* runs in December. Ballet Florida presents its *10th Anniversary Gala* in February, with choreography by Michael Smuin, Lar Lubovitch and William Soleau. Performances are at 8 PM on Fridays and 2 PM and 8 PM on Saturdays.

Subscriptions are available from $40 to $318. For ticket information, call 659-1212 or (800) 540-0172.

BOCA BALLET THEATRE COMPANY
131-B S.E. Mizner Blvd.
Boca Raton   395-6167

Co-artistic directors Dan Guin and Jane Tyree are husband-and-wife dance partners who manage this not-for-profit civic dance organization founded in 1990. The emerging Company promotes collaboration among professionals, pre-professionals and student dancers through three productions a year — two full-length ballets and a mixed-repertoire. Well-known are its Thanksgiving weekend productions of the holiday dance classic *The Nutcracker,* a collaboration with Southern Dance Theatre of Orlando. Historically, the Company performs at Olympic Heights Performing Arts Center and in outdoor community concerts at the Mizner Park Amphitheater; 1995 marked its debut at the Griswold Theatre at Florida Atlantic University. The Company's repertoire includes *Romeo and Juliet, Les Sylphides* and *Coppelia,* and 1995's summer production of *Giselle.* Two premieres you'll undoubtedly see again in mixed-rep include *Just Swinging,* an upbeat new work inspired by the music of Benny Goodman, with choreography by Dan Guin. *Gaugy Concerto,* choreographed by national dancer Christopher Fleming to music composed by Dr. David Goldstein of Tampa, illustrates the power of suggestion from the painting "Pas de Deux." French-born artist Jean-Claude Gaugy, whose gallery is in Royal Palm Plaza, gave the Company its program signature and the inspiration for *Gaugy Concerto.*

The organization's volunteer board is relatively young. Most officers and directors are working professionals and business owners. Some are parents of aspiring dancers; others are dance lovers.

The School of Boca Ballet Theatre celebrated its second anniversary in September as the area's only non-profit dance training studio open to the public. Tyree and Guin teach a development system necessary for classical ballet and concert dance, with instruction in ballet technique, pointe, variations, boys' class, jazz technique and partnering. Pre-ballet and adult classes are also offered. Income from the School supports its operations and Company programs. Ballet program prices vary by production, from $12 to $20.

CALDWELL THEATRE COMPANY
7873 N. Federal Hwy., Levitz Plaza
Boca Raton   Box Office: 241-7432, 930-6400

Born in Boca Raton in 1975 and raised from infancy by local diehard theater fanatics, this professional equity regional theater is bulging with patrons clambering for more space. Performances are usually sold out, and there's a waiting list for tickets. Supporters have raised almost $3 million of the $7 million needed to build a Caldwell Theatre Center with a second 450-seat stage on a parcel adjacent to its parking lot. The theater offers a handful of dynamic drama and comedy productions each winter, plus a Theatre in the Schools Program, a summer series and special productions each spring during the annual Mizner Festival.

Artistic director Michael Hall peruses current on- and off-Broadway releases, occasionally wedging a new work into the schedule. Subscriptions are $100 for four winter programs. Individual tickets are $35 for opening night, $28 for regular performances and $25 for previews. Group discounts are offered and student "rush" tickets, when available, are $5. Tickets go fast, and seating is limited to 305.

Caldwell's summer trio included the Florida debut of *You Should Be So Lucky*. Carbonell Award-winning actress-singer Avery Sommers returned in her one-woman musical *But Not For Me* in the fall of 1995.

The 1995-'96 season opened in October with an Arthur Miller adaptation of Henrik Ibsen's drama *An Enemy of the People*. Plans for other shows include the musical *Hustlin' After Dark*, a '70s magazine of entertainment, and the drama *The Country Girl* by Clifford Odets.

DUNCAN THEATRE
Palm Beach Community College
4200 Congress Ave.
Lake Worth   Box Office: 439-8141

From international ballet to an evening of Shakespeare, contemporary music and a chamber series, Duncan audiences expect and receive an adventure. The upcoming Professional Guest Artist Subscription Series opens in January 1996 with the world premiere of *Earth Studies*, a multi-disciplinary work choreographed by Demetrius Klein that tells tales through music, dance and song. The season continues with Mark Morris Dance Company, *Momix: BASEBALL,* Russia's St. Petersburg Ballet, *Jelly Roll! The Music and The Man* and the Pascal Rioult Dance Theater in the spring. The series concludes with a theatrical event to be announced. Individual tickets are $15 to $30. Subscriptions for the seven events are $97, $125 and $153. Concerts begin at 8 PM.

Duncan Theatre also gears a quartet of Friday night concerts especially for families.

The Chamber Music Series offers five events: St. Lawrence String Quartet, Virtuosi Wind Quintet, Prague Chamber Orchestra, Brno Chamber Orchestra and the Ying String Quartet. Individual tickets are $12 to $20; reserved series seats are $50. Concerts begin at 3 PM.

FLORIDA ATLANTIC UNIVERSITY
500 N.W. 20th St.
Boca Raton   Box Office: 367-3758

Take time to acquaint yourself with the Department of Music concerts in the FAU Theatre (a.k.a. Griswold Theatre), part of the new Dorothy F. Schmidt Center. Orchestral, band and choral performances are offered. Concert and festival times vary. Tickets are $5 through the box office or TicketMaster outlets.

Commercial programs through Concert Showcase Productions take place in the FAU Center Auditorium, off Glades Road and east of I-95. Performances are at 8 PM.

FLORIDA PHILHARMONIC ORCHESTRA
3401 N.W. Ninth Ave. Box office: (305) 561-2997
Fort Lauderdale   *(800) 226-1812*

The state's largest performing arts organization celebrated its 10th anniversary in September 1995, with Music Director James Judd conducting and guest artist James Galway on flute. The Philharmonic tailors programs for a Masterworks series, featuring world-renowned guest artists; the Prelude series of classical favorites and emerging artists; and Mostly Matinees, a narration format of symphonic repertoire introduced in 1994. Like many other symphony orchestras reaching for a broader audience

base, the Philharmonic relies on an alternative series, Peter Nero at the Pops, to shore up its $9 million budget.

The classical and pops series generate 150 concerts a year in seven South Florida venues, including Kravis Center, FAU Center and a chamber music series at the Eissey Campus Theatre. The organization operates with an umbrella board of governors representing markets in Palm Beach, Broward and Dade counties.

Judd will devote the 1995-96 season to A Celebration of Three Centuries, a programming theme that traces symphonic repertoire. Historical music selections from Purcell, Handel, Mozart, Verdi, Shostakovich, Prokofiev and Mahler will be featured.

Judd and the orchestra have two commercial CDs on the Harmonia Mundi label, a Walton program released in 1991 and 1994's *Mahler's Symphony No. 1*.

Nationally syndicated radio broadcasts of the *Alamo Classical Music Hour* include the orchestra's performances and, in April of 1995, the state-sponsored the Philharmonic's debut in "Performance Today" on National Public Radio. The orchestra and its 150-member Florida Philharmonic Chorus also appeared on public television during 1994, in holiday broadcasts of Handel's *Messiah*.

Following the 1995 season opener with James Galway, other programs in the Masterworks series include James Judd conducting, Pinchas Zucherman, violin; Theo Alcantara conducting, Andre-Michel Schub, pi-

ano; James Judd conducting, The Romero Family, guitar; James Judd conducting, Florida Philharmonic Chorus; Carl St. Clair conducting, Cho-Lang Lin, violin; James Judd conducting, Maria Joao Pires, piano. Subscriptions are $82 to $259. The Masterworks series plus the Galway concert cost $89 to $275. Concerts begin at 8 PM.

Concerts in the Prelude Series are at 8 PM, and subscriptions are $69 to $159. Concerts for Peter Nero and the Pops are at 8 PM with subscription from $75 to $189. Pops Matinee concerts are at 2 PM with subscription rates between $39 and $99. The noted performances are at FAU. For information on programs at other venues, call the box office, 930-1812.

FLORIDA SYMPHONIC POPS INC.
100 N.E. First Ave.
Boca Raton   *391-6777*

Founded in 1951 as a municipal band of 20 volunteers, the pops expanded into a professional 65-piece orchestra with seasonal performances at FAU Center Auditorium. The organization includes the Voices of the Pops, a professional chorale of 14 members. "Boca Pops" also plays for the city's annual Fourth of July concert and city-sponsored outdoor concerts at Mizner Park Amphitheater.

Several prospects auditioned in 1994 for the role of music director to replace retiring conductor Derek Stannard, whose last season is 1995.

Boca Pops' series includes eight concerts with the following guest artists or themes: Toni Tennille, Skitch Henderson, "A Beatles Evening," Pete

Photo:Michael Price

Henri Matisse's charcoal on paper creation "Girl at the Piano," 1925, is on display at the Boca Museum of Art.

Fountain, Burt Bacharach, Melissa Manchester, Byron Stripling and "The Best of Broadway."

All concerts begin at 8 PM on Wednesday and Thursday. Subscription tickets are available at the box office, 100 N.E. First Avenue. For individual tickets, call 367-3737.

KLEIN DANCE
3208 Second Ave. N., No. 10
Lake Worth   *964-9779*

Demetrius Klein touched down in Lake Worth in 1987, and the paw prints of the dance troupe he founded have stirred a pattern of happy feet ever since. *The Village Voice* calls thirtysomething Klein, "a sensual, miraculous dancer whose every move is fully wrought and interpreted, beautifully phrased, precisely weighted, brilliantly executed." Harvard Sum-

mer Dance Center knows where to find Klein, who also teaches at schools with lesser names. Jacob's Pillow Dance Festival welcomed Kleins in the summer of 1995, and New York grows impatient expecting him at least once a year.

Klein Dance performs a seasonal series of modern works, many in the experimental lane. The company of nine tours the rest of the year. It wound up the *Forgotten Spaces* community-based project in fall 1995 in Lincoln, Nebraska.

A creative post-modern choreographer nationally recognized for innovation, Klein segued from the delicate art of wrestling in high school to the Cincinnati Conservatory of Music. The forceful physicality of sports and the subtle grace of ballet bear his own stamp of cosmic inquiry, as students learn in the school he founded to instruct both professional dancers and beginners.

Klein Dance also stages productions for other performance artists. For the third consecutive year, Klein Dance received designation as an official Cultural Olympiad event through the Atlanta Committee for the Olympic Games' Regional Designation Awards in the Arts.

Through an endowment by the John D. and Catherine T. MacArthur Foundation, Klein Dance coordinated Soles Reaching Souls, a dance education initiative during the 1994-95 season with two other regional companies: Grupo Folklore Latino, a West Palm Beach company of student dancers that explores the diversity of Hispanic dance cultures; and Olufemi II Dance Theatre, a Riviera Beach-based African-American dance theater. With goals of promoting ethnic dance traditions and serving needs not met in public arts education, the three companies collaborated on dance classes and lecture demonstrations.

A MacArthur Foundation grant also enables Physical Prayer, a series of workshops on sensitive subjects, dealing with unexplored roles of the artist in society. Klein is collaborating on Physical Prayer with playwright John F.X. Warburton.

The Klein Dance Company Fall Concert is held in the Rinker Theatre at Kravis Center. The company also performs at Kravis Center. A holiday tradition, Klein Dance will perform *Messiah* at the Duncan Theatre in December. For exact dates and ticket information, please call 964-9779.

For information on Soles Reaching Souls, contact Klein Dance; Grupo Folklore Latino, 4907 Regina Court, West Palm Beach, 642-0834; or Olufemi II Dance Theatre, 1417 W. 10th Street, Riviera Beach, 848-7926.

LOIS POPE THEATRE COMPANY
262 S. Ocean Blvd.
Manalapan   585-3433

Another example of local philanthropy that generates public support, this professional theater receives funds from Palm Beach County, administered through the Cultural Council's Tourist Development Cultural Activities Grant program. The theater, which seats 250, also offers a 10-film movie series on Monday nights.

The season will open with *Not Waving*, a comedy by Gen LeRoy, then continues with *Below the Belt*, a comedy by Richard Dresser; a timeless Nuremberg trial drama by Romulus Linney; and *Bag Babies*, a social comedy by Allan Stratton.

Performances are at 8 PM Tuesday through Saturday and 7 PM on Sunday, and 2 PM matinees are held Wednesday and Sunday. Theater tickets are $21 to $25. Movies are $7 for evening shows and $5 for matinees. Call for information on subscription series prices.

MIAMI CITY BALLET
777 S. Flagler Dr.
West Palm Beach   *Box Office: 930-3262*

Known as "the Miami miracle" since it was conceived in a private dining room in Coral Gables, Miami City

Ballet is still relatively young for the national and international acclaim it garners. Entering its ninth season, the professional company derives its reputation from classical expressions of tradition and innovation. Ballet lovers will identify a distinct visual presence rooted in the legacy of George Balanchine, a unique footprint courtesy of Artistic Director Edward Villella.

The company's tri-county series of four major programs appears at Kravis Center, Broward Center, Bailey Concert Hall in Davie and Dade County Auditorium in Miami.

Audiences are dazzled whenever the company delivers sequences of the 20th-century Balanchine work *Jewels*. Program III in 1995, dubbed The Suzanne Farrell Festival, featured *Diamonds, Agon* and *Apollo*.

Miami City Ballet presented its 1995 season premiere in November featuring works by Balanchine, Turner and Jimmy Gamonet De Los Heros. The company's annual holiday performance of Balanchine's 19th-century *The Nutcracker* followed.

Also on the schedule are performances of *Bugaku, Purple Bend, Surfacing* and *Company B* as well as *Square Dance, Bach in Three Movements, Nous Sommes* and *The Four Temperaments*.

Concerts at Kravis Center begin at 8 PM on Friday, 2 PM and 8 PM on Saturday and 1 PM on Sunday. For information on programs at other venues, please call the box office at the previously listed number or (305) 532-7713.

OLD SCHOOL SQUARE CULTURAL ARTS CENTER

The Crest Theatre
51 N. Swinton Ave.
Delray Beach   Box Office: 243-3183

Once upon a time, Delray's 1896 one-room schoolhouse grew into a two-story elementary school. Built in 1913, it served as the stage for touring vaudeville troupes during the Roaring Twenties. Decades later, when the abandoned inner-city school was a whisker away from the wrecking ball, the nonprofit Old School Square Foundation took baby steps toward preserving the historic site and thrusting it center-stage once again. Today the rescued building complex is the cultural cornerstone of downtown Delray Beach, transformed into an award-winning theater, art museum and educational and performance venue.

Public funds helped save the once-doomed buildings, which now stand on the National Register of Historic Places. A model project credited with revitalizing the central business district, Old School Square received na-

Palm Beach County Cultural Council's ArtsLine gives updates on arts and attractions year round. To hear what's going on, call (800) 882-ARTS.

Insiders' Tips

tional recognition in November 1994 as one of three winners in the Culture Builds Communities competition of the International City/County Management Association. Private donations turned Old School Square into showcase facilities now coveted by numerous regional performing arts groups.

Formerly the 1925 high school auditorium, The Crest Theatre today seats 300 and functions as a professional-quality venue. Renovation achieved an expanded stage and realigned seats for better sight lines from the audience chamber. To honor Delray's Centennial, the 1995-96 season is devoted to Americana, featuring *Boomers*, a multimedia event celebrating the stars of the '50s and '60s; *Mark Twain On Stage*, starring John Chappell; *Zora Neale Hurston*, starring Phyllis McEwen; *Oh Henry!*, a tribute to the late composer Henry Mancini; *Quilters*, a musical about pioneer wives and daughters; and *Freddy Cole In Concert*.

Performances are at 2 PM and 8 PM. Individual tickets cost $20 for evening shows and $15 for matinees. Call the box office for subscription information. Please see the Museums and Galleries section in this chapter for happenings at Old School Square's Cornell Museum of Art and History.

PALM BEACH INVITATIONAL INTERNATIONAL PIANO COMPETITION
P.O. Box 3094
Palm Beach 33480   833-8817

This annual event will celebrate a decade of world-class ivory-tickling when the three-day Spring '96 com-

petition takes place (see our Festivals and Annual Events chapter). The 1995 event featured adjudicated performances by 16 pianists from 11 countries at the Flagler Museum in Palm Beach. Contestants hailed from Argentina, China, England, Israel, Italy, Korea, Latvia, the Republic of Georgia, Russia, Ukraine and the United States. Honorariums are generous: The winner earns $15,000, plus a recital at Lincoln Center in New York. Tickets are $20 for one performance and $5 for each additional performance. Piano Competition Guild members pay $15.

Several months prior to the competition, the Guild presents weekly Sunday Salon and Living Room Concerts at the Four Seasons Ocean Grand Hotel, 2800 S. Ocean Boulevard, Palm Beach. Sunday programs running through February begin at 4 PM, and tickets are $20. Call for more information.

PALM BEACH OPERA
415 S. Olive Ave.
West Palm Beach   Box Office: 833-7888

This professional opera company offers first-rate international favorites at Kravis Center, including democratic nods to French, German and Italian classics. Prices for the subscription series are $45 to $600; individual tickets are $18 to $110.

Operas include *Le Nozze Di Figaro* by Mozart, Verdi's *La Traviata* and *Turandot* by Puccini. Performances are at 8 PM Friday, 1:30 PM Saturday, 7 PM Sunday and 1:30 PM on Monday. For more information, please call.

Photo: Timothy Morrissey

Klein Dance has been an artistic innovator both here and on tour nationwide.

PALM BEACH POPS

231 Bradley Pl.   832-7677
Palm Beach   (800) 448-2472

This 65-member professional orchestra performs under the direction of founder and music director Bob Lappin. Emerging as a force to preserve the music of American composers, Lappin and the Pops perform at Kravis Center and Florida Atlantic University in Boca Raton. Also an accomplished pianist, Bob Lappin guest conducts other pops ensembles elsewhere in Florida and around the country.

In June 1994, the orchestra was invited to perform in New York City at Avery Fisher Hall in Lincoln Center. Also that summer, Lappin and the Pops performed at the Phipps estate on Long Island in a concert to benefit North Shore Hospital.

Founded in Palm Beach, the orchestra expanded its series to Boca Raton, where subscription sales have more than doubled since Lappin recruited Joseph Ferrer as vice president and general manager.

The 1995-96 subscription season includes a Tribute to Andrew Lloyd Webber and Other Broadway Composers in October at Kravis Center and at FAU with guest artists Bonnie Schon and David Chaney.

Look for Grammy Award-winning recording artist Maureen McGovern followed by Robert Klein, actor/comedian.

Listen to Vic Damone in March. Later, enjoy Lappin and his Jazz All-Stars' salute to Duke Ellington.

Palm Beach Pops subscription tickets are $102 to $450 at Kravis Center and $102 to $300 at FAU. You may order by mail, phone or FAX. Call the previously listed numbers or FAX orders to 832-9686.

REGIONAL ARTS FOUNDATION

P.O. Box 3444
West Palm Beach 33402   Box Office: 832-7469

A 21-year-old institution, the Foundation presents classical music series at the Kravis Center. Programming includes many of the leading symphonies, conductors and world-class virtuoso artists you would see lighting the neon in the most sophisticated cultural meccas. The Los Angeles, Royal and Israel philharmonics were some of the 1994 season's highlights. Call the box office for program and ticket information.

ROYAL PALM DINNER THEATRE

303 S.E. Mizner Blvd.
Royal Palm Plaza   392-3755
Boca Raton   (800) 841-6765

Entering its 19th year as an equity operation, Royal Palm is the Gold Coast's first year-round professional theater. It produces musicals, comedies and revues on two stages. Often called "The First Lady of Florida Theater," producer-actress Jan McArt opened Royal Palm in the face of skeptics who argued that the region wasn't ready for year-round theater. She has proven them wrong every year since, whether producing sellout shows, starring on stage or collecting awards

from the regional arbiters of the good, the bad and the funny.

The Main Stage ended its run of *Fiddler on the Roof* in time to open *Little Me*, a musical comedy by Neil Simon, which was followed by *My Fair Lady*.

Internationally acclaimed *La Cage aux Folles* is a French-flavored musical written by Jean Poiret with music and lyrics by Jerry Herman. Heavily laced with leggy Parisian naughtiness and glamor, it takes the stage in February. Also scheduled are *Take Me Along* and Eugene O'Neill's *Ah Wilderness*. In the summer of 1996, be sure to watch for the Tony Award-winning Gershwin musical *Crazy For You*.

Performances in the main theater are 8 PM Tuesday through Saturday and 6 PM Sunday. Seating is limited to 250 patrons, and dinner is served two hours prior to show time. Tickets are $38 to $48. Seating is limited to 100 for Jan McArt's Rooftop Cabaret, with shows at 8:15 PM Wednesday through Saturday and 6:15 PM on Sunday. Tickets are $23 to $29. To verify prices and show times, call the box office.

ROYAL POINCIANA PLAYHOUSE

70 Royal Poinciana Plaza
Palm Beach   Box Office: 659-3310

Presentations of PTG-Florida Inc., the Broadway Series appears in rotation in Palm Beach, Fort Lauderdale, Miami, Orlando and Tampa. The Palm Beach series opened in the fall of 1995 with *Greater Tuna*, which was followed by *An Inspector Calls*. *Laughter on the 23rd Floor* takes the stage in January, and *Stomp* follows. For ticket information, call the box office.

The Kravis Center hosted *Jekyll & Hyde* in December and in 1996 will feature The Pointer Sisters' *Ain't Misbehavin'*, *Carousel* and *Damn Yankees*. For ticket information, call (800) KRAVIS-1.

THE HARID CONSERVATORY
2285 Potomac Rd.
Boca Raton   Reservations: 997-8846

A professional dance and music conservatory, The Harid has programs at the Conservatory as well as regional venues such as Morikami Museum, The Crest Theatre, Olympic Heights Performing Arts Theater and Broward Center.

The Harid's extensive schedule includes Music at the Morikami, The Harid Philharmonia, Faculty Recitals, Student Recitals, Music & More at Harid, Cello Week, Special Music Events, Dance Events and Collaboration Concerts.

You may buy tickets in person at The Harid reservations desk, which is open Monday through Friday, 9:30 to 11:30 AM and 1:30 to 4:30 PM. You may also make reservations by phone and mail your payment, which must be received 10 days prior to a performance. Group rates for 20 or more are available by calling 997-5322. Tickets are half-price for children younger than 12 and for full-time students with an ID.

THE SOCIETY OF THE FOUR ARTS
2 Four Arts Plaza
Palm Beach   655-7227

Founded in 1936 by a group of islanders, the nonprofit organization encourages the appreciation of art, literature, music and drama. Prominent society architect Maurice Fatio designed the original building, which houses the Society's library. The section on Art Galleries and Museums has information on the Society's exhibition schedule.

An earlier building designed by Addison Mizner evolved as the Gallery Building, which houses art exhibitions. Concerts, lectures and films take place in a modernized auditorium.

Concerts are at 8 PM. Take in the Katsaris Piano Quintet from Germany in January, the National Arts Center Orchestra with Trevor Pinnock conducting and guest artist John Kimura Parker in February and the Borodine Quartet from Russia in March. Sunday afternoon concerts in January and February will feature the Bergonzi String Quartet.

Lectures are offered each Tuesday at 3 PM in the Gallery Building during January, February and March, featuring experts in the arts, media, entertainment or government. Lecture tickets are available to the public one week in advance for $15. The Gallery and Auditorium are open from December to mid-April, Monday through Friday from 10 AM to 5 PM and Sunday from 2 to 5 PM. Concert tickets are available to the public a week in advance for $20 at the gallery reception desk. For information on ticket availability, call 655-7226.

The film series of American and foreign classics is Friday at 3 PM and 8 PM during January, February and March. Tickets are $3 and are available at the door.

Museums and Galleries

To collect and flaunt or to exhibit only the coveted treasures of others? Such is the difference between the majors and minor-league art museums. Fortunately, we have collections to flaunt as well as the coveted treasures of others to exhibit at destinations such as Boca Raton Museum and the Norton Museum of Art in West Palm Beach.

If you fly into Palm Beach International Airport, begin by noting the Art in Public Places exhibition sponsored by Palm Beach County Cultural Council, 471-2901. The Regional Artist Gallery is on Level 2 at the west end of the Main Terminal.

BOCA RATON MUSEUM OF ART
801 W. Palmetto Park Rd.
Boca Raton 392-2500

Housed in a one-story building since 1962, the Museum has plans for a $17 million expansion involving a move to 700 Banyan Trail, off Military Trail and north of Glades Road. The board bought the 11-acre parcel and former IBM warehouse site for $2.3 million in 1993.

Major Venues

Bailey Concert Hall, Broward Community College, 3501 S.W. Davie Road, Davie; I-95 to I-595 W.; seating accommodates 1,197 patrons; (305) 475-6884.

Broward Center for the Performing Arts, 201 S.W. Fifth Avenue, Fort Lauderdale; I-95 to Broward Boulevard and exit east; seating capacity is 2,700 in the Au-Rene Theatre and 600 in Amaturo; (305) 462-0222.

Caldwell Theatre, 7873 N. Federal Highway in Levitz Plaza, Boca Raton; take I-95 to Yamato Road, then exit east to U.S. 1 and go north; 241-7432 or 930-6400.

Crest Theatre at Old School Square, 51 N. Swinton Avenue, Delray Beach; take I-95 to Atlantic Avenue and exit east; 243-3183.

Delray Beach Playhouse, 950 N.W. Ninth Street, Delray Beach; 238 seats; 272-1281.

Duncan Theatre, Palm Beach Community College, 4200 Congress Avenue, Lake Worth; I-95 to Sixth Avenue S. and exit west; seating accommodates 720; 439-8141.

Edward M. **Eissey Theatre**, PBCC north campus, 3160 PGA Boulevard, Palm Beach Gardens; I-95 to PGA Boulevard, exit east; 625-2345.

Florida Atlantic University Center Auditorium, Glades Road east of I-95; box office: 367-3737 or 367-3758.

Lois **Pope Theatre**, 262 S. Ocean Boulevard, Manalapan; take I-95 to Lantana Road and exit east to Highway A1A; 585-3433.

Olympic Heights Performing Arts Center, on the campus of Olympic Heights High School, Lyons Road north of Glades Road, west of I-95.

Parker Playhouse, 707 N.E. Eighth Street, Fort Lauderdale; I-

95 to Sunrise Boulevard, exit east; 1,200 seats; (305) 763-2444.

Quest Theatre and Institute, 444 24th Street, West Palm Beach; 832-9328.

Raymond F.**Kravis Center for the Performing Arts**, 701 Okeechobee Boulevard, West Palm Beach; take I-95 to Okeechobee Boulevard and exit east. For box office information, call 832-SHOW; outside the area code, (800) KRAVIS-1.

Royal Palm Dinner Theatre, 303 S.E. Mizner Boulevard, Boca Raton; I-95 to Palmetto Park Road, east to Federal Highway and south to Royal Palm Plaza; 392-3755, (800) 841-6765.

Royal Poinciana Playhouse, 70 Royal Palm Plaza, Palm Beach; I-95 to Okeechobee Boulevard, east to Olive Avenue, north to El Campeon Bridge and east to Palm Beach; 850 seats; 659-3310.

Sunrise Musical Theatre, 5555 N.W. 95th Avenue, Sunrise; take I-95 to Commercial Boulevard in Fort Lauderdale and exit west; 4,086 seats; (305) 741-7300.

West Palm Beach Auditorium, 1610 Palm Beach Lakes Boulevard, West Palm Beach; I-95 to Palm Beach Lakes Boulevard, exit east; 7,000 seats; 683-6012.

The master plan calls for 180,000 square feet devoted to new galleries, crafts and workshops, an art school, a restaurant, ballroom, sculpture garden, a 750-seat theater and space for an antique auto museum. George Bolge, the museum's new executive director, is busy redirecting energies toward the expansion effort, while moving forward with scheduled events for this season.

You'll enjoy a variety of events and exhibitions. The Boca Museum will display the exhibit Jean-Pierre Pincemin: A Retrospective December 15 through January 23 and circulate it to select museums in America and abroad. The exhibit is the first comprehensive survey of this contemporary French artist and will include paintings, sculptures and prints. A grant from the French Government's Ministry of Foreign Affairs helped finance the exhibit.

THE CORNELL MUSEUM OF ART AND HISTORY

51 N. Swinton Ave.
Delray Beach 243-7922

The Cornell occupies the portion of Old School Square Cultural Arts Center that faces Atlantic Avenue. Named for philanthropists Harriett and George Cornell, the museum enhances the centerpiece quality of the national award-winning complex. For more background on Old School Square, see this chapter's Cultural and Performing Arts Organizations section.

The Cornell Museum features major painting, sculpture and graphics exhibits as well as other exhibits of historic and educational interests. The Cornell also houses a permanent collection of Military Miniatures on loan from Edwin S. Reynolds. More than 6,000 hand-painted military collectibles, model craft and soldiers comprise Reynolds' display From the Normans to Norman Schwarzkopf, illuminating 1,000 years of battlefield history.

The Cornell Museum of Art and History is open Tuesday through Saturday, 11 AM to 4 PM and Sunday from 1 to 4 PM. Call for information on upcoming exhibits.

EISSEY CAMPUS GALLERY

Palm Beach Community College
3160 PGA Blvd.
Palm Beach Gardens   625-2328

New in spring 1995, the Art Gallery is an 1,800-square-foot space on the ground floor of PBCC's new $6 million Humanities Building. Museum director Alessandra Gieffers, an associate professor, oversees annual exhibitions plus activities at the art education studio and a 250-seat lecture chamber.

A Visual Arts Faculty Exhibition is set for January.

Watch for Folk, Outsider and Native Art in February. Guided tours of the museum and current exhibitions are offered Monday through Friday at 2 PM.

FLORIDA HISTORY CENTER MUSEUM

805 N. Federal Hwy.
Jupiter   747-6639

Enjoy a variety of exhibits at the Florida History Center and Museum. The center is open from 10 AM to 4 PM Sunday through Wednesday. Call for ticket information.

HIBEL MUSEUM OF ART

150 Royal Poinciana Way
Palm Beach   833-6870

This lovely public museum is dedicated to 78-year-old Singer Island artist Edna Hibel, who started painting when she was 10 and still paints every day. The museum houses a 300-piece collection of Hibel's work, which was donated by Ethelbelle and Clayton Craig of Boston with the condition that the works be displayed in a museum open to the public. This museum changes its exhibits three or four times a year. Hours are Tuesday through Saturday from 10 AM to 5 PM and Sunday from 1 to 5 PM. Call for information.

THE INTERNATIONAL MUSEUM OF CARTOON ART

Mizner Park
127 N.W. 13th St., Ste. 4
Boca Raton   391-2200

After 20 years of outgrowing its New York digs and after rejecting alternative sites in Boston and Washington, D.C., the museum board settled on Mizner Park's south flank. At the December 1994 ground-breaking of its $4.5 million first phase, a kazoo band played while everyone's beloved cartoon characters marched through the tented gathering.

Beetle Bailey saluted his creator, museum founder Mort Walker, and Garfield actually hugged alter ego Jim Davis. Spider Man, Snoopy, Fred Flintstone, Popeye and Olivoyle mingled with politicians, business and civic leaders — literally hundreds of well-wishers ogling an architectural model of the building to house the world's largest collection of cartoon art. West Palm Beach-based Schwab, Twitty & Hanser architectural firm designed the two-story, 45,000-square-foot complex.

Phase I is scheduled for dedication in January 1996, including more than two dozen galleries, the Education Wing, Library, Gift Shop and Cafe. Another $10 million will complete facilities for the permanent collection of more than 100,000 original drawings and 10,000 books as well as videos and films on animation. Major galleries will display permanent exhibitions devoted to major themes and special exhibitions. And the Education Orientation Center will offer programs for adults, teens, children, scholars and researchers. Call for information on this fun-raising activity.

See this chapter's sidebar on this highly touted museum.

THE MORIKAMI MUSEUM
AND JAPANESE GARDENS

4000 Morikami Park Rd.
Delray Beach   *495-0233*

So how Japanese is The Morikami? Take a camera and you'll look like a tourist. . . .

A television viewer saw a documentary broadcast in Japan that featured the only place in the United States devoted completely to the study and preservation of Japanese culture. The man from Tokyo made the journey here to see for himself that Morikami Park really is like being in Japan. Stories also abound of Japanese nationals living in the States who journey to the Morikami whenever they are homesick. Insiders can learn even more about The Morikami in the chapter on Festivals, since full-flavored annual celebrations such as Hatsume Fair and Bon Festival are among its most attended events.

Still, assets of the museum and gardens are as varied as the greenery nestled among 200 acres of Morikami

Park, named for the man who farmed in the region during the early 1900s with others of Boca Raton's Yamato Colony. When competition from Caribbean pineapple growers forced many of the Japanese out of business, George Morikami diversified into vegetables and land itself, quietly acquiring small parcels of real estate. He donated 200 acres to Palm Beach County, along with his dream for a park dedicated to Yamato pioneers that would interpret Japanese culture for future generations. The Parks and Recreation Department owns and operates the Morikami, with help from a private, not-for-profit group of volunteers, The Morikami Inc.

On any given day, the guest register reflects visitors hailing from dozens of other states and foreign countries. Regardless of whether they expect to kill an hour in the library, waltz through an exhibit or picnic on the grounds, the response is almost always some version of "Let's come back when we can spend the whole day." A mile-long nature trail acquaints you with pine stands and a cypress head, while four picnic pavilions are named for pioneer Yamato Colony families. The pavilions are first-come, first-served, but groups may reserve the large Lake Biwa pavilion near the park entrance. For details, please call the county's parks department, 964-4111.

The Morikami's unique *bonsai* collection near Yamato-kan bridge includes Florida miniatures, while its surrounding stroll garden gives previews of other highlights on the grounds: the George Sukeji Morikami stone memorial, the Challenger Astronauts memorial, the Peace Pole, the Koro-en/Dan Nelson Memorial Garden and the Allan S. Austin Memorial Waterfall Overlook.

The Museum includes the original Yamato-kan site, fashioned after an imperial villa and built when the park opened in 1977. Its one-story rooms overlook a dry landscape interior courtyard and pebble garden, where artfully positioned formations symbolize water elements as counterpoint to carefully placed plantings. Yamato-kan accentuates the site's permanent historical exhibition of the original farming colony — a venture promoted by Henry Flagler's Model Land Company, an offshoot of his Florida East Coast Railroad. Displays of playthings instruct young children in everyday aspects of Japanese life. Hakata dolls, for example, are a low-fired unglazed bisqueware series of hand-painted figurines molded in poses such as spinning thread, serving sake, scouting for oysters or reading to a child.

The Morikami introduced its new 32,000-square-foot museum in 1993.

Morikami Museum galleries feature changing seasonal exhibitions of world-class quality that reflect traditional and modern culture. More than 100,000 visitors a year view its permanent collections of Japanese artifacts — a delightful group of toys plus historical displays, contemporary crafts, representative everyday objects and a rare library collection.

Enjoy a wide variety of exhibits and presentations. Through the beginning of March 1996 take in Kindred Spirits: Japanese Mingei and Shaker Craft, which will be followed by Folding Images: Japanese Screens from the Liza Hyde Collection as well as A Distinctive Elegance: Japanese Lacquer Boxes from the Elaine Ehrenkranz Collection.

Museum classes include the crafts of *origami, ikebana, bonsai, sumi-e* ink painting, the tea ceremony, kite and toymaking, Japanese language, martial arts and many more unique opportunities.

Take time out for tea in the Seishin-an Tea House, an authentic chamber with a 45-seat viewing gallery to observe this traditional art.

A 225-seat theater accommodates performances, lectures and movie screenings and is available for cultural, community and business group activities. The Donald B. Gordon Memorial Library, with a reading room and thousands of volumes, is open Wednesday through Friday, 10 AM to 5 PM.

High-tech? You betcha, at the Infotronic Gallery multimedia resource center. User-friendly computers have touch-screens for fingertip access to videos, photographs, music and literature about Japanese culture.

The Cornell Cafe offers homestyle Japanese food, snacks and beverages, 11 AM to 3 PM. It also hosts numerous private dinner parties and luncheons. Overlooking Morikami Pond, the Cornell serves an elaborate brunch of exotic Japanese delicacies on the third Sunday of each month, 10 AM to noon, for $9.

In the Museum Store, don't think of it as "buying Japanese;" dwell in-

Front of Boca Raton Museum of Art building.

stead on merchandising for the Museum — a worthy cause for education and culture. You'll be delighted with authentic gift items from Japan such as books, toys, dolls, greeting cards, jewelry, pottery, lacquerware, utensils and more. The store is open 10 AM to 4:45 PM, and proceeds benefit The Morikami.

The Morikami Museum is open daily *except* Monday from 10 AM to 5 PM. Other exceptions are Thanksgiving, Christmas, New Year's Day, Easter and the Fourth of July. Admission is $4.25 for adults, $2 for children ages 6 to 18 and $3.75 for seniors. Admission to the museum is free on Sundays from 10 AM to noon. Morikami Park is open seven days a week including holidays, from sunrise to sunset, and admission is free.

Guided tours of the museum and grounds are available if planned in advance. Parking is plentiful on the grounds, just a short walk from the museum and gardens. To reach the Park, take I-95 to Yamato Road, exit west to Powerline Road and turn right; the entrance is between Clint Moore Road and Linton Boulevard. For reservations and information, call 495-0233.

The Morikami's master plan calls for an ambitious future that is quite likely, given its growing base of loyal supporters. Plans call for a Japanese inn or *ryokan* for visitors who want to stay overnight in authentic surroundings; a working demonstration farm to produce rice, bamboo, pineapple crops and winter vegetables and to reenact turn-of-the-century life at Yamato Colony; a historic Sundy Feed Store, moved to the site to be restored and used to house farming artifacts; a full-service Japanese restaurant; an artists-in-residence program to demonstrate crafts and conduct workshops in authentic *minka* and other buildings brought from Japan and reconstructed on-site; an amphitheater for performing arts events and outdoor exhibits; and a horticultural center.

NORTON MUSEUM OF ART
1451 S. Olive Ave.
West Palm Beach   832-5196

Palm Beachers are understandably proud of the Norton's growth from gallery to world-class museum. Plans call for a $20.5 million expansion including double the number of exhibit galleries and more than double the square footage. About $12 million in cash and pledges from private donors and corporations signal the project is well on its way to completion by 1997. Ralph Norton founded the institution in 1941. The challenge for architect Chad Floyd will be to integrate Marion Sims Wyeth's neoclassic original with downtown neighbors that are part residential, academic and commercial.

Barbara and Melvin Nessel of Palm Beach donated 81 works of 20th-century art, including paintings by Pablo Picasso, Marc Chagall, Henri Matisse, Willem do Kooning, Helen Frankenthaler, Joan Miro, Frank Stella, Adolph Gottlieb and Hans Hofmann; and sculptures by Max Ernst, Alexander Calder, Henry Moore, Louise Nevelson and Giorgio di Chirico. They're sure to be comfortable in the Norton's eclectic company.

Hours are Tuesday through Saturday from 10 AM to 5 PM and Sunday 1 to 5 PM. The recommended donation is $5 during the regular season, mid-November through mid-April, and $4 off-season. Children younger than 12 and with an adult are admitted free.

You may arrange a 15-percent group discount by calling the education department, 832-5196, at least three weeks in advance.

SCULPTURE CENTER AT THE ESPERANTE
222 Lakeview Ave.
West Palm Beach   471-2901

Exhibitions feature sculptures by students from the Palm Beach County School of the Arts. Call for information.

THE SOCIETY OF THE FOUR ARTS
2 Four Arts Plaza
Palm Beach   655-7227

Take in a variety of exhibitions including, Redefining Genre: French and American Painting, 1850-1900, set for January; Imperial Russian Porcelain from the Raymond F. Piper Collection, scheduled for February 10 through March 10; and Arthur J. Stone: Master Silversmith, a project of Art Access, a collaboration of the American Federation of Arts (AFA) with support from the Lila Wallace-Reader's Digest Fund, which will also run for a month starting February 10.

American Art from the Currier Gallery of Art exhibition is scheduled from March 16 to April 14, featuring paintings, sculpture, furniture and decorative arts from the Colonial era to the 20th century. A National Endowment for the Arts assisted the AFA event.

The 18th Annual Gifted Child Art Exhibition of the Exceptional Student Education Department of Palm Beach County is on deck February 22 through March 28.

Don't overlook the artwork that supersedes the dramatic impact of all others in Florida, sunrise and sunset:

Sunset Celebration is an art and crafts show featuring local and national artists exhibiting sculpture, paintings, photography and jewelry behind a backdrop of nature's centerpiece. Sailfish Marina sponsors the complimentary Thursday events, 6 to 9 PM. For information, please call (800) 446-4577.

WHITEHALL — THE HENRY MORRISON FLAGLER MUSEUM
1 Whitehall Way
Palm Beach   *655-2833*

Henry Flagler built Whitehall as a wedding present for his wife Mary Lily Kenan in 1901. The residence cost $2.5 million to construct, and another $1.5 million was spent to furnish what the press called "the Taj Mahal of North America." After Flagler's death in 1913, Whitehall sat out the winter season. Mrs. Flagler, who remarried and then died in 1917, left the mansion to a niece who sold the site to investors. Whitehall operated as a luxury hotel with a 10-story tower addition overlooking Lake Worth from 1925 to 1959. Flagler's granddaughter Jean Flagler Matthews spearheaded an organization that acquired Whitehall, restored the residence and opened The Henry Morrison Flagler Museum in 1960.

Listed on the National Register of Historic Places as an architectural landmark, Whitehall showcases the opulent lifestyle of the railroad magnate and Standard Oil Company partner (with John D. Rockefeller). Besides its period rooms restored with original Louis IV furnishings, separate collections contain paintings, porcelains, silver, crystal, dolls and costumes. Numerous chambers display archives that illustrate local history during the pioneer era Flagler dominated.

Whitehall's extravagant appointments offer a much-coveted destination for cultural arts organizations, concerts, charity galas and special exhibitions. The Palm Beach Invitational piano competition takes place here every spring.

Again in 1995, Palm Beach Pops selected Whitehall for a black-tie gala that drew supporters such as U.S. Supreme Court Justice Sandra Day O'Connor, San Francisco real estate baron Brian Burns, sugar queen Tina

The Jewish Community

In South Florida, Judaism is more than religion, it's culture. And the South Palm Beach County Jewish Federation, founded in 1979, caters to the cultural needs and welfare of the entire Jewish community.

Its many divisions on the Richard and Carole Siemens Jewish Campus also focus on philanthropic, social and educational advancement, and it promotes understanding between various local organizations and the community in general. Theses divisions include the Adolph and Rose Levis Jewish Community Center, Ruth Rales Jewish Family Service, Donna Klein Jewish Academy, Jewish Association for Residential Care and Menorah House Society.

Adolf and Rose Levis Jewish Community Center

Many parts make up the whole of the Adolph and Rose Levis Jewish Community Center, such as the health and fitness department; the cultural arts department; the Betty and Marvin Zale Early Childhood Learning Center; the family department; JCC Camp Ted Weisberg; and the adult services department.

The health and fitness facilities rival those of surrounding health-club facilities and show that physical fitness is just as important as community fitness. It is 7,000 square feet, with a wide range of cardiovascular equipment: stationary bikes, step and rowing machines, treadmills, free weights and other workout stations. Aerobics classes, karate and Israeli folk dancing are on the roster for the 3,100-square-foot aerobics studio. Other facilities include racquetball and squash courts; tennis courts; a double gymnasium; lighted softball and soccer fields; swimming pools; sauna and steam rooms; and locker rooms. Memberships are available for Jewish and non-Jewish residents, alike.

Zinman Hall, a 500-seat theater and the Nathan D. Rosen Museum Gallery host events for the cultural arts department. The gallery hosts artists from around the world; the Jewish Community Festival of Arts, Books and Culture; and Judaic traveling exhibits.

And every age group will find something at the JCC to serve its needs. Tots from 6 months old to pre-kindergarten can choose from programs in the Early Childhood Learning Center or in the family department; children and teens can participate in the family department's after-school programs, Kids Club, youth groups and special events. For adults, the family department offers single-parent programs and family holiday events and pool parties. And the adult services department has a variety of offerings suitable for young adults to more senior adults. These programs include a professional and business Jewish networking group; a social program for young adults with special needs, a 50-plus adult department; and programs and classes for elder members.

Federation/United
Jewish Appeal Campaign

The largest philanthropic campaign in South Palm Beach County is the annual Federation/United Jewish Appeal Campaign. In 1995, it raised $12.2 million from more than 17,000 contributors. Proceeds benefit the local Jewish community, Israel and Jewish communities worldwide and help provide Jewish education and counseling, and rescue and resettlement for Jews everywhere.

Education

Education is a key component of the Federation.

In 1979, the South County Jewish Community Day School opened with 50 students. Now, enrollment passes 600 students in kindergarten through 8th grades at the school, which since has been renamed Donna Klein Jewish Academy. It perpetuates Jewish and American values, ethics, culture and traditions, all the while providing a high-quality Jewish and secular education experience.

The Jewish Education Commission develops and implements South County Jewish educational programs, including the Academy for Jewish Studies, which has a lecture series and has a Yiddish library with texts and tapes available; Elderhostel, part of a network of more than 1,4000 colleges, universities and other educational institutions that offer residential academic programs for people over the age of 60; and Florence Melton Adult Mini-School, a two-year curriculum.

And the Sally and Lester Entin Holocaust Pavilion is a living lesson on the horrors of the Holocaust and the 6 million Jewish victims. The teaching exhibit has the Albert and Pearl Ginsberg Wall of Remembrance, which outlines the Holocaust with 22 photographs and text. The pavilion also includes an outdoor chapel. Every year, more than 6,000 children from public and private schools visit the pavilion to learn the meaning of the Holocaust.

Special Needs

The Ruth Rales Jewish Family Service provides counseling to clients of all ages, with the goal of strengthening and preserving family life. Support groups that it offers address compulsive eating, children of divorce, effective parenting for couples and single parents, new mother/new babies, separation/divorce, widows/widowers and other individual and family issues.

The Family Service also has special services for the area's elderly residents, including providing a link between the elderly residents in need of assistance and out-of-town relatives; the Diamond Club for ages 75 and up; a grandparenting program that helps create surrogate grandparent relationships; and a volunteer service to help the home-bound.

The Jewish Association for Residential Care provides three group homes for 22 adults with developmental disabilities.

The Menorah House Society is dedicated to helping to enrich the lives of residents of the 120-bed, Menorah House, a private skilled-care nursing facility that is owned by Hillhaven Inc. The Society provides religious services and programs and activities for residents.

The Gould Council provides programming for residents of the Shirley H. Gould House, government subsidized housing for low-income and handicapped elderly residents. Residents have complete access to the Siemens Campus and facilities.

To contact the South Palm Beach County Jewish Federation, write to 9901 Donna Klein Boulevard, Boca Raton 33428, or call 852-3100. The fax number is 852-3150. The address for the Delray Beach satellite office is 5869 W. Atlantic Avenue, Delray Beach 33445, 499-6262. The fax number is 498-91069.

Fanjul, Republican fund-raiser Gay Hart Gaines, Home Depot wizards Bernard Marcus and Kenneth Langone, and Sensormatic chairman Ron Assaf. Tiffany and Company provided the table favors.

Whitehall's major rooms reflect the look of Versailles and other historic European styles: the Marble Hall, the Italian Renaissance Library, Louis XIV Music Room, St. Mark's Hall, the Swiss Billiard Room, Elizabethan Breakfast Room, Francis I Dining Room and Louis XVI Salon. The Louis XV Ballroom was famous for the "Bal Poudre" the Flaglers gave in honor of George Washington's birthday in 1903. Fourteen guest chambers interpret Mary Lily's preoccupation with styles of 18th-century France, Colonial America and Art Nouveau.

Also on the grounds of Whitehall is the 1886 Rambler — Flagler's private railway car restored in 1967.

ATLANTIC AVENUE GALLERY STROLL
Delray Beach

Our Festivals and Special Events chapter introduces Art and Jazz on the Avenue, a giant Thursday night party that Downtown schedules four times a year to showcase new exhibitions, live entertainment, contests and special happenings at restaurants and boutiques.

In addition, several Atlantic Avenue galleries collaborate year round to offer special evenings for art lovers.

They include Artcetera, Carlynn Gallery, Cornell Museum, Forms… A Southwest Gallery, Lyons Gallery, Shared Visions and Z-Mod. For information on upcoming Gallery Strolls, call the Delray Beach Joint Venture, 279-1381, or the Chamber of Commerce, 278-0424.

CALIFORNIA FINE ARTS
140 W. Glades Rd.
Boca Raton   *392-7220*

Rick and Janet Swahn opened California Fine Arts in 1992, a secondary market specialist affiliated with more than 600 fine art sources. Relocating from San Diego, the Swahns buy, sell and trade with publishers, galleries, artists and dealers.

They carry the work of Joan Miro, Marc Chagall, Erte, Peter Max, Yuroz, Zhou Brothers, Isaac Maimon, Salvador Dali, Orlando Agudelo Botero, Romero Brito, Howard Behrens, Eyvind Earle and many others.

The 4,000-square-foot gallery showcases original paintings, sculp-

The $55 million Kravis Center for the Performing Arts opened nearly debt free in 1992.

ture and limited-edition serigraphs by major contemporary artists.

Palm Beach County Cultural Council's ArtsLine gives updates on arts and attractions year round. To hear what's going on, call (800) 882-ARTS.

GALERIE MIHALIS
365 E. Palmetto Park Rd.
Boca Raton   367-1532

Peggy and Mihalis Gourgourinis opened their fine art gallery about six years ago, as Boca was planning some major infrastructure improvements to make way for downtown revitalization. Peggy, who has 20 years experience in the business, has been active as both head of the Palmetto Park Merchants Association, and also a member of the Visions 90 committee and the Downtown Business Alliance.

She's especially bullish on the city's potential and its appeal as a cultur-ally advanced and sophisticated destination.

"We were surprised at how culturally aware Boca is, with so many flourishing entities. I'd like to see more galleries come here ... Palmetto would be like a Rodeo Drive. We've lived in Europe and California and never seen anywhere as nice as Boca, with so much potential. We'll have a real jewel of North America."

Gourgourinis has a jewel already, a repository of major American and international artists — many Impressionists as well as Realists. She works with decorators and art collectors to find just the right pieces, and the gallery also handles art restorations and picture framing.

Business is keeping pace with downtown's progress, she says, so Galerie Mihalis is doubling its size — adding an additional 1,500 square feet of space.

Artists-in-Residence

Palm Beach County attracts its share of world-class artists who visit on vacations or for their own exhibits, then decide to move here.

Meet sculptor **Esther Wertheimer**, who divides her time between homes in Boca Raton and Montreal, a foundry in Bridgeport, Connecticut, and global travel for permanent installations of her work and lecture engagements. Wertheimer works in large bronze figures that people many of Canada's metropolitan plazas and landmarks, including the collection of the Musee d'Art de Joliette in Quebec.

Educated at Montreal Museum of Fine Arts, the International Academy in Austria and Academia di Belle Arts in Florence, Italy, Wertheimer has numerous awards and development grants from government agencies in Italy, Canada and Japan. Her work is extremely popular in the Far East, especially Singapore and Japan, where the municipal government of Fukuoka commissioned a work to commemorate its centennial in 1992. Other permanent works in Japan are the Sports Centre in Hamura City and Symphony Hall in Katsushika-ku, Tokyo.

When Canada dedicated its new embassy in Tokyo in the fall of 1993, Wertheimer was the only Canadian artist asked to exhibit in its gallery. Speaking at opening ceremonies were Canadian ambassador David Rose and His Imperial Highness Prince Takamado. The proud owner of his own Wertheimer piece, "Carlotta III," the prince said, "Among the great majority of sculptures that simply crouch in quiet poses with no movement, her works seem to leap up in motion. They are vibrant with life."

Favorite subjects are dancers, lovers and parents with children — all captured in the rush of lively spirits. Wertheimer coveted the role of ballerinas as a young child, though she was too petite to consider a professional career. She often gains inspiration from people's actions under duress — the kind she saw in the 1989 pro-democracy protests in Beijing. The ordeal in China inspired a series of six sculptures, including an 18-foot piece called "Democracy."

Elsewhere in the United States, Wertheimer's sculpture decorates the grounds of Sun Bank in Coral Springs, California.

Placed in downtown Boca Raton in 1994, a 23-foot piece called "Water Babies" accentuates Royal Palm Plaza outside the Hall of Frames Gallery. Wertheimer sculptures also are on display at the Curzon Gallery inside the Boca Raton Resort and Club and at Gloria Waldman's Artcetera, 640 E. Atlantic Avenue in downtown Delray Beach.

Donald Neal displayed sketching genius as a young child in the migrant farming community of Belle Glade, an unlikely cradle for the provocative material he produces. He studied with regional art-

International Museum of Cartoon Art

(by Lisa Goddard)

Beetle Bailey, Garfield, Charlie Brown and thousands of other cartoon characters have come to life in comic strips, books, magazines and movies over the years, making us laugh, cry, think and wonder. These characters will live on forever, not only in the hearts and minds of millions of people, but in a permanent home in Boca Raton in the International Museum of Cartoon Art.

Now under construction in the downtown Mizner Park shopping, restaurant and office complex, the museum relocated to Boca after 20 years in metropolitan New York. It is the country's only museum devoted to all forms of cartoon art. When completed in late 1997, it will house the world's largest collection of original works of cartoon art in all genres.

More than 150,000 works on paper, 10,000 books, 1,000 hours of animated film and numerous collectibles and memorabilia are part of this collection. Forms include comic strips and comic books, editorial cartoons, magazine and book illustrations, animation, caricatures, sports cartoons, advertising cartoons, graphic novels, greeting cards, panel cartoons and sculpture. Some of the distinguished and legendary cartoon artists whose work is part of the museum's permanent collection include Thomas Nast, Herblock, Charles Schulz, Charles Addams, Mort Walker, Walt Disney, Hal Foster, Winsor McKay, Charles Dana Gibson, Richard Outcault, Jim Davis and Peter Arno.

Photo: Stephanie Murphy

At the groundbreaking for the International Museum of Cartoon Art: "Beetle Bailey" with Mort Walker, Jim Davis and "Garfield"

Located on a 1.5-acre site, the two-story museum will feature 25 galleries, the Cartoon Hall of Fame, a changing exhibition gallery, an education orientation center, classrooms, a library/research center, a video center, a theatre, a resident cartoonist's studio, Toonville, the Laugh Center and an area depicting how color comics are printed. A "mini-opening" of the first floor with modular, temporary gallery spaces designed to showcase a portion of the museum's collection, is slated for March 1996. One million visitors, residents and tourists are expected to see the museum annually once the entire facility is open.

Already, the museum has created and hosted a variety of exhibitions throughout South Florida to introduce the public to its new cultural facility and give them a taste of what's to come. *Glasnost, The Story of America in Cartoons, The Artist and the Baseball Card, Masters of Cartoon Art, Cartoons from Russia* and *100 Years of the American Newspaper Comic Strip* are some of the exhibitions held in the area.

The museum also has presented a variety of programs to area children, including curriculum materials and cartoon art in schools, cartoon art classes, exhibition study guides, a workshop for Palm Beach County teachers, college/university internships in archival studies, collections, management and business/merchandising, docent training and a children's cartoon contest.

To reach out to the community, the museum has participated in numerous local civic activities, such as the Dixie Manor Summer Camp, Boca Festival Days, Boca Holiday Parade, SunFest, Meet Me Downtown, the Delray Affair and the Florence Fuller Child Development Center and YMCA after-school programs. In addition, a Speaker's Bureau has been established to service chambers of commerce, civic organizations, service clubs, economic councils and schools.

Mission Statement

• To make accessible to the general public the largest collection of original historic and contemporary cartoon works in the world and continually to acquire such works.

• To provide on-site and community outreach education opportunities for students and training for teachers.

• To conduct seminars and courses for students and the public on all aspects of cartoon art, its history, humor, message, technique and social and historical significance.

• To be an information center for scholars, industry and professionals.

• To organize special changing exhibits featuring the profession's most acclaimed and aspiring artists.

• To create an international tourist attraction that is both educational and entertaining, allowing the museum to play a significant role as a contributor to the region's tourist economy.

Sarge tagged along at the ceremonies to start construction on the International Museum of Cartoon Art.

• To achieve fiscal soundness through optimum self-sustaining programs, innovative earned income resources and efficient private philanthropy.

History

In 1960, Mort Walker, creator of "Beetle Bailey", recognized the need to preserve and exhibit the cartoons that have become a collective memory of our civilization as individuals, cultures and societies. Walker gathered and preserved cartoons that would otherwise have been lost or destroyed because there was no repository for them, and sought funding to build a museum to house this growing collection. The William Randolph Hearst Foundation provided start-up grants of $100,000, and the Mead mansion was rented as the museum's first site in Greenwich, Connecticut. The museum, chaired by Walker, moved to larger quarters in Rye Brook, New York in 1974 and remained there for 18 years.

During its first years, thousands of families, tourists, collectors, students, reporters, cartoonists and community groups visited the museum. Growing attendance, an expanding collection of all cartoon art media and a significant rise in participation in its public and educations programs enhanced the museum's reputation as a serious and critically-acclaimed cultural institution.

In 1990, the museum's board of trustees renamed the museum the International Museum of Cartoon Art and decided to find a new home, one that would give it a larger, more modern facility and a supportive place to grow. Once established in Boca Raton, the museum established a new board of trustees and organized active advisory boards in the areas of editorial cartoons, animation, comic books, advertising cartoon art and international cartoons. Business, fund raising, architectural, education programs, exhibition schedule and marketing/public relations plans have been developed, and nearly 200 volunteers have worked to serve the museum's new community. Ground was broken on Phase I of the museum's $15 million facility in December 1994. The board of trustees is comprised of a number of well-known area business and civic leaders, as well as recognized experts in the cartoon art and entertainment fields such as Garfield creator Jim Davis, Walt Disney marketing and entertainment president Thomas Elrod, Mother Goose and Grimm creator Mike Peters, Momma creator Mell Lazarus and King Features Syndicate President Joseph F. D'Angelo. Founder Mort Walker will continue to serve as chairman.

Museum Founder Mort Walker

At the age of 12, Mort Walker sold his first cartoon. By 14, he was selling gag cartoons on a regular basis to such magazines as "Child Life", "Inside Detective" and "Flying Aces". At 15, he was a comic strip artist for a metropolitan newspaper, and by the age of 26, he was the No. 1 gag cartoonist in the country in volume of sales.

Walker's most popular creation is the Army's worst and funniest private Beetle Bailey. Originally known as "Spider" and featured in a college setting, the strip was sold to King Features in 1950, where his name was changed to Beetle. Walker added the Bailey in honor of The Saturday Evening Post Editor John Bailey, and the strip started running in 12 newspapers. Within six months, 25 papers carried the strip, and when Beetle was inducted into the Army after the eruption of the Korean War, popularity of the strip soared. Today, "Beetle Bailey" appears in more than 1,800 publications worldwide.

Born Addison Morton Walker in El Dorado, Kansas, in 1923, Walker became the chief editorial designer at Hall Brothers at age 18. He used a light, playful style that has characterized the company's greeting card division, Hallmark Cards. He was drafted in 1943, serving as a private, corporal sergeant and at the time of his discharge in 1946, a first lieutenant. It was in the Army that Walker says he picked up ideas for cartoon characters. After his stint in the Army, Walker enrolled at Missouri University, where he held the position of editor-in-chief of the Missouri Showme magazine. In 1948 he graduated with a degree in humanities.

Though his first 200 cartoons were rejected, Walker finally came up with "funny guy" we now know as Beetle Bailey, and he hasn't stopped since. He is also the creator of "Hi and Lois" (1954), "Sam's Strip" (1961), "Boner's Ark" (1968), "Sam and Silo" (1971), "The Evermore's" (1982), "Betty Boop and Felix" (1984) and "Gamin and Patches" (1987).

Among Walker's many honors are the National Cartoonists Society's prestigious Reuben Award in 1953 for "Beetle Bailey" and the NCS Best Humor Strip award in 1966 and 1969 for "Beetle Bailey" as well. In 1955, he won the Banshee's famous "Silver Lady" as the outstanding cartoonist of the year. He served a two-year term as president of the NCS from 1959-60 and currently is a member of the NCS Executive Council and chairman of the NCS Ethics Committee. Walker is also national chairman of Cartoonists for Literacy.

ists, encouraging instructors at Palm Beach Community College and later at the Norton School of Art in West Palm Beach. Moving on from drawing and sculpture, Neal defies labels with a startling style of painting that challenges surrealism to explain itself.

The Cornell Museum at Old School Square is among area galleries that regularly showcase Neal's entrancing paintings, many which sparkle and blaze with bold uses of *trompe l'oeil*. His work accuses the world and indicts its abusers, his super-realism usually raising more questions than answers.

Born in the Jura mountain region of France, **Jean-Claude Gaugy** arrived in the world 300 years after tradition stamped the arts onto his family countenance. Originally channeling his vision into sculpture, Gaugy studied at Beaux Arts in Paris, the School of Sculpture in Moscow and the School of Design in Rome — then held an apprenticeship with Henry Moore. An early believer was Salvador Dali, who sponsored Gaugy's first exhibition in Paris when the artist was a puppy of 17.

Jean-Claude and his wife, Michelle, moved to Boca Raton nine years ago and established Gaugy, a gallery at 301 Patio de Fuente in Royal Palm Plaza. Visitors acquaint themselves with his unique, stand-alone medium of paintings on wood he carves in a style of linear expressionism. Also found in international collections, including the Musee Luxembourg in Paris, Gaugy exhibits frequently in Europe. The government of Luxembourg showcased his work in 1994, and Germany hosted five exhibits the same year.

Gaugy's painting "Pas de Deux" inspired other artists to create a ballet ensemble work, "Gaugy Concerto," which had its premiere in spring 1995 during Boca Ballet Theatre's spring medley. Guests at an après-ballet reception included yet another unusual ensemble —

Bill and Lois Warren, whose art collection contains the original painting, along with the artist, the choreographer, the composer and the dancers who brought the work to life.

Gaugy gallery is open by appointment in the summer and during season Tuesday through Saturday from 10 AM to 5 PM. For information on fall activities, please call 338-5224.

Inside
Education and Child Care

You don't need to twist a Palm Beach countian's arm to make him or her admit that folks here have a lust for learning that's as big as their lust for living. It's a passion we pass along to our children.

Palm Beach County's schools are among the state's best without a doubt, but in the county's high-growth areas in the north, west and south, heavy enrollments have classrooms beginning to bulge at the seams. Fortunately, some of the state's best private schools are here too, so parents can select the type of instruction that best serves their children's needs and goals.

you on where your child will attend classes. If your child has special needs, punch #2 for exceptional student services.

If you're still looking for a home, most Realtors take the time to find out which schools serve their respective neighborhoods. If you want to check out your child's school before making your move, feel free. Just be sure to call ahead and set up an appointment, and remember to register at the office when you pay your visit. That's not to make sure you get the "A" tour . . . it's to prevent the embarrassment of having a security officer detain you.

Public Instruction

Boca Raton Elementary School opened in 1924 to educate children whose parents worked for the Mizner Development Company. Today the county is burgeoning with high-tech, cutting-edge schools that prepare students to meet the technological age with confidence.

If you're considering moving into the area and have school-age children, the number to remember is 434-8000. Wait for the prompt, then punch #4. That will connect you to the county's pupil assignment office in West Palm Beach. These kind folks can advise

Private Schools

Excellent private and parochial schools abound in Boca Raton and its nearby communities and serve students from pre-kindergarten through 12th grade. Space doesn't permit mentioning them all, but here's a representative sample of some of the best:

ST. ANDREW'S SCHOOL
3900 Jog Rd.
Boca Raton   483-8900

Founded as a boarding school for boys by the Rev. Hunter Wyatt-Brown in 1962, St. Andrew's School brings the best of the northeastern boarding-school tradition to the Sunshine State on a spacious, bucolic campus that hums with activity.

St. Andrew's offers a coed program for day students and residents in grades 6 through 12. The school is accredited by the Florida Council of Independent Schools, the National Association of Episcopal Schools, the Educational Records Bureau, the Cum Laude Society and more. Its international student body represents all faiths and several continents. Ninety-nine percent of graduates go on to four-year colleges and universities, some on National Merit Scholarships.

Class size within the school's Bahamian Colonial-style buildings averages 15 students per classroom. Step outside and you'll quickly learn the school's sports facilities are as impressive as its student/faculty ratio, with a gymnasium, pool, baseball and softball diamonds and plenty of fields for soccer and lacrosse. The extracurricular height of autumn is football season, and on crisp Saturday afternoons Don Jones Memorial Field is a swirl of red and gold, with players, coaches, cheerleaders, proud parents, alumni and even a few bagpipers cheering the Scots on to victory.

St. Andrew's carries on the proud tradition of its sports teams and a wide variety of clubs and other extracurricular activities such as the school newspaper, drama and film clubs and much more.

The annual cost to attend is $9,650 for middle school students, $10,550 for the upper school and $19,600 for boarding students.

POPE JOHN PAUL II REGIONAL HIGH SCHOOL

4001 N. Military Tr.
Boca Raton 994-8998

Opened in 1982, the school now known affectionately by its students as "Pope" came as an answer to the prayers of parents who wanted to obtain a Catholic high school education for their children but found the drive to Cardinal Gibbons High in Fort Lauderdale or Cardinal Newman High in West Palm Beach a bit much to bear.

Staffed by an order of Carmelite brothers and priests, the school quickly attained a sterling academic reputation and, like fine wine, simply gets better with age.

On the athletic field, the girls' teams garnered the lion's share of attention in the school's early years, but the Eagles' boys programs have caught up. Today, students of both sexes have the opportunity to excel in an array of individual and team sports.

There are plenty of opportunities for students to enjoy interest and service club activities, and the school presents many opportunities for students to grow as individuals by offering community service to the area's less fortunate citizens.

The cost to attend is $3,650 annually for students who are members of parishes in the school's service area, $4,700 for nonmembers.

ZION LUTHERAN CHRISTIAN SCHOOL

959 S.E. Sixth Ave.
Deerfield Beach (305) 421-3146

Zion Lutheran started small but over the past two decades has grown and prospered. The school offers a va-

Calusa Elementary School students re-create pioneer days.

riety of classes and services and an interscholastic sports program comparable with large private schools but keeps its class sizes small and retains its family atmosphere.

Zion offers day-care and preschool programs for newborns up to pre-kindergarten-age children and grade-level programs for kids in kindergarten through grade 12.

The school's administrators point with pride not only to the low student/teacher ratio but to the school's outstanding music, art and sports programs as well. Among the activities offered are drama programs, vocal and handbell choirs, school band and competitive teams in football, boys and girls basketball, baseball, volleyball, tennis, soccer, golf and track and field.

Annual tuition rates are $3,100 for kindergarten through grade 5, $3,450 for grades 6 through 8 and $4,050 for grades 9 through 12.

HIGHLANDS CHRISTIAN ACADEMY
501 N.E. 48th St.
Pompano Beach (305) 421-1747

Like Zion Lutheran, Highlands Christian is a school that has moved past the growing pains without losing the warm, supportive atmosphere that first made it popular among local families. The school offers classes for students in grades K through 12 and enjoys a high college placement percentage among its graduates.

Among its extracurricular offerings are choir and band and an athletic program that offers competitive opportunities for elementary school through high school students.

The school is a member of the Florida Association of Christian Colleges and Schools and the Florida Association of Non-Public Schools. The cost to attend ranges from $1,725 for half-day kindergarten to $2,690 for full-day sessions and from $2,990 for the elementary grades to $3,385 for high school students.

PINE CREST SCHOOL AT BOCA RATON
2700 St. Andrews Blvd.
Boca Raton   852-2800

When Boca Raton Academy closed its doors in 1987, Pine Crest School of Fort Lauderdale stepped in to revitalize the campus and transform the school into a lower-division branch campus, serving students in pre-kindergarten through grade 8.

Graduates of Pine Crest-Boca Raton are encouraged to continue their education at the parent Pine Crest School in northeast Fort Lauderdale, which was started in 1934 as a winter tutorial program by renowned educator Dr. Mae McMillan and has grown into a highly respected independent school.

Pine Crest-Boca Raton students enjoy a variety of educational opportunities, from the regular curriculum to the a diverse enrichment program, which offers coursework in values, classical studies, computers, art, instrumental instruction and physical education. Students who need additional assistance can benefit from special help sessions, and students whose fluency in English is less than satisfactory can benefit from the English as a Second Language Program. Students can also elect to participate in an extensive after-school enrichment program that offers courses ranging from baking to rocketry.

Campus life is enhanced by the library and media center, dining hall, computer lab/classroom, 750-seat student activities center, fine arts building, swimming pool, tennis center, gymnasium and plenty of playgrounds and playing fields.

More than 30 of the faculty have master's degrees, and the school is accredited by the Southern Association of Colleges and Schools, the Florida Council of Independent Schools and the Association of Independent Schools of Florida.

Annual tuition ranges from $7,110 for pre-kindergarten to $8,130 for students in grade 8.

CLERISY ACADEMY
625 N.E. Mizner Blvd.
Boca Raton   368-6083

One of the newcomers to the education scene in Boca Raton, Clerisy Academy, a private school open to all faiths, caters to the needs of academically gifted students.

The school, which operates as a nonprofit corporation and a subsidiary of First United Methodist Church in Boca Raton, opened its doors in 1993 to students ages 5 to 10. A facilities expansion in March 1994 permitted the school to include students through age 13.

Clerisy Academy's master teachers hold advanced degrees or are specially trained to work with gifted children. Class sizes are limited to 16 per master teacher and full-time assistant, allowing the student-teacher ratio to be maintained at or below 8-to-1.

The yearly tuition ranges from $4,200 to $4,450.

ST. JOAN OF ARC SCHOOL
501 S.W. Third Ave.
Boca Raton   392-7974

Balance is a key concept at Boca Raton's oldest Catholic elementary school, and its administrators point to the teamwork among its teachers, counselors and religious educators to

Photo: Visual Dynamics/Jeffrey Toll

Donna Klein Jewish Academy offers a high-quality program of individualized secular and Judaic studies.

help its students post consistently superlative scores on standardized national tests.

The school's campus is compact but well-stocked, with a library and media center, computer center, science lab, auditorium and physical education and recreation areas.

Special after-school help sessions for students who need extra guidance, and optional enrichment courses for those who can benefit from the extra challenge, augment the classroom program. The school also offers activities such as a glee club, cheerleading and organized sports competition in basketball, baseball and softball.

Enrolling at St. Joan of Arc is sometimes tough because of the school's popularity; it's not uncommon for prospective students to be placed on a waiting list. Applicants on this list are chosen based on three criteria: St. Joan of Arc School appears to be a suitable educational placement for the child; the child's siblings already attend the school; and the family is a member of St. Joan of Arc Church or another local Catholic parish.

Tuition is $2,520 annually. Families with more than one enrolled child pay reduced tuition for other children attending.

St. Paul Lutheran School
701 W. Palmetto Park Rd.
Boca Raton   395-8548

On the edge of the city's Old Floresta neighborhood is St. Paul's Lutheran School, which, like nearby St. Joan of Arc, has long served the children of the community.

The school is well known for its commitment to Christian education and service, its fine arts and sports programs and the high Scholastic Aptitude Test scores its students consistently post. Among the extracurricular activities are the choir and operetta; special events include the Children's Christmas Service and Grandparents' Day.

The school is accredited through the National Lutheran School Association's Florida/Georgia district. The annual tuition is $3,100.

Advent Lutheran School
5001 N.E. Fourth Ave.
Boca Raton   395-3635

Just north of the business and governmental hub of the city, Advent Lutheran School is popular among families living throughout Boca Raton and in Delray Beach.

The school is a member of the National Lutheran School Association's Florida/Georgia district and serves students in grades 1 through 8. In addition to its academic program, the school offers competitive sports and a music program that includes a handbell choir, band and chorus. Students also produce a newspaper and yearbook.

The annual cost to attend grades 1 through 5 is $2,500 for church members, $3,100 for nonmembers. Grades 6 through 8 cost $2,650 for members, $3,250 for nonmembers.

Donna Klein Jewish Academy
9701 Donna Klein Blvd.
Boca Raton   852-3300

This widely respected school opened in 1979 as the South County Jewish Community Day School. At that point, it had only 50 students.

Current enrollment is more than 10 times that number, with students ranging from kindergarten to 8th grade. Focus is given to academics, with emphasis on both Jewish and secular studies.

The current annual cost to attend kindergarten is $5450; 1st grade, $5750; 2nd grade through 4th, $5900; and 5th through 8th grades, $6350. For more information on the school, see our sidebar called The Jewish Community in the Arts and Culture chapter.

NORTH BROWARD SCHOOL
AND LIGHTHOUSE POINT ACADEMY
3701 N.E. 22nd Ave.
Lighthouse Point   *(305) 941-4816*

Only a minute or two south of Deerfield Beach along the east side of U.S. Highway 1 is the bedroom community of Lighthouse Point. Located in the city's center, alongside City Hall, these two private schools stress the importance of the basics, small classes and a warm environment for learning.

Founded as a preschool in 1957, North Broward School grew and added grade levels. In 1977, Lighthouse Point Academy was created.

North Broward School offers a Montessori curriculum pre-kindergarten through grade 8 for students whose parents prefer a private school environment to enhance their children's academic and creative opportunities. Lighthouse Point Academy, which serves the same grade levels, educates average to gifted children who experience difficulties in a traditional classroom setting.

Both schools are accredited by the Southern Association of Colleges and Schools and the Florida Council of Independent Schools. North Broward School's academic program is built on mastery of language arts, mathematics, science, social studies and Spanish. Lighthouse Point Academy's curriculum focuses on reading, spelling, English, mathematics, social studies and science. Students at both schools participate in physical education, art, music and computer courses. Interested students may participate in an extracurricular sports program (grades 5 through 8), honor organizations and clubs.

Costs at both schools vary by grade level and payment plan. North Broward School's tuition averages $5,160 for pre-K and kindergarten, $5,306 for grades 1 through 5 and $5,496 for grades 6 through 8. Tuition at Lighthouse Point Academy averages $9,786. Tuition does not include book, uniform and transportation costs.

UNITY SCHOOL
101 N.W. 22nd St.
Delray Beach   *276-4414*

Established in 1964, Unity School is a place for achievers age 2½ through grade 8.

Students gain admission to the school's elementary and middle schools by scoring in the 80th percentile or higher on standardized tests and must maintain a 3.0 grade-point average.

The challenging academic program offers a student the opportunity to succeed within his or her own individual learning style.

Students in grades K through 8 also are given the opportunity to participate in the Odyssey of the Mind program, which gives them the chance to work with a team of creative thinkers to solve a variety of problems. Groups present their creativity in multilevel competitions in an effort to promote team cooperation and camaraderie.

Extracurricular activities for students in the elementary school include intramural athletics, drama, Chess Club, Choir Chimes, chorus and student council.

For middle school students, extracurricular activities include band, chorus and choir chimes and a variety of intramural sports including flag football, basketball, tennis and volleyball.

A Montessori preschool, featuring a 6-to-1 student-teacher ratio, is also available. Admission requires that children be toilet trained and up-to-date on necessary immunizations.

Tuition for the three schools ranges from $3,450 to $5,775 annually.

Child Care

To say Palm Beach County offers a selection of child-care facilities is something like saying Imelda Marcos owned a few pairs of shoes or that there are a few banks in the Bahamas. There is quite a selection of child-care facilities out there!

As of July 4, 1995, concerned parents here got the chance to breathe a bit easier as they contemplated their child-care options. On that date, a 1991 law took full effect, mandating that licensed day-care centers must provide a worker certified with a Child Development Associate credential for every 20 children under the center's care. To earn a CDA credential, applicants must go through a minimum of 600 hours training and experience.

Previous portions of the law mandated increased minimal training for all child-care workers, from 20 to 30 hours.

If you are searching for a child-care provider for your child, stop by the centers you're contemplating unannounced to inspect the center's facilities. Ask to check the school's license and any other accreditation certification it may have. There are reputable accreditation centers with stringent criteria, including teacher-child ratios more stringent than the state requires, and teacher-education and program requirements.

During the visit, observe carefully the interaction between staff members and children and how the children interact with each other. How are disputes handled? How are special-needs children accommodated? How are meal and snack times handled? Are the children given creative opportunities?

Don't be shy about asking many questions. If the child-care provider seems reluctant or unwilling to answer your questions fully, move on. There are plenty of facilities out there whose operators are willing to answer your toughest questions, meet all the necessary state requirements and provide tender, compassionate care for your children.

If you are visiting the area and need child-care services, check first with the

Photo: Richard Rolan

Budding engineers create a poster on a multimedia computer as part of a weeklong Florida Atlantic University program aimed at getting high-schoolers interested in the sciences.

concierge or desk clerk at your place of lodging. Some hotels offer child-care programs, and others work with local centers to provide daily services. Two places that provide supervised children's programs include The Breakers in Palm Beach and Jupiter Beach Resort in Jupiter. See our Accommodations chapter for information about these lodgings.

Palm Beach County also has its share of nationally known facilities. A few you might recognize are KinderCare Learning Centers, LaPetite Academy and Adventure Bay Early Learning Centers.

Day-care centers are subject to specific city and county ordinances and are regulated and inspected by the Florida Department of Health and Rehabilitative Services. The state agency monitors centers for care-giving and health standards as well as for teacher and attendant licensing and screening.

The types of day-care facilities in Florida are many: nonprofit facilities, community centers, workplace centers, church centers and commercially operated facilities. For information about specific agencies, call or write **Child Care Resource Referral**, 551 S.E. Eighth Street, Delray Beach 33483, 265-2423.

Photo: FAU Relations

Sorority members ride a float in Florida Atlantic University's homecoming parade.

Inside
Colleges and Universities

One of the reasons the quality of life here on Silicon Beach (so called because of the high-tech industries here) is so good is the effect and influence higher education has on our lives. A student can go from kindergarten through a doctorate here in Palm Beach County, and more top-flight colleges are located just outside the county limits. He or she then can walk into a satisfying, high-paying, prestigious career in a variety of fields.

But our colleges and universities do much more than simply offer degree programs. They add to the community through superior continuing education opportunities, cultural and athletic events and other outreach programs.

Palm Beach County

FLORIDA ATLANTIC UNIVERSITY
777 Glades Rd.
Boca Raton 367-3000

Among Florida's nine state universities, Florida Atlantic, established in 1961, is considered a baby next to some of the grizzled old-timers like Florida State (established 1851) and the University of Florida (1853) But, my, how that baby's grown!

FAU, which opened the doors to its 850-acre campus in 1964 and was elected to regular membership in the Southern Association of Colleges and Schools and fully accredited in 1967, originally had been planned as a commuter school to serve upper-division undergraduates, graduates and doctoral students. But with the need for public higher education rising, the college added freshman and sophomore classes in 1984 and also has added residence halls and expanded its athletic program.

In its short lifetime, FAU has developed a sterling reputation in the academic community as a university with rigorous standards and a penchant for excellence and innovation. Its separate schools of study focus on the arts and humanities, education, the liberal arts, the physical sciences, urban and public affairs, business, engineering, nursing and the social sciences.

FAU also has forged strong ties with the community through programs such as the Lifelong Learning Society, the largest senior learning center in the United States. There are also hundreds of low-cost professional development and continuing courses available through the university's EdVentures program. Small business owners can receive assistance and training through the FAU Small Business Development Center.

PALM BEACH COMMUNITY COLLEGE, SOUTH CAMPUS

3000 St. Lucie Ave.
Boca Raton   367-4500

The oldest of Florida's 28 public junior colleges, Palm Beach Community College has served the community since 1933.

PBCC has offered courses in the southern part of the county since 1971. The South Campus, nestled on the northern edge of Florida Atlantic University's property, became a permanent campus in 1989. Other sites are the Central Campus in Lake Worth, Glades Campus in Belle Glade and the Edward M. Eissey Campus, named to honor the college's current president, in Palm Beach Gardens.

The college offers a broad number of majors leading to Associate in Arts and Associate in Science degrees, one-year certificates, and an array of courses in its diverse, active Department of Continuing Education.

PBCC students may also participate in a variety of competitive sports.

LYNN UNIVERSITY

3601 N. Military Tr.
Boca Raton   997-0770

In 1962, just across the tracks from where Florida Atlantic University was beginning to push itself from the sand, a two-year Catholic college for women, Marymount College, also began to grow. For its first few years, the school, set on a peaceful campus dotted with Florida live oaks, grew fitfully then faltered. Donald Ross, president of Wilmington College in Delaware, visited the school early in the 1970s, hoping to acquire a significant portion of the school's library

holdings but found he liked the campus and the energy in the surrounding community. Instead of raiding the college's resources, Ross helped it back onto its feet and eventually became its president. Marymount became the College of Boca Raton in 1971 and grew to become a four-year, coed school. In 1991, the college changed its name to Lynn University to honor the contributions and support of benefactors Christine and Eugene Lynn.

Lynn University offers associate's and bachelor's degree programs in a variety of areas and master's programs in hospitality, international management, health-care administration, sports, and athletic administration, geriatric-care management and biomechanical trauma.

PALM BEACH ATLANTIC COLLEGE

901 S. Flagler Dr.
West Palm Beach   650-7700

Lying at the crossroads between Palm Beach and West Palm Beach, at the foot of the Flagler Bridge, Palm Beach Atlantic is a pulse point in central Palm Beach County's action.

The college, which enrolls about 2,000 students, has added a graduate division that includes a program in business administration designed for working professionals.

Undergraduate majors include Biblical and theological studies, and educational and general studies.

NORTHWOOD UNIVERSITY

2600 N. Military Tr.
West Palm Beach   478-5510

Northwood University, plain and simple, means business. Every course

Make Your Future Happen...

Lynn University knows what it takes to succeed in today's global world! Discover your exciting future with **real programs** that help to prepare you for **real jobs** in a **real world** — a dynamic world that is expanding and changing constantly. Prepare for many of the fastest growing professions; choose from our many timely academic programs:

Aviation, Business, Communications, Education, Fashion, Interior Design, Design, Health Sciences, Hotel/Restaurant, Liberal Arts, Sports/Recreation, and Hospitality.

Graduate programs available are: Biomechanical Trauma, Eldercare Administration, Geriatric Care Management, Hospitality Administration, International Management, Sports and Athletic Administration, and the Master of Education in Varying Exceptionalities and ESOL.

A full complement of Professional and Continuing Studies is conveniently scheduled for the working adult. New is the Bachelor of Science in Nursing (RN to BSN). Other opportunities include Human Resource Management, Management Information Systems, and International Business.

LYNN UNIVERSITY

Office of Admissions
3601 North Military Trail, Boca Raton, Fl. 33431 U.S.A
(407) 994-0770 • (800) 544-8035

offered at the 500-student school is tied in some way to the world of business and commerce.

The West Palm Beach school is one of three campuses of the university. The others are in Cedar Hill, Texas, and Midland, Michigan, plus there are Northwood extension centers throughout the country.

The school offers an Associate in Arts, Bachelor of Business Administration and Executive Master of Business Administration degrees.

REGIONAL SEMINARY
OF ST. VINCENT DE PAUL
10701 S. Military Tr.
Boynton Beach   732-4424

The major seminary serving the Catholic Diocese of Palm Beach and the Archdiocese of Miami (southern Florida's minor seminary is St. John Vianney College Seminary, in Miami), the Seminary of St. Vincent de Paul offers Master of Divinity and Master of Arts degrees.

Broward and Martin Counties

To the north and south of Palm Beach County, Broward and Martin counties also offer exceptional educational opportunities within a reasonable drive. Among them are:

BROWARD COMMUNITY
COLLEGE, NORTH CAMPUS
1000 Coconut Creek Pkwy.
Coconut Creek   (305) 973-2240

Many of BCC's North Campus students are from Boca Raton or southwest Palm Beach County and find the commute to Coconut Creek is a snap.

Serving southeastern Florida since 1960, BCC also operates major campuses in Davie and Pembroke Pines. The Central Campus in Davie is also a host site for Florida Atlantic and Florida International University courses.

North Campus is home to the college's program in Electronic Engineering Technology, named winner of the 1993 Department of Education Secretary's award for Outstanding Vocational-Technical Education.

NOVA SOUTHEASTERN UNIVERSITY
3301 College Ave.
Davie   (305) 474-7300

Nova University celebrated its 30th birthday in 1994 with a name change, reflecting its merger with the Southeastern University of the Health Sciences. With the change, Nova Southeastern University became an even more diverse school, offering an undergraduate program plus extensive graduate and professional programs in osteopathic medicine, pharmacy, psychology, family therapy, education, business and entrepreneurship, oceanography, medicine and law.

The college offers an extensive sports program for its undergraduates and is the home of the Miami Dolphins' training facility.

ART INSTITUTE OF FORT LAUDERDALE
1799 S.E. 17th St.
Fort Lauderdale   (305) 463-3000

An offspring of the Art Institute of Pittsburgh, the AIFL is a private, proprietary college offering two- and four-year degree programs in a variety of majors including visual communications, fashion design, interior design, travel and tourism, photography, culinary arts and photography.

Photo: FAU Relations

Students work in a chemistry lab at Florida Atlantic University. For some, this is the first step toward careers in medicine, pharmacology and other science-based fields.

One very popular aspect of the school is its continuing education program, which provides modestly priced eight-week experiential learning programs in areas such as cartooning, computer graphics, culinary arts, photography and more.

HOBE SOUND BIBLE COLLEGE

11298 S.E. Gomez Ave.
Hobe Sound 546-5534

Twenty-five miles north of West Palm Beach, Hobe Sound Bible Col-

lege sits next to Jupiter Island on the Palm Beach-Martin County line.

The 200-student college awards one-year certificates, Associate in Arts and Bachelor of Arts degrees in a variety of Biblical and theological areas, missions and more.

Inside
Government

Thirty-seven municipalities comprise Palm Beach County, the largest county east of the Mississippi River and home to almost a million residents within its 2,000 square miles. Boca Raton anchors South County, with the Village of Tequesta 47 miles to the north. West Palm Beach, the county seat, sits midway between Boca and Tequesta.

In addition to serving residents of incorporated areas, Palm Beach County serves more than 80,000 residents in unincorporated western Boca and more than 50,000 west of Delray Beach's city limits.

The **Southeast Palm Beach County Administrative Complex**, 345 S. Congress Avenue, Delray Beach, 276-1200, houses divisions of several major departments: Health Department, tax collector, voter's registration, property appraiser, supervisor of elections, planning/building/zoning, and satellite offices for county commissioners from Districts 4, 5 and 7.

The South County sheriff's substation is also at 345 S. Congress Avenue, and the non-emergency number is 278-2644. The Crime Stoppers hot line is (800) 458-TIPS.

The county health department operates an office nearby, 225 S. Congress Avenue, 274-3100. In the same complex is Palm Beach County Community Services' office of human services, 274-3130.

The **Administrative Complex Annex**, 501 S. Congress Avenue, has the Property Appraiser's office. Call 276-1250 for information on homestead exemption and departments related to land, buildings, condominiums and tangible personal property. In the same location is the Tax Collector's office. Call 930-7922 for auto and boat registrations and title changes, hunting and fishing licenses; 930-7923 for occupational licenses; and 930-7927 for property tax information.

The regional **South County Courthouse**, 200 W. Atlantic Avenue, Delray Beach, houses circuit and county satellite courts, 274-1400.

Elected Officials and Agencies

Palm Beach County

In 1984, voters expanded county government initiatives by adopting a "Home Rule" Charter. Effective since January 1, 1985, the charter allows the county to determine ordinances and laws, as long as they aren't in conflict with federal and Florida law. Voters may initiate procedures to create new local laws or amend existing ones. The

Palm Beach charter provides for recalling county commissioners for cause, and has procedures for voters to modify or amend the charter.

A seven-member **Board of County Commissioners** serves staggered four-year terms. Ken Foster of District 6, named chairperson in November 1994, presides over meetings and serves as the county's ceremonial representative. Vice Chair is Burt Aronson of District 5. Other Commissioners are past chairperson Mary McCarty of District 4; Maude Ford Lee, District 7; Warren Newell, District 3; Carol Roberts, District 2; and Karen Marcus, District 1.

Elected from single-member districts, commissioners meet on the first, third and fourth Tuesdays of each month in the Jane M. Thompson Memorial Chambers on the sixth floor of the **County Governmental Center**, 301 N. Olive Avenue, West Palm Beach. Government and Education Television broadcasts county commission proceedings live. Cable providers for access are Comcast Cablevision in Boca Raton (Channel 20) and parts of West Palm Beach (Channel 35); Adelphia for west Boca, Highland Beach and west-south-central areas in the county (Channel 20); Leadership Cable for Delray Beach (Channel 20); Tele-Media Co. for Boynton Beach, Century Village-Boca and parts of West Palm (Channel 20). In addition, the Palm Beach County Public Affairs Department publishes *Channel 20 Highlights* monthly.

Useful numbers include **Public Affairs**, 355-2754, and the **Governmental Center**, 355-2040. Palm Beach County also recently established a phone network to expedite communications about services and other useful information. Call the **County Information Line** at 355-6848, or toll-free from South County, 930-5125.

The **County Citizens' Service Line**, 355-4314 or 930-4314, is open 24 hours a day, seven days a week. Staff members are available to assist callers weekdays from 8 AM to 5 PM. On weekends, holidays and evenings, leave a message for a return call the next business day. The TDD line for hearing-impaired callers is 355-4415. Residents may report nonmedical and non-law enforcement situations to the **Emergency Operations Center**, 233-3500.

County Administrator Robert Weisman oversees more than 20 departments and offices that provide services and related programs. County Attorney Joe Mount and Internal Auditor Fred Jenkins are also accountable to the Commission. Herman Brice oversees Fire-Rescue services, whose professionals provide fire-fighting, prevention, emergency medical assistance and advanced life support. The county and each municipality respond to respective 911 *emergency* calls. The county's *non-emergency* **Fire-Rescue** administrative number is 233-0010, or 278-9970 in South County.

Constitutional officers include Sheriff Charles McCutcheon (former Under Sheriff as well as Boca Raton's police chief for 10 years), State Attorney Barry Krischer, Public Defender Richard Jorandby, Clerk of the Circuit Court Dorothy Wilken, Property

Appraiser Gary Nikolits, Supervisor of Elections Jackie Winchester, Tax Collector John Clark and Chief Judge Jack Cook.

In spring 1994, Palm Beach County's judiciary — criminal and civil divisions of Circuit and County Court, administrative staffs, Probate and Juvenile courts, custody investigations, youth affairs, victim services, witness management, jury assembly, interpreters and courthouse security — completed its move into a new $125 million courthouse at 401 N. Dixie Highway, West Palm Beach.

Palm Beach County's **Sheriff's Department** remains at 3228 Gun Club Road, West Palm Beach, 688-3000. Near the Governmental Center and the Courthouse are the headquarters for the State Attorney and the Public Defender, 451 N. Third Street, West Palm Beach.

County administrative offices and Channel 20 are among those remaining in the Governmental Center. On Dixie Highway, across from the new facility, work is under way to restore the 1916 courthouse.

Independent of the County Commission, the seven-member, nonpartisan **Palm Beach County School Board** is elected to govern the county's educational system. The Board meets on the first and third Wednesdays each month at 6 PM in the Winona Jordan Board Chambers, 3300 Forest Hill Boulevard, West Palm Beach. Channel 20 broadcasts the proceedings live.

Members from Districts 1 through 7 are Gail Bjork, Paulette Burdick, Chairwoman Jody Gleason, William Graham, Vice Chair Bob Hayes, Diane Heinz and Dr. Sandra Richmond.

The Palm Beach County School Board voted this summer to replace School Superintendent Monica Uhlhorn a year before her contract was to expire. Seldom free of controversy during four years on the job, Uhlhorn agreed to a $300,000 buyout offer from the board.

Her effectiveness was under fire even before a nationally televised documentary used Uhlhorn's administration to illustrate what's wrong with public education in the United States.

The school board appointed an acting superintendent from district administration while searching for a replacement.

Call the **Board of Education**, 434-8000, or Public Information, 434-8228.

The **Palm Beach County Library System** headquarters is 3650 Summit Boulevard, West Palm Beach, 930-5115. The **Southwest County Regional Library** is 20701 95th Avenue S., off Glades Road in west Boca, 482-4554. Hours are 10 AM to 9 PM Monday through Thursday, 10 AM to 5 PM on Saturday and 1 to 5 PM on Sunday. Hours at the Delray Beach branch, 7777 W. Atlantic Avenue, 498-3110, are 10 AM to 8 PM Monday through Wednesday and 10 AM to 5 PM Thursday through Saturday. Proof of residency is required to obtain a county library card; noncounty residents pay a $15 fee.

For information on the Bookmobile, Talking Books, Books By Mail and the county program of the **Florida Literacy Coalition**, call 265-0299.

Photo: Stephanie Murhpy

Palm Beach County's new, grand courthouse opened two years late, but better late than never.

The **Tourist Development Council** has an office in West Palm Beach, 233-1048; film liaison, 233-1000, and visitor information services, 233-1020, also are available.

Besides the 37 county municipalities, other taxing entities independent of the County Commission include the **South Florida Water Management District**, 686-8800; **Health Care District**, 659-1270; and various drainage and inlet districts. A *Telephone Guide to County Services* offers useful numbers.

Palm Beach County regulates water service from its headquarters at 2030 E. Congress Avenue, West Palm Beach. For information, call 278-5135. For information on county recycling programs, call 471-2700.

Major Municipalities

Trivia: Boca Raton's population inside the city is 66,000 in an area just more than 27 square miles. Median household income is about $45,000. Delray Beach is 15-plus square miles, with a population of 49,500 and median household income of about $32,000. Boynton Beach is 15-plus square miles, with a population of 49,000 and median household income of about $29,000. Lake Worth has a population of almost 30,000 in 5 square miles, and median household income is about $22,000. Palm Beach has only 9,800 islanders rattling around a 12-mile strip. Median household income is about $62,000, keep the change. And West Palm Beach has a population of almost 70,000 occupying 54 square miles, with a median household income of about $27,000.

Boca Raton

Boca Raton voters selected a Council-Manager system 30 years ago, with

• **303**

a mayor and four nonpartisan members elected at large for two-year terms. Mayor Carol Hanson serves with Deputy Mayor Steven Abrams and Council members Wanda Thayer, Esther Dance and Susan Whelchel. The City Council meets the second and fourth Tuesday at 7:30 PM in Council Chambers, City Hall, 201 W. Palmetto Park Road, 393-7700. The Council sets policy, determines municipal ordinances, adopts its budget and collects taxes and fees.

City Council appointed City Manager Donna Dreska in 1994. Previously, she served as assistant city manager under the late Richard Witker.

Departments include public safety, parks and recreation, library, engineering, public works and community development. **City Hall** houses most departments at 201 W. Palmetto Park Road, 393-7700. The **Citizen Inquiry Line** is 393-7914.

Police Department headquarters are across from City Hall at 100 N.W. Boca Raton Boulevard. Divisions include road patrol, crime investigations, internal affairs, K-9 unit, marine patrol, motorcycle patrol, underwater teams and community education assistance. For *non-emergencies*, call 338-1333.

Boca Raton Fire-Rescue teams of paramedics and firefighters provide residents with 24-hour protection. In addition, the city offers educational programs, fire prevention training, investigations and building code inspections. For *non-emergencies*, call 395-1127.

Boca Raton Public Library is at 200 N.W. Boca Raton Boulevard. Services include books for adults and juveniles, videos, children's programs, copy machines, microfilm reader-printers and a TDD unit for the speech- or hearing-impaired.

Library hours are 9:30 AM to 8:30 PM, Monday through Thursday; 9 AM to 5 PM, Friday and Saturday; noon to 8 PM on Sunday. For more information, call 393-7852. Library cards are available with proof of residency such as driver's license or voter's registration. The library also issues cards for a $35 fee to people who live outside the city limits.

Boynton Beach

Boynton Beach has a manager-commission form of government and a majority of new officials since elections in March. Newcomers include Mayor Jerry Taylor, Commissioner Shirley Jaskiewicz and Commissioner Sidney Rosen. They serve with Mayor Pro-tem Lynne Matson and Vice Mayor Matt Bradley.

City Manager is Carrie Parker, whose administration includes an assistant city manager, the city attorney, the city clerk, and directors for planning, finance, utilities, recreation and parks, personnel, public works and development. The non-emergency number for **Boynton Beach Police Department** is 732-8116; and the **Boynton Beach Fire Department**, 375-6035.

Boynton Beach City Library is at 208 S. Seacrest Boulevard, 375-6390. Hours are 9 AM to 8:30 PM Monday through Thursday, 9 AM to 5 PM on Friday and Saturday.

Palms adorn the modern facade of the South County Courthouse on W. Atlantic and Fourth avenues in Delray Beach.

The City Commission meets the first and third Tuesday at 6:30 PM at City Hall, 100 E. Boynton Beach Boulevard, 375-6000.

Boynton Beach will celebrate its centennial in 1996. The city's namesake is Major Nathan Boynton of Michigan, who fought in the Civil War.

Delray Beach

Delray Beach, with about 49,000 residents, also governs itself with a town commission. City Manager is David Harden. Mayor Tom Lynch serves with Vice Mayor Jay Alperin and Commissioners Ken Ellingsworth, David Randolph and Barbara Smith. **City Hall** houses most departments at 100 N.W. First Avenue, 243-7000.

The City Commission meets on Tuesdays at 6 PM at City Hall.

Delray Beach Public Library is at 29 S.E. Fourth Avenue, 276-6462. Summer hours are 9:30 AM to 9 PM on Mondays and 9:30 to 5 PM Tuesday through Saturday. After Labor Day the library is open three days a week only. Please call to verify days and times.

Police Department headquarters are at 300 W. Atlantic Avenue. For non-emergencies, call 243-7800.

The non-emergency number for **Delray Beach Fire Department** is 243-7400.

Highland Beach

The boutique-size Town of Highland Beach covers 3 miles of oceanfront between Boca Raton and Delray Beach. A residential community with a Holiday Inn as its only commercial structure, the township governs itself from **Town Hall**, 3614 S. Ocean

Photo: Stephanie Murphy

Boca Raton's City Hall is located at 201 W. Palmetto Park Road.

Boulevard, Highland Beach. Delray Beach assumed fire-rescue service for the township, which in prior years contracted with Palm Beach County. For information, call Town Hall at 278-4548.

Lake Worth

The city has a manager-commission form of government. Officials are Mayor Rodney Romano, Vice Mayor Bob Dovey and Commissioners Retha Lowe, Tom Ramiccio and Lloyd Clager. The City Commission meets the first Tuesday at 4 PM and the third Tuesday at 6 PM at City Hall, 7 N. Dixie Highway, 586-1600.

The non-emergency number for **Lake Worth Police Department** is 586-1611, and the **Lake Worth Fire Department**, 586-1711.

Lake Worth Public Library is at 15 N. M Street, 533-7354. Hours vary seasonally. Please call for details.

Palm Beach

Palm Beach governs itself from the Mediterranean Revival **Town Hall**, constructed in 1925, on South County Road. Contemporary-style police headquarters lie immediately northeast of the restored Town Hall that houses the mayor, town manager, town clerk, zoning and other departments. For information, write P.O. Box 2029, Palm Beach 33480, or call 838-5400.

The Town has a manager-council form of government. Mayor Paul Ilyinsky serves with Council president Lesly Smith, president pro-tem Jack McDonald and Councilmen Samuel McClendon, Leslie Shaw and Allen Wyett.

The Town Council meets the second Tuesday at 9:30 AM at Town Hall, 630 S. County Road, 838-5400.

The non-emergency number for **Palm Beach Police Department** is 838-5454, and the **Palm Beach Fire Department**, 838-5420.

West Palm Beach

About three years ago, West Palm revised its system from manager-commission to a strong mayor form of government. The city's first elected mayor, Nancy Graham serves with Commission president Mary Hooks and Commissioners Joel Daves, Howard Warshauer and Alfred Zucaro.

The City Commission meets every other Monday at 6 PM at City Hall, 200 W. Banyan Boulevard, 659-8000.

The non-emergency number for **West Palm Beach Police Department** is 837-4000, and the **West Palm Beach Fire Department**, 835-2900.

West Palm Beach has a new landmark: a computer-controlled fountain, outside the main library, 100 E. Clematis Street, 659-8010. Hours are 10 AM to 7 PM on Mondays and Tuesdays, 10 AM to 5:30 PM on Wednesdays and Thursdays and 10 AM to 5 PM on Saturdays. The library is closed on Fridays and Sundays.

The city celebrated its centennial in 1994.

State of Florida

Democratic Gov. Lawton Chiles is serving his second term of office at the State Capitol, Tallahassee, Florida 32399. You may call him at (904) 488-4441.

Palm Beach County's Legislative Delegation "lives" at the Governmen-

tal Center, 301 N. Olive Avenue, West Palm Beach. You can contact legislators at the following respective addresses and phone numbers:

State Senators include Robert Wexler, 2500 N. Military Trail, Boca Raton, 994-6505; W.G. Myers, 50 Kindred Street, Suite 301, Stuart 34994-3058; 283-3133; Ken Jenne II, 612 S.E. Fifth Avenue, Suite 3, Fort Lauderdale 33301, (305) 467-4332; Matthew Meadows, 3741 W. Broward Boulevard, Suite 206, Fort Lauderdale 33312, (305) 327-6200; Jim Scott, 2000 E. Oakland Park Boulevard, Fort Lauderdale 33306, 833-9231; Tom Rossin, 505 S. Flagler Drive, Suite 1001, West Palm Beach 33401, 837-5400.

State Representatives include Ron Klein, 8177 W. Glades Road, Boca Raton 33434, 482-8560; Suzanne Jacobs, 990 S. Congress Avenue, Delray Beach 33445, 274-4690; and Bill Andrews, 217 N.E. Fourth Street, Delray Beach 33483, 276-5823; Rick Minton, 2300 Virginia Avenue, Suite 200, Fort Pierce 34982, 595-1380; Tom Warner, 957 S. Federal Highway, Stuart 34994, 223-5010; Sharon Merchant, 721 U.S. Highway 1, Suite 110, North Palm Beach 33408, 840-3147; Addie Greene, 330 Clematis Street, Suite 205, West Palm Beach 33401, 837-5252; Lois Frankel, 1645 Palm Beach Lakes Boulevard, Suite 290, West Palm Beach 33409, 681-2597; Ed Healey, 50 S. Military Trail, Suite 205, West Palm Beach 33415, 640-6161; Debbie Sanderson, 4800 N.E. 20th Terrace, Suite 401, Fort Lauderdale 33308, 995-0036.

The Department of Health & Rehabilitative Services has toll-free protective services assistance at (800) 962-2867 or TDD calls, (800) 453-5145.

The Florida Highway Patrol has stations in Lantana, 540-1145, and at the West Palm Beach interchange of Florida's Turnpike, 640-2830. The Division of Driver Licenses has offices at 571 N. Military Trail, West Palm Beach; 14570 S. Military Trail, Delray Beach; 1299 W. Lantana Road, Lantana; 3185 PGA Boulevard, Palm Beach Gardens; Florida Highway Patrol Station, 1839 E. Main Street, Pahokee; 4320 S.E. Federal Highway, Stuart; 8495 Federal Highway, Port St. Lucie; 3220 S. Federal Highway, Fort Pierce; and 668 U.S. Highway 1 N., Tequesta. For information, call (800) 303-7288.

For general State of Florida information, call 837-5000.

Federal Government

U.S. Senators include Bob Graham, 44 W. Flagler Street, Miami, (305) 536-7293, or 241 Dirksen Senate Office Building, Washington, D.C. 20510, (202) 224-3041; and Connie Mack, 777 Brickell Avenue, Miami, (305) 530-7100, or Hart Senate Office Building, Washington, D.C., (202) 224-5274.

U.S. Rep. Harry Johnston has offices as 1501 Corporate Drive, Boynton Beach, 732-4000, or 204 Cannon House Office Building, Washington, D.C., (202) 225-3001.

Reach U.S. Rep. Clay Shaw at 1512 E. Broward Boulevard, Suite 101, Fort Lauderdale, (305) 522-1800; 222 Lakeview Avenue, Suite 162, West Palm Beach, 832-3007; and 2267 Rayburn House Office Building, Washington, D.C., (202) 225-3026

U.S. Rep. Alcee Hastings can be contacted at 2701 E. Oakland Park Boulevard, Suite 200, Fort Lauderdale, (305) 733-2800; 5725 Corporate Way, Suite 208, West Palm Beach, 684-0565; and 1039 Longworth House Office Building, Washington, D.C., (202) 225-1313.

U.S. Rep. Mark Foley has offices at 4440 PGA Boulevard, Palm Beach Gardens 33410, 627-6192; or 506 Cannon House Office Building, Washington, D.C. 20515, (202) 225-3121.

The **Social Security Administration** has an office at 310 S.E. First Street, Delray Beach. Hours are 8:30 AM to 3:30 PM weekdays. For information, call (800) 772-1213.

The **Veteran's Administration** offers employment assistance at 8895 N. Military Trail, Palm Beach Gardens, and an outpatient clinic at 301 Broadway, Riviera Beach, 845-2800.

The **National Weather Service** provides a local forecast 24 hours daily at 686-5650.

The **Office of Immigration and Naturalization** is at 4360 Northlake Boulevard, Palm Beach Gardens, 626-8151.

The U.S. Government offers toll-free information at (800) 347-1997.

Information on the postal service, occupational and other licensing procedures appear in the Service Directory.

Inside
Mizner Park

The year 1995 will be remembered as The Year We Moved From Park Into Overdrive on this issue. One index of that progress is real optimism coming from the lips of formerly-fierce opponents.

What issue, you ask?

There was a time when stand-up comics went around saying the quickest way to start an argument in Boca Raton was to mention real estate developer Tom Crocker and/or Mizner Park, the mixed-use urban phenomenon that made its breathless debut in December 1990. Crocker owns Mizner Park through an entity of Crocker & Company in a joint venture with mega-pension fund Teachers Insurance and Annuity Association (TIAA).

For more than five years, Crocker and Mizner Park drew praise, criticism, envy, derision, applause, controversy, congratulations, discourse, wagering, hypothesizing and wishful thinking.

Today, the pair draws thumbs up and in some corners respectful relief because a lot of discussions about new elements in downtown redevelopment have parentheticals of "aligned with" or "leading to" or "meshing with" and "expanding with" Mizner Park. It's not necessary to speculate whether current phases are compelling enough to be stand-alone destinations the way Mizner Park has performed to this point. But it is useful to recognize that it was immensely convenient if not predestined for Mizner Park to be in place if later projects were to complement.

So if someone says Mizner Park arrived ahead of its time, fewer people would argue the point — even if they disagree — because, finally, the rest of downtown is participating in the vision that saw Mizner Park as its catalyst, even when Mizner Park was too green for the job.

Says Marta Batmasian, an owner of Royal Palm Plaza, "Mizner Park is a beautiful monument . . . some people will stay mad about it for 20 years, but then it will be OK."

Go back to the late 1980s. Tom Crocker had paid $28.5 million for a dilapidated property and razed the existing Boca Raton Mall. The city was kicking around ideas for a mixed-use project that would revitalize its 344-acre downtown and trying to think of ways to mix cultural components into the equation. Several cultural groups, including the Boca Raton Museum of Art and Caldwell Theatre, were interested in locating downtown.

Recognizing the economic advantages of having private sector involvement, the city started talking with developers, including Crocker. The Boca Mall site seemed ideal for the concept of Mizner Park, and Crocker was attracted to the public-sector financing advantages. So Crocker proposed that the Community Redevelopment Agency (CRA) buy his land; he, in turn, would develop the project and pay for its common area maintenance until 1996. Crocker's financial partner in the development is TIAA. The 30-acre village was the first of its kind in the Southeast United States and called for 125,000 square feet of specialty retail space; an eight-plex cinema; 102,000 square feet of professional office space; 200,000 square feet of Class A office space; more than 200 residential units; and museums and theaters to be built out over 10 years.

Critics of the deal said the city shouldn't get into the real estate business, though voters approved the measure on referendum after Crocker took the initiative to call for a special election. The CRA borrowed money from Gulf Breeze, a Florida Panhandle municipality, at tax-free rates and issued tax-free redevelopment bonds to buy the land from Crocker. Eventually, the city will repay the bondholder with tax increment financing in the revitalized downtown area — the difference between property taxes as they were assessed at the origin of redevelopment and tax assessments after new construction has generated more revenue. After the city has paid off the bonds sometime next century, the project will become a pure revenue stream.

Others criticized the failure of Mizner Park to draw the cultural tenants, but it was those groups themselves that changed their minds about locating downtown.

To put the issue into perspective, it might help to recall that Mizner Park was envisioned as a commercial/cultural mixed-use project with certain elements to arrive over the course of 10 years. The International Museum of Cartoon Art is well on its way to completion, and the north end of Mizner Park still remains available for cultural tenants who might choose to move there.

What Crocker achieved otherwise is significant. He intuited correctly that the redevelopment project had to address existing market need, which meant not simply putting a Band-Aid on an outdated mall or creating another facility in the already mall-dominated landscape.

It meant creating a destination for dining and leisure time rather than just retail. Several restaurants, the advanced cinema and the unique bookstore combined to create a place to

Photo: B. Shepard

Mizner Park offices, apartments and shops surround a fountain-adorned plaza.

visit while people browsed and shopped. These destinations were complemented by the outdoor atmosphere and human scale for landscaping, parking and the streetscape. The size of tenant spaces were also considered: boutique-size bays for retail and comfort zones for professional offices.

The result is that people who have never seen many other parts of Boca Raton usually find their way to Mizner Park — to see, to be seen, to browse, to buy, to soak up the Boca mystique. Mizner Park has nearly 50 tenants, including many of the original lessees who opened shop in early 1991. The space is 96 percent leased on retail, which comprises about 55 percent of the total nonresidential development. About 94 percent of the office and professional space is leased.

The Magnet

Crocker is among developers and other entrepreneurs who anticipated that a sophisticated, appealing lifestyle would be very important to drawing new business investment in Boca Raton and South County. The arrival of Fortune 100 and Fortune 500 member headquarters here proves global markets can be managed from any location. Projects of the Mizner Park genre sweeten the deal when decision

makers have narrowed relocation to two or three possibilities.

Crocker believes the choice to be here demonstrates we don't have to rely on residential property taxes. Rather, "we can continue to build a tax base beyond building more homes by attracting tenants who are taxed at a bigger rate. Commercial is less costly to maintain, with bigger returns."

Certainly, piquancy arrived downtown with the July 1995 opening of Mezzanotte, the standing-room-only South Beach supper club that opened on the first floor of the NationsBank building on Palmetto Park Road. A town that averted its eyes from an anatomically correct statue in Mizner Park this year, now welcomes a club that embraces an upbeat, almost-anything-goes approach. Dining was the raison d'être when owner Tom Billante opened the first Mezzanotte in Miami Beach, and fine Northern or "high-tech" Italian cuisine is still the focus, according to Boca Raton club manager Ron Del Signore.

"We still feature the best food anywhere, but after nine o'clock, people start feeling at home. Our clientele has to do with our attitude: upbeat, no dress code, be comfortable; the help dances with the customers and there's some tabletop dancing."

In 1995, Billante will also open Mezzanotte in Mexico City as well as

Insiders' Tips

The best place in Boca Raton to stargaze is Mizner Park. Previous sightings include tennis star Steffi Graf; tennis star Andre Agassi and his girlfriend, actress Brooke Shields; and fashion designer Nicole Miller.

Photo: B. Shepard

The Mizner Park Amphitheatre is surrounded by a lawn on which spectators can picnic while watching a performance.

one in Coconut Grove at The Mayfair in August.

Del Signore says, "We look forward to growing with the expansion of Mizner Park. There will be development west of us with office space and retail and more residential nearby too. This is a perfect location."

Jacobson's Department Store

One new tenant who apparently concurs with Del Signore's "perfect location" assessment is Jacobson's Department Store, an 80,000-square-foot upscale retailer that will locate at the southeast corner of Mizner Park. Crocker & Company will begin construction later this year and estimates the store will open in November 1996.

Jacobson's selected the site more than three years ago but was unable to

move forward with development because a downtown property owner and a group of residents filed a lawsuit blocking commercial use of city-owned land that was earmarked for cultural use. Jacobson's considered alternative sites in Delray Beach before going back to its original plan to be in Mizner Park, and the dispute was resolved with another referendum in 1995.

County Commissioner Mary McCarty, whose district covers Boca Raton, was a city commissioner in Delray Beach before its downtown had gained the current positive momentum reflected in winning the All-America City award, the Florida Main Street designation and a *Florida Trend* magazine review of "The Best Run Town in Florida."

Reflecting on the way Boca is turning the corner to go forward, McCarty says, "Boca's downtown has gotten off square one because voters told them to, the way they did in Delray a few years ago. Delray tends to take a stand on things . . . they don't call for a special election after every spat. Boca fell into a pattern of hiding behind referendums on issues, which lessened their momentum. Jacobson's should have been there two years ago."

About that time, then-Mayor Bill Smith spearheaded an analysis of Boca's municipal operations, which the private sector produced. Regarding the controversial Grace Commission Survey, which critics discounted as a tool of special interests, McCarty said, "That survey was a bold move on Bill Smith's part, and Boca will benefit a lot long-term from a document that looks strictly ay financial matters. That would be a fine legacy. His downfall was in allowing one campaign to point out deficiencies at a time voters were fed up with both sides. It wasn't a level playing field."

McCarty believes progress will pick up because voters attach more middle ground to Mayor Carol Hanson, who was elected in March 1995. Says McCarty, "Things have calmed down. There's not the same old baggage. The battles lines have blurred."

Downtown developer Keith O'Donnell thinks the city's maturity as a market, as Boca reaches buildout, also contributed to the turnaround. "If you look beyond special interest groups, most people in the city are prudent. Smith's survey showed responsibility to identify cost savings in running government. The start of

change, whether pro or con, comes from government paying attention. We may be a wealthy city, but we need to be fiscally responsible. The Grace study may have been a milestone, a rallying point. Now, Carol Hanson is doing well. Being timely is in her favor."

The attention to redevelopment is nothing if not timely. We even have economic indicators in our favor. Commercial real estate used to be a bad word in South County, where the vacancy rate in existing office and industrial space was pushing 39 percent. The glut of existing space is being absorbed at more than a quarter-million square feet a year, as existing tenants expand and new ones move in.

O'Donnell, of Southcoast Partners, is a veteran commercial broker and now a principal in the company developing the Parkwood Properties sites in downtown Boca. He was with Arvida when Mizner Place was developed at Palmetto Park Road and S.E. Fifth Avenue.

O'Donnell estimates the absorption of commercial space to be about 350,000 square feet annually, ongoing. His conservative estimate of supply is two and a half years. "We're entering the opposite end of the cycle toward an equilibrium of 10 percent. This is a growth market, which depends on supply. Now that we're almost absorbed, we're looking at a potential shortage."

With built-in demand for South Florida "as long as we're only an hour from the Miami Airport and equal distance from good connections at both Palm Beach and Fort Lauderdale air-

Photo: Tom Knibbs

Mizner Park has it all—retail shops, offices and apartments.

Source: The News

This model depicts the International Museum of Cartoon Art at Mizner Park.

ports," corporate executives come here on weekends or seminars and they start thinking they could move their businesses here.

Tenants who need large quantities of space are drawn to some of the high-quality parcels vacant since IBM consolidated some divisions. For more modest size Class-A space, they'll be looking at new projects such as the one O'Donnell's company is building.

Says McCarty, "We've reversed the problem; now we need to be building new. That's essential if we are to grow beyond the retirement community level for contributions to the economy. High passive income is very limiting. Active income is a vital component of where we want to go."

She participated in Initiatives '95, an unprecedented county-sponsored summit on small business issues versus corporate matters. McCarty says, "That effort sends a very strong message reinforcing a national trend to use dollars to lure businesses. The po-

tential is there for tremendous impact, to cut unemployment in half in only two years. South County becomes very attractive to both corporate and small business because we have a multilayered work force. We have very educated technical people, and we have unskilled labor. That's important."

Marta and Jim Batmasian, owners of Royal Palm Plaza, began investing in South Florida 10 years ago, buying more than 100 acres in and near downtown Boca Raton. They are the second-largest landowners, behind the city, and most of their properties are contiguous parcels in and around the pink plaza. Unlike Crocker, the Batmasians bought existing developments to manage and maximize.

Says Jim, "Downtown are many positives these days, especially the three major apartment projects and Jacobson's. To achieve a true village atmosphere requires every detail to be in place, so the city should consider incentives.

Photo: Mizner Park Leasing Office

The Mizner Park Amphitheatre hosts many performances.

"Mizner Park didn't help the situation immediately, but now we definitely see a difference. People are excited about the residential downtown . . . that's the reason for the momentum. And it's generating investment from large and small merchants who envision a captive audience of customers living within walking distance. Mizner Park acquainted people with downtown. Now that the novelty is worn off, we're seeing newcomers coming along. And it's not a wholesale operation like Sawgrass Mills. The ones coming are in tune with the boutique environment."

Mizner Park echoes the contemporary trend toward mixed-use development applications to reverse suburban sprawl. Historically, the concept of "living above the store" was born out of economic necessity. And while Mizner Park may not draw too many starving artists, the concept is the same, whether uptown or backstreet, upscale or affordable.

Inside
Business

The Palm Beaches are home to Fortune 100 and500 corporations; large, medium and tiny private firms; chain operations; ma and pa independents; and boutique-size services. As a region, we rave appropriately when big fish move in, but we're even more bullish on the entrepreneurial little guy of either sex who owns a business or works for one that falls into the small business category of fewer than 100 employees.

That's because half of Palm Beach County's work force clocks in somewhere other than a Fortune 500 address. They are the army of productivity that drives more than 28,000 small businesses.

International trade is emerging as one of the strongest engines in South Florida, and others in the fast lane of the general high-growth mode are business services, health care and commercial real estate. Besides healthy export activity, we're seeing foreign businesses investing here with a presence or even a headquarters. The after-market is seen in increased international tourism. Conversely, the proximity to Latin America draws prospects interested in that market to open offices in the region.

Palm Beach County

The county trades cash for full-time new jobs that are created from a relocation or expansion. The county's effort to encourage economic development led to Initiatives '95, a summit for businesses and government to explore areas

Area Chambers of Commerce

GREATER BOCA RATON CHAMBER OF COMMERCE
1800 N. Dixie Hwy., P.O. Box 1390
Boca Raton 33432-1892

395-4433; Fax 392-3870

GREATER BOYNTON BEACH CHAMBER OF COMMERCE
639 E. Ocean Ave., #108
Boynton Beach 33435

732-9501; Fax 734-4304

GREATER DEERFIELD BEACH CHAMBER OF COMMERCE
1602 E. Hillsboro Blvd.
Deerfield Beach 33441-4389

(305) 427-1050; Fax (305) 427-1056

GREATER DELRAY BEACH CHAMBER OF COMMERCE
64 S.E. Fifth Ave.
Delray Beach 33483

278-0424; Fax 278-0555

GREATER FORT LAUDERDALE CHAMBER OF COMMERCE
512 N.E. Third Ave., P.O. Box 14516
Fort Lauderdale 33302

(305) 462-6000; Fax (305) 527-8766

JUPITER/TEQUESTA/JUNO BEACH CHAMBER OF COMMERCE
100 U.S. Hwy. 1 N.
Jupiter 33477

746-7111; Fax 746-7715

GREATER LAKE WORTH CHAMBER OF COMMERCE
1702 Lake Worth Rd.
Lake Worth 33460

582-4401; Fax 547-8300

GREATER LANTANA CHAMBER OF COMMERCE
212 Iris St.
Lantana 33462
585-8664

GREATER MIAMI CHAMBER OF COMMERCE
1601 Biscayne Blvd., Omni Complex
Miami 33132-1260

(305) 350-7700; Fax (305) 371-8255

MIAMI-DADE CHAMBER OF COMMERCE
9190 Biscayne Blvd., #201
Miami 33138

(305) 751-8648; Fax (305) 758-3839

CENTRAL PALM BEACH COUNTY CHAMBER OF COMMERCE
6728 Forest Hill Blvd.
West Palm Beach 33413-3306

642-4260; Fax 642-1721

CHAMBER OF COMMERCE OF THE PALM BEACHES
401 N. Flagler Dr.
West Palm Beach 33401

833-3711; Fax 833-5582

NORTHERN PALM BEACHES CHAMBER OF COMMERCE
1983 PGA Blvd., # 104
Palm Beach Gardens 33408

694-2300; Fax 694-0126

PALM BEACH CHAMBER OF COMMERCE
45 Cocoanut Row
Palm Beach 33480
655-3282

GREATER POMPANO BEACH CHAMBER OF COMMERCE
2200 E. Atlantic Blvd.
Pompano Beach 33062

(305) 941-2940; Fax (305) 785-8358

SUNCOAST CHAMBER OF COMMERCE
2001 Broadway, # 301
Riviera Beach 33404
842-7146

such as capital formation, trade, procurement and regulations.

Job Growth Incentive Fund

This year, the Job Growth fund has paid businesses more than $2.3 million for new job creation, with

The Four Seasons Ocean Grand Hotel has six luscious acres of oceanfront property about 15 minutes from Palm Beach International Airport.

Boca businesses benefiting from about half that amount. BellSouth Mobility, for instance, received $390,000, while the National Council on Compensation Insurance gained $195,000 for opening a customer service operation in Boca.

So what are all these companies doing here? Some are making money, others are making history. Boca Raton, especially, has plenty of blue-chip stock speckling the so-green landscape, reflecting the high quality of corporate newcomers that followed IBM: NCCI, Sony, Rexall Sundown and Sensormatic. One reason is a relatively well-educated population from which to recruit

employees — from professional-level executives to the labor force. High-tech firms that deal in information need computer-literate people. Here, they also find people with some decision-making experience and judgment.

Big Blue

It can be said that the arrival of IBM Corporation at Yamato Road in 1967 was the cantilever that enabled Boca Raton to "imagineer" itself from rich resort town to the enviable high road other high-tech players followed. Tom Watson Jr., son of IBM's founder, credited Boca's quality of life as the factor that prompted the company's decision to manufacture mainframes in the middle of nowhere. Then came a think tank that perfected enough software technology for Boca to replace BASIC as a first language. A milestone was reached in August 1981, when IBM launched its first personal computer from the Boca Raton development laboratory. That product created a whole new personal computer industry and established an industry standard for PC technology.

At its peak, IBM Boca Raton employed more than 9,500 people in its South County sites. Today, the operation is primarily software development. The company employs approximately 2,700 permanent and 700 contracted workers, including technical staff at the OS/2 support center. IBM Boca Raton has a 585-acre main campus with a portion set aside as an environmental preserve. There is a total of 21 buildings, and all missions are conducted at the main site — Marcel Breuer's design that, like an IBM innovation, seemed futuristic when new and now seems timeless.

Key missions include Personal Software Products and Personal Operating Systems. The IBM Boca Raton Programming Center, run by laboratory director John Schwarz, houses one of IBM's most vital software teams that focuses on new markets, technologies, processes and skills.

The most visible product is IBM's award-winning operating system OS/2 Warp, released in fall 1994. The marketplace response: More than 2.5 million copies have been shipped in the United States and worldwide.

Other key missions in Boca are Manufacturing Systems Products to make manufacturers more competitive and efficient; Manufacturing Technology Center for solutions on the manufacturing floor; Worldwide Communications Solutions, developing products for the industry including telephone companies; Special Needs Systems, to develop computer-based systems for those with disabilities; and IBM PC Company Latin America, to coordinate marketing activities throughout Latin America.

A perennial leader in technology, IBM Boca Raton inventors received 99 patents in 1994, for a total of more than 550 since the site was established in 1967. This is the second year IBM has led the field in total number of U.S. patents issued . . . 1,298, a record for any one year.

Scott Paper Company

The verdict is in regarding the latest Fortune 100 company to select Boca Raton for a headquarters, though discussion continues on Scott Paper Co.'s plans after the move.

The $4.4 billion Scott Paper signed a 10-year lease with Crocker Realty Trust for 30,000 square feet of space at Crocker Square, 2650 N. Military Trail. The global headquarters will employ about 100 people, occupying one full floor and part of another. Scott Paper Co. CEO Albert Dunlap cemented the decision with a residential purchase at Addison Estates, a

Photo: The News

*Tri-Rail carries commuters to different stops along its route from
West Palm Beach to Miami.*

gated 13-home enclave adjacent to the grounds of the Boca Raton Resort and Club.

Crocker Realty Trust

Crocker Realty Trust, a public real estate investment trust trading on the American Stock Exchange, has a property portfolio of 4 million square feet of space in 14 cities throughout the Southeast United States. Boca Raton, Delray Beach and Fort Lauderdale are three of them.

In the Boca market, its assets include One Boca Place, 2255 Glades Road; Crocker Financial Plaza, 5550 Glades Road, and Crocker Square, 2650 N. Military Trail. Developer Tom Crocker says all three are 97 percent leased and the balance of the portfolio is 92 percent leased. In Delray, Crocker has The Arbors where Office Depot bought its corporate headquarters after first leasing two of the five buildings from Crocker. The Fort Lauderdale space is downtown's Broward Financial Center.

Independent of the realty trust, Crocker owns Mizner Park through a separate entity of Crocker and Company and Teachers Insurance and Annuity Association.

An important trend is growing in South County that began in Boca and is extending to nearby communities. Crocker is among those who have capitalized on it. The arrival of major headquarters here — of the multibillion-dollar level of Grace, Scott and Office Depot . . . speaks very well to the future. It proves that global markets can function and produce and be managed from any location and that an appealing lifestyle can be very important to drawing them.

Says Crocker, "Whether a Grace or a Scott remains intact corporately or stays here forever is beside the point. The important thing is, they chose to be here. It shows we can continue to build a tax base, beyond building more homes, by attracting tenants who are taxed at a big rate. Commercial is less costly to maintain, with bigger returns."

The Global Connection

AGES Group of Companies in the Arvida Park of Commerce is poised to top $200 million in revenue for this year. Air Ground Equipment Sales employs 250 worldwide with about 175 at world headquarters in Boca Raton. The corporation's purchase of 115,000 square feet of office-warehouse in Boca Raton made a nice dent in the existing commercial inventory.

One AGES group trades in jet engines, avionics and spare parts for large commercial aircraft. Another division sells, leases and buys turboprop commuter planes. More than half of AGES' market is domestic, with 30 percent in Europe and the rest in Asia and Latin America. Founded by Robert Fessler in West Babylon, New York, in 1979, AGES moved to Boca Raton for the same reason many companies choose: The nature of its after-market commerce makes it feasible to locate headquarters vir-

The Greater Boca Raton
Chamber of Commerce invites you to

Visit us in Cyberspace!

Internet home page:
http://bocaraton.com

Do you have access to the Internet? If you do, you can visit us in Boca Raton. You can check out the sights, hit the beach, find the best hotels, and shop 'til you drop -all from the comfort of your own computer! You can find us on the World Wide Web at http://bocaraton.com.

The Greater Boca Raton Chamber of Commerce brought Boca Raton "on-line" so that visitors from all over the world have access to this unique, vibrant area. We have a feeling that if you visit our virtual Boca Raton community site on the Internet, you'll be compelled to visit the real thing.

And when you do get here, be sure to stop by the Chamber. We look forward to seeing you - in person. Virtual cheers!

GREATER
BOCA RATON
CHAMBER OF COMMERCE

1800 North Dixie Highway, Boca Raton, FL 33432
Phone: 407-395-4433 ❖ Fax: 407-392-3780 ❖ E-Mail: Chamber@bocaraton.com

tually anywhere there's telecommunications, a sales force, storage space and a distribution system. Boca posed a considerable temptation, especially when compared to New York's chilly business environment. Fessler's parents retired to Florida many years ago. Familiar with Boca Raton's charms, he decided to AGE gracefully right here.

Before you imagine moss growing on Fessler's bottom line, AGES is regularly winging it to the Bahamas since acquiring Fort Lauderdale-based Paradise Island Airlines in May. The airline was leasing a fleet of 50-passenger Dash-7 turboprops from AGES at the time Resorts International sold its interests in Paradise Island to a South African corporation. Bahamian regulations prohibited the airline from being transferred to the new owners. Since the airline's only destination was the island, and its private 3,000-foot runway accommodates only the Dash-7s, AGES and its planes acquired a spare airline.

Downtown Redevelopment: Boca Raton

In 1995, downtown shows concrete signs of moving forward with momentous and controversial projects that even opponents are beginning to applaud. Like it or not, there's plenty to celebrate:

Jacobson's Department Store, expected to be 80,000 square feet, is set for construction at the southeast corner of Mizner Park. Estimates call for completion by fall 1996.

Its groundbreaking was a hoot, but the International Museum of Cartoon Art will be a serious addition to the city and the county. It's rising rapidly at the southwest quadrant of Mizner Park, with the current phase of 55,9000 square feet set for dedication in late 1995. See more on the museum, including a sidebar, in the chapter on Arts and Culture.

NationsBank Tower is the first phase of the Parkwood Properties development, discussed elsewhere in this chapter. The bank interior was remodeled, and plans call for an outer facelift and new landscaping.

The U.S. Trust Building is proposed for 8,000 square feet of space on two floors, east of Mizner Boulevard between Palmetto Park Road and Royal Palm Road.

Mizner On The Green, a development by Trammell Crow on land purchased from Arvida Company, is a residential townhome project under construction east of Mizner Boulevard overlooking the Boca Raton Resort's golf course. Leasing is hot, and occupancy is expected by fall.

With its focus on becoming an "urban village," the city has invested $42.5 million to improve drainage, roads and landscaping downtown. The improvements complement mixed-use Mizner Park, where the picture is brighter than ever. With about 50 retail tenants, 96 percent of the space is leased. Of the office and professional space, about 94 percent is leased. Of its 136 rental apartments in Phase I, 98 percent are leased. Phase II, another 136 units, is complete and 95 percent leased. Prices range from $800 to $3,000 for a penthouse, with one-, two- and three-bedroom units and townhomes.

Long before Mizner Park, the linchpin of downtown redevelopment was considered to be the corner of Palmetto Park Road and Federal Highway. The Barbar Group, original developers of Woodfield Country Club and its sellout forerunner Woodfield Hunt Club, spent years and a small fortune to get approval for a mixed-use center on the same site. A casualty of the era when the

Resolution Trust Corporation was lunching on live projects, Barbar Group in 1991 sold the 9.5 acres of downtown to Parkwood Properties Corp., a New York investment company.

Parkwood Properties contracted with Southcoast Partners as a third-party developer with Codina Bush Klein Oncor International to create a new linchpin that does justice to that location. That will come in Phase IV of the 460,000-square-foot mixed-use project, when Southcoast Partners builds a 150,000-square-foot office building with a smattering of retail

Delightful Delray

Greater Delray Chamber of Commerce president Bill Wood heads an organization that's quite proud of its role in the city's overall renaissance, the many successes of Downtown, numerous annual events the Chamber sponsors, and the robust economy that results from thriving groups of merchants.

Bruce Gimmy, owner of The Trouser Shop, heads the Atlantic Avenue Merchants Association, one of the groups that the Chamber assists to improve business opportunities.

Wood's job is made easier by having such a unique and dynamic municipality to promote. Delray's many homeruns in recent years include being named an All-America City in 1993, by the National Civic League and the Allstate Foundation; the Delray Beach Tennis Center winning "Facility of the Year" in '93, courtesy of the United States Tennis Association; winning "No. 1 Beach in Palm Beach County" according to *South Florida Parenting* magazine; "Best Swimming Beach in the Southeast," in *Travel Holiday* magazine; Veterans Park being named "Best Playground in Palm Beach County," in *Florida Parenting* magazine; the national "Culture Builds Communities" award for Old School Square last fall, given by the International City/County Management Association; the "Project of the Year Award" for the Decade of Excellence Project, by the American Society of Civil Engineers; winning the Florida Main Street designation for the city's Pineapple Grove neighborhood, a 24-block area northeast of Atlantic and Swinton avenues; and Florida *Trend* magazine dubbing Delray Beach "The Best Run Town in Florida."

The Chamber's biggest annual event, the spring Delray Affair, has long been named a Top 20 Event by the Southeast Tourism Society and a Top 100 Event in North America by the American Bus Association. Numerous other community-wide efforts showcase a city that flaunts its assets and troubleshoots problems with grass-roots solutions.

Wood can afford a bemused look if someone asks Downtown's vacancy rate . . . tenancy has been full for so long, it's hard to recall when there wasn't a waiting list for storefronts on Atlantic Avenue.

Delray Beach Joint Venture

Part of the reason for that winning streak is chalked up to "Delray's secret weapon," the Delray Beach Joint Venture, a public-private collaboration among the Chamber, the city's Community Redevelopment Agency (CRA) and the Downtown Development Authority (DDA), a special taxing district.

In the fall of 1992, Wood, CRA director Chris Brown and DDA chairman Michael Listick, a local attorney, decided to create an unprecedented entity, the Joint Venture, and to hire a Downtown Coordinator to focus on mobilizing the momentum that was building among businesses, cultural, civic and special interest groups.

The Chamber, the CRA and the DDA approved contributions toward an operating budget that was marketing-driven, and set their cap on a coordinator who could fill the bill and whatever vacancies remained.

Marjorie Ferrer was hired in January 1993 from a field of more than 350 applicants. She and her family had relocated to Palm Beach County after 25 years in Miami, where her professional background in marketing, merchandising and administration included private industry and nonprofit organizations.

Ferrer had been an apparel buyer for a major retailer for 15 years, had run operations at a major tourist attraction, Miami Seaquarium, for four years, managed gift shop merchandising at Miami MetroZoo for two years, and was marketing director of magnet programs in Dade County Public Schools.

So planning dynamic events suitable and enjoyable for thousands of people, children of all ages and assorted pets was like skating on cake. And getting Atlantic Avenue to doll up for such events was like inheriting an entire street of store windows to decorate with music and fun . . . a natural for a pro from Jordan Marsh. One of the best examples of Ferrer's efforts are the quarterly Art and Jazz on the Avenue events, which are discussed in our chapter on Festivals.

If you ask what accounts for the success of the Joint Venture — measured in part by requests from other cities for Ferrer to share how she does it and how she gets it financed — some say she's an accomplished multiplexer who listens to government agencies, special interest groups and business owners; that she identifies mutual ground in their diverse messages and motives; and that she fashions events that are a win-win that will move them forward.

Ask Ferrer about her job, and she says she's "like a chef who tries to keep the Bearnaise sauce from separating."

During Summer Nights on the Avenue and the myriad number of events she coordinates throughout the year, it's clear she knows the Avenue from eyelash to whisker, precisely where all the electrical outlets are located for special-effects, lighting and live music scenarios. She's never without a portable radio to expedite communications with staff members from the Chamber, volunteers and police officers who patrol the events on bicycle. Even in the midst of 25,000 people strolling the Avenue, she makes it look like a walk in the park.

Chamber Opportunities

Through networking, idea-sharing, membership meetings, special programs and workshops, the Greater Delray Chamber of Commerce forums ease the process of developing business contacts.

For information on membership in the Chamber, call Bill Wood at 278-0424. You can stop by the office, 64 S.E. Fifth Avenue, for a calendar of activities and Chamber-sponsored events. While you're there, pick up a free Downtown Directory of the marvelous shops along Atlantic Avenue.

The Chamber also houses the Joint Venture, which has been very successful in generating long-term sponsorships among local businesses for numerous regular events. For information on Joint Venture activities and ways you or your business can be involved, call 279-1381.

space. Timing is estimated to be about two years from now. But since new, Class-A institutional quality space has dwindled and demand is increasing, the pace may be accelerated.

Now in Phase II, Southcoast Partners is ready to break ground on a five-story, 55,000-square-foot building at the corner of Palmetto and Southeast First Avenue, facing east. About 25,000 square feet is expected to be home for Merrill Lynch, and Southcoast is in discussion with banks and other financial institutions regarding the penthouse. In Phase I, Southcoast reno-

vated the interior of NationsBank office tower at 150 E. Palmetto Park Road and plans to update the exterior and refurbish the landscaping. The tower is almost completely occupied, with a new tenant ready to open: South Beach restaurateur Mezzanotte recently opened its restaurant-nightclub on the first floor of the bank building.

Phase I also included Smith Barney's striking new build-to-suit headquarters at Southeast First Street and First Avenue.

Part of the third phase likely will take a while, though it promises to bring permanent, long-term rewards to downtown: a pedestrian link to a future spine across Palmetto Park Road that bridges the shopping and business sectors to the north and south. The brick, landscaped connector road eventually would link Mizner Park and Royal Palm Plaza with the shopping corridor east and west along Palmetto. Delays for the spine are partly because the Community Redevelopment Agency and the developer are dealing with 14 property owners, the issues of eminent domain and the potential for lawsuits. The other is getting owners to agree on one of three alternative designs and locations.

The rest of the third phase is an eight-story rental apartment complex similar to Mizner Tower, with ocean and golf course views. The 106-unit building will be at Mizner Boulevard and Southeast First Avenue, where the bank drive-through area is now. The developer expects the apartments to be available within 18 months.

Principals of Southcoast Partners are Keith O'Donnell and Bill Morris, both experienced veterans of development and commercial real estate with Arvida Corp. As a third-party operation, they work with banks and investors to supervise and troubleshoot procedures for obtaining permits that comply with vested property rights.

City of The Arts: West Palm Beach

West Palm Beach has considered a "City of the Arts" promotion to capitalize on a wave of cultural deposits that include the $55 million Kravis Center for the Performing Arts and the $20 million expansion of the Norton Museum of Art. Morikami Park and Japanese Gardens proved too tempting for the American Orchid Society, which decided to move its headquarters from West Palm Beach, "the Orchid City," to Delray Beach.

Wackenhut Corporation, a multinational firm that trades on the New York Stock Exchange, announced plans to move its headquarters from Coral Gables to Palm Beach Gardens in early 1996. About 175 of its 300 employees will make the move, and Wackenhut will hire another 125. The firm is a major provider of private security and investigative services for government and industry.

Skopbank of Finland owned the majority of Downtown/Uptown, a vacant 77-acre parcel that borders the Kravis Center in West Palm Beach. Other owners include Lennar Corp., the Florida Department of Transportation, First Union National Bank and local investor Bert Moerings. Among the parties interested in buying and developing Downtown/Up-

Photo: Stephanie Murphy

Philanthropist Eadie Steele and Delray Beach Joint Venture's downtown coordinator Marjorie Ferrer share a few moments.

town are shopping mall giant Melvin Simon and office building investor Gerald Hines.

While the county seat is West Palm, many tend to think of Boca as the county cushion, due to its free-spending populace, 40 percent share of the corporate tax base and magnetic draw for visitors and relocating newcomers. Said seat and cushion are in the midst of a pillow fight over which is the best location for a major convention center — a matter the County Commission will decide in October 1995.

West Palm Beach is going after the project with money in both fists: offering $11.5 million in land it would donate for the site and $250,000

needed for operations the first year. Officials see the complex as a cornerstone from which to cantilever underpinnings for repairing a blighted downtown.

Rather than trying to "buy" the convention center, Boca is selling itself with lower crime statistics, stronger destination appeal, equal proximity to Palm Beach and Fort Lauderdale International Airports, and its location at the Congress Avenue interchange of I-95, complete with park and ride lot.

The biggest news about the proposed Boca Raton site is that it's the first issue ever to achieve a united stand among the three major cities of South County: Boca

Raton, Delray Beach and Boynton Beach all have pulled together to endorse the 62-acre Knight Enterprises property as the best site.

On prospects for a convention center in South County, Crocker says, "I hope it works. Considering all our contributions to the bed tax, we deserve a major civic investment. The fundamentals are good at the Knight property, especially access and proximity to South County's attractions, and there's a large bed base. In the north, ingress and egress are difficult and the bed base is nil."

Bellwether Employers

Of the leading employers, two are in Palm Beach: Fanjul Family Holdings, one of the Big Sugar empires which employs 2,000; and Flagler Systems Inc., owner of The Breakers resort and other real estate which employs 1,100. Two other sugar conglomerates in the area are U.S. Sugar Corp. in Clewiston, employer of 2,500; and Sugar Cane Growers Co-Op in Belle Glade, with more than 750 employees.

Besides Palm Beach Newspapers Inc., the largest employer based in West Palm Beach is the Ecclestone Organization, a real estate developer that employs 625.

Also included is paving contractor Hardrives Inc. of Delray Beach, founded more than 40 years ago by George and Wilma Elmore, who often are lauded for their philanthropy and activism on behalf of the cultural arts. Hardrives, which em-

ploys 380, has the unusual headquarters on S. Congress Avenue that resembles an underground bunker. Employment leaders based in Boca are included elsewhere in this chapter.

Boynton Beach can claim an employment leader, too, the agricultural operation DuBois Farms founded in 1937, which employs 500. And when you see a white 18-wheeler on I-95 with the name Armeillini Express Lines Inc., think flowers as well as trucking.

As for trucking, you can't travel very far on I-95 or Florida Turnpike's without spotting the red-white-and-blue fleet of Shaw Trucking, a family-owned company that will celebrate its 40th anniversary next year. With projects in Palm Beach, Broward and Dade counties, Shaw Trucking has annual sales of $13 million these days — a mud puddle shy of the record years of earth-moving for real estate developers creating master-planned communities of the mid-1980s.

Before engineers, architects, space planners, builders and interior decorators have their way — and before salespeople and buyers get involved — Shaw Trucking's fleet of delivery trucks, transport vehicles and heavy equipment is demolishing, excavating and delivering building materials: tons of topsoil, silica, chattahoochee, gravel, egg rock, mulch and mason sand.

Founded *Where The Boys Are* in Fort Lauderdale in 1956, Shaw's two trucks delivered materials to the movie set, then took off on a telling

Insider Profile: John Temple

In the overall experiences that explain Boca Raton today, you'd have to give the past two decades more weight than any other half-century or more. And you'd have to give John Temple more credit than any team of business leaders for engineering the high-profile projects that dominated those years and also set the stage for the momentum of today.

Temple, an executive of Arvida Corp. from 1975 to 1987, was its president during the glory days that set the master-planned and manicured standard for the way much of Boca looks today. He left Arvida to launch Temple Development Co., a consulting firm and developer of projects you'll hear about for a long time to come.

The biggest to date, which we discuss in our Real Estate chapter, is Presidential Place. So you might worry that Temple has gone fishing and Boca has no captain. You'd be right on one count: He chases giant bluefin tuna around Bimini in a 60-foot custom Jim Smith that he and buddy Scott Morrison bought from Bill Knight. You'd be wrong on count two, because Temple remains very involved in key projects that affect Boca long-term.

John Temple

One is the Boca Raton Resort and Club, the city's third-largest employer behind IBM and Boca Raton Community Hospital. Chicago-based real estate developer VMS Realty Corporation bought the resort hotel from Arvida Corp. in 1983, a deal Temple crafted as Arvida's president. Initially, the transaction put VMS Realty in charge as general partner for Boca Raton Hotel & Club Limited Partnership. Temple became a managing director, motivated partly because buyers at Presidential Place are eligible for membership in the Resort's exclusive Premier Club.

A power struggle developed in 1993, which coincided with an ambitious expansion as part of a larger plan to refinance $150 million of indebtedness. Temple perceived correctly that a proxy squabble could complicate the Resort's master agenda and took the initiative to clarify who was in control. The result was that Boca Raton Management Company (BRMC) took over as general partner for Boca Raton Hotel & Club Limited Partnership and Temple became one of five BRMC directors who control operations at the Resort.

With the refinancing completed the same year, the Resort proceeded with expansion plans that include its conference center.

Historically, Arthur Vining Davis — ArViDa — bought the hotel and adjacent property in 1956 for $22.5 million, then a record in Florida real estate deals. Arvida Corp. owned and operated the hotel from 1958 to 1983 and added its tower and conference center during the $14 million expansion begun in 1969. The $20 million Boca Beach Club addition enhanced the destination package in 1980, with a windfall of amenities when the Resort acquired Boca Country Club in 1988.

Beginning in 1990, the Resort invested $10 million annually on property upgrades and maintenance and in '91, another $11 million to renovate several sites, including decor and equipment in the existing convention center, a facelift for the 14,000-square-foot Great Hall and $1.5 million for the Top of the Tower Italian Restaurant. Also new for the conference center is the 5,200-square-foot Galleon Room, a flex space with 20-foot ceilings that can be split into two venues. The existing 2,900-square-foot Valencia Ballroom has new carpets, wall coverings, lighting and audiovisual gear.

Long term, Temple and company plan to invest an additional $60 million in capital improvements: building a new and larger conference center and related space; improved club facilities; another 18-hole signature golf course; more spa space; a new activities center; additional retail shops and restaurants; and a larger, more luxurious motor yacht to ferry passengers between the two hotels.

Temple believes expanding the conference center is essential for the Resort to remain competitive in the meetings industry. And he thinks it would complement a new exhibition-size convention center such as the one proposed for the Knight Enterprises site in north Boca.

"I'm very supportive of a convention center in South County, especially since we generate 40 percent of the county's tourist tax dollars," he said. "If the project is approved for the Knight site, the whole county will benefit. And anything that enhances Boca is good for the hotel. We're also pleased the Premier Club is prospering, with a lot of new programs to make it more effective as a club."

Meanwhile, Temple Development Co. and Shubin Properties are well on their way with the 52-acre Florida Atlantic University Research and Development Park. Temple and partner Bill Shubin, another Arvida alumni, are developing more than 400,000 square feet of space. They're ready to top off a 30,000-square-foot building for their first tenant, V.O.C. Analytical Lab, a materials and water-quality testing outfit whose principal executive is a graduate of FAU. With enough growth in recent years to absorb existing commercial space, FAU Research Park will be in the catbird seat as other newcomers arrive needing new space.

Temple's latest residential endeavor is developer of The Ocean Club at lush Key Biscayne in Miami. The 57-acre project of 835 condominium units will be a private beach club community estimated at $500 million at buildout. The first building is permitted, and a sales office is ready to open. Temple's partner in The Ocean Club is financier George Soros of New York, a Wall Street billionaire.

Temple also is managing partner for the 1,200-acre Towne Park Joint Venture, a master-planned community in western Boynton Beach, still in the planning stages. Temple's Recreational Development Team consults on international projects and has advised on the use of more than 40,000 acres held by the MacArthur Foundation.

Other business interests include a piece of Pete's goldmine restaurant in west Boca; a mixed-use project in Telluride, Colorado; investments in South Beach; and a board position with Atlantic Gulf Communities, a public company formed from defunct General Development Corp.

By the time he tackled Presidential Place, Temple had evaluated plum parcels in California, Hawaii, Australia, the Caribbean, Michigan's upper peninsula and Florida. Signature Arvida projects associated with his tenure include The Addison and Mizner Village.

Temple and a team of Arvida associates collaborated with the Bass brothers of Fort Worth, Texas, to acquire Arvida in a leveraged buyout. A year later, after the merger with Walt Disney Company, Temple headed Arvida/Disney, assisting the entertainment empire in its real estate development plans.

Temple was nibbling choice oysters in the world's primo destinations long before the Arvida years. He picked up an MBA at Stanford University

Photo: Stephanie Murphy

Presidential Place is adjacent to the Boca Beach Club, where buyers enjoy concierge and room service.

after a tour in the U.S. Navy and a math degree at the University of Washington, his home state. Numbers always counted, especially when he went to work in real estate acquisitions for Kaiser Aluminum in California, at one time managing $300 million in Kaiser property assets. A colleague, Chuck Cobb, persuaded Temple to join him in Florida after Cobb was recruited as Arvida's CEO.

Looking back on Boca Raton, Temple said, "When I came in the mid-1970s, the attitude was no growth, no density, no business . . . a gang mentality of no. . . ."

Looking ahead, he sees things are very diversified: "We're beyond just a resort city, however grand . . . with light industry, a growing population, one of the best shopping environments you can imagine, terrific restaurants and a dominant cultural focus. We're seeing the maturing of Boca. Downtown redevelopment. Royal Palm Plaza and Mizner Park. The city is in buildout, so you see a lot of razing. Royal Palm Yacht Club is a phenomenal success. . . . Imagine, a community that began in 1959 going through such rebirth now. More than 100 homes have been redone out of 700 total. Of course the hype chases the high-end, but resales in any price range in the city will do well."

Active in civic, cultural and charitable activities, Temple is founding chairman of the Palm Beach County Development Board. He and his wife, Catherine, are past chairs of the Alexis de Tocqueville Society — whose members contribute $10,000 annually to United Way of Palm Beach County.

Temple, 57, has three grown children and a 6-year-old son and 1-year-old daughter.

His wife heads Samiani Inc., a retail buying and consulting company.

Home is Harbour Point in Boca Raton, a short walk from the Boca Raton Resort and Club. Their vacation retreat is an 1874 Victorian-style bungalow a block from the center of town in Telluride, Colorado.

odyssey of tire marks. Today, the insignia on Shaw's private fleet witnesses the shredding of demolition debris from Hurricane Andrew, the 1992 storm that flattened Homestead; hauls building material to Barry University and ferries fill for new soccer fields at Nova Southeastern University in Southwest Broward; and excavates lakes at a former nursery west of Military Trail in Delray Beach in preparation for bringing in materials for streets, utilities and homesite pads for a new subdivision, Via Delray, under way by Financial Florida Developers Inc. at Palm Beach Bath & Tennis.

Major Employers in Boca Raton

Boca Raton's major employers include 24 headquarters operations.

AGES Group of Companies, 645 Park of Commerce Way, 998-9330; world headquarters for air ground equipment sales; employs 170;

Programmers test multimedia software that is running on IBM's OS/2 operating system.

Alfred Angelo, 791 Park Commerce Boulevard, 241-7755; bridal manufacturer and distributor; employs 140;

Arvida Company, 7900 Glades Road, 479-1100; headquarters for national real estate developer; employs 400;

Astraltech Americas Inc., 5400 Broken Sound Boulevard, 995-7000; replicate all formats of compact discs, duplicate and distribute video tapes, audio and CDs; employs 100;

Athletic Club of Boca Raton, 1499 Yamato Road, 241-5088; full-service fitness center; employs 100;

BellSouth Mobility, 5201 Congress Avenue, 995-8859; public firm specializing in mobile telecommunications; trades on the New York Stock Exchange (BellSo); employs 300;

Bloomingdale's, 5840 Glades Road, Town Center, 394-2000; department store; employs 400;

Boca Raton Community Hospital, 800 Meadows Road, 395-7100, private; employs 1,950;

Boca Raton Marriott, 5150 Town Center Circle, 392-4600; 12-story, 256-room hotel and conference center, centerpiece of the 28-acre mixed-use shopping destination Boca Center; employs 190;

Boca Raton News, 33 S.E. Third Street, 395-8300; seven-day local morning newspaper; employs 220;

Boca Raton Habilitation Center, 755 Meadows Road, 391-5200; service organization to rehabilitate the physically and mentally disadvantaged; employs 117;

Boca Raton Resort and Club, 501 E. Camino Real, 395-3000; 223-acre luxury resort and convention center; employs 1,850;

Boca Raton Transportation, 1450 N.W. First Avenue, 368-8333; headquarters for commercial taxi, bus, van and limousine fleet; employs 120;

Boca Research Inc., 1377 Clint Moore Road, 997-6227; headquarters for the public firm that develops modems and computer enhancement services; trades on Nasdaq (BocaRs); employs 300;

Brothers Gourmet Coffees, 2255 Glades Road, One Boca Place, 995-2600; an upscale coffee distributor; employs 94;

Burdines, 5700 Glades Road, Town Center, 393-4400; department store; employs 400;

Casi-Rusco, 1155 Broken Sound Parkway N.W., 998-6100; developer of access control systems; employs 95;

City of Boca Raton, 201 W. Palmetto Park Road, 393-7700; one of 37 municipalities in Palm Beach County; employs 1,250;

Coiltronics Inc., 6000 Park of Commerce Boulevard, 241-7876; headquarters for an electronic manufacturer that produces transformers and inductors; employs 75;

Core International, 6500 E. Rogers Circle, 997-6044; manufactures disk drives; employs 75;

CRC Press, 2000 Corporate Boulevard N.W., 994-0555; headquarters for medical textbooks; employs 180;

Custom Marble Inc., 1160 S. Rogers Circle, 994-0566; headquarters for wholesale manufacturing supplier of vanity tops and whirlpool spa tubs; employs 59;

Embassy Suites Hotel, 661 N.W. 53rd Street, 994-8200; a seven-story, 263-suite hotel; employs 140;

Encore Service Systems Inc., 1080 N.W. First Avenue, 392-1122; headquarters for air-conditioning and major appliance service; employs 200;

Federal Express, 5900 Park of Commerce Boulevard, (800) 238-5355; package shipment and air mailings; employs 100;

Florida Atlantic University, 777 Glades Road, 367-3000; the main campus of the institution, part of the state university system since its founding in the mid-1960s; employs 2,014;

Globe Communications, 5401 Broken Sound Boulevard N.W., 997-7733; headquarters for tabloid publisher; employs 170;

IBM Corporation, 1000 N.S. 51st Street, 443-2000; multinational public conglomerate involved in research and development of computer products, cradle of the PC; trades on the

Royal Palm Plaza is a popular shopping destination in downtown Boca Raton.

New York Stock Exchange (IBM); employs 2,700;

ITW MIMA, 1081 Holland Drive, 241-8222; packaging machinery and stretch wrapping systems; employs 140;

JW Charles Securities Inc., 980 N. Federal Highway, 338-2600; stock brokerage; employs 200;

Kraft Foodservice, 7598 N.W. Sixth Avenue, 994-8500; sale of food products to hotels, restaurants, hospitals, schools and jails; employs 160;

LDDS Communications, 1515 S. Federal Highway, Suite 400, 392-2244; headquarters for long distance communications; employs 300;

Levitz Furniture Corporation, 6111 Broken Sound Parkway N.W., 994-6006; headquarters for publicly held furniture retailer; trades on the New York Stock Exchange (Levitz); employs 175;

Lynn Insurance Group, 2501 N. Military Trail, 994-1900; headquarters for North America's leader in the forest products insurance industry; employs 280;

Lynn University, 3601 N. Military Trail, 994-0770; main campus of the private university; employs 225;

Macrotel International Corporation, 6001 Park of Commerce Boulevard, 997-5500; headquarters for manufacturer of business telecommunications systems; employs 60;

Mark, Fore & Strike, 6500 Park of Commerce Boulevard N.W., 241-1700; headquarters for retailer of sportswear and casual clothing; employs 200;

McDonald's Corporation, 5200 Town Center Circle, Suite 600, 391-8003; regional headquarters for fastfood restaurant chain; employs 62

Model Imperial Supply, 1243 Clint Moore Road, 241-8244; headquarters of wholesale distributor of fragrances; employs 175;

Monier Roof Tile, 135 N.W. 20th Street, 395-1770; manufacturer of roof tiles; employs 80;

Mutual of America, 1150 Broken Sound Parkway N.W., 241-4000; insurance and national technology center; employes 150;

National Council of Compensation Insurance, 750 Park of Commerce Drive, 997-1000; headquarters for the rate maker of worker's compensation; employs 800;

Norbar Fabrics, 7670 N.W. Sixth Drive, 997-0800; wholesaler and decorative fabric jobber; employs 100;

Patten Corporation, 5295 Town Center Road, 391-6336; headquarters for public company involved in land sales and financing, which trades on the New York Stock Exchange (Patten); employs 70;

PCA Health Plans, 301 Yamato Road, Suite 4200, (800) 688-3144; health maintenance organization; employs 164;

Pepsi-Co International, 1200 N. Federal Highway, Fourth Floor, 392-7008; Latin American headquarters for the soft-drink company; employs 30;

Production Truss & Fabrication Corporation, 161 N.W. Fourth Street, 391-59556; maker of prefabricated wall panels and roof and floor trusses; employs 100;

Radisson Suites Hotel, 7920 Glades Road, 483-3600; a 200-suite hotel that anchors the upscale mixed-use Arvida Parkway Center; employs 125;

Rexall Sundown Inc., 851 Broken Sound Parkway, 241-9400; headquarters for the public firm that manufactures, markets and distributes vitamins; trades on Nasdaq (Rex/Sun); employs 600;

Saks Fifth Avenue, 5820 Glades Road, Town Center Mall, 393-9100; specialty retailer; employs 200;

Scott Paper Company, NYSE, 2650 N. Military Trail, Boca Raton; global headquarters of world's largest tissue maker; employs 100;

Sears, 5900 Glades Road, Town Center, 338-1100; department store; employs 246;

Sensormatic Electronics, 6600 Congress Avenue, 995-6000; manufactures devices employed in article surveillance; trades on the New York Stock Exchange (Sensormt); employs 500;

Sheraton of Boca Raton, 2000 N.W. 19th Street, 368-5252; a five-story, 193-room hotel; employs 120;

Siemens Credit Corporation, 5300 Broken Sound Boulevard N.W., 994-7400; manager of corporate services; employs 53; total of 2,000 employees at all Siemens and Tel-Plus companies;

Siemens Nixdorf Printing Systems, 5500 Broken Sound Boulevard, 997-3100; sales and service of laser printers; employs 100;

Siemens Rolm Communications Systems, 5500 Broken Sound Boulevard, 994-8800; PBX related communications; employs 175;

Siemens Stromberg-Carlson, 900 Broken Sound Parkway, 995-

Florida's Stock In Trade

Palm Beach County is home to more than 40 of the public companies rated among the top 250 in the state this year by *Florida Trend* magazine. According to their calculations, Palm Beach County also claims four of the top five financial performers, based on revenue gains: Appletree Companies Inc., Hydron Technologies Inc., Crocker Realty Investors Inc. and Top Source Technologies Inc. We're sharing *Trend's* list of home-base winners, with designations for trading on the New York Stock Exchange, American Stock Exchange, Over-The-Counter, National Bulletin Board and National Market System:

American Media Inc., NYSE, 600 S. East Coast Avenue, Lantana 33462, 586-1111;

Appletree Companies Inc., OTC, 2255 Glades Road, Suite 200-E, Boca Raton 33431, 995-0605;

BE Aerospace Inc., NMS, 1400 Corporate Center Way, Wellington 33414, 791-5000;

Boca Research Inc., NMS, 6413 Congress Avenue, Boca Raton 33487, 997-6227;

Brothers Gourmet Coffees, NMS, 2255 Glades Road, Suite 200, Boca Raton 33431, 995-2600;

Clinicorp Inc., ASE, 1601 Belvedere Road, Suite 500-E, West Palm Beach, 684-2225;

Computer Products Inc., NMS, 7900 Glades Road, Suite 500, Boca Raton, 33434, 451-1000;

Crocker Realty Investors Inc., OTC, 433 Plaza Real, Suite 335, Boca Raton 33432, 395-9666;

CV REIT Inc., NYSE, 100 Century Boulevard, West Palm Beach 33417, 640-3155;

Diversified Communications, ASE, 601 Clearwater Park Road, West Palm Beach 33401, 655-9101;

Dycom Industries Inc., NYSE, 450 Australian Avenue S., Suite 860, West Palm Beach 33401, 659-6301;

Empire of Carolina Inc., ASE, 5150 Linton Boulevard, Delray Beach 33484, 498-4000;

Engle Homes Inc., NMS, 123 N.W. 13th Street, Boca Raton 33432, 391-4012;

Financial Benefit Group, NMS, 7251 W. Palmetto Park Road, Boca Raton 33433, 394-9400;

Florida Public Utilities Co., ASE, 401 S. Dixie Highway, West Palm Beach 33401, 832-2461;

FPL Group Inc., NYSE, 700 Universe Boulevard, Juno Beach 33408, 694-4704;

Grace (W.R.) & Company, NYSE, One Town Center Road, Boca Raton 33486-1010, 362-2000;

Hilcoast Development Corporation, OTC, 100 Century Boulevard, West Palm Beach 333417, 471-5700;

Hydron Technologies Inc., NMS, 941 Clint Moore Road, Boca Raton 33487, 994-1701;

Innkeepers USA Trust, NMS, 5255 N. Federal Highway, Suite 100, Boca Raton 33487, 994-1701;

Integracare Inc., NMS, 551 S.E. Eighth Street, Delray Beach 33483, 274-0204;

Investors Insurance Group, ASE, 7200 W. Camino Real, Boca Raton 33433, 391-5043;

Jerry's Inc., NBB, 1500 N. Florida Mango Road, Suite 19, West Palm Beach 33409, 689-9611;

JW Charles Financial Services, 980 N. Federal Highway, Suite 210, Boca Raton 33432, 338-2600;

Marbledge Group, NBB, 1777 Seventh Avenue N., Lake Worth, 33461, 585-7400;

Milastar Corporation, OTC, No. 9 Via Parigi, Palm Beach 33480, 655-9590;

Milestone Properties Inc., NYSE, 5200 Town Center Circle, Boca Raton 33486, 394-9533;

Model Imperial Inc., NMS, 1243 Clint Moore Road, Boca Raton 3487, 241-8244;

Office Depot Inc., NYSE, 200 Old Germantown Road, Delray Beach 33445, 278-4800;

Oriole Homes Corporation, ASE, 1690 S. Congress Avenue, Delray Beach 33445, 274-2000;

Patten Corporation, NYSE, 5295 Town Center Road, Boca Raton 33486, 391-6336;

Prime Management Group Inc., NMS, 1051 S. Rogers Circle, Boca Raton 33487, 997-4045;

Rexall Sundown Inc., NMS, 851 Broken Sound Parkway, Boca Raton 33487, 241-9400;

RT Industries Inc., OTC, 7280 W. Palmetto Park Road, Suite 306, Boca Raton 33433, 750-6600;

Safeskin Corporation, NMS, 5100 Town Center Circle, Suite 560, Boca Raton 33486, 395-9988;

Scott Paper Company, NYSE, 2650 N. Military Trail, Boca Raton 33487, (610) 522-5000;

Sensormatic Electronics, NYSE, 6600 Congress Avenue, Boca Raton 33487, 995-6000;

Servico Inc., ASE, 1601 Belvedere Road, West Palm Beach 33406, 689-9970;

Solitron Devices Inc, OTC, 3301 Electronics Way, West Palm Beach 33407, 848-4311;

Sports/Leisure Inc., NMS, 2650 N. Military Trail, Suite 230, Boca Raton 33487, 995-7416;

Todhunter International, NMS, 222 Lakeview Avenue, West Palm Beach 33401, 655-8977;

Top Source Technologies Inc., ASE, 2000 PGA Boulevard, Palm Beach Gardens 33408, 775-5756;

TPI Enterprises Inc., NMS, 777 S. Flagler Drive, West Palm Beach 33401, 835-8888.

5000; network supplier of telephone digital switching equipment; employs 1,300;

SIRS Inc., 1100 Holland Drive, 994-0079; publishers of educational materials; employs 180;

South Palm Beach County Jewish Federation, 9901 Donna Klein Boulevard, 852-3100; nonprofit organization providing recreational, educational and cultural programs for families and individuals of all ages; employs 1,000;

Sony Professional Products, 6500 Congress Avenue, 998-9922; manufacturer and distributor of professional audio and video recording studio equipment; employs 210;

Trammell Crow, 6400 Congress Avenue, 997-9700; residential and commercial real estate developers; employs 60;

Unisys Corporation, 7700 W. Camino Real, 750-5800; Latin American headquarters for computer marketing; employs 77;

W.R. Grace & Company, One Town Center Road, 362-2000; world headquarters for the largest specialty chemical company, a leader in health care and other niche businesses; trades on the New York Stock Exchange (Grace); employs 450;

West Boca Medical Center, 21644 U.S. Highway 441, 488-8000; private regional hospital; employs 703.

The Greater Boca Raton Chamber of Commerce

Says M. J. "Mike" Arts, executive director: "Boca Raton has a thriving economy. The business community is dynamic, energetic and involved. The continued expansion and revitalization of downtown will have a tremendously positive effect on our community and will help expand and maintain our prosperous economy for many years to come."

Today's Chamber has a professional staff working as a team with business owners and community volunteers to improve business opportunities and preserve the quality of overall growth throughout the city. The volunteer, not-for-profit organization is the only organization in South County that works full-time to better the business climate, enhance the quality of life and create new jobs.

Photo: Palm Beach County Convention and Visitors Bureau

Shop and browse on Palm Beach's world-famous Worth Avenue.

The Chamber dates to January 1952, when the late city council member and Realtor, W.P. Bebout Sr., was appointed temporary chairman of a committee to organize a Chamber. The goal was letting tourists know about Boca Raton. Until 1953, members met in the Community Church downtown, near the present-day NationsBank drive-through lanes. They complemented government and in some cases took the lead on items such as stop-sign installations, railroad crossings and traffic light synchronization.

Meanwhile, the Chamber carried on a "drive" for new members, literally from the running board of the 1925 fire engine Old Betsy, riding around town and ringing her bell. Then, the whole Chamber fit on Betsy at one time: four attorneys,

one dentist, one banker, a savings and loan executive, three insurance agents and two accountants. Today, the Chamber has more than 1,700 members who employ more than 45,000.

Still popular as a home base for visitors to collect maps and ask for directions, the Chamber also positions itself as the city's economic barometer. The way some businesses stretch to become agents of prosperity within their own commercial activity, the Chamber pushes itself to bolster economic stability overall. Its strategy is fostering the growth of existing and new businesses, with almost a dozen volunteer committees promoting community growth through business development, education, public affairs, special events and leadership. As the Chamber advises in its yearly publication, *The*

Photo: Woodbury & Associates

IBM has a strong presence in the community.

Greater Boca Raton Annual, "Membership in the Chamber is a blue-chip investment in your company. Take advantage of the opportunities. . . ."

One is networking, made easy by the Chamber's idea-sharing business card exchanges, Network '95, mini-trade shows, membership breakfasts, special program luncheons and monthly small business workshops. These forums ease the process of developing business prospects through working with other civic-minded professionals.

Another advantage is prospecting: Only Chamber members may advertise in the *Annual*, the monthly newsletter *The Reporter* and the Chamber's home page on the WorldWideWeb. Listings in the *Annual* are alphabetical and categorical so your message reaches thousands of newcomers inquiring about Boca Raton.

The Chamber also provides leads groups, called The Chamber Connection, and MASTERMINDS, a program designed for CEO-level, peer group networking. Membership keeps you up to date on the business community and legislative news through publications, committee meetings and other forums.

Another advantage is that the Chamber can save you money, offering eligibility for group buying power on LDDS/Metromedia long-distance service, Airborne Express overnight delivery, HIP Health Plans of Florida's HMO plan, John Alden Life Insurance Company's PPO, long-term disability and dental plan and the United Chambers Insured Plan.

The Chamber's community events — including the Meet Me Downtown arts and entertainment festival, Boca Festival Days and Boca Business Expo — are a great way to get acquainted and get involved.

Finally, there is no way to put a price on the advantage you gain from representation: "You are ensured a voice in legislative issues that affect your business on local, state and national levels. Your tax-deductible investment guarantees that the opportunity for continued growth, prosperity and success remains in Boca Raton."

Keys to the City

Thanks to the initiative of the Greater Boca Raton Chamber of Commerce, the city has its own site on the Internet for cyberphiles to plumb. Notes on the business community, housing and shopping are some areas of interest that computer users can explore, even before you set foot in Boca Raton.

This is one of the first chamber organizations in the country to stake a claim on the public's curi-

Insiders' Tips

Don't feed any alligators you might encounter; they lose their natural fear of humans when they are fed.

Photo: David Becker

Sunrise over the beach.

osity. To tour the city in cyberspace, proceed via Prodigy to the WorldWideWeb and type http://BocaRaton.com. For more information about http://BocaRaton.com, call the Greater Boca Raton Chamber of Commerce, 395-4433.

Here We Come, Ready or Not

And why not join the Chamber before you move here? If your company is relocating to Boca Raton or you've considered opening your own business here, Chamber membership is a great first step. For details on applying for membership in the 1,700-member organization, call the number above and ask for Marketing Director Kerry Jennings. You can send a message e-mail to "Chamber@BocaRaton.com."

The All New Delray Beach, The Realization Of a Dream...

Become A Part Of The Dream.
Delray Beach Florida, Where Our Business Is Your Business.

Delray Beach is nestled between the cities of Palm Beach and Boca Raton in Palm Beach County. This renaissance city of unique shops and early 20th century architecture has truly blossomed over the past ten years.

Delray Beach has completely rebuilt their historic downtown main street, built a brand new 8,300 seat stadium and tennis complex, restored the cultural arts center, provided facilities for several new corporate headquarters, and now boasts a wide selection of fine restaurants, hotels, galleries and other amenities.

Corporations and Downtown/Mixed Use Developers are invited to share and experience Delray's unique assets. So become a part of the dream, in the all new beautiful Delray Beach. *Where Our Business Is Truly, Your Business.*

DELRAY BEACH
FLORIDA
★★★★★
All-America City
®
1993

For More Information About The All New Delray Beach Call:
Delray Beach Chamber Of Commerce/Downtown Development Authority 407•278•0424
Delray Beach Community Redevelopment Agency 407•276•8640 • City Of Delray Beach 407•243•7000

A Commitment to Care.™ Dedicated to being a leading provider of packaging and specialty chemical products and services that improve the quality of life for people throughout the world. Committed to our employees, the environment and the communities in which we live and work. We're Grace and we're proud to have our global headquarters in beautiful, dynamic Palm Beach County, Florida.

W. R. Grace & Co. Headquarters
One Town Center Road, Boca Raton, FL 33486-1010

Inside
Real Estate

The biggest single residential sale in Boca Raton during the last two years was the $5 million transaction for a Por La Mar residence hugging Lake Boca Raton. The property moved in June — always hot for temperature and almost always lukewarm for sales. Ask local experts in the high end and they'll say the buyer got a bargain. Arguably the best waterfront parcel in the city, only dinghy distance from the Atlantic Ocean through the Boca Inlet, the double lot with 150 feet of deepwater lake frontage sports a finger pier for two 80-foot yachts and enough bulkhead for another 100-foot vessel. The seller's fleet — 67-foot summer-home yacht, 36-foot sportfishing craft, assorted tenders and 33-foot speedwagon — was not cramped.

Award-winning Boca architect Derek Vander Ploeg anointed the two-story residence with just the right mix of Mizneresque pixie dust to make it complement the Boca Raton Resort and Club — a dog-paddle across the lake. Enclosed space of 10,000-plus square feet meshes well with 4,000 square feet of lakefront patio, diving pool and spa; the double-gate electronic entrance has a 6,000-square-foot motorcourt, generous porte cochere, fountains, walls and six-figure landscaping.

Welcome Aboard

The kicker in the industry is, a boat captain made the sale — a nautico who paired his real estate license with Fort Lauderdale yacht brokerage Peter Kehoe & Associates last year. John Dial has 17 years experience on the bridge, including two at Hilton Head, South Carolina. He relocated to Boca Raton with Stoltz Management Company to operate boats belonging to its subsidiary, Luxury Homes Inc. Dial got into real estate sales three years ago and expanded his waterfront focus last year when Kehoe and Luxury agreed to collaborate.

The best way to show waterfront homes is from the water, so lots of Realtors skipper their own boats or borrow a craft when the need arises. While Boca has some excellent high-end Realtors, the yacht brokers are in Palm Beach and Fort Lauderdale. Kehoe was the first major player to cast a line toward a bollard in Boca territory, creating a yacht division at Luxury Homes. Dial remains one of the few salts in the Southeast with captain experience and licenses to sell both real estate and yachts.

Neighborhoods

Waterfront is one big reason people move to Florida, and the limited

Design a million-dollar dream from $700,000.

Amid the legendary vistas and amenities of The Polo Club Boca Raton, million dollar dream homes become a reality, starting at only $700,000 at Vintage Oaks, the crown jewel in South Florida's most sparkling golf and country club.

Once you've seen Vintage Oaks' unsurpassable custom homes, you wouldn't dream of living anywhere else.

The features are remarkable, the craftsmanship exquisite. Floors of Saturnia stone and marble. Rich granite countertops. Floor-to-ceiling windows. Dramatically shaped rooms, including lofty circular foyers and octagonal libraries. Stunning courtyards. Personal fitness areas. Enormous custom-organized closets. Huge, hedonistic master baths.

All this and more surrounded by stunning golf and water views and the incomparable lifestyle of The Polo Club. Two championship golf courses, a 90,000 sq. ft. Clubhouse, 29 clay tennis courts, fitness and beauty Spa, gatehouse and patrolling security, and a social life second to none.

From $700,000 to over a million. Please call 407-496-4904 prior to coming so Security can admit you through the gates. Broker participation is warmly welcome.

VINTAGE OAKS

THE POLO CLUB BOCA RATON

Golf, tennis and social equity memberships readily available.

amount of real estate on the ocean, the Intracoastal, lakes and canals creates its own permanent demand for those properties. It's also very subjective which exposure is best — 180-degree panoramic Atlantic, point-lot for your boat or quiet canal tucked away from wakes and the fast-lane.

New construction on the water is scarce, but what there is, is terrific. Here are some must-see properties to whet your appetite and tickle your checkbook, including waterfront, inland villages, country clubs and private communities.

We open out of order to introduce **Le Sanctuaire** — the first "custominium" — Mark Rothenberg's striking building on the ocean at 3425 S. Ocean Boulevard, Highland Beach, across the street from St. Lucy's Catholic Church.

Le Sanctuaire is only four stories and only one residence per floor, Rothenberg's concept for a custom home environment in a condominium setting all about privacy. Inside the gated entry with underground parking are private elevators controlled by card-key access to deliver you into your living room. Three homes are available. The first floor is offered furnished at $1,475,000 with 3,000 square feet under air and 2,000 square feet of private walled-in courtyard. The third floor has 5,200 square feet under air for $1,695,000 and the fourth is 4,000 square feet under air with 2,200 feet of balcony, for $1,795,000. Both are in the finishing stages of turnkey.

Floor-to-ceiling, 180-degree views of the ocean and generous ceilings enhance the feel of a luxury home, yet the storm shutters and property management services match the convenience of condo living. Le Sanctuaire has a pool on the southeast corner and cabanas with mini-kitchens, bathrooms and shower. Brito & Cohen of Coral Gables are the architects. Mark Rothenberg is a Floridian who likes to quote research guru Lew Goodkin: "We can build more golf courses, but all the ocean you see is all the ocean you'll ever see."

3600 SOUTH OCEAN BOULEVARD
3600 S. Ocean Blvd.
Palm Beach

New in 1995, this property is in high demand among buyers eager for oceanfront. The gated address of 24 two- and three-bedroom condominiums is an eyelash north of The Ritz-Carlton Palm Beach.

The building is more than 65 percent sold, with first-floor units and penthouses among the early favorites. Apartments are available in four floor plans from 2,400 to 5,000 square feet, with private elevator entries for each home, covered parking, a heated pool and spa and private beachfront. Prices are $414,000 to $695,500 in the six-story mid-rise, a Stoltz Bros. development.

THE ADDISON
1400 S. Ocean Blvd.
Boca Raton

Arvida Corp. developed The Addison, twin 16-story towers on a choice 10-acre site on the ocean. The luxurious condominiums were quick sellers when the '80s building was new, and resales at The Addison remain in demand. Prices are $550,000 to $2 million with more than 15 currently available. Choices include units that sold as-is and others very customized — 2,160 square feet for a two-bedroom, for example, and up to 3,100 square feet for a three-bedroom. Key advantages are amenities, service and a location with perennial appeal. To see the building, take I-95 to the Palmetto Park Road exit and go east to Highway A1A. The Addison is south of Camino Real.

ADDISON ESTATES
455 Addison Park Ln.
Boca Raton

The 13-home enclave created by master builder Dan Swanson in 1992 is the only single-family housing option on the apron of the Boca Raton Resort. Addison Development Corp. also arranged for buyers to be eligible to join the amenity-rich Premier Club. Addison Estates sold out in less than two years at minimums of $800,000, and the first resales listed for more than $1 million. The new CEO with Scott Paper bought one this year.

THE ARAGON
2494 S. Ocean Blvd.
Boca Raton

Boca Raton's newest luxury oceanfront address, also south of Camino Real, is priced from $1 million to $5 million. The 10-story Aragon actually is three buildings with 46 residences, from two-story courtyard homes to penthouses with roof-top gardens. The building was about half sold when the developer received the certificate of occupancy in March. Buyers have plenty to choose from, with the option to interpret a custom spin on 12 oceanview floor plans.

The wing buildings have four two-story units with their own swimming pool and spa and private garden. Wing buildings have two residences per floor, with only one per floor in the third building. Try on its centerpiece penthouse for size — 8,751 square feet of enclosed space, 4,903 feet of terrace and a roof garden with its own swimming pool, spa, gazebo, entertainment area and cabana bath. Then make an offer in the vicinity of $4,750,000.

BOCA GROVE PLANTATION
7003 Mandarin Dr.
Boca Raton

One of the best long-term values in suburban country club living, the 350-acre community is retaining its original low density with a total of only 400 homes. Approaching build-out and maturing very gracefully, Boca Grove has a few new homes on line and resales are very solid. A desirable mix includes estate homes, patio homes, villas and luxury condominiums, with prices from $250,000 to more than $3 million. Award-winning builder Diane Courchene of Courchene Development produced many of the newer estates. For lasting classic beauty, the Boca Grove Clubhouse has few rivals. The main entrance to Boca Grove is on Glades Road west of I-95, opposite Florida's Turnpike interchange.

Photo: Stephanie Murphy

This estate residence in Boca Grove Plantation shows the area's prevalent interest in grandeur. This custom design uses the pediment as its signature element.

BOCA POINTE
6943 S.W. 18th St.
Boca Raton

Much of Boca Pointe's 1,100 acres is playground and the rest is home for a variety of lifestyles: condominium, garden apartment, coach, single-family, patio and custom estate home. Prices vary from $100,000 to more than $1 million, with amenities of golf, tennis, clubhouse, fitness center and swimming. Markborough Properties, a Canadian developer, created the community, and renovations keep it competitive. Resales remain popular in many of the villages that sold out in the early 1980s. New construction is under way at Villa Sonrisa, an attached product ranging from $136,900 to $168,900; El Dorado, with courtyard zero-lot-line homes from $399,000 to $485,000; and custom

single-family at La Corniche, from $300,000 and $400,000.

Boca Pointe is west of I-95 and south of Palmetto Park Road, with the main entrance at Powerline Road and S.W. 18th Street. Villa Sonrisa is in the section east of Powerline Road on S.W. 18th Street west of Military Trail. The Prudential Florida Realty has a sales office on-site and many of its agents also live at Boca Pointe.

BOCA WEST COUNTRY CLUB
20540 Boca West Dr.
Boca Raton

One of Arvida's flagship communities with gated security and elaborate landscaping, Boca West began earning a reputation for championship golf as early as 1969 when its first two 18-hole courses carved sand traps out of 1,440 acres on Glades Road,

Photo: Tom Ervin

Homes at The Sanctuary, one of Boca Raton's most exclusive communities, have views of the Intracoastal Waterway.

between I-95 and Florida's Turnpike. The golf legend prompted early sales at Bridgewood, the first of 54 villages, when it opened in 1974. Residents enjoy a lifestyle that began as the club model, with a total of four golf courses, 39 tennis courts, bicycle trails, a health and fitness club, aquatic park and fine dining. The community sold out early and resales continue to be in demand.

This year, Boca West completed the first phase of a $22 million renovation of amenities to please 9,000 residents. Homes begin about $70,000 and climb fast, with a choice of mid-rise condominium, townhomes, villas and single-family. Inside Boca West is its ultra-exclusive village, The Island, tucked away over a bridge which has a separate guard staff and motorized gates. Resales of the existing 10 homes are always in demand, and Stevenson Development is finishing the last one this summer. Arvida also has a branch office on-site.

BROKEN SOUND

5200 St. Andrews Blvd.
Boca Raton

Arvida Corp. opened its 1,000-acre country club in 1987, with a clock-tower decorating the striking entrance at Yamato Road and St. Andrews Boulevard, west of I-95. The masterminds of master-planned communities, Arvida sold out Broken Sound years ahead of schedule. Like the developer's earlier hits, Broken Sound stands out for its scope of landscap-

Old Floresta

It might be said that one of Boca Raton's haunts, literally, is smack-dab in the middle of the Old Floresta neighborhood in Boca Raton.

The historic district, built in the early part of this century, is home to 29 houses designed by architect Addison Mizner. And a ghost from its past sometimes seems to be hanging around still. No, this isn't a scary ghost. This spirit tends to be partial to the sound of pianos playing, light laughter and the tinkling of glasses.

At least that's what Lavender House owner Suzy Wiberg thinks.

Wiberg and her husband, Ewald, own the 1926 house that architect Herman Von Holst once called home. Von Holst hung his hat there for 25 years after buying the house and 28 others from a bankrupt Mizner. After he purchased the homes, Von Holst, who had taken over the Chicago practice of Frank Lloyd Wright, named the homes so gardeners could identify them.

"I guess they didn't have street numbers," Wiberg, whose home is the second of two Old Floresta houses to be added to the National Register of Historic Places, mused in an interview with *The News* in Boca Raton.

The first Old Floresta/Mizner home to be put on the register is on Hibiscus Street. It was owned by Fred and Lottie Aiken. Fred Aiken was Boca Raton mayor from 1929 to 1939. Today, it is owned by Geri and Jerry

Ludeman, who got the home on the list by restoring it without changing much of Mizner's original design or materials. On the patio today, one can still see the same fountain sculpture that was there when the Aikens owned the home.

The first homes in Old Floresta were built in the 1920s as cottages to house employees of Mizner's Cloister Inn, on the grounds of the present day Boca Raton Resort and Club. The neighborhood begins off Palmetto Park Road, west of the Boca Raton Museum of Art, and is contained between N.W. Ninth Terrace to the west and Paloma Avenue to the east. And the houses are well-rooted on streets named for tropical flowers: Alamanda, Oleander, Hibiscus, Azalea and Aurelia streets.

According to information from the Boca Raton Historical Society, Mizner built Old Floresta for executives of his land development company and "the less well-to-do," reserving more-opulent designs to beach-area dwellings.

Mizner is known for his use of the Mediterranean Revival style in architecture. Typical features in homes of his design include Dade County pine floors and pecky cypress ceilings for durability, strategically placed windows for cross-ventilation without air-conditioning, and balconies and wrought iron for the Mediterranean look that Mizner believed suited South Florida.

The curious can drive around the neighborhood; it's not gated. This allows for a peek at the exterior and the gardens.

To learn more about Old Floresta and Addison Mizner's work in the Boca Raton area, contact the Boca Raton Historical Society at 395-6766.

Ewald and Suzy Wiberg sit outside their historic Old Floresta home in Boca Raton.

ing, decorative streetscape features and overall attention to quality. A total of 29 communities include lifestyle choices from single-family estate home to villas, patio homes and quad-style condominiums. Prices are $200,000 to more than $2 million. Broken Sound neighborhoods are tailored for every size family, especially people with children. Some newer villages are Tanglewood, Grand Oaks, Vintage Estates and Bermuda Run.

GRAND BAY ESTATES
1018 Grand Bay Ct.
Highland Beach

Few communities have sold as fast as Addison Estates described above. Dan Swanson's partners in that venture, Stuart and Howard Wexelman, are developing Grand Bay Estates, a collection of 19 one- and two-story estate homes inside the gates of Boca Highlands condominium. Home sites are available on the Intracoastal. Grand Bay has a deepwater marina, private club and lighted tennis facilities. Estates begin at $1.5 million. To visit, take Yamato Road east to U.S. Highway 1 and south to Spanish River Boulevard; cross the bridge to Highway A1A and turn north.

LES JARDINS
St. Andrews Blvd.
Boca Raton

The garden spot for sure, Les Jardins is gated with large single-family estate homes in a secluded park environment. Only 122 residences decorate 105 acres, with 18 acres of green space. Large families have plenty to choose from, with half-acre homesites, sidewalks and pristine landscaping. The community was an immediate sellout, and a handful of resales are from $500,000 to $1.5 million.

MIZNER VILLAGE
500 S.E. Fifth Ave.
Boca Raton

Residential choices vary from condominiums in Mizner Tower to those in the mid-rise Mizner Court, on the west side of the Intracoastal Waterway off Palmetto Park Road. Arvida was the developer and both properties are a short walk from the Boca Raton Resort and Club and its nearby Golf Villas, where people stay by the week, the season or even year round. Mizner Court is available from $250,000 and Mizner Tower has units from $750,000 to more than $1 million. The developer of The Aragon recently offered $14 million for the seven-acre parcel next to Mizner Tower, so we can expect more new construction near the Resort.

OCEAN PLACE ESTATES
4401 S. Ocean Blvd.
Highland Beach

As noted earlier, new construction on the ocean is scarce. Ocean Place Estates fills the bill nicely for buyers such as the new CEO at W.R. Grace & Company who succumbed to the $3.6 million turnkey charms of the Arielle model. Addresses within the gated enclave of 11 custom homes begin at $2.5 million. Sites are available and construction is under way on two other recent sales — one buyer, a young man who distributes designer sunglasses, and the other, a designer of yachts. The development team, many of whom are aligned with Cushman & Wakefield, plan another "spec" residence, probably for less than $3 million.

THE POLO CLUB BOCA RATON
5100 Champion Blvd.
Boca Raton

The largest clubhouse in the area, at 90,000 square feet, makes a certain statement in a city very preoccupied with country clubs and multiples of amenities. Other attractions that generate heavy sales are 29 clay tennis courts, two championship golf courses and an equestrian center. Home to tennis legend Chris Evert and her family, The Polo Club draws visitors and buyers from all over the world. Almost 20 villages offer buyers the gamut in housing styles, with plenty of resales.

Knightsbridge is one of the few villages within The Polo Club Boca Raton with new construction opportunities. Only 30 homes are in the final phase, and prices begin at $595,000.

Hidden Cove has three new courtyard models under construction by Tuscan Harvey Homes, priced from $595,000.

Vintage Oaks properties are available from $700,000 to more than $1 million. Builders at Vintage Oaks include Marlex Housing, Vintage Properties Inc., Charlse Custom Homes, Wyndsor Building & Design, National Custom Homes Inc. and Leonard Albanese & Sons.

To visit The Polo Club, take I-95 west to Military Trail and go north past Clint Moore Road to the entrance on Champion Boulevard.

PRESIDENTIAL PLACE
800 S. Ocean Blvd.
Boca Raton

A whisker longer and you'll miss out on the last two residences available at the Prez, the seven-story commander-in-chief among new oceanfront condominium projects. A total of only 42 residences enjoy 700 feet of private beachfront adjacent to the Boca Beach Club, the oceanside presence of the Boca Raton Resort. Buyers at Presidential receive the initiation fee and first-year dues in the Resort's Premier Club, with the use of its world-class amenities. A concierge attends to residents' requests as if they were hotel guests — room service, maid service and personal trainer. Individual beachfront cabanas come with each home, outfitted with sundeck, sitting room with wetbar, bathroom and full-size shower, and wiring for cable and telephone service from the owners' residences. Noted designer Alfred Karram is responsible for five turnkey residences at Presidential. His family-owned firm also created the lobbies and public areas. Judy Howard of J/Howard Design produced three, including one that's still available.

Prices on the last two homes are $2.25 million and $2.6 million. The developer is Presidential Place Partners Ltd., whose principals John Temple and Mike Post are from the Arvida school. Temple was president of Arvida Corp. during development of The Addison and

Mizner Village, to name two, and Post managed the construction. You can read more about John Temple's new projects in the chapter on Business.

The buyer profile at Presidential Place reflects a lot about the contemporary luxury marketplace: 30 percent are European; the average age is early 50s with some in their 30s; about 25 buyers are single; one owns a professional hockey franchise, and another deals in baseball.

ROYAL PALM YACHT & COUNTRY CLUB
500 E. Camino Real
Boca Raton

One of the untold stories is the extent of teardowns and large-scale renovations in Arvida's first Boca Raton residential development. It dates to 1959, when winter residents who belonged to the Boca Raton Resort provided steady traffic for the emerging estate-style, second-home market. The community lies south of Camino Real between Federal Highway and the Intracoastal Waterway. One gated entrance is Federal and S.W. 18th Street; the other is on Camino Real at the circle opposite the entrance to the Resort. Streets are curving and wide, and buyers like the choice of waterfront exposure, interior lot and golf course sites.

The teardown trend began with waterfront lots and coveted other lots as demand increased. Of 700 estate homes in the community, more than 100 are renovations. Developers have invested $1 million or more for a house, just to tear it down.

THE SANCTUARY
4400 N. Federal Hwy.
Boca Raton

When it opened in 1980, The Sanctuary set the standard for exclusivity, security, glamour and turnkey. The community of 96 single-family estate residences is on the west side of the Intracoastal Waterway buffered from the fast lane by a 27-acre natural wildlife preserve and mangrove hammock. The Sanctuary appeals to yachters who need deepwater flex space, so the thirst for waterfront fueling the teardown craze also is swallowing many of its choice point lots. Security includes guard gates at the main entrance on Federal Highway and at a second entrance on Spanish River Boulevard, roving road patrols inside and electronic marine surveillance at the waterway.

SANTA BARBARA
20580 N.W. 28th Ter.
Boca Raton

Following the trend to capture Californians on the go in the early '90s, the developers introduced this 70-acre single-family community inspired by the mission style of the West Coast. Santa Barbara sold out promptly, but resales are available. Priced from $240,000 to $360,000, options include patio homes, villas and courtyard residences. The developers were Marlex Housing and Ahmanson Developments Inc., a subsidiary of the financial stronghold Home Savings of America Inc. Since Boca Raton is approaching buildout per its comprehensive plan, it is one of the last new planned communities inside the city limits. Buyers are happy to be across the street from Town Center mall. Santa Barbara has 240 residences and buyers are members of the $1.8 million Santa Barbara Club, with tennis courts, a fitness center and the swimming pool overlooking an interior lake. The entrance is north of Glades Road on Powerline Road.

ST. ANDREWS COUNTRY CLUB
7227 Clint Moore Rd.
Boca Raton

The country club adopted the mystique of Scotland's famous links to relay its commitment to upper-crust exclusivity. Resales are in demand in this gated community, which allows only single-family estate homes. Amenities are golf, tennis, fitness and fine dining. Prices are from the $400,000s to $2 million.

WOODFIELD COUNTRY CLUB
3650 Club Pl.
Boca Raton

Inside the city limits and poised from the outset to be the country club with as much promise as any around, Woodfield got caught in the window that the Resolution Trust Corp. slammed on many sound and well-planned developments in the late 1980s. Infrastructure and the traffic-stopping landscape were in place, and residents enjoyed some top-flight amenities. The 830-acre master-planned community was only about 25 percent developed when construction stopped on one of four clubhouses. While the media blamed the inept lender, the RTC and the developer, residents continued to enjoy their beautiful community.

Fortunately, the window is wide open again since a new developer rescued Woodfield from the RTC's clutches. The promise is there, even more so, as the market discovers a very desirable country club inside the city limits with the buzz of new construction going on. New homes in Woodfield create a likely alternative to older club communities, and a new clubhouse, The Cascades, is the next best thing to a Caribbean vacation. It's a head-spinner in a city where competition among amenities is extra stiff. The landscaping also reflects the millions poured into upgrading Woodfield overall. New properties are coming on line in villages such as Windsor Bay, Coventry, Carlton Place, The Enclave, Briarcliffe, Mayfair and Kensington. Resales remain popular, with prices in a wide range of housing styles from the $200,000s to $2 million-plus.

Other Great Places To Live

ANDOVER
2660 Hampton Bridge Rd.
Delray Beach

New in 1987 and popular ever since, Andover resales remain in demand among families fond of traditional single-family homes, spacious lots and the signature element the original developers put on a pedestal . . . the natural asset of abundant trees! It's still possible, for less than $300,000, to live in this 70-acre gated community in a heavily wooded hamlet off Old Germantown Road.

Original developers Tom Fleming and Bill Maher avoided removing native vegetation wherever possible and planned the community's winding roads according to tree trunk placement. They were so committed to the concept, they relocated more than 400 mature trees that were threatened during the excavation phase and accepted buyer's plans on the condition of moving rather than sacrificing trees.

The community of 154 residences averages one-third-acre homesites. The granite face of the entrance wall is repeated with slate-styled Bomanite accenting the sidewalks, and electronic surveillance monitors security at the gate. Otherwise, it's trees that stand watch at the community tennis courts and playgrounds. To see Andover, exit I-95 west to Congress Avenue and go south; bear right on Old Germantown Road and the entrance will be on your left.

THE BANYANS
Clint Moore Rd.
Boca Raton

A sellout community when Arvida Co. introduced it five years ago, The Banyans arrived to fill the growing demand for another village like Broken Sound. Resales can be had for the low $200,000s in this community of 310 detached zero-lot-line patio homes. Homes are 1,700 to 2,400 square feet with two-car garages. Some have lake views, and there's a large neighborhood pavilion with a free-form swimming pool, whirlpool spa, spacious sun decks and covered cabana. Twin banyan trees, the namesake, grace the guarded entry gate. To visit The Banyans, take the Congress Avenue exit of I-95 south to Clint Moore road; turn right and go west for two miles past Military Trail. The entrance is on your right, east of Powerline/Jog Road. You can also exit Florida's Turnpike at Glades Road going east, turn left onto Powerline Road and then left again at Clint Moore Road.

Newport Bay Club
17053 Newport Club Dr.
Boca Raton

A contemporary playground lifestyle surrounds this gated community of four different villages, all enjoying a vicinity that reads like a Who's Who among prestigious luxury addresses in Boca: St. Andrews Country Club, Woodfield Country Club, The Polo Club, Fieldbrook Estates, Season's at Boca Raton, The Colonnade at Glen Oaks, Broken Sound and The Banyans. Also nearby are Andover, Foxe Chase and Rabbit Hollowe in Delray. Earlier communities at five-year-old Newport include The Estates and the Hampton Club, where resales on two-bedroom residences are available for $225,000.

In 1993, a new developer took over 47 lots at lender-held Copper Lake, an 86-lot enclave that was half complete. Copper Lake has single-family detached homes with one- and two-story styles priced from $185,000. Also relatively new are homes at The Tides, a 39-lot parcel of zero-lot-line detached residences priced from $225,000. Another creation by a later developer, The Tides runs from the Newport clubhouse to the eastern border of St. Andrews Country Club.

Newport Bay Club is all about loving tennis. During development, the racquet sports program was under professional management with an ongoing sales campaign to encourage outside membership growth to complement the pace of community buildout. Newport Bay Club has a full-time tennis pro to oversee private lessons, clinics, tournaments and special events.

There are eight lighted tennis courts, including one championship court with a grandstand, two indoor racquetball courts, a half-court for basketball, a pro shop, men's and women's shower/locker rooms and saunas. The heated, short-course Olympic-size swimming pool and a fitness center complete the sports package.

Besides pricey neighbors, Newport Bay enjoys the convenience of Regency Court Shopping Center at Yamato and Jog roads, the Jog Road Center and the luxury carwash/gourmet store Plaza Real. The entry to Newport Bay Club is off Jog Road just north of Old Clint Moore Road, about 10 minutes from the I-95 interchange at Linton Boulevard and Florida's Turnpike exit at Glades Road.

Frenchman's Creek
Donald Ross Rd.
Palm Beach Gardens

Talk about staying power: Frenchman's Creek was a golfer's dream destination in the 1970s and very popular throughout the mid-1980s, maintaining sales leadership even when market conditions were otherwise flat. The 770-acre community by Haft-Gaines Associates was essentially sold out far sooner than originally expected. Its first 15 years, and a decade before residential sales began, Frenchman's Creek was known for two 18-hole championship golf courses set in a heavily wooded glen about a mile from the ocean. Less than a handful of zero-lot-line homesites are available through Exclusive Realty, 627-5100, and they are priced from $250,000.

Resales on existing homes are from $350,000 to " a few million dollars," with choices among townhomes, zero-lot-line, patio homes, villas and custom waterfront estates. Amenities include an oceanfront Beach Club in Juno Beach, new in 1991 and designed by noted architect Kenneth Hirsch, featuring a resort-style swimming pool, sun deck and private beach; the 67,000-square-foot main clubhouse with a full-service spa and fitness center; and 17 Har-Tru tennis courts. Some homes have private docks, and there are slips available for lease at Frenchman's Creek Marina. The Yacht Club overlooks the deepwater marina, where slips can accommodate vessels of more than 100 feet. An on-site sales office at Frenchman's Creek, 694-8500, has current resale prices. To visit Frenchman's Creek, take I-95 to Donald Ross Road and go east; the entrance is on your right.

And Just A Few More . . .

With more than 300 neighborhoods in Boca Raton alone, stretching from the ocean to the Everglades and covering a range of housing styles more innovative than many parts of the United States have ever experienced, the Gold Coast beckons you to explore: single-family homes, estate compounds, villas, patio homes, courtyard homes, condominiums and townhomes.

In your travels to see all of the above, make time also for Wellington, west of West Palm Beach out Forest Hills Boulevard; Bankers' Row in Delray Beach; Old Floresta in Boca Raton (see this chapter's sidebar); Mission Bay, west of Boca Raton at Glades Road and U.S. 441; Bocaire, on Military Trail north of Clint Moore Road; and Weston, the 10,000-acre Arvida town in west Broward County.

Affordability Can Be Found Here Too

With annual residential sales volume averaging more than $500 million, just in South Palm Beach County, it's no wonder developers and builders scramble to be innovative with products and savvy with niche marketing. The marketplace bears average home prices of $185,000 in Boca Raton, while the national average is $145,000.

Still, there's demand for affordability since the hospitality and service industries are among the fastest growing population sectors. Traditionally, many people who worked in Boca Raton couldn't afford to buy homes here, but that picture is changing as developers and brokerages take steps to close the gaps. One company, ironically named Luxury Homes Inc., is prepared to dispose of the myths surrounding luxury.

Explains Broker Robert Mitchell, vice president of Luxury Homes, "There's so much attention to country clubs and luxury communities that 'average people' are too often forgotten. We know there are teachers, policemen, firemen, middle management executives and small business owners who can only dream about living in a community of millionaires. But they need just as much help when it comes to buying and selling a home. We're in the business of providing service, regardless of price range."

Proof of progress in affordability is shown by the growing presence of communities with FHA financing options.

Boca Rancho garden homes was an early sellout for that reason and because the developer, Stoltz Bros., offered attractive closing terms on homes priced from $67,500. With the combined advantages, buyers found purchasing at Boca Rancho more affordable than many rentals, since the average total of closing costs and down payment was $3,900. The community of 120 two-bedroom units is in a two-story configuration of four to a building, with gated courtyard and screened-patio entries.

Realtors

The Realtor Association of South Palm Beach County speaks for a membership of 2,500 to 2,700 real estate professionals. Offices for the association are in the Potomac Building, 3200 N. Military Trail, Suite 100, Boca Raton, 33431, 997-8266.

In 1993, a consolidation campaign successfully bridged the administrations and support services of the Boca Raton, Delray Beach and Boynton Beach Realtor associations. The territory of the umbrella organization, affecting more than 360 professional offices, is the Hillsboro Canal north to Hypoluxo Road. A full-time staff person operates a satellite office at 639 E. Ocean Avenue, Boynton Beach.

The original Boca Raton association dates to 1956; it received its charter from the National Association of Realtors in 1957.

The Florida Association of Realtors has headquarters in Orlando. The FAR Governmental Affairs Office is in Tallahassee, (904) 224-1400. FAR's Legal Hotline is a valuable service for members, who can receive complimentary advice on any aspect of real estate law by calling 439-1409. Hours are 8 AM to 6 PM.

Executive director of the South County Association is Robert Golden. Meryl Thurman is director of communications and editor of the association's weekly industry newsletter.

Current officers are Debby O'Connell, president; Alberta McCarthy, president-elect; Bill Richardson, vice president; Pat Noenert, secretary; Jay Abbott, treasurer; and Myra Mueller, past president. Directors include John Breithart, Kenneth Davis, Herb Gimelstob, Jeri Ann Harrington, Bill Harris, Jerry Lehman, Beth Pomeranz, Ron Shulman, Conrad Sittler and William Tison Jr.

Brokerages

Boca Raton's real estate community is enormous, with more than

Photo: Stephanie Murphy

Boca Raton Synagogue dedicated its new temple on Montoya Circle in suburban Boca in December 1994.

2,500 members in the Association of Realtors. In recent years, firms vying for top-dollar sales volume include Arvida Realty, Coldwell Banker, Gimelstob Realty/Better Homes and Gardens, Luxury Homes Inc. and The Prudential Florida Realty.

The following companies are noted for their market share, based on dollar-volume, sales domination in certain neighborhoods or other qualifying characteristics.

ARVIDA REALTY SALES LTD.
555 S. Federal Hwy.
Boca Raton   391-9400

Don't confuse the brokerage with the namesake developer, Arthur Vining Davis, whose company began its first Boca Raton residential community in 1959 and is credited with setting the standard for our famous manicured master-planned excellence. As Boca Raton proper approached buildout and Arvida had less to develop, project sales expanded to become a general real estate brokerage.

Agents still dominate sales at most Arvida communities, such as Royal Palm Yacht & Country Club, Broken Sound and Boca West, and lead the field in many others. For more than five years, Arvida Realty has been No. 1 in dollar volume sales in the area. In the area of luxury homes, which includes homes from $750,000 and up, it outsells the competition.

However, Arvida Realty goes beyond the scope of luxury homes. Listings here include condominiums that start at $40,000 to properties that run well into the millions.

Arvida Realty's office network includes sites at the Boca Raton Resort and Club, which the parent company once owned; one at Boca West; one at Glades Road and St. Andrews Boulevard; one at Clint Moore and Jog roads; and one at S. Federal Highway and S.W. Fifth Avenue.

In summer 1995, Arvida Realty set up a public information kiosk at Town Center mall, with interactive Multiple Listing Service data. The kiosk has a TOUCHPARADISE computerized home preview center. The company also publishes a *Guide to Paradise* at least nine times a year.

The head of Arvida Realty is Fred DeFalco, who shepherds 175 agents.

COLDWELL BANKER

101 N. Federal Hwy.
Boca Raton   391-9097

If you like 'em large or want a name you knew outside Florida, Coldwell Banker has a hemispheric presence of 2,000 offices backed up with two decades of stability in this region. The tri-county area has two dozen offices, including three in Boca Raton and another in Boynton Beach. Coldwell Banker is especially active in western Boca.

GIMELSTOB REALTY INC./ BETTER HOMES AND GARDENS

7777 W. Glades Rd., Ste. 100
Boca Raton   451-9800

One of the largest independents in Florida, Gimelstob has 26 offices in four counties, from Port St. Lucie south to Kendall. Sales volume for 1994 was $801,375,000. Herb Gimelstob began the company in 1984, with one associate and an office in a trailer, and aligned with Better Homes and Gardens the following year. He became acquisitive, buying small brokerages throughout the region and expanding the operation to offer one-stop services in mortgages, title insurance and homeowner's insurance. Gimelstob also acquired the Gold Coast School of Real Estate last year, merging his in-house school into the training system.

Aggressive, tough, energetic and controversial, Herb Gimelstob is also well-taught. When he needed an executive administrator for his expanding operation, Herb recruited his own former mentor Elaine Hall — now Mrs. Gimelstob and his business partner.

LIMITED EDITION INTERNATIONAL REALTY

443 Plaza Real, Mizner Park
Boca Raton   362-5270

Curbside at Boca Raton's high-profile shopping and leisure destination, Limited Edition draws passersby who admire offices appointed like a luxury residence: 12-foot ceilings, arches, 18-inch marble flooring, stone columns, art deco wall sconces and chandeliers.

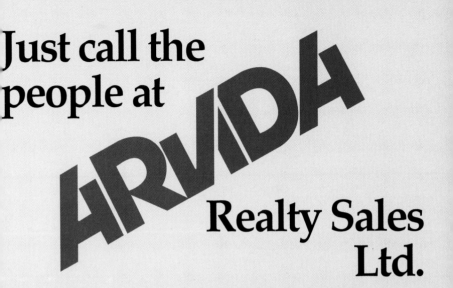

Just call the
people at

ARVIDA

Realty Sales
Ltd.

Nobody knows Boca Raton better than Arvida Realty Sales.
Nobody *sells* it better, either.

In this ever-changing competitive marketplace, it's just good sense to do business with the people who are *the dominant real estate force in Florida's paradise.*

We have the numbers to prove it. Most importantly, we have the people who do it. And, we actually accomplish this with fewer real estate specialists than our nearest competitors.

Professionalism. Experience. Arvida.

The team of real estate specialists at Arvida Realty Sales average 13 years experience each.

The dollar volume of their closings, per individual, put them near the top of residential sales people...not just in Boca Raton, but in the entire United States.

The depth of experience and professional education of the team ranks among the highest in the industry. Nationwide. Not just in Boca Raton.

Many Arvida people are former owners or managers of their own real estate firms. They are the best of the best.

*H*ere's what experience looks like.
This is what it means.

More solutions, fewer problems.
You'll sell your home faster. You'll find the home you're looking for quicker.
You'll have a business partner working for you. Not just a sales agent.

We are leaders in sales. Leaders in the community. Leaders in the industry.
Nationwide. Worldwide.
Phone today. Start living your dream in Paradise tomorrow.

Just call the people at

ARVIDA
Realty Sales Ltd.

The Dominant Real Estate Force in Florida's Paradise

At Arvida, every seller's listing gets exposure.

In such a dynamic, ever changing market, Arvida Realty Sales' marketing and advertising thrust is total inventory coverage.

- MLS (Multiple Listing Service), exposure to more than 10,000 Realtors®.

- Arvida Realty Sales' *Guide to Paradise*, published a minimum of nine times annually with distribution of more than 400,000.

- Local and regional newspapers with a combined circulation of over 110,000 monthly.

- *TOUCHPARADISE®*, the computerized home preview center displayed exclusively at Boca Raton's Town Center Mall, visited by over 6.2 million shoppers annually.

While recognizing the importance of marketing Boca Raton properties to people from across town to across the nation, Arvida Realty Sales is an important player in the world-wide marketplace.

Selectively and strategically, Arvida markets the globe.

From its national and international hub – the world-renowned Boca Raton Resort and Club, the firm has not one, but two offices. No other real estate firm is represented there.

- Boca Raton is introduced to more than 228,000 guests annually by way of two staffed information offices, hotel product displays and an exclusive 24-hour television channel in every room.

- Buyers and sellers are assisted through an assortment of professional organizations, referral networks, world trade center computerized bulletins and the Internet, the *de facto* global electronic bulletin board.

- Arvida Realty Sales is linked to departments of commerce, foreign trade offices, brokerage and investment firms and embassies.

- Professional associations are maintained with powerful real estate leaders and developers around the globe.

Boca Raton is business.

It's the city of choice for the headquarters of more Fortune 500 companies than any other Florida city.

It is education.

It has a modern graduate-level state university, a four-year private university, excellent public and private schools.

Boca Raton is culture.

A genuine artistic interest prevails with a wide range of venues and a staggering number of programs, art galleries and theatres, outdoor concerts and festivals and craft fairs.

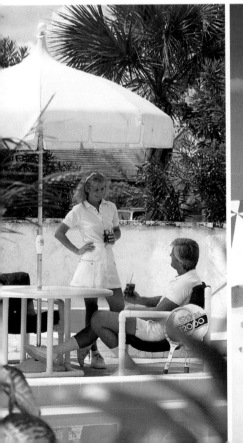

The Arvida Mosaic - The dream realized.

Following the death of its founder in 1962, the legacy of Arvida continued over the next three decades. The Arvida Corporation patterned a strategy to satisfy enlightened consumers who sought a high quality of life and a superior physical environment. Thus the comprehensively planned community concept was born.

Nowhere in Florida are there more imaginative choices for residential living than in Boca Raton. And most were planned by Arvida:

- *The Addison*
- *Boca Inlet*
- *Boca West*
- *Broken Sound*
- *Estancia*
- *Lake House South*
- *Millpond*

- *Mizner Village*
- *Paseos*
- *Royal Palm Yacht & Country Club*
- *The Sabals - Sabal Point,*
  Sabal Ridge, Sabal Shores
- *Timbercreek*
- *Town Place*

As families came to live and play in Boca Raton, it evolved from a winter resort area to a year-round community attracting major businesses. Again, Arvida fulfilled the dream by creating a wide range of business communities: office parks mixed-use commercial centers, retail centers, warehouse and research facilities; each combining beauty with function which has become the trademark of an Arvida development.

- *Arvida Park of Commerce*
- *Arvida Executive Center*
- *Arvida Financial Plaza*

- *Arvida Parkway Center*
- *Town Center*
- *The Village Square*

Boca Raton. **We call it Paradise.**

It's a town that's special and different. It's cosmopolitan and manicured. It has a grand history of excellence and residents who ensure that the tradition be preserved. It has its own executive airport; is 30 minutes from both West Palm Beach and Ft. Lauderdale International airports and 60 minutes to Miami International Airport.

Boca Raton. **It is a variety of lifestyles.**

From the coastal neighborhoods along the Intracoastal Waterway to oceanfront estates and high-rise condominiums; from charming in-town family neighborhoods to sprawling all-amenities-included communities to the west; from contemporary villas and garden apartments to stately mansions with tennis courts and horse stables, housing costs run the gamut from under $100,000 to the millions.

Boca Raton. It has a unique look.

You can see the influences everywhere. It's the romantic legacy of the Mediterranean-style of architecture from the Addison Mizner era of the 1920's.

It is different here.

You can feel it. It's warm, inviting and dedicated to preserving the influences and flavor of the past while forming a partnership with the environment to assure an exceptional quality of life today and tomorrow.

Boca Raton and Arvida.

It was 1958 when the man behind the name, Arthur Vining Davis, envisioned the life one could lead here and purchased the Boca Raton Hotel and Club, a one-mile stretch of beach and thousands of acres of land to the west. Wishing to perpetuate the influence of architect Addison Mizner, Davis focused on creating the definitive haven for those who wanted a glorious lifestyle, and a wonderful place to raise families.

Arvida, an acronym for Arthur Vining Davis, was then formed to develop the vast land holdings and to make Boca Raton the cornerstone of residential living, unequaled anywhere in Florida.

That year, 1958, saw the development of the first Arvida community, Royal Palm Yacht and Country Club, one of the most luxurious communities of its kind. Soon to follow was the Royal Palm Plaza, a collection of the first "designer" shops in Florida. Boca West became the west golf course for the guests of the Boca Raton Hotel. Then came a totally new concept in living, the beachfront condominium, which became one of Florida's greatest commodities. Sabal Point, Sabal Ridge and Sabal Shores were among the first of the condominiums to carry the Arvida name.

Boca Raton is relaxation.
Exotic foliage, quiet courtyards, sculptured fountains enhance the experience of world-class shopping and fine dining.

It is recreation.
Winter polo matches, celebrity tennis tournaments, dozens of championship golf courses, miles of pristine beaches and more acreage of public parks than any other city in Florida.

Boca Raton is year-round outdoor living.
It's subtropical – average temperature 74 degrees. Miles of pathways all over town beckon the bicycle riders, the rollerbladers, the joggers and the walker of all ages.

Boca Raton.
You'll call it Paradise, too.

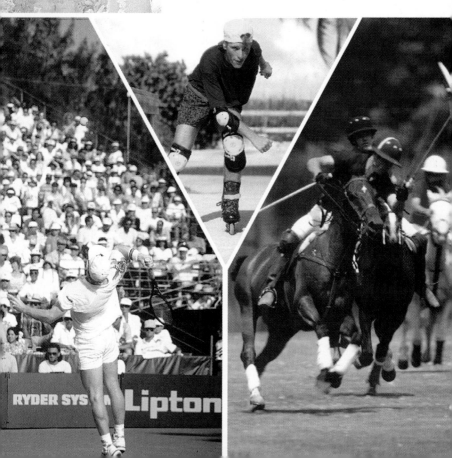

The people behind the name.

They are your neighbors. Your friends. They belong to your clubs. Shop in your stores. Their children attend your schools. They're your Hometown Realtors®.

Each Arvida specialist maintains a personal sphere of valuable contacts from past customers and clients, as well as contacts through a variety of civic, charitable and social organizations.

These specialists also conduct ambitious personalized marketing campaigns that focus upon particular communities, neighborhoods, or a myriad of other "niche" markets.

Arvida people know every nook and cranny of the city. For 37 years the people of Arvida have helped families buy and sell homes in every sector of this city and surrounding areas.

Leaders are obligated to be innovative and competitive.

Arvida Realty Sales is unlike any other real estate firm in the country. Its philosophy is entrepreneurial in spirit – one in which the company forms a partnership with its real estate specialists, while providing a foundation of support services.

Make the right call.
"Just Call the People at Arvida"

People also see architectural models of some of its properties, and the interactive video system, allowing potential buyers to enter important criteria — price, size, neighborhood, style, etc. — and shop for homes by touch. With a lengthy career in Boca's high-end, partners Carroll Hahn and Jack Meneely specialize in properties priced from $500,000.

Relationships with developers generate new opportunities. For example, when construction began on the last available parcel in The Island at Boca West, a private isle inside Boca West Country Club, developers Judy Chefan and Steve Chefan Jr. (Judy's son) asked Carroll Hahn to market it. Listed for $2,495,000, it carries the mystique of this quiet glen hidden over a bridge with separate guard staff and motorized entry gates.

LUXURY HOMES INC.

Boca Bank Corporate Centre
7000 W. Palmetto Park Rd.
Boca Raton 395-9800

Founded in 1986 by pioneers in Boca's high-end market, Luxury Homes began by marketing mansions built on speculation. Following its acquisition by Delaware-based Stoltz Bros. Ltd. in 1990, Luxury Homes expanded to market residential properties in all price ranges and communities.

Other Stoltz Bros. affiliates include a commercial realty, property management firm, business brokerage, construction firm and land acquisition division. The parent company owns Boca Bank Corporate Centre and Northern Trust Plaza, both Class-A office complexes.

The staff of 75 works from the corporate office and branches downtown and near the beach. Luxury Homes is a sales leader in Les Jardins, Woodfield Country Club, Sea Ranch Club and The 3600 Building in Palm Beach, to name a few.

Luxury Homes also has a comprehensive third-party sales division to handle transactions involving REO (real-estate-owned), corporate-owned, estate-owned and guardian-held properties.

PREMIER ESTATE PROPERTIES INC.

351 E. Palmetto Park Rd.
Boca Raton 394-7700

Four brokers own the two-year-old firm, which restricts itself to listings in excess of $1 million. Its chosen niche is Hillsboro Beach to Manalapan, both waterfront and country club properties. The firm is especially active in The Sanctuary and Royal Palm Yacht Club.

Founders of Premier Estates are twin brothers Gerard and Joseph Liguori and Carmen D'Angelo Jr. All three are polished, thirtysomething very quick studies who learned the high-end business from some of the most respected and successful top-producers in town — Corinne Brinkman and Dorothy Snyder, who founded Luxury Homes Inc., and Jane McAllister, a former Realtor of the Year whom they invited to be a partner.

THE PRUDENTIAL FLORIDA REALTY

2301 Glades Rd.   994-8886
Boca Raton   (800) 325-7232

Based in Clearwater with 65 offices statewide and 11 in Palm Beach County, Prudential Florida is a good example of a large solid company with corporate support for regional and nationwide marketing. The company maintains a strong position in Boca's central corridor, west of I-95, and the Boca Pointe area to the southwest.

Sanctuary Realty, 4400 N. Federal Highway in Boca Raton, became a Prudential Florida subsidiary last year, though the firm retained its name and specialty in waterfront homes from Boca to Palm Beach. The family-owned brokerage emerged in 1979 to sell new residences within The Sanctuary, where the concept of turnkey mansions began. The Sanctuary appears later in the Neighborhood portion of this chapter. Sanctuary Realty sales manager Bill Barnes, a veteran of both Arvida Realty and the Gimelstob organization, teaches a course for Prudential Florida about Boca's 317 neighborhood communities, complete with maps.

The Rental Landscape

The hotbed of business expansion regionwide and the momentum from downtown redevelopment in several cities forms a dynamic combination that is fueling the first wave of new multifamily rental construction in five years.

Many newcomers are buying resales and new homes in various price ranges right away, while others are taking longer to tour the marketplace.

Fortunately, some attractive new rental properties are just now coming on line, including Trammell Crow's Mizner on the Green. New this summer are Mizner Park Tower and the Valencia and Tarragona Townhomes, and at least one other developer plans to build upscale new rentals downtown.

The location of these properties and sales statistics in general resales confirm a larger trend: the reversing of western urban sprawl by retrofitting the east. After more than a decade of pushing west with new construction, the momentum is shifting, with eastern neighborhoods the target of new activity. In Boca, that's partly because we bump into the Everglades sooner than west of Delray and Boynton. The "River of Grass" bends farther east in South County, brushing the flanks of neighborhoods just west of Mission Bay and Loggers Run.

Marta and Jim Batmasian, who own 100 acres of downtown Boca Raton including the exclusive Royal Palm Plaza, see the trend reflected in more vitality downtown, with downtown residential construction part of the impetus.

Says Marta, "The residential base is generating investment among large and small merchants because they realize people who rent these apartments will be only a few steps from their stores. The impact from residential activity is very encouraging. Also, we're seeing more year-round residents and fewer closed shutters. The houses and condos that used to be occupied by snowbirds on the east side .

. . many of the old-timers are passing away. The younger affluent people with children tend to be a year-round population. The average retiree can afford much less here than in the past. The marketplace is replacing them with younger professionals, especially on the east side."

Noting two high-profile purchases in recent months — Scott Paper CEO Albert J. Dunlap's at Addison Estates and Grace Company CEO Albert Costello's at Ocean Place Estates in Highland Beach — she said the sales successes there and at addresses such as Presidential Place are part of the reason so many developers are producing new rental projects on the east side.

"The job incentive program is bringing companies from other states, and a lot of newcomers naturally equate Florida with water . . . even if they aren't into boating. The east has always appealed to tourists . . . now, affluent executives and young professionals are renting and buying here too."

Mizner Park

Downtown Boca activity has been building since 1990, with Mizner Park as the catalyst for spreading the urban village gospel of "living above the store." When the five-story mixed-use urban phenomenon opened with retail and professional spaces on the first floor, Phase I of residential development included 136 rental apartments on the upper floors — the Villa Hibiscus and Villa Poinciana Apartments. Mizner Park leasing executive Chris Becker says they're 98 percent leased. There are one-, two- and three-bedroom floor plans from $750.

Phase II is now complete with another 136 units, and Becker says the new apartments are 95 percent leased, with prices from $800 to $3,000 for a penthouse. Available are one-, two- and three-bedroom, single-level floor plans in the nine-story Mizner Park Tower, and two-bedroom, three-level townhomes at Valencia and

Tarragona Townhomes. Apartments have views of the Mizner Park courtyard and the ocean, many with private balconies. Community amenities for apartments include a parking garage with remote-controlled access to reserved spaces. Townhomes have their own one-car attached garage.

Private facilities include a roof-top swimming pool, wet and dry saunas and a fitness center. The clubhouse has a library, fireplace, kitchen and planned social activities. There's a doorman and concierge service, Mizner Park's on-site professional management staff and 24-hour security patrol. Apartments and townhomes are walking distance to fine dining, the beach, the public library, City Hall, shopping throughout downtown, concerts at the Mizner Park Amphitheater and the on-site AMC movie theater.

Mizner Park residential projects are a joint venture development by Crocker & Company and Teachers Insurance and Annuity Association. To visit, take I-95 to Palmetto Park Road and go east, turning left onto Northeast Mizner Boulevard two blocks west of U.S. Highway 1. Mizner Park runs north from Northeast Second Street. For information, call 362-0606.

Southcoast Partners

The chapter on Business discusses the company developing the Parkwood Properties sites at U.S. Highway 1 and Palmetto Park Road. Part of Phase III, due mid to late 1996, is an eight-story rental apartment complex similar to Mizner Tower with ocean and golf course views. The 106-unit building will be at Southeast Mizner Boulevard and Southeast First Avenue, where the NationsBank drive-through is now.

Mizner on the Green

At publication time, Mizner on the Green was under construction and still too new to have a leasing office or a brochure. The $25 million rental community is by nationally respected residential developer Trammell Crow and its joint-venture financial partner, an out-of-state pension fund. Trammell Crow bought the 8.7-acre parcel for $5.6 million from Arvida Corp. and closed on the site in March.

If you want a location that matches Mizner Park and surpasses anything else in the vicinity, consider Southeast Mizner Boulevard across from the south end of Royal Palm Plaza, where residential townhomes with one- and two-car garages will overlook the championship links of the Boca Raton Resort and Club. The first of 246 three-story townhomes in a choice of one-, two- and three-bedroom floor plans are to be ready by October 1995. The Mizneresque elevations will resemble Trammell Crow's award-winning rental village San Marco at Broken Sound, described below in a summary of rentals.

Designers of upscale Mizner on the Green are Danny Powell and KTGY, the Fort-Lauderdale based offices of California-based international resort and hotel architects

Corbin/Yamafuji & Associates. The community comprises 19 buildings in an Old World pattern of urban-scale configuration. One-bedrooms will be 825 square feet under air and 1,184 gross square footage; and two-bedrooms will be 1,170 square feet under air and 1,785 gross. Three-bedroom units will be available in two sizes: 1,475 square feet enclosed with 2,156 gross and 1,790 square feet enclosed and 2,500 gross square footage.

Leasing prices at Mizner on the Green for corresponding sizes will start at $975, $1,200 and $1,625. A swimming pool and clubhouse will overlook the golf course, with the village within walking distance to shopping throughout downtown, the beach and dining.

Development partner Greg Iglehart of Trammell Crow expects a leasing office to open by the end of August 1995 to accept rental deposits. He anticipates delivering a building a week beginning October 1.

Elsewhere in selected South County locations, Trammell Crow is building The Vinings of Boynton, 252 units west of I-95 and north of Woolbright Road; The Vinings of Delray Beach, 228 units near the Laver's Racquet resort south of Linton Boulevard; and another 69-unit project west of Town Center mall in Boca.

Existing Trammell Crow rentals include The Vinings I and II at Town Place in Boca and a series of garden apartment communities: Town Colony, Boca Colony and Boca Place.

Trammell Crow also has a fine history in the for-sale marketplace, with area properties including Majorca near Town Center mall, Cedar Cay and Timbermill in Broken Sound and Sea Colony in Jupiter.

Smaller Apartments and Townhome Communities

BOCA PALMS
APARTMENTS AND TOWNHOMES
22300 S.W. 66th Ave.
Boca Raton   488-1510

A large gated community in the west, Boca Palms had the advantage of significant renovations from July 1988 to November 1994, when the owner was Delaware-based Stoltz Bros. Prior to selling the community to Pennsylvania Real Estate Investment Trust, the developer began a $40 million overhaul to complete construction of 338 new garden and lake villa apartments and townhomes and to renovate the existing 182 apartments and 80 courtyard townhomes. Floor plans of one-, two- and three-bedroom units are available. Amenities include guard-gated security, lighted tennis courts, three fitness centers, three swimming pools including two heated, three whirlpool spas, covered parking and a wide range of activities for tenants of all ages. The community is convenient to the Sawgrass Expressway and Florida's Turnpike and west of I-95. To visit Boca Palms, take Palmetto Park Road west to U.S. Highway 441; turn left to Southwest Third Street, then right at 66th Avenue.

CASABLANCA
815 W. Boynton Beach Blvd.
Boynton Beach   734-7092

With a choice of one-bedrooms priced from $650 and two-bedroom units from $780, Casablanca has the convenience of proximity to Boynton Beach Mall. Lake views look great from the screened patios and Casablanca has lighted tennis courts, a fitness center, a swimming pool and recreation deck. The nearness to I-95 makes Casablanca ideal for tenants who work almost anywhere in Palm Beach County. To visit, take I-95 to Boynton Beach Boulevard; the entrance is immediately west on the right. Leasing office hours are Monday through Friday, 10 AM to 6 PM; Saturday, 10 AM to 5 PM and Sunday, noon to 5 PM.

PALM COVE APARTMENT HOMES
1805 Palm Cove Blvd.
Delray Beach   *243-6455*

Scenic and so convenient, Palm Cove has lake views and eight floor plans, including some with lofts, starting at $700. Apartments have screened terraces and storage, walk-in closets, roman tubs and full-size washers and dryers. In addition to plentiful parking, enclosed garages are available. There's concierge service, a clubhouse and fitness center, swimming pool and whirlpool spa and lighted tennis courts. Minutes from I-95, Palm Cove's entrance is off Linton Boulevard just west of Congress Avenue. Leasing office hours are Monday through Thurs-

day, 9 AM to 7 PM; Friday, 9 AM to 6 PM; Saturday, 10 AM to 5 PM; and Sunday, 1 to 5 PM.

PRESIDENTIAL GOLFVIEW
1860 N. Congress Ave.
West Palm Beach   *689-1995*

Managed by Trammell Crow Residential Services, the four-story complex offers great value in condo rentals with views of the Presidential championship golf course. Prices begin at $530, with one- and two-bedroom units available. Amenities include three lighted tennis courts, private balconies and a heated swimming pool. To visit, take I-95 to Palm Beach Lakes Boulevard and go east to Congress Avenue; turn left and the entrance will be on your right.

SAN MARCO AT BROKEN SOUND
5555 N. Military Tr.
Boca Raton   *997-6700*

Great value and a gorgeous setting make these two- and three-bedroom villas and townhomes very popular. The gated community has a clubhouse, fitness center, views of lakes and the golf course, two swimming pools, two lighted tennis courts and numerous standard features that contribute to the "upgrade" atmosphere. San Marco units have remote-controlled attached garages and in-home alarm systems. Prices start at $1,125, and furnished corporate apartments

Insiders' Tips

Be aware of sea lice conditions before you swim in the ocean.

are available. For the flavor of what to expect at Mizner on the Green, visit San Marco: Take the Yamato Road exit of I-95 west to Military Trail and turn right. San Marco at Broken Sound is on the left.

THE VININGS AT TOWN PLACE
21409 Town Lakes Dr.
Boca Raton   *338-6861*

Villa-style Mediterranean units are available in one-, two- and three-bedroom floor plans in this Trammell Crow community near Town Center mall. Amenities include two swimming pools, spa and tennis courts, a fitness center and indoor racquetball courts and festive barbecue area. Call 338-6861 for current availability and prices or visit Monday through Friday from 9 AM to 6 PM, Saturday from 10 AM to 5 PM and Sunday, noon to 5 PM. To visit The Vinings, exit I-95 west at Palmetto Park Road; turn right at Military Trail, then left at the first traffic light, which is Verde Trail South. The entrance will be on your right.

Inside
Philanthropy

Giving is a major force here . . . it's one of the engines that fuels business activity and one of the busiest vehicles of our social process. Individuals — both wealthy and less-so — corporate giants and businesses of all sizes donate money, in-kind services and professional expertise for the myriad institutions that measure our progress as a civilized community: charities, not-for-profit cultural organizations, social service agencies and public-private collaborations.

Corporate Giving

Good community relations, good employee relations and tax-attractive charitable contributions or expense write-offs . . . these are some of the results of what appears at first blush to be a product-driven endeavor: Pepsi-Cola sponsoring an arts and crafts show, American Airlines donating airfare for an orchestra's guest artists, Miller Brewing Co. and Continental Airlines sponsoring a rodeo that benefits a scholarship foundation.

Some businesses favor educational institutions, especially if they seek the long-term benefits of stabilizing and promoting a technical or business curriculum that produces future hires. Some favor charities for a variety of reasons, including personal experiences with certain illnesses and

paybacks or loyalty to business associates. Often, they promote aspects of a balanced lifestyle that they deem appealing, even necessary, to recruit top executives for a corporate relocation.

IBM is always generous to communities where its people are employed, often taking their employees' leads to identify which groups and causes should receive donations in any given year. Its technology base explains IBM's consistent support of educational programs, notably in math and science. Explains Norman Ostrowski, site manager of external programs, "We also strive to be the industry leader in community service. We understand how important we are to the communities where IBM does business . . . and we recognize that it's difficult to separate business goals from community needs."

The corporation also gives to the arts as an application of education — sometimes money, sometimes computer equipment. In the past, IBM's employees and retirees donated more than $200,000 in one year alone to Palm Beach County arts groups.

Notes Palm Beach cultural leader Joseph Ferrer, who lives in Boca Raton, "The presence of IBM has helped shape the city and the region for more than 27 years . . . fostering an environment that attracted other prestigious corporate citizens in recent years."

IBM has been generous with the Boca Raton Museum of Art, Kravis Center for the Performing Arts, Boca Ballet Theatre Company, the Florida Philharmonic, the Museum of Science and Discovery in Fort Lauderdale and the Greater Miami Opera.

Says Ostrowski, "We try to maintain a balance . . . with support for environmental issues, social services, health care and the cultural arts. Consistent with our business objectives, IBM's mission is to be a national asset and a recognized world leader in the area of corporate social policy by addressing societal issues."

To that end, the company and its employees contributed $3.3 million in cash and equipment to South Florida community organizations in one recent year.

Certain businesses mesh well with the cultural arts, whose support groups tend to have above-average disposable income ... a big plus with the opportunity to share the gold mine of names and addresses on a group's mailing list.

Citibank is a division of Citicorp, the nation's largest financial institution and a global presence reflected by its banking establishments in 94 countries around the world.

Especially in New York, Citibank, has a reputation for involvement with the cultural arts. Here, says business development specialist Sage Wallace, Citibank takes culture seriously as a vital component to any vibrant community.

Thus, Citibank created a special promotion of a joint exhibition for the International Museum of Cartoon Art to support its ambitious development campaign. Citibank also works with the pops orchestras in Palm Beach and Boca Raton to sponsor special events.

George Snow Scholarship Fund

Founded in 1982 as a memorial to the late George Snow, a prominent real estate developer (see this chapter's sidebar), the George Snow Scholarship Fund has grown at a rate clearly reflected in the expanding base of community and business support. In 1995, grants to students totalled $67,500; the total of Snow awards to young people to date is $398,000.

The Snow Fund administers programs including the Hometown Hero Scholarships, the William Santangelo Scholarship for single parents returning to school, and the new Arts Scholarship, which George Snow's sister, Sandra, established this year in memory of their father, G.B. An ongoing commitment includes at least one $1,000 grant annually to each public high school in Palm Beach County.

See the chapter on Festivals and Annual Events for information on Frontier Family Days rodeo, the organization's primary fund-raiser held the first weekend in November.

Corporate sponsors include Continental Airlines, Miller Brewing Co., WRMF-FM Radio, NationsBank, Palm Beach County Tourist Development Council, Mario's of Boca,

Domino's Pizza, Synadyne, Vern's Electronics, Sherwood Pontiac-GMC Truck-Honda, Publix Supermarkets, Cheney Brothers, Statewide Plumbing, Mobil Oil, County Ice, Rancho Deluxe, Human Resource Development Worldwide, Sun-Sentinel, Strawn and Monaghan Attorneys, Builders Square II and Koala Care Inc. Accommodations for out-of-town cowpokes are donated by the Holiday Inn Camino Real and the Holiday Inn Highland Beach.

JM Family Enterprises Inc.

Far beyond the bevy of beautiful imports that stop on a dime and draw envious stares from every direction is an amazing corporate culture rooted in the principles of founder Jim Moran.

The automotive empire headquartered in Deerfield Beach, ranked by *Forbes* magazine as the 30th-largest privately owned company in the United States, includes Southeast Toyota — the world's largest distributor of Toyotas. SET distributed 201,204 cars last year, surpassing any country in Europe.

Jim Moran is chairman and Pat Moran is president of JM Family Enterprises, parent of more than 20 related businesses that provide automotive products and services for dealers, drivers and passengers. With revenue of $4.1 billion and 2,004 employees, the organization includes JM Lexus of Margate, the largest volume Lexus dealership in the United States; the distributor of selected General Motors vehicles in France, Monaco, Andorra, Martinique and Guadeloupe;

the auto industry's first computerized data processing network for dealers; Florida's largest provider of extended service contracts; and the first import captive finance company in the United States.

JMFE is also big on giving.

Active in charitable gifts, community projects and sponsorship of cultural arts groups in Palm Beach and Broward counties, JMFE supports similar endeavors in Jacksonville and Mobile, Alabama, its other major corporate bases.

Education, including the work it does for the Snow Fund, is a primary focus of JMFE's charitable giving and community relations programs, many targeted at at-risk youth to provide basic education and skills that might improve their chances in life. One particular priority is the **Youth Automotive Training Center of Broward Inc.**, founded by Jim Moran in 1984. The nonprofit corporation provides free training in the basics of automotive repair, academics and life skills development for unemployed, underprivileged and minority youths.

Says Pat Moran: "Our charitable giving efforts focus on the young people of our community, because the children of today will be our leaders of tomorrow. There can never be too much guidance and support for kids. Now, more than ever before, it is the responsibility of businesses to pick up where families and schools have left off in helping children stay on the right track.

"Organizations such as The Haven, that are dedicated to providing the services that young people need

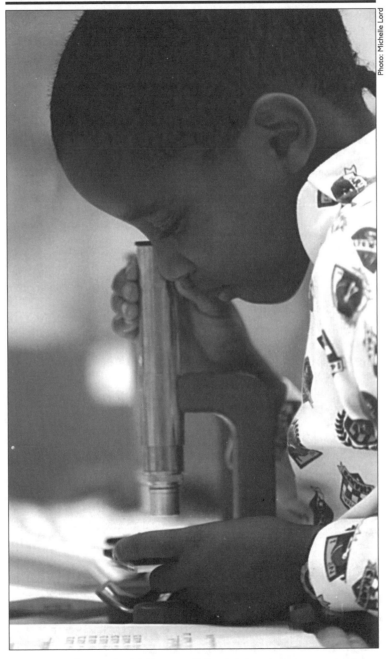

Photo: Michelle Lord

Palm Beach County schoolchildren can display their knowledge at events such as the Magnet Fair.

to thrive, help make a difference in the quality of life in Boca Raton," Moran added. "One of the things I admire most about The Haven is, they take care of the kids who otherwise would have slipped through the cracks; those who would not have been able to meet their fullest potential."

JMFE supports numerous cultural resources such as Palm Beach Youth Symphony Orchestras, the Morikami Museum and Boca Raton Historical Society; and community institutions such as Children's Place, Florence Fuller Child Development Center, Boca Raton Community Hospital and Aid to Victims of Domestic Assault.

JMFE is South Florida's largest corporate contributor to the United Negro College Fund; other philanthropic efforts extend to Saluting Today's African-American Achievers, Barton's Boosters, WPEC Channel 12's "Helping Our Kids" and Florida Atlantic University. Sponsorships in the Jacksonville area include Portfest, the Jacksonville Symphony's *Starry Nights at Metro Park* concert series, Gator Bowl, Light Up Jacksonville, the Jacksonville Jazz Festival, Museum of Science and History, WJCT Public Television membership drives, Otis F. Smith Foundation, Children's Home Society,

Habitat for Humanity, the Urban League and many others.

Target Stores

The Minneapolis-based quality discount retailer has 611 stores in 32 states. The largest division of national retailer Dayton Hudson Corporation, Target Stores is a generous contributor to community organizations in the cities where it does business. Target's commitment is to give 5 percent of the company's annual taxable profits to community organizations for programs focused on enriching family life. In 1994, that amount nationwide totalled more than $8.8 million disbursed to more than 2,000 nonprofit groups.

For the second consecutive year, Target Stores has given Boca Ballet Theatre Company $3,000. Erika Ayres, team relations leader of Target Stores in this region, says as a family store, Target's goal is to provide both financial and volunteer support to community programs that help strengthen families. Boca Ballet Theatre Company is working to achieve this goal.

Small and Midsize Businesses

Good relationships with other businesses help a smaller business become better known among new customers. And a good community image gradually propels sales their way. For that reason, and because business owners also want the place they call home to prosper, businesses of all sizes take turns helping each other's causes.

Giuliano Lorenzani, owner of Boca Raton Travel & Cruises, gets involved with providing airfare for guest artists as well as donating incentives and travel-related prizes for auctions, raffles and other fund-raising activities for Boca Ballet Theatre Company.

Other corporate and midsize business support for the dance company includes Shell Oil Company Foundation, Blockbuster Entertainment, JM Family Enterprises, Southeast Toyota, First Union Foundation, Saatchi & Saatchi and the Community Foundation for Palm Beach and Martin Counties.

BookFest, which moved to Delray Beach this year, has a new corporate sponsor, Levenger, the powerhouse purveyor of materials for serious readers founded by Steve and Lori Leveen. Levenger, which is discussed in our Business and Shopping chapters, has a great motto: "Sell globally, give locally."

The Adolph and Rose Levis Jewish Community Center

The nonprofit JCC is a major force in South County, creating a modern hub of humanity, services and dynamic programs for people and families of all ages. Activities are designed to enhance Jewish identity, education and community life.

Benefactors in various monetary categories supplement the resources the JCC makes available to the community in an incomparable campus setting at 9801 Donna Klein Boulevard, Boca Raton, 852-3200.

Specific programs target early childhood, active adults and less-active seniors, children and teenagers, cultural interests, sports, health and fitness, and members with disabilities.

Facilities include a 7,000-square-foot fitness center with state-of-the-art cardiovascular equipment; an aerobics studio with daily schedules for step and low-impact aerobics classes, circuit training, yoga, karate and Israeli folk dancing; racquetball and squash courts; six plexi-pave lighted tennis courts; a double gym for leagues and open play; private locker rooms for adults and children; steam rooms and saunas; two softball fields and a soccer field; two outdoor Olympic-size swimming pools (one heated), and tot wading pools; three playgrounds; teen, "tween" and adult lounges in the youth wing; a 500-square-foot child-care/baby-sitting area; and rooms available for rent for bar and bat mitzvahs, weddings, conferences, birthdays and other special occasions. Meeting rooms can accommodate small and large groups in addition to a 500-seat auditorium and 220-seat banquet facility.

Zinman Hall is the JCC's 500-seat state-of-the-art theater. The hub of members' social calendars, Zinman Hall has hosted Kirk Douglas, Dr. Ruth Westheimer, Joel Grey, and numerous other celebrities and entertainers.

The Nathan D. Rosen Museum Gallery is the magnet for bringing artists from around the world, Judaic touring exhibits, local artists and the Jewish Community Festival of Arts, Books and Culture — an annual, week-long event at the Richard and Carole Siemens Campus of the JCC (see our Festivals and Annual Events chapter). The festival hosts leading Jewish literary personalities, and a book fair showcases contemporary and classical Jewish authors. For information on the next festival, call Zinman Hall Box Office, 852-3241.

The School of Visual and Performing Arts offers specialized classes by a professional staff. Courses include pottery, silk painting and dance. The Florence and Irving Blickstein Craft Room is for art and pottery, and there's also a senior adult lounge.

The JCC operates the JCC Thrift Shops, upscale resale stores in east Boca at 2 S.E. First Street, 368-3665, and in west Boca Raton at 23024 Sandalfoot Plaza Drive, 451-4437.

The Adult Department offers Judaic programs including hands-on workshops and classes relevant to the Jewish lifestyle: Kosher cooking classes, Hebrew Ulpan, Cafe Israel, Israeli folk dancing and Mitzvah Maker Community Service projects.

Activities for couples in their 20s to 40s include road rallies, movie premieres, nights of comedy, dancing, sports, lectures and cultural events. Projenet, the Professional Jewish Network, hosts monthly lectures and programs that are ideal for newcomers in the community.

Additional programs take place at the Betty and Marvin Zale Early Childhood Learning Center and the JCC Camp Ted Weisberg.

The sports, fitness and health center, which rivals any in the Southeast United States, includes the Richard Davimos Racquetball Complex, the Len and Marianne Minkoff Family Cardiovascular Facility, the Roxane and Larry Philips Gymnasium and the Patricia and Harold Toppel Aerobics Studio.

Programs at the center include adult leagues in softball, basketball, flag football, tennis and racquetball; skill training in basketball, soccer and T-ball; children's classes; aerobics classes and water aerobics; tennis; racquetball and squash; competitive and recreational swimming; karate; free weights; lectures and workshops on nutrition; and a shape class for teenagers. A variety of services such as personal training, massage therapy, facials and private lessons is also offered.

The staff offers programs for all ages, at all levels of ability and interest.

"Special needs" individuals have a special department of their own at JCC, where people with disabilities are offered social, recreational, educational and cultural programs. The professional staff works to integrate children and adults into general classes wherever possible. Programs include Sunday Social Scene for young adults with learning disabilities; Insight for the visually impaired; Interface for adults with mild and moderate developmental disabilities; and SHHH,

Self Help for Hard of Hearing Individuals Inc.

See our Retirement chapter for more information on JCC programs for those 50 and older, including information on the Kaplan Jewish Community Center in West Palm Beach.

Individuals

If you get sufficiently involved to attend some of the black-tie charity galas famous in Palm Beach and Boca Raton, you'll think you're dreaming or stuck in a rewind of fashions à la Academy Awards. The difference is, the diamonds you'll see aren't borrowed from Harry Winston.

A woman, a former New Yorker who spent many years in the fashion business, was attending an afternoon tea at Boca Country Club with a friend. They brought along a change of clothes so they could go on to the Tennis Center for the finals of the Delray Beach Winter Championships. Walking down the hall in jeans and a blazer, the woman commented to her companion how she felt bare without her gems, and maybe she'd put them back on. Her friend said relax, "Don't worry, we're only going to a tennis match. People know we have jewelry."

Yes, people who relocate to the Palm Beaches bring along a certain style of doing business, a unique social process and certain expectations about the cultural and social services they want in a hometown. In some cases, they try to recreate nuggets of civilization as they knew it back home, so the organizations they launch in Florida are rooted in the way things were done elsewhere. Thus, they want scouting activities for children or grandchildren, museums, orchestras, libraries and dance companies. And they want them badly enough to pay for them personally or persuade friends and business associates to ante up.

One wealthy widow whose generosity favored the cultural arts got mad when her banker dragged his feet about underwriting a party for one of her favorite causes. So she said she was moving her trust fund and closing out her accounts, unless of course he wanted to reconsider. He did, since the interest alone was more than she was able to spend in a year.

It would be tough to even list all the philanthropists who make a big difference, but we mention a few here because you'll see and hear their names often in your travels around the Palm Beaches.

Count Adolph and Countess Henrietta de Hoernle

The royal couple are among the most well-known of our many generous souls . . . known for sizeable cash donations and for the wide variety of their favorite causes. The de Hoernle name can be seen on the restored Florida East Coast Railroad Depot in Boca Raton, an historic site renovated by the Boca Raton Historical Society, and the American Red Cross headquarters on North Federal Highway. Boy Scouts of America, The Haven — a home for abused teenagers — and the Migrant Association for South Florida are among the causes favored with significant donations by Count and Countess de Hoernle. "Rita" to her friends, Countess de Hoernle is a lovely study in no-nonsense: You'll see her browsing at Razzmatazz, a well-turned-out consignment boutique, on the same day she's pledged a quarter-million dollars to one pet cause and chaired a black-tie gala for yet another.

Jean Spence

A successful entrepreneur who with her late husband founded an international furniture design empire, Jean moved to Florida from New York in the mid-1950s. She began investing in real estate much earlier, buying a five-story brownstone on 73rd Street between Fifth and Park avenues. In Boca and Ocean Ridge, the Spences bought oceanfront acreage, land by the Boca Raton Community Hospital, parcels along Federal Highway and a retail furniture center in North Palm Beach. They moved to Gulf Stream in the mid-1970s, buying an historic estate on 14 acres between the Intracoastal Waterway and Highway A1A.

Having traveled the world on business for decades, the Spences accumulated an extensive and very eclectic art collection of paintings, sculpture, antiques and archeological artifacts.

After her husband's death in 1986, Jean immersed herself in numerous charitable groups including the American Heart Association, Lynn University, the Alexis de Tocqueville Society of United Way, Boca Raton Community Hospital and the Council of 100.

She has served as a director for Caldwell Theatre, the Boca Raton Museum of Art, the Florida Philharmonic, Boca Pops, Bethesda Memorial Hospital, the Friends of Philosophy of the University of Miami, Sinfonia Virtuosi and Chorus of Florida, the American Red Cross, Palm Beach Council of the Arts, the Humanitarian Society, the Junior League of Boca Raton and the Daily Bread Food Bank.

Jean remains the quintessential hostess whose invitations are among the most coveted all season. Several times a year, she hosts black-tie gatherings for 100 or more guests, or private dinner parties for an ex-president who might be in town to go fishing or play tennis. The home itself would astound the most sophisticated and discriminating art dealer, and the lush shaded grounds are a sight to gasp over. Jean herself is the real work of art, and the organizations that gain her loyalty are doubly blessed with her business acumen.

Caridad Asensio

"Cari" as everyone calls her was honored this year by President Clinton as a recipient of a JCPenney Golden Rule Award. She has worked miracles on behalf of disadvantaged range-line farming families for 18 years.

Asensio has been the *Sun-Sentinel* "Volunteer of the Year," and was named by the Junior League and First United Bank as "Boca Raton Volunteer of the Year." A native of Cuba who came to the United States dur-

Meet George Snow

George Snow came to Boca Raton in the late 1950s from Pennsylvania, a family man with young children and teaching credentials. He got a job teaching math at the former Seacrest High School, now Atlantic High, since Boca Raton teenagers were several years away from a high school of their own. To supplement his income, Snow started building houses, two or three at a time, leapfrogging with his family into whichever one hadn't yet sold. He cultivated the business cautiously, gradually, never overextending, always with a backup plan — such as what to do after a hurricane wiped out his construction trailer. And all the while, he added a dozen houses, two dozen, 50, a few hundred . . . finally more than 2,000 new homes in Boca Raton. The demand for new housing came courtesy of faculty members

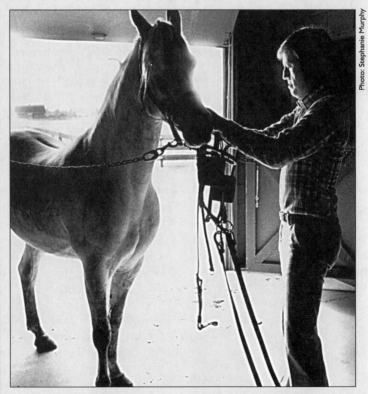

Photo: Stephanie Murphy

The late George Snow retired from land development to enjoy his horse ranch and sports, including powerboat racing. He started a helicopter charter business favored by network TV film crews. In this shot, he readies Bali for a carriage ride.

joining Boca's new state university (FAU), physicians on the charter staff of the new community hospital (Boca Raton Community Hospital) . . . and then in the late 1960s, the arrival of IBM Corp.

Snow's success enabled him to bid on commercial construction jobs such as Royal Palm Plaza, St. Gregory's Episcopal Church, Furniture Plaza (the site of City Furniture/Waterbed City on Federal Highway) and others. Moving into choice development opportunities such as Horseshoe Acres, where he built his own 40-acre gentleman's ranch on a private lake, he also moved on community projects such as donating the land for Meadows Park Community Pool. Though he had long since left teaching, Snow maintained an intense interest in issues affecting the public schools and remained an activist who devoted personal time to mediate disputes such as those triggered by unrest over busing.

Snow was able to semi-retire in his early 40s to pursue hobbies such as powerboat racing and helicopter flying, initiating a charter service favored by some of the Miami and West Palm Beach television network affiliates. In November 1980, he took a broadcast film crew to remote Caya Lobos Island in the Bahamas to cover a controversial story about a stranded band of Haitian refugees. Snow's helicopter disappeared during the return flight, and hundreds of friends and family spent the next few months in intensive air searches over the Atlantic Ocean, chains of islands, even the Bermuda Triangle. A German tourist on one of the islands later found a piece of what is presumed to be a remnant of the crashed helicopter, but no other evidence surfaced to confirm the fate of Snow and his passengers. George's children and friends of the family set up the Snow Scholarship Fund in memory of his dedication to young people and education.

ing the 1960s, Cari at one time worked as a teaching assistant at Boca Raton High School. She became a social/health educator in the Migrant Child Education Department of the Palm Beach County school system and worked at Hagen Ranch Elementary School prior to retirement. Cari and her husband Manuel live in Boca Raton.

In 1989 she founded the Migrant Association of South Florida (MASF) to assist seasonal farm workers. MASF operates a housing initiative to place families in mobile homes; a thrift shop; and a warehouse storage-distribution system to provide emergency food, clothing, bedding, appliances and furniture for migrant families.

Caridad, which is Spanish for "charity," also is the namesake for Caridad Health Clinic, founded in 1992 in a double-wide trailer at U.S. Highway 441 and W. Boynton Beach Boulevard. The clinic treated 400 patients in its first three months of operation, using donated equipment and sparse contributions for lab tests and prescriptions. The clinic "staff" is all volunteers . . . 56 doctors, 105 dentists, 40 nurses and 106 dental assistants. A salaried nurse-administrator coordinates schedules, arranging for everyone to serve once a quarter. Open Saturdays and Wednesday nights, the clinic has two exam rooms, three dental chairs, a laboratory and storage area and a reception desk. There's no waiting room, so patients sit outside, either in cars or underneath shade trees.

Caridad Clinic has effectively outgrown its temporary quarters. Through significant donations in 1995, Asensio received enough money to purchase a parcel for a new clinic. A steering committee will oversee the expansion, including a campaign to raise $1,150,000 for an 8,500-square-foot permanent clinic and a future building for educational, preschool and community awareness programs. For information on MASF and Caridad Clinic, call 274-4027 in Delray Beach.

Eadie Steele

A 12-year resident of Tropic Harbor in Delray Beach, and a native of Rye, New York, the former Eadie Anderson used to visit her parents after they retired to Boca Raton in the early 1950s. Her dad, Harold, was an advertising executive and an early leader of the Chamber of Commerce. Eadie lived awhile in California and spent World War II in Chicago. Widowed and working in merchandising for a retailer, she took a job as advertising manager for Carson, Pirie Scott & Company department store. Then, after a tour in charge of sales for a commercial photography stu-

dio, Eadie founded her own advertising agency, Steele & Associates, in the Windy City's retail catalog hub, which she operated for 29 years. After closing her agency, Eadie was recruited by reinsurance conglomerate Marsh & McClennan to run their direct-mail campaign, and she spent 10 years there before "retiring."

Still a consultant for the department store, Eadie recalls the day Mr. Pirie tossed down something of a gauntlet: "To celebrate our 100th anniversary next year, I want Carson, Pirie Scott to have something nobody has ever seen before." Well, the storyteller delivered. Eadie sat down and designed a giant mosaic that told in tiny tile pictures the true tale of "Mrs. O'Leary's Cow and the Great Chicago Fire."

The model was produced as a limited-edition collectible round platter in 1984, illustrating how, on October 8, 1871, during a very long, hot, dry spell, Mrs. O'Leary's cow sits contentedly chewing her cud, munching along until she inadvertently kicks over a lantern, igniting her shed and precipitating the Great Chicago Fire. She tries to flee the fire, the now-famous Water Tower in the background, but ends up being dispatched to heaven. To redeem herself, she returns as an angel to help develop the world's largest inland port, then heads for the stock yard where she wins a Blue Ribbon for "class." Standing on the new city's blueprint, she sees the Wrigley Building, the Tribune Tower and the Glass House. At that point, she winks coyly at you, as if to say, "Who would believe this little ol' cow could have started all this."

Well, seventysomething Eadie Steele hasn't stopped telling stories or building images and dreams. In Palm Beach County, she worked diligently on behalf of Habitat for Humanity before common sense told her to slow down or face an awkward halt. Having met Delray Beach Downtown Coordinator Marjorie Ferrer through Habitat, Eadie called her one day to volunteer her services to the Delray Beach Joint Venture.

She inherited a carton containing two-and-a-half years of newspaper clippings in no particular order and got a tear in her eye when she realized nostalgically it had been 50 years since she worked with an Exacto knife and glue pots.

To date, the results of Eadie wanting to keep busy are three giant volumes of Delray Beach that come to life and all but dance off the pages. More than chronologies, they are story books of a city's Renaissance, all the pieces interwoven and reflecting the balance you see all around Eadie's adopted town.

She is quite sure the secret to Delray's success has been redevelopment through renewal rather than change. And ever the shy soul of diplomacy, she predicts, "We'll be copied by Boynton, and we've got Boca scared to death!"

Eadie finished her project while recuperating from a broken hip, so we can only wonder and stay tuned for more stories after she gets the full use of both sea legs.

Chris Evert

People outside the Palm Beaches have followed the legendary tennis star, who played a doubles match with former President George Bush to celebrate her induction this year into the International Tennis Hall of Fame in Newport, Rhode Island. Everyone knows she grew up and perfected her baseline domination of clay courts at Holiday Park in Fort Lauderdale, then went on to a meteoric 16-year run of seven French Open titles and 18 Grand Slam wins. Locally, anyone who can takes advantage of opportunities to advertise that Evert and her family live at The Polo Club - Boca Raton.

What singer Michael Bolton and other celebrities know is, Evert and her husband Andy Mill devote a lot of time to raising money for specific causes. Chris Evert Charities Inc., a division of Evert Enterprises founded in 1989, sponsors numerous fundraisers to benefit campaigns against substance abuse, such as Ounce of Prevention Fund of Florida.

One of the most high-profile charity bashes each year is the fall Chris Evert/Ellesse Pro-Celebrity Tennis Classic at the Boca Raton Resort and Club, presented by Perry Ellis. Scheduled for October 28 and 29, 1995's event includes tennis matches with talking heads and other famous rackets and a black-tie gala that guests paid $750 a person to attend in 1994.

Past participants include Bolton, Cheryl Tiegs, Nicolette Sheridan, President Bush, Regis Philbin, John Oates, the late Vitas Gerulaitis,

Brooke Shields, Linda Evans, Chevy Chase, Olivia Newton John, John Lloyd, Johan Kriek, Flo Jo and Al Joyner, Mary Pierce, Carling Bassett Seguso, Robert Seguso, Betsey Nagelsen, Wendy Turnbull, Fred Stolle, Gina Tollesen, Gary Carter, Burt Reynolds, Bud Collins, Alan Thicke, Pete Rose, Martina Navratilova, Mark McCormack, Scott Record, Tracy Austin, Danny Sullivan, Mary Carillo and LeRoy Neiman.

The event is held to raise money to fight drug abuse in Florida and to afford improved opportunities for at-risk infants and their families. Agencies that benefit include the Drug Abuse Foundation of Palm Beach County, Broward-based Families in Transition, Casa Madonna in Dade County, and Ounce of Prevention Fund of Florida Inc. For information, write Chris Evert Charities, 7200 W. Camino Real, Boca Raton 33434, or call 394-2400.

Other Notable Contributors

Elsewhere, people of note, influence and affluence lend their names to numerous causes important to the quality of life in Palm Beach County:

Ivana Trump served as honorary chair for Hope House of the Palm Beaches Inc., which assists women and children infected with the HIV virus and AIDS.

Xiomara Ordonez co-chaired the Hispanic Cultural Arts gala.

Judy Messing and Lois Kniznik co-chaired the annual fund-raiser for the Joseph L. Morse Geriatric Center in West Palm Beach.

Laurence Levine chaired the 1995 gala to benefit the Palm Beach County School of the Arts Foundation Inc.

Brian and Eileen Burns and Bernard and Billi Marcus co-chaired this year's gala to benefit the Palm Beach Pops. Held at Whitehall - Henry Morrison Flagler Museum, the black-tie event produced Tiffany & Company favors for guests. The lady with the happy feet that couldn't stop dancing raised the question, "Does the Supreme Court boogie all the time or just in Palm Beach?" It was Supreme Court Justice Sandra Day O'Connor, who bought the first two tickets for herself and husband John.

Marion Pearson entertains a group at the Mae Volen Senior Center.

Inside
Retirement

If you're on the shy side of 100, listen up. Much of middle-aged America dreams about retirement in Florida, and nowhere is the good life more promising than in Palm Beach County.

Like other segments of our population, retirees are relatively more affluent, well-educated, well-traveled and sophisticated than their counterparts in many other regions of the country.

From housing choices to leisure pursuits, the high standard of living energizes a marketplace that eagerly caters to the whims of folk over 50. Government responds, too, with special programs to address the volume of mature interests reflected at the polls. Religious groups and community organizations also give their elders the nod, devoting vast resources to educational, cultural and recreational activities.

Resources

Regardless of whether you, your friend or someone in the family is an "older adult," "senior citizen" or "elder," the following organizations and agencies can offer useful advice about services and assistance for retirees and others:

AMERICAN ASSOCIATION OF RETIRED PERSONS (AARP)
Regional information *(813) 576-1155*

The American Association of Retired Persons is a not-for-profit and nonpartisan service organization for people 50 and older. By design and mission, AARP helps members achieve goals of independence, dignity and purpose.

AARP **West Boca Chapter 2643** meets at 1 PM on the second Tuesday of each month at Our Lady of Lourdes Parish, 22094 S.W. 57th Avenue; **Boca Raton Chapter 1091** meets at 11:30 AM on the second Monday of each month at the Community Center, 150 N.W. Crawford Boulevard; **Boynton Leisureville Chapter 3190** meets the third Wednesday of the month at 1:30 PM at 1807 S.W. 18th Street, Boynton Beach; **Greater Palm Beach Chapter 196** meets at 1 PM on the first and third Fridays of each month at Howard Park Senior Center, Parker Avenue, West Palm Beach; **Greater Northern Palm Beach Chapter 4736** meets the third Tuesday of the month at 7 PM at Community Medical Center, 3360 Burns Road, West Palm Beach.

Members are welcome at meetings but attendance isn't required. Benefits include educational opportunities, insurance advantages and information about travel. Current dues are $8 per year.

AGENCY FOR HEALTH CARE ADMINISTRATION

1495 Forest Hill Blvd., Ste. A
West Palm Beach   433-2688

This agency acts on behalf of Floridians to inspect nursing homes and ACLFs. Complaint evaluations are available upon request.

ALZHEIMER'S ASSOCIATION

6401 Congress Ave., Ste. 265
Boca Raton   998-1988
National helpline   (800) 621-0379

This support group provides patients and families with information and referrals.

AREA AGENCY ON AGING

8895 N. Military Tr., Ste. 201C
Palm Beach Gardens   694-7601

The agency helps coordinate many local services, including housing options, for folks age 60 and older. It also sponsors community events. Call for details.

CATHOLIC CHARITIES INC.

135 S.E. Fifth Ave.
Delray Beach   274-0801
Main office, West Palm Beach   775-9560

An affiliate of the Diocese of Palm Beach, Catholic Charities provides information on adult day care and numerous other services in Palm Beach County.

CENTER FOR GROUP COUNSELING

22455 Boca Rio Rd.
Boca Raton   483-5300

The center offers free or low-cost psychological help for seniors and others with problems in daily living.

CENTERLINE

P.O. Box 3588
Lantana 33465   (800) 930-1234

A service of The Center for Information and Crisis Services, Centerline provides community resources referrals 24 hours a day.

DEPARTMENT OF HEALTH AND REHABILITATIVE SERVICES

111 S. Sapodilla Ave.
West Palm Beach   837-5138

The department's Aging and Adult Services branch maintains a list of state-licensed housing facilities. Call for information.

ELDER HELPLINE

Palm Beach County
Div. of Senior Services   (800) 930-4050

DOSS' helpline provides information and referrals to many government, private and nonprofit organizations. Homebound seniors may apply for personal care, home meals, homemaker assistance, respite for caregivers and adult day care. Other services include transportation, group meals, education and recreational activities. Elder Helpline also broadcasts Mondays and Wednesdays at 10:30 AM on Channel 20, the county's educational TV station (Channel 35 for Comcast viewers, Channel 24 for Leadership).

FAMILY TOUCH

102 N.E. Second St., Ste. 236
Boca Raton   394-0213

Bruce and Faye Berkowitz are just starting up a new business employing a concept that evolved during the past few years when they lived in New York. They have acquaintances who comment on the frustration and stress

of having elderly parents living in Florida, sometimes alone and frequently lonely. No matter how many times these grown children visit or call, there's never enough peace of mind.

Berkowitz decided there is a niche market for people who would hire surrogate children to visit elderly parents, grandparents, in-laws or aunts and uncles in their absence. At the time of our publication, he and his wife expected to be operational by Labor Day of 1995.

Family Touch will concentrate its efforts to visit people who are maintaining an independent lifestyle at their own homes. They'll make reports to family members, including any suggestions about health care or personal needs. Several packages are available: half-hour or hour-long visits, from one to four times a month. Prices will begin at a range of $145 to $405 a month.

GOLDEN YEARS DAY CARE INC.
6870 N. Federal Hwy.
Boca Raton   *241-6983*

Golden Years is a private facility that provides activities for seniors with physical limitations including Alzheimer's disease. Golden Years is a CORF — comprehensive outpatient rehabilitation facility, also offering physical therapy for patients referred by physicians. Transportation is provided for clients in the center's vicinity.

LIFELONG LEARNING SOCIETY
Florida Atlantic University
500 N.W. 20th St.
Boca Raton   *367-2410*

The Lifelong Learning Society confirms there is no statute of limitations on an inquiring mind. Its mission is "to provide mature men and women with intellectual and physical wellness programs which foster personal growth, maintenance of mental and physical vitality and cultural fellowship."

Headed by Director of Development, Alvin White, the Society also supports FAU's mission of teaching, research and public service. While the Society campaigns for its own permanent center, University professors currently teach in an FAU classroom. Former Massachusetts governor and presidential candidate Michael Dukakis has also led LLS sessions in the past.

NATIONAL ASSOCIATION OF SENIOR FRIENDS

The Palm Beaches Medical Center
2201 45th St., West Palm Beach
General info.   *881-2675*
Local chapter schedule   *881-2676*

Local chapters offer information and plan wellness activities.

PALM BEACH COUNTY MEDICAL SOCIETY

3540 Forest Hills Blvd., Ste. 101
West Palm Beach   *433-3966*

This society offers physician referrals (see our Health Care chapter for other referral options).

REAL TALK

Palm Beach County Div. of Senior Services
From Boca Raton   *392-5000*
From Palm Beach   *433-5000*

DOSS also sponsors the Sixty-Plus section of this automated information system accessed by phone. The Real Talk directory appears in the front of the West Palm Beach/Boca Raton Yellow Pages. Once connected, dial the four-digit Real Talk code that corresponds to the type of information you want. For example, Help At Home for Seniors is 3346; Nursing Home Placement is 3344.

RETIRED AND SENIOR VOLUNTEER PROGRAM

6653 Jog Rd.
Boca Raton   *995-0042*

Housed in the First Union Bank building, this program matches folks who want to help with volunteer organizations. To learn about opportunities in the public school system, call 434-8713.

Photo: Michelle Lord

The Mae Volen Senior Center offers many activities for Boca Raton's older residents.

SERVICE CORPS OF RETIRED EXECUTIVES
1050 S. Federal Hwy.
Delray Beach   *278-7752, 278-0277*

Members of SCORE volunteer their time and expertise by advising and helping people running or starting a new business. Sponsored by the Small Business Administration, it's open to any retired executive.

SENIOR PLACEMENT SERVICES OF SOUTH FLORIDA
1164 E. Oakland Park Blvd.
Fort Lauderdale   *(800) 866-8677*

This private business rates housing and health-care facilities in Palm Beach, Broward and Dade counties. For a free copy of its annual guide, call or visit its offices.

SOCIAL SECURITY ADMINISTRATION
301 S.E. First St., Delray Beach
3650 Shawnee Ave., West Palm Beach
General info.   *(800) 772-1213*

If you need to visit, business hours are 8:30 AM to 3:30 PM weekdays. Otherwise, call the toll-free number between 7 AM and 7 PM.

Senior Centers

MAE VOLEN SENIOR CENTER
1515 W. Palmetto Park Rd.
Boca Raton   *395-8920*

This center does a superb job of providing a social hub for adults who enjoy keeping mentally and physically active. About 300 people a day participate in weekday recreation, including hot lunches, from 8 AM to 4:30 PM. The private, nonprofit organization promotes wellness through health screenings and lectures on nutrition, while offering numerous services for the homebound.

Its fleet of 18 buses also provides transportation — about 100,000 rides a year — so people 60 years and older can get to medical appointments, the Center or the supermarket. Less active seniors and Alzheimer's patients are welcome to participate in Mae Volen's senior day-care program.

ADOLPH AND ROSE LEVIS JEWISH COMMUNITY CENTER
9801 Donna Klein Blvd.
Boca Raton   *852-3225*

The Adult Department invites one and all, "Over 50" to centenarians, to enjoy the myriad programs: educational, physical, social, travel and cultural activities.

Boca Raton's main campus on Donna Klein Boulevard, and the Delray Beach satellite location at 5869 W. Atlantic Avenue, have hundreds of classes and programs to fit any lifestyle and level of activity — whether you're ready to jog with the president or devote the afternoon to improving your couch-potato skills.

Highlights include singles 50-plus programs, a Couples Club, lectures and classes, support groups and a weekly calendar of special events.

Some of these include Senior Maccabi Games, the Federation Follies and Burlesque Revue, summer camp, field trips and odysseys, dances and more.

The adult lounge is appropriately called "A Center for Life," offering activities designed to broaden horizons and enrich any lifestyle. Laura Hochman manages the diverse seniors programs.

The Levis Center is part of The South Palm Beach County Jewish Federation, an organization that offers services to people of all ages. See our sidebar on the Federation in the Arts and Culture chapter.

THE HAROLD AND SYLVIA KAPLAN JEWISH COMMUNITY CENTER OF THE GREATER PALM BEACHES

3151 N. Military Tr.
West Palm Beach   *689-7700*

Much like the Levis JCC in South County, the Kaplan JCC offers a myriad of programs for family members of all ages. Adult programs include educational, physical, social, travel and cultural activities. The 20-year institution has a 93,000-square-foot campus that was new in 1991. The executive director is Gerald Weisberg.

THE JOSEPH L. MORSE GERIATRIC CENTER

4857 Fred Gladstone Dr.
West Palm Beach   *471-5111*

Opened in July 1983, the 280-bed Joseph L. Morse Geriatric Center provides long-term care to the elderly, three-quarters of whom are indigent. There are alternative services through Morse-Evans Home Health Care Agency and the Schaffer Adult Day Care Center, which enables older citizens to reside in their homes longer.

TEMPLE BETH EL

333 S.W. Fourth Ave.
Boca Raton   *391-8900*

An interfaith program, cosponsored by St. Joan of Arc Catholic Church and First Presbyterian Church of Boca Raton, operates

here, offering senior day care on Wednesdays from 9:30 AM to 2:30 PM. The program takes the summer off. For information on schedule the rest of the year, call Cis Rader, 994-0752.

Retirement Living

Where to live runs the gamut from multimillion-dollar mansions in gated country clubs to varying levels of mobile home parks that cater to seniors. Options abound for institutional living conditions that suit both able-bodied and disabled adults, covering every level of activity and medical limitation in between.

One memorable retiree, a former Realtor and self-proclaimed "reactionary Republican from the Midwest," spent his mid-90s living alone in Royal Palm Yacht and Country Club and summering at his mountain home in North Carolina. He began putting in a new swimming pool at age 93, bought a new Jaguar at age 94 and regularly appeared in a tuxedo for theatrical productions and musical concerts.

For those who don't "age in place" quite so flamboyantly, scenarios vary from near-independence in an environment of sublime luxury to virtual incapacity within a regimen of custom care. Besides checking prices and the official view on credentials and ratings, a personal tour should be considered essential before selecting your or a family member's living arrangements.

Because She Wanted
The Best For You.

When you were young, Mom made sure everything was perfect for you. Now, you can return the favor because The Sunrise Atrium at Boca Raton provides the perfect setting for comfortable, secure elder care.

We offer services with your loved one in mind–from superior Assisted Living care to our Special Needs Program for people with Alzheimer's disease or other memory disorders.

At Sunrise, we believe that retirement should be worry–free for both you and Mom, and we take very seriously the trust placed in us by families nationwide.

To find out more about our affordable Assisted Living community, call us or mail the coupon today.

 **(407) 750/7555**

THE
SUNRISE ATRIUM
AT BOCA RATON
AN ASSISTED LIVING RETIREMENT RESIDENCE

Rental Communities

ADVENT SQUARE
4798 N. Dixie Hwy.
Boca Raton 391-7207

This interfaith ministry of Advent Lutheran Church is an independent self-care rental community with 30 apartments — but few vacancies — for residents of any creed.

Advent Square offers meals, utilities, housekeeping, transportation, activities and an emergency alert system. Basic costs for a standard apartment with two occupants include an entry fee and monthly rent. Contact administrator Virginia Wainwright for further details.

BOCA TEECA LODGE
5800 N.W. Second Ave.
Boca Raton (800) 344-6995

Daily, weekly and monthly accommodations are available at Boca Teeca Country Club, a condominium community in north Boca primarily popular with retirees. Forty-six rooms are available for $49 a day or $59 a day for poolside, between April 15 and December 15. Then, rooms are $99 and $109. Amenities include access to the private golf course, free tennis, men's and women's exercise rooms, a large swimming pool heated in the winter and a recreation hall with pool table and Ping Pong.

CASA DEL MAR
22601 Camino Del Mar
Boca Raton 750-7100

This luxurious rental community for independent residents also operates an assisted-living section. Hamilton House in Fort Lauderdale is a companion property. Casa Del Mar combines 154 independent-living and 60 assisted-living residences on a 12-acre campus near the Camino Del Mar golf course. Units are arranged in low-rise Mediterranean-style garden apartments that feature extra storage, washers and dryers, living rooms, kitchens and separate dressing areas in the master bedroom.

Amenities include a private dining room for entertaining friends and family, a heated swimming pool, library, video room, cocktail lounge, fitness spa and a creative arts studio.

PROSPERITY OAKS
11381 Prosperity Farms Rd.
Palm Beach Gardens 694-9709

This 27-acre complex offers 228 luxury senior rental apartments with kitchens, housekeeping service, 24-hour emergency service and numerous activities. There's no endowment fee or admission fee, and nearby is a 120-bed Heartland Health Care Center.

Oak Pointe at Prosperity Oaks also offers assisted-living programs in the same luxurious environment.

THE VERANDA CLUB
6061 Palmetto Cir. N., Boca Del Mar
Boca Raton 368-2122

This upscale suburban residence has the lovely neighborhoods of master-planned Boca Del Mar as a backdrop for graceful retirement living. Veranda Club's 192 one- and two-bedroom units have fully equipped kitchens and separate climate control. Rent includes continental breakfast and dinner, weekly housekeeping, 24-

hour security, transportation and an activities program.

Condominium Communities

The following condominium communities cater to retirees:

CENTURY VILLAGE AT BOCA RATON
19296 Lyons Rd., Boca Raton   852-7806
CENTURY VILLAGE EAST
2400 Century Blvd.
Deerfield Beach   428-7095
CENTURY VILLAGE
2751 N. Haverhill Rd.
West Palm Beach   471-9677

Two Century Village condominium communities in Palm Beach County, one in Deerfield Beach and a fourth at Pembroke Pines in Southwest Broward County offer a unique country club lifestyle that is home to several thousand contented residents.

Boca Raton's Century Village, developed in the late 1970s and early '80s, is home to more than 10,000 in 5,700 apartments in 16 individual neighborhoods of mid-rise buildings. A system of lakes creates numerous waterfront views that complement the amenity-rich recreational lifestyle. Neighborhood centers have swimming pools and tennis courts, and The Hamptons 18-hole championship, a par 72 golf course, is practically next door. Amenities include a multimillion-dollar clubhouse with planned activities for all comfort levels — from competitive swim-

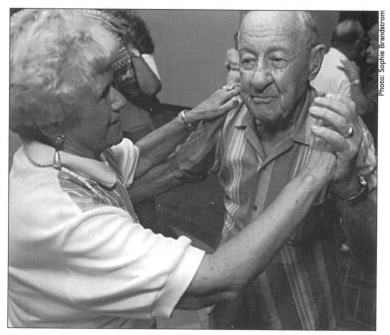

Photo: Sophie Brandstrom

Retirees kick up their heels.

mer to couch potato. There's a 1,250-seat auditorium-theater managed by a professional staff that books year-round programs with nationally known guest artists. The clubhouse has an indoor heated pool, an outdoor pool and sundeck, party rooms, a game room, health club and saunas, as well as activity rooms for cards, billiards, music, lectures and meetings. There's also a center to coordinate fishing, sailing, tennis and shuffleboard.

Century Village has its own tram system that connects to the county's PalmTran bus routes with scheduled outings to shopping destinations, the nearby Levis Jewish Community Center, temples, adult education classes at the universities and unlimited cultural offerings in Boca, Delray and West Palm Beach.

The community has 24-hour manned security at the entry gates and plenty of interior street and walkway lighting, so residents are comfortable strolling to evening activities.

Resale opportunities include one-bedroom, one-bath apartments from about $35,000 to two-bedroom, 1½-bath apartments from the mid-$50,000s. Two-bedroom, two-bath apartments range up to more than $100,000.

Smaller than Century Village but representative of its country club lifestyle, are adult condominium communities in suburban Delray, including King's Point (499-3335), High Point of Delray (496-0377), and Heritage Park (499-7744).

Adult Congregate Living Facilities (ACLFs)

THE ELYSIUM OF BOCA RATON INC.
2600 N.W. Fifth Ave.
Boca Raton   368-6222

With 35 years experience, Elysium managers John and Mary Fiorilla are veterans in the skilled-nursing care business. They offer affordable, fully assisted living in an atmosphere that rivals many country clubs. Private and semiprivate accommodations are available for as many as 144 residents.

Contact administrator Hugh Quigley or staff nurse Claire Bojanoski for details on limited nursing services and respite- and day-care programs. Like most ACLFs, fees depend on the length of stay and degree of required personal attention. Residents must be ambulatory or able to transfer themselves to and from a wheelchair.

STRATFORD COURT OF BOCA RATON
6343 Via de Sonrisa del Sur, Boca Raton
General information   392-5940
Assisted-living information   394-6385
Rental information   392-2772

Marriott Senior Living Communities operates choices in several Palm Beach County locations, as well as in Fort Myers and Palm Harbor on the Gulf coast. Operations range from independent-living to assisted-living programs and nursing home accommodations.

All three categories of lifestyle care are available in different centers at Stratford Court in suburban Boca: rentals for residents who are able to function independently; assisted-living programs for residents who need

Photo: Visual Dynamics/Jeffrey Toll

*Young and old share times together on the Richard and
Carole Siemens Jewish Campus.*

help on various levels with medication, bathing, dressing or getting around; and skilled nursing care for those who need it.

THE HORIZON CLUB
1208 S. Military Tr.
Deerfield Beach 481-2304

Similar to Stratford Court, The Horizon Club is a full-service community. For toll-free information, call (800) 223-9624.

BRIGHTON GARDENS OF BOYNTON BEACH
1425 S. Congress Ave.
Boynton Beach 369-7919

Another Marriott Senior Living Community, Brighton specializes in a variety of assisted-living programs.

BRIGHTON GARDENS OF WEST PALM BEACH
2090 N. Congress Ave.
West Palm Beach 686-5100

The West Palm Beach affiliate of the Marriott Senior Living Community has various programs for assisted living.

SUNRISE ATRIUM AT BOCA RATON
1080 N.W. 15th St.
Boca Raton 750-7555

Owners Paul and Terry Klaasen opened Sunrise Atrium six years ago to offer fully-assisted living for two special needs groups. The parent company, Sunrise Assisted Living, has a 14-year history in Fairfax, Virginia.

They are licensed for 220 residents and usually have more than 200 who may be frail, confused or otherwise not able to live independently.

The five-story complex devotes much of the fifth floor to extra security for patients with advanced Alzheimer's. The fourth and part of the fifth floor have patients with less severe memory loss. And the first through third floors are for alert patients who need personal help with taking medication, bathing, dressing or getting around.

Dancers take a spin at the Mae Volen Senior Center Independence Day Dance. The center sponsors a dance every month.

Sunrise Atrium attempts to balance freedom and security as a nursing home alternative for patients who don't need skilled nursing care. Prices, from $1,965 to $2,665 a month, includes 24-hour personal care needs, room, meals, transportation and utilities except for the telephone.

Other Life-care Communities

Several developers operate life-care facilities, including Adult Communities Total Services (ACTS) and Life Care Retirement Communities Inc. Residency requires an upfront payment and monthly fees to cover living accommodations and medical treatment if a resident becomes ill.

ACTS' life-care operations in Boca Raton include **St. Andrews North**, 6152 Verde Trail, 487-5500; **St. Andrews South**, 6045 Verde Trail, 487-6200; and **Edgewater Pointe Estates**, 23315 Blue Water Circle, 391-6305.

HARBOUR'S EDGE
401 E. Linton Blvd.
Delray Beach   272-7979

This ACLF is the high-end benchmark among area life-care providers. Its Intracoastal Waterway site, luxurious accommodations and premium health-care facilities reflect the lifestyles of its affluent residents. Amenities include reserved inside parking, valet and concierge, a cock-

Photo: Stacey Porter

tail lounge, the Harbour Light Theater, a heated swimming pool, indoor and outdoor whirlpool spas, sauna, steam room, exercise and locker rooms, The Chart Room for private dining, party rooms for cards and pool and guest rooms. Each residence has a fully equipped kitchen and a washer and dryer.

Services include a daily meal in The Edgewater Dining Room, special diets and tray service, weekly housekeeping, scheduled transportation, planned activities, a security staff, basic cable TV, a library, beauty and barber shop, banking services, a professionally staffed health center and emergency nursing services in your apartment.

Harbour's Edge was developed and is managed by Life Care Services Corporation of Des Moines, Iowa. Current entrance fees are $212,000, a substantial portion of which can be recovered by you or your estate under the membership plan.

Inside
Health Care

Florida has acquired a reputation as a healthy place to visit and live, overcoming its previous image as an isolated outpost when it came to obtaining sophisticated, state-of-the-art medical care.

Rare, particularly thorny or perplexing maladies are routinely referred to a physician at one of the state's world-class teaching hospitals: the University of Miami School of Medicine at the UM/Jackson Memorial Medical Center or the University of Florida's Shands Teaching Hospital at the J. Hillis Miller Health Science Center in Gainesville. Many of the state's physicians are trained at one of these two centers. The University of Florida also trains many of the state's dentists and veterinarians.

Referral Services

In most cases, finding a physician to handle your and your family's health-care needs is simple. Decide what kind of physician — family specialist, internist, pediatrician or gynecologist — will best serve your health needs. Then, as a first rule of thumb, remember to establish a relationship with your doctor when you're healthy. Word of mouth is sometimes a good way to find a physician, and some hospitals offer referral services. Otherwise, a call to one of the local professional medical associations might be just what the doctor ordered.

Medical Associations

PALM BEACH
COUNTY MEDICAL SOCIETY
3540 Forest Hill Blvd., Ste. 101   433-3940
West Palm Beach   276-3636

Call between 9 AM and noon or 1 and 5 PM weekdays for referrals and other helpful information.

BROWARD COUNTY
MEDICAL ASSOCIATION
5101 N.W. 21st Ave., Ste. 510
Fort Lauderdale   (305) 938-5006

For convenience, some folks from the southern end of Palm Beach County drive to Broward County for medical care. Broward's referral service is open between 9 AM and 5 PM weekdays.

Dental Associations

DENTAL REFERRAL SERVICE INC.
(800) 917-6453

For assistance in locating a dentist, this nonprofit nationwide referral service, can be of help between 8:30 AM and 9 PM weekdays and 9 AM to 3 PM Saturdays.

CENTRAL PALM BEACH
COUNTY DENTAL ASSOCIATION
659-1880

Folks in the Palm Beaches, in the area between Lantana Road and 45th Street only, can call this regional service for assistance.

Hospitals

When an emergency strikes, there's no time for referrals, just the need to get good help quickly. The following is a selection of Palm Beach County hospitals.

BOCA RATON COMMUNITY HOSPITAL
800 Meadows Rd.
Boca Raton   393-4060

Boca Raton Community Hospital takes its middle name very seriously. Since opening its doors in 1967, the hospital has built strong ties to the community it serves. In addition to its role as a private health-care provider, BRCH is a proactive wellness center, serving the community's health needs through innovative programs. BRCH provides nurses for all public schools within Boca Raton and medical services for migrant workers in the far western portion of the county, and it supplies food for Extra Helpings, which distributes leftover prepared and perishable food to nonprofit agencies that feed the hungry. BRCH also offers the Living Library, which provides speakers for local schools.

Among the specialties at the hospital are the Lynn Regional Cancer Center; medical, surgical, pediatric and maternity and cardiac-care services; and a full education and support center.

WEST BOCA MEDICAL CENTER
21644 S.R. 7
Boca Raton   488-8000

West Boca Medical Center has served the growing western Boca communities since 1986 and gets high marks for its patient-centered care. The 185-bed acute-care, private facility offers complete medical, surgical, pediatric and maternity services. Located in an area populated by many young and growing families, the center's pediatric and maternity services are especially noteworthy, particularly the Level III Neonatal Intensive Care Unit and the BirthCare Pavilion. Other related specialties include the 24-hour emergency services provided by the Pediatric After Hours Care Center at the Children's Pavilion. Another special program is the Diabetic Care Program, a six-week program for newly diagnosed diabetics and those who have had the disease longer but require more specialized instruction to assist in their own care.

BETHESDA MEMORIAL HOSPITAL
2815 S. Seacrest Blvd.   737-7733
Boynton Beach   278-7733

In addition to its full-service, 362-bed acute-care facility, Bethesda, named to *Modern Healthcare* magazine's 1994 list of the top 100 U.S. hospitals, also offers a 19,000-square-foot health and fitness center that provides cardiac rehabilitation and general fitness programs. Other special services and programs at this public hospital include a cardiac catheterization unit; Pain Management Center; 55 Plus, a lifestyle and preventive health club that provides

screenings and preferred rates on diagnostic tests and hospital services; and New Day, a program for seniors dealing with grief or depression.

At the other end of the spectrum, Hello, Baby! is a comprehensive childhood education program for the whole family. Topics in the series cover Lamaze birthing techniques, newborn care, breast feeding, baby massage and more.

DELRAY COMMUNITY MEDICAL CENTER
5352 Linton Blvd.
Delray Beach   498-4440

Delray Beach Community Medical Center is the designated Level II trauma unit for the southern part of Palm Beach County. This private hospital's specialties in cardiovascular and orthopedic medicine — the Chest Pain Emergency Room, Heart Center and Orthopedic Center — reflect its emphasis on providing top-flight medical services in a timely manner.

Neurological services also are a high priority at this 211-bed facility, which features headache and sleep disorder treatment units.

JFK MEDICAL CENTER
5301 S. Congress Ave.
Atlantis   965-7300

Since 1966, JFK has been the hospital of choice for many residents of the south-central portion of Palm Beach County.

The private, 369-bed center offers specialty services in the areas of cardiovascular diseases and oncology. It's also known for its extensive outpatient services, including a surgical unit and diagnostic breast-imaging center.

GOOD SAMARITAN MEDICAL CENTER
1300 N. Flagler Dr.
West Palm Beach   655-5511

Since it opened its doors in 1920, "Good Sam" has been a quality

Photo: Boca Raton Community Hospital, Inc.

Boca Raton Community Hospital has provided health care for Palm Beach Countians since 1967.

BOCA RATON COMMUNITY HOSPITAL, INC.

General Information 800 Meadows Road	395-7100
After Hours Minor Emergency Center 600 S. Dixie Hwy	368-1606
Center For Breast Care 690 Meadows Rd	362-5000
Education Center 800 Meadows Rd	393-4063
Emergency Services 800 Meadows Rd	395-7100
Fitness Center 600 S. Dixie Hwy	395-1640
Home Health 745 Meadows Rd	393-4040
Imaging Center 690 Meadows Rd	750-4708
MRI Center 690 Meadows Rd	393-4048
Nutrition Counseling 745 Meadows Rd	393-4074
Occupational Therapy 800 Meadows Rd	393-4060
Speech-Language Department 745 Meadows Rd	393-4071
Voice and Swallowing Center 745 Meadows Rd	393-4071
Physician Referral Service 800 Meadows Rd	393-4087
Radiation Oncology-	
Lynn Regional Cancer Center-Boca Raton 800 Meadows Rd	393-4111
Lynn Regional Cancer Center-Delray Beach 16313 S. Military Tr.	637-7200
Rehabilitative Services-	
Physical Therapy-Main Hospital 800 Meadows Rd	393-4060
Therapy Center Of Boca Raton Community Hospital	
880 NW 13th St	391-3871
Social Services 800 Meadows Rd	393-4150
SurgiCenter Plus 800 Meadows Rd	393-4119
Women's Center 690 Meadows Rd	362-5000

healthcare provider for thousands of Palm Beach countians.

The 341-bed private hospital in downtown West Palm Beach, just moments from Palm Beach, offers specialty units in sleep disorders, perinatology and pediatrics, orthopedics and oncology. Its Good Samaritan Cancer Unit is supported by the Duke University Medical Center.

ST. MARY'S HOSPITAL
901 45th St.
West Palm Beach   *844-6300*

Like Good Samaritan, St. Mary's has provided excellent care to Palm Beach County folk for decades — since 1938.

St. Mary's, a nonprofit hospital, is the designated regional trauma center for the north-central part of the county and offers a Level II and III Neonatal Intensive Care Unit, a psychiatric unit including outpatient care and a physical rehabilitation center. Construction has begun on a pediatric emergency room to upgrade the 433-bed hospital's 24-hour emergency services.

Also on hospital grounds is the Hanley-Hazelden Center at St. Mary's, a nonprofit center for the treatment of alcoholism and other addictive disorders.

Related Regional Services

Mental Health Facilities

The following mental health facilities provide services for children, adolescents and adults.

Photo: Boca Raton Community Hospital, Inc.

Boca Raton Community Hospital offers Smart Heart blood pressure and cholesterol screening in conjunction with Boca Raton Fire-Rescue.

THE RENFREW CENTER

7700 Renfrew Ln.
Coconut Creek   (800) 332-8415

Just a stone's throw from Boca Raton is the Renfrew Center, an 11-acre facility that offers specialized mental health programs for women.

Originally, the 40-bed center was opened as an inpatient center for women suffering from eating disorders. Today, it assists women with a variety of mental health needs, including care for depression, obsessive and compulsive disorders, anxiety, substance abuse and counseling for those suffering the effects of living in dysfunctional or abusive families.

The center offers inpatient, outpatient, day and residential care and a transitional living program that allows patients to reside at the center and participate in therapy and still attend school, look for work or locate a new residence.

The center also provides support groups and community outreach programs for women.

SANDY PINES HOSPITAL

11301 S.E. Tequesta Ter.
Tequesta   744-0211

Sandy Pines specializes in the treatment of childhood psychiatric disorders. It also offers support groups and outpatient care for adults and children with bipolar affective disorder, panic disorder and similar afflictions.

FAIR OAKS HOSPITAL

5440 Linton Blvd.
Delray Beach   495-1000

Fair Oaks is a psychiatric institution offering care for adults, adolescents and children. It also provides geriatric care and offers a chemical dependency unit, an adult unit, a summer day camp and Silver Sands Senior Care.

Walk-in Medical Centers

In addition to full-service hospitals, Palm Beach County is replete with acute-care, walk-in facilities.

Non-emergency medical centers are usually open seven days and evenings a week and specialize in after-hour and

weekend care for folks with sore throats, hay fever, sprained ankles and bumps and bruises that aren't severe enough to warrant a visit to an emergency room but are too bothersome to put off until the family physician's office opens.

Many of these facilities accept insurance, and many also have diagnostic, laboratory and X-ray services on site.

BOCA RATON COMMUNITY HOSPITAL AFTER-HOURS MINOR EMERGENCY CENTER
600 Dixie Hwy.
Boca Raton   368-1606

DELRAY PHYSICIANS CARE CENTER
2280 W. Atlantic Ave.
Delray Beach   278-3134

FIRSTMED WALK-IN MEDICAL CENTER
1786 N.W. Second Ave.
Boca Raton   368-6920

MINOR EMERGICENTER
750 S. Federal Hwy.
Deerfield Beach   (305) 421-8181

PRIME MEDICAL DOCTORS WALK-IN CENTER
Mission Bay Plaza
20401 S.R. 7
Boca Raton   479-1777

NORTHLAKE MEDICAL CENTER
4239 Northlake Blvd.
Palm Beach Gardens   626-9190

SFHCA WALK-IN MEDICAL CENTER
7301 W. Palmetto Park Rd., Ste. 108B
Boca Raton   347-1300

Plastic and Reconstructive Surgeons

For various personal reasons, many people in Palm Beach County

You're Looking Good

A new wrinkle surfacing in aesthetic plastic surgery is more deliberate communication between doctors and patients about procedures, techniques and expectations.

Motivated to save face in the controversy over the alleged risk of silicone, plastic surgeons remind us sterile saline-filled implants remain a safe alternative for breast augmentation.

Determined to look their best, men and women of all ages are investigating what's new in facelifts, eye repair, body contouring, altered noses and skin rejuvenation: chemical peels derived from sugar cane, multilayer facelifts, open-structure rhinoplasty, transconjunctival blepharoplasty, musculocutaneous flaps, circular waistlifts, medial eyelids and higher coronals.

Some folks are surprised to learn their new best friend is an old-fashioned idea espoused by leading plastic surgeons from Boca Raton to Stuart. A *Palm Beach Illustrated* poll of 10 area specialists indicates strong agreement about the importance of increased attention to pre- and postoperative skin care.

The newest policy in the Boca Raton practice of Dr. Lawrence M. Korpeck is incorporating a regimen of skin care into the surgical approach: "Most experts feel facelifts and peels alone don't produce optimal results. There's new concern for the quality of the skin and the importance of aftercare.

"We give pre- and post-op facials using seaweed and other natural ingredients, because a cleaner, healthier surface is important. After a lift to correct the jowls or a saggy neck, a peel of the outer layer reveals a better texture; a post-op facial cleans ointments out of the pores."

In South Florida, where sun-damage is prevalent, the advent of chemical peels less aggressive than traditional Phenol appear to be a godsend.

Multiple applications of widely used trichloroacetic acid (TCA) over a few weeks can accomplish the same results as deeper-penetrating Phenol, and do it more safely. However, doctors caution that TCA in a solution of 50 percent or more, has greater scarring potential than Phenol.

The mildest peel is media-darling glycolic, a fruity acid wash derived from sugar cane. Glycolic acid solutions have an advantage over comparable substances like Retin-A, which creates photosensitivity.

Still, patients are advised, even a relatively mild acid wash can produce devastating results if applied improperly because there is no control over the healing process.

Because consumers are so curious about new products, and glycolic acid wash — the new kid on the block among chemical peels — is now available from several leading cosmetics manufacturers, Dr. Frederick Barr of West Palm Beach believes the marketplace is ripe for confusion and potential misapplication.

"Even though they are so potent, peels have overtaken the market, which is unfortunate. Twenty years ago, a trio of doctors perfected the acid treatment, but the patent was dropped in 1992. So it's being touted as the next `fountain of youth.' What plastic surgery provides is selections, within everyone's personal limitations, not a fountain of youth."

Barr emphasizes that what's new in plastic surgery is really what's old.

"The foundation has been refined to allow a patient greater expression and a more natural, balanced look. Facelifts, especially, now include more techniques in one sitting — face, neck, eyelids, forehead; because the forehead ages just like the rest of the face."

Opinions favor finesse over flaunt to avoid what is sometimes called the "windblown" face — brow work that broadcasts you sat on a thumbtack.

As Barr states, "Good work is subtle; it will be hard to discern."

With his South Palm Beach County practice limited strictly to faces, Dr. James R. Shire strives for the most natural look possible, ostensibly to appear as if a patient had never even had surgery.

Shire believes it's ironic the anatomical or deep facelifts took some time to become state-of-the-art. "If you think about a woman who is pregnant, what happens to her skin after it's been stretched over the abdomen? Eventually, it goes back to where it was. If you stretch just the skin on a face, it won't last — for the same reasons. Deep facelifts go to the foundation and lift the muscle, then the skin."

According to Dr. Steven Schuster, practicing in Boca/Delray, the recuperative period for a deep facelift is only slightly longer than a superficial skin procedure, yet the results are impressive — lasting up to three or four years longer. "In the past, a lift would last 5 to 10 years; with a deep lift, it's more like 8 or 14 years."

"No longer a fad, no longer experimental, it's now the standard for reshaping an abnormal area (love-handles, heavy thighs, a flabby belly) by making a quarter-inch incision that's hidden in the body. You can sculpt the extra fat with no telltale signs."

Another procedure applauded for its lack of evidence is the transconjunctival blepharoplasty, a new eyelid surgery especially practical for younger patients, even children. Done on an outpatient basis, the incision is made inside the eyelid.

Stein's partner, Dr. Richard Schwartz, said the technique is "recent and very popular because you have no visible scar."

Through very specific training and continuing education, he added, "We continue to be able to offer refinements in eyelid and facelift procedures, and contouring of other areas. One refinement is the musculocutaneous flap, which uses a segment of tissue combining skin, muscle and fat, that is relocated from the belly or back, then sculpted for a new breast."

In breast reconstruction, Stein noted refinements in tissue expansion: "Along the idea of an inflatable balloon to stretch out existing skin, adding shaped fat relocated from another area (a tummy tuck). It involves more extensive surgery, but is appropriate on an individual case basis. Not only is it standard procedure, there are more shapes, sizes and materials to choose from."

A more recently used material in body contouring is Autologen, produced in a Massachusetts laboratory by Boca Raton-based Autogenesis Inc.

According to Dr. Orrin Stern of Boca Raton Plastic Surgery Center, autologen hasn't been on the market long enough to judge its effectiveness. "Bovine was the source of collagen; and later it came from pigs. Neither substance lasts very long. This company takes human skin, processes it to remove the collagen; then it's injected into your own wrinkles. Because it's your own, the body is more likely not to reject it."

When it comes to rejection, not all plastic surgeons accept what their colleagues have to say about advancements in the field, whether it regards procedure, technique, material, equipment or policy.

"I must emphasize that as time goes by, safe, sound procedures — not pie in the sky — are where it's at. A good plastic surgeon will always put the safety of a patient first. Working with what we already know, there now is more honesty about what's available when a patient asks, 'How do I get rid of these wrinkles?' There's better communication about what patients expect."

are deeply concerned about looking their very best. Perhaps that's why plastic and reconstructive surgeries (see this chapter's sidebar) are not uncommon here in the land of The Best of Everything.

In part, because Palm Beach countians are generally active and outdoorsy folks, mishaps associated with a rigorous recreational lifestyle — a bump resulting from a broken nose received in a touch-football game or a chin scar from a bad-hop grounder on the softball diamond — routinely occur and are treated via plastic or reconstructive surgery.

Also, despite repeated warnings from members of the medical community, some folks do not heed the fact that overexposure to the sun — especially South Florida's tropical rays — can cause skin cancer. Not surprisingly, plastic surgeons in this area devote a good part of their businesses to removing cancerous and precancerous lesions.

The following is a sampling of Palm Beach County surgeons who offer both plastic and reconstructive surgeries:

LAWRENCE KORPECK, MD, FACS
9980 Central Park Blvd. N., Ste. 124
Boca Raton   483-6850

PAMELA LOFTUS, MD
900 N.W. 13th St.
Boca Raton   394-7494

DANIEL MAN, MD
851 Meadows Rd.
Boca Raton   395-5508

MARK SCHRIEBER, MD
2623 S. Seacrest Blvd.
Boynton Beach   738-0727

ORRIN STERN, MD
CRISTINA KEUSCH, MD
950 Glades Rd.
Boca Raton   368-9455

JEFFREY WISNICKI, MD
13005 Southern Blvd.
Wellington   798-1400

Inside
Daycations

In a county that bills itself "The Best of Everything," one might wonder why anyone would ever want to explore outside our borders, but we'd urge you to give it a try if only for a day — although some of our suggestions are better spread over a weekend. On the map, our little peninsula looks too narrow to offer much, but we beg to differ.

There are two ways to make your daytrips: by land and by water (yes, there are some excellent water-bound excursions to choose from).

The Florida Keys

Key West

It's not without a touch of irony that Conchs (Keys natives) call Key West "The Last Resort." Part of it is simple: Key West is the last of the delicate string of coral beads that make up the Keys. The other part is the laid-back lifestyle for which the islanders of the Conch Republic are noted . . . visitors just can't be too serious here. If you decide to drive down to Key West, be sure and stop at the end of Whitehead Street, where the southernmost-point-in-the-U.S. marker is located. Other points of interest in America's southernmost city include the **Hemingway House**, 907 Whitehead Street, 294-1575, where the Nobel Prize-winning author occasionally worked. The house is still maintained to reflect the days Hemingway lived and worked here, right down to the six-toed cats that call this place home. Not far away are several interesting spots of historical interest: **Harry S Truman Little White House Museum**, 111 Front Street, 294-9911; **Audubon House and Gardens**, Whitehead and Green streets, 294-2116; **Key West Shipwreck Historeum**, 1 Whitehead Street, 292-8990; the **Curry Mansion**, 511 Caroline Street, 294-5349; and the **Mel Fisher Maritime Heritage Society Museum**, 200 Greene Street, 294-2633, where many of the artifacts recovered from the *Atocha* and *Margarita* are on display.

The biggest attraction on the island is free: **sunset** at the Mallory Dock, Duval and Front streets. Buskers, from a barechested bagpiper, magicians and musicians to a fireeater, do their thing; artists and craftspeople display their wares; and there are plenty of cool drinks and snacks available for nibblers.

After sunset it's dinner time, and the restaurants on the island have plenty of bounty from the seas with which to tempt their guests. Here are a few favorites:

JIMMY BUFFETT'S MARGARITAVILLE CAFE
500 Duval St.   292-1435

Cheeseburger in Paradise? You bet; it's here on the menu, along with lots of great seafood and sandwiches. For Parrotheads, a stop here is *de rigueur*. Besides, You Know Who just may be hanging out.

SLOPPY JOE'S
201 Duval St.   294-5717

This was Hemingway's hangout during the 1930s. Today, Sloppy Joe's is known for frozen drink specialties, burgers and sandwiches and live music. Like Margaritaville, Sloppy Joe's is extremely popular with tourists; both are must-see places.

LA LECHONERA
3100 Flagler Ave.   292-3700

Located outside the Old Town area, this delightful little Cuban restaurant specializes in pork dishes, as its piggy-motif decorations attest.

The Other Keys

Should your travels not take you as far as Key West, there's still much to see, do and sample in the rest of the Keys.

KEY LARGO

Originally named *Cayo Largo*, or Long Island, by Spanish explorers, Key Largo is the first key visitors reach as they leave the mainland. It's heaven on earth to divers and snorkelers and home to John Pennekamp Coral Reef State Park, the first undersea park in the United States. If diving or snorkeling to watch more than 650 varieties of fish is underwhelming, you also can tour the 21-mile park by glass-bottom boat.

ISLAMORADA

Originally known as *Isla Morada*, or Purple Island, Islamorada's claim to fame is its location as a fishing mecca and the staging area for many fishing tournaments. If you have time on your drive, stop at the **Green Turtle Inn**, 664-9031, at mile marker 81.5. Famous for its green turtle chowder (Try it; you'll like it!) and freshly caught seafood specialties served in comfortable surroundings, it's well worth the stop.

MARATHON

The heart of the middle Keys, Marathon is the start of the famous (though many would say infamous) Seven-Mile Bridge. Now that a new bridge has made travel easier, the old bridge has gained the distinction as the world's longest fishing pier (although it has become a favorite spot for moviemakers as well).

BIG PINE KEY

As the heart of the lower Keys, Big Pine Key is the refuge for Key deer, a species of white-tailed deer that reaches doglike sizes at maturity. This area also is home to a variety of reptiles and birds as well as numerous fish species.

Photo: Investments Limited

Royal Palm Plaza in downtown Boca Raton is a popular shopping destination.

"The Grove"

"The Grove" is the artsy, bohemian part of Miami, snuggling up alongside Biscayne Bay. There, the drinks are cool but the entertainment is hot, hot, hot. The stars come out at Planet Hollywood — at Mayfair in The Grove — but you'll find cool folks scoping out the action and watching the human parade from bistros, cantinas and cafes throughout the area, but especially where Main Highway, Grand Avenue and McFarlane Road meet.

There are two ultra-chic shopping centers at the intersection: Mayfair and Cocowalk. There also are loads of one-of-a-kind shops, bicycle and in-line skate rentals, restaurants, galleries, theaters and other fun things to do within easy walking distance. Friday and Saturday evenings tend to be dominated by the high school and college crowd, but Sunday is a fabulous day to visit and linger on through sunset.

If you want to check out natural and man-made scenery, take a little drive along Bayshore Drive and Tigertail Avenue. Bayshore Drive runs along the bay and is a favorite workout route for bikers, runners and in-line skaters. Dade County's power elite live in the breathtaking homes along these two streets.

Miami Beach: A City of Contrasts

Take the beach exit off I-95 across the Julia Tuttle Causeway to Miami Beach — just across Biscayne Bay, but a whole world away. Like Miami, Miami Beach is a city of contrasts. The beach area still is a mecca for elderly residents, but many of the old retirement hotels have been restored to their 1920s and '30s heyday grandeur. Especially beautiful are the pastel art deco buildings along **Ocean Drive**, which captivated audiences on *Miami Vice*.

It's very busy and touristy here on the weekends, and during the season it's pretty hectic, but it's always enjoyable. In the summer and at off-peak times, it's fabulous even for claustrophobes. The choices and varieties of food here are plentiful and the quality is good.

But if a day in the sand or doing the club scene doesn't enthrall you, you don't even need to leave your car to have a great time on the beach. Cruising Ocean Drive and Washington Avenue is fun; the people-watching is always good here.

Welcome to Naples

Most Gulfside communities are known to be casual and gracious, and Naples is pleased to behave accordingly. While booming development in recent years cost the city its best-kept-secret status, the languid pace still beckons invitingly to visit for a day or several.

A peek at Naples today versus the 1980s will cause some double-takes: If you remember a drowsy hamlet of provincial snowbirds from the Midwest, you'll be astounded at one of the fastest growing metropolitan areas in the United States. One reason is Fort Myers' expanded regional airport and daily direct flights from major U.S. cities. People on the Gold Coast and the Treasure Coast who contemplated a getaway to Naples used to hesitate at the uninviting drive: south through highway traffic to begin the boring and awkward trek across two-lane Alligator Alley west from Fort Lauderdale. Marshes, snakes, canal banks and wildlife straying onto the road — plus no service stations for 78 miles — made for a grim trip. On I-75, the trip is a breeze.

Now, Naples' natural attributes get the attention of a wider range of weekend visitors and residents. Some people who live in west Broward or Palm Beach counties even commute to jobs in Naples.

Naples matured as a "Southern suburb" that largely reflects the conservative values of fans from the Midwest. It draws people with money who flaunt it less, but who also like fine accommodations.

Thus, Naples' posh **Ritz-Carlton** is a popular destination among international and resort travelers as well as convention planners.

Gulf beaches are a pleasant diversion, especially for shellers and aimless beachcombers just out for a stroll at sunset. Shallow, usually calm wa-

Allilgators sun themselves at the Arthur R. Marshall Loxahatchee National Wildlife Refuge.

ters are bathtub warm and ideal for skiing, sailing and almost any watersport. The city has some exciting diversions for every lifestyle: boating, golf, tennis, shopping and dining.

Shopping could be a major pastime, with its charming **Olde Naples** area: **Third Street S.** and **the Avenues** just a short walk from the beaches, and the upscale **Wa-**

terside **Shops** at Pelican Bay off U.S. Highway 41. You'll find Jacobson's Department Store and Saks Fifth Avenue's first resort-size establishment, smaller than the traditional department store you find at many malls.

Then there's **The Village On Venetian Bay**, a Mediterranean-flavor shopping destination all its own with 50 specialty shops, art gal-

Photo: Cynthia Thuma

leries and restaurants — all perched on decks over the waterway. The Village is so picturesque, it's been interpreted in oil by local artist Rachel Kennedy. There's an info line for The Village that gives shopping hours and special events: (813) 261-0030.

Waterfront areas popular for shopping include **Dockside Boardwalk**, **Crayton Cove**, the **Old Marine Marketplace** at Tin City, and **Hibiscus Center**. And if you're bargain hunting, check out the **Coral Isle Factory Stores**.

Definitely consider dining at **Maxwell's** or **Bayside Grill**, both at The Village on Venetian Bay. There also are plenty of familiar chains, including **Outback Steakhouse**.

After shopping and dinner, those hungry for culture may sample the **Philharmonic Center for the Arts** at Pelican Bay, home to the Naples Philharmonic and the west coast venue for Miami City Ballet.

An appealing climate, amenities and quality of life create great demand for the charms of Naples, either for lunch and an afternoon of shopping or to linger all weekend on the Gulf of Mexico.

Cruise the Intracoastal Waterway

There are few more relaxing ways to spend a leisurely afternoon or evening than cruising the Intracoastal Waterway. The *Ramblin' Rose Riverboat*, which departs from its dock at Veterans Park, 801 E. Atlantic Avenue, Delray Beach, 243-0686,

offers a wonderfully relaxing yet informative cruise. Sight-seeing and dinner cruises are available.

Sight-seeing cruises leave at 11 AM and return at 3 PM Monday through Friday and cost $15.95 for adults, $4.95 for children. On Saturday, cruises depart at 11 AM and return at 2:30 PM; the cost is $13.95 for adults, $4.25 for children. Sunday cruises depart at 2 PM and return at 4:30 PM and cost $9.95 for adults, $3.75 for children.

A Sunday brunch cruise is available, which leaves at 11:30 AM and returns at 1 PM; it costs $18.95 for adults, $10.95 for children.

Dinner cruises board between 6:30 and 7 PM and depart for a 7 to 10 PM cruise Friday and Saturday evenings; the cost is $29. From Sunday through Thursday, boarding again takes place between 6:30 to 7 PM for a 7 to 9 PM dinner cruise that costs $24.14.

Hooray for Hollywood (Florida)

Hollywood, like many cities in southeastern Florida, was started by a man with a dream. Like Addison Mizner, who conjured up Boca Raton, fellow Californian Joseph Wesley Young envisioned Hollywood-by-the-Sea as a world-class resort and a great place to call home.

After falling back on its heels a bit, Hollywood is moving again toward fulfilling Young's visions. A real magnet is its Broadwalk, which attracts visitors — many of them French-speaking Canadians — in droves.

Photo: Associaated Press file photo

It's only a two-hour drive to watch the space shuttle lift off at the John F. Kennedy Space Center.

Other favorite spots are the state-operated **John Lloyd Park** and county-operated **Topeekeegee Yugnee Park** (just call it T-Y Park). Both are popular with hikers, bikers and nature lovers. John Lloyd Park features an ocean beach, and T-Y Park offers a lake for swimmers and boaters to enjoy.

Cultural festivals, art shows and other open-air activities are held at Young Circle — at Hollywood Boulevard and Federal Highway.

Surf City and the Space Coast

Take a leisurely two-hour drive north on I-95 and you'll reach Brevard County, home of Florida's best surfing beaches and the Kennedy Space Center.

Many of the beaches in Brevard County still have a rugged look, with sea oats waving in the wind and salt spray kicking up off the waves. Surfers could hardly love it more.

The surf scene gravitates to the Cocoa Beach pier area, home of the **Easter Surf Festival** every April.

Head inland, though, and you'll find the **John F. Kennedy Space Center**, an enduring symbol of man's attempt to control his universe and his destiny.

An excellent stop for adults and children alike is **Spaceport USA** at the Space Center, 452-2121, with dual IMAX theaters and an enthralling exhibit area that includes many of the actual space capsules used by American and Russian space explorers. There's also a full-scale replica of a space shuttle. The Spaceport USA adventure also includes a bus tour of the Space Center and a visit to launch sites from the Mercury and Gemini eras — the early days of America's space program.

Simulation programs are the drawing card at the **Astronaut Hall of Fame** in Titusville, 6225 Vectorspace Boulevard, 269-6100. The center uses virtual technology to permit participants to experience weightlessness and pilot a shuttle simulator. A model space shuttle simulates the feel of a trip into space.

The Hall of Fame also displays and provides historical information and personal effects and memorabilia of America's pioneers in space.

For those who prefer flying heroes from a different bygone era, Titusville is also home to the **Warbird Air Museum**, 6600 Tico Road, 268-1941, displaying aircraft from World War I and II, the Korean War and the Vietnam War.

Perhaps the greatest thrill of visiting the Brevard County area is getting to watch a space shuttle launch. To keep abreast of information and scheduling on anticipated and upcoming launches, call (800) KSC-INFO. Viewing areas are along Highway A1A in Cape Canaveral and Cocoa Beach and on U.S. 1 in Titusville. *Florida Today*, the daily newspaper serving the Space Coast, provides excellent launch-day viewing information and tips.

Sea It In a Day

SeaEscape and Discovery cruises make a trip to the Bahamas a breeze. Why pile like sardines into a plane to fly to Grand Bahama Island when you can lounge on deck and sip cold drinks with little umbrellas in them or do the limbo to the sounds of a steel band? Or if those mundane albeit relaxing pursuits bore you, just saunter down to the on-board casino and try your hand at your favorite game of chance.

SeaEscape cruises leave Port Everglades for Grand Bahama on Sunday, Monday, Wednesday and Friday at 7 and 8 AM and return from 7 to 9:30 PM. The cost is $69 plus $49 port charges. Meals are included and drinks may be purchased on board. Call (305) 476-9900 for further information.

Discovery Cruise Line ships sail to Freeport, Bahamas, from Port Everglades and the Port of Miami. Cruises depart and return from Fort Lauderdale on Sunday, Monday, Wednesday and Friday and from the Port of Miami on Monday, Tuesday and Thursday through Saturday.

Cruises on Friday, Saturday or Sunday depart at 6:45 AM and return to port about 6:45 PM and cost $69.99 plus $49 port charges. Cruises on Monday through Thursday depart at 7:45 AM, return at 11 PM and cost $79.99 plus $49 port charges. Meals are included. Call (305) 525-7800 for further information.

Inside
South Florida Media

Because Boca Raton and the Palm Beaches are so vibrant and diverse, the area's need for fast, accurate information is great. And, like its population, that need is growing daily.

But we don't want just the facts, ma'am; we want to know the issues and how they might affect our lives. We also want to know about our lively arts and culture scene, the world-class business communities, educational, medical and child-care issues, and the wide variety of national and local sports that happen here.

The needs of the area's information consumers have been met largely through a wide selection of newspapers, television and radio that stretches from Miami to the Martin County line, just north of Palm Beach Gardens.

Newspapers

Dailies

THE NEWS

33 S.E. Third St.
Boca Raton 395-8300

From the flamingo on the mast to the tightly written, entertaining stories and eye-catching photos and graphics, *The News* has its finger on the pulse of South County, and it shows it in its pages.

The News, a Knight-Ridder newspaper, goes heavy on local coverage but doesn't ignore the world, national and regional stories of importance to South County's well-educated, upscale, savvy readers who want to keep informed but whose on-the-go lifestyles limit their reading time.

Written in a sprightly manner and tightly edited, *The News'* sports section keeps close tabs on the local scene, from area pro team events to youth league results and features.

Local stories provide perspective on topics related to city government and neighborhood news and events.

The "Society Monday" section is lively and widely read, and the daily "Essentials" section offers lifestyle stories and news of interest to South County families. Each day's section follows a theme such as Generation X, Parent & Child, Business Extra or Weekend Preview.

THE MIAMI HERALD

I Herald Plaza
Miami (305) 350-2111

The flagship paper of the Knight-Ridder chain offers a daily Palm Beach County edition to supplement the *Herald's* world-class global, national and state coverage in each edition of Florida's newspaper of record.

The *Herald's* investigative reporting is among the nation's best, and some of its most lively writing can be found in the "Living & Arts" section. Youngsters will love "YO" (Youth Only), which explodes from the back page of Wednesday's "Living & Arts." Other gems are Sunday's *Tropic* magazine, with Pulitzer Prize-winner Dave Barry's column, and the Thursday "Food" section, whose selections reflect South Florida's cosmopolitan, outdoorsy lifestyle. Especially worth checking out each week is Viviana Carballo's "Kitchen Tropicale" column. And Friday's *Weekend* tabloid is an excellent compendium of what's happening in the Dade-Broward-Palm Beach area.

Another *Herald* product is *El Nuevo Herald*, a Spanish daily that offers an alternative source of information for South Florida's Hispanic communities. Call it *El Nuevo* when you ask for it at your local newsstand.

THE PALM BEACH POST

2751 S. Dixie Hwy.   820-4100
West Palm Beach   (800) 654-1231

A member of the Atlanta-based Cox family of newspapers, the *Post* keeps tabs primarily on Palm Beach County but maintains a watchful eye on the surrounding counties as well.

The paper's coverage of governmental news and local issues is especially strong, particularly on those centered in the West Palm Beach area.

The sports section is comprehensive, offering a nice mix of big-time sports and high school coverage.

PALM BEACH DAILY NEWS

265 Royal Poinciana Way
Palm Beach   820-4100

Ask for the *Palm Beach Daily News* by name and you may find paper vendors are unfamiliar with this distinctive Cox paper that publishes every morning during the season (Thanksgiving through Easter) and twice a week in the off-season. Call it *The Shiny Sheet* and you'll get immediate name recognition.

The Shiny Sheet, named because it was once printed on a glossy stock paper to minimize ink ruboff on Palm Beachers' hands and expensive clothes, follows the news and society happenings in Palm Beach, the magnificent community some call "Fantasy Island."

Sunday's "Lifestyle" is a highlight, loaded with news about the arts, society and cutting-edge fashion trends.

THE SUN-SENTINEL

200 E. Las Olas Blvd.
Fort Lauderdale   (305) 356-4000

Despite its Broward background, *The Sun-Sentinel* — owned by Chicago's Tribune Company since 1963 — has spread its roots into South County.

Among its strengths are its local columnists, coverage of local and educational issues and investigative reporting.

Its sports section offers a special Sunday football section during the fall and other themed sections throughout the year.

PALM BEACH DAILY BUSINESS REVIEW

328 Banyan Blvd.
West Palm Beach   832-0386

The *Review*, like its sister publications in Broward and Dade counties, is a Monday-through-Friday survey of law, business and real estate issues and events.

Don't make the mistake of thinking this publication is stodgy and dull; the paper's writing consistently has teeth, and the *Review* has the guts to take on some stories the other dailies won't touch.

Non-Dailies

PALM BEACH GAZETTE

P.O. Box 18469
West Palm Beach 33416   844-5501

The *Gazette*, a weekly, bills itself as "Tomorrow's Black newspaper today." The *Gazette* is a lively publication, an eloquent voice for Palm Beach County's African-American citizens, and an active participant in community events.

Some of its best work is reflected in its enterprising reporting and editorials. The *Gazette* also offers a variety of features, including cooking and sports.

PALM BEACH TODAY

234 S. County Rd., Ste. 2
Palm Beach   655-8667

Palm Beach Today is a weekly publication filled with the names and faces who give the area its dazzle and pizzazz. It also provides listings of society events throughout the county and offers some excellent articles on Palm Beach County history.

THE TOWN CRIER

12794 W. Forest Hill Blvd., Ste. 14
Wellington   793-7606

The Town Crier covers communities in west-central Palm Beach County, including Wellington, the Palm Beach Polo and Country Club and Loxahatchee. The news and sports sections are well-written and cover their communities exceptionally well. Editorials are lively and thought-provoking.

The Town Crier hits lawns and newsstands every Thursday.

LA VOZ HISPAÑA

3242 S. Dixie Hwy.
West Palm Beach   659-1833

As a gateway to The Americas, South Florida's population is swelling with new residents from Spanish-speaking countries. *La Voz Hispaña*, a free weekly, provides news and features of interest to Hispanics. Regular features include immigration, health, society, sports, the poetry corner and cooking and nutrition.

EL LATINO SEMANAL

4325 Georgia Ave.
West Palm Beach   835-4913

El Latino Semanal, a weekly broadsheet, serves the Hispanic communities of Dade, Broward and Palm Beach counties, with offices in West Palm Beach and Hialeah.

The paper is strong on world and Latin American news that impacts Hispanics living in South Florida, many of whom still have relatives living in their native countries. Other standing features include arts and literature, religion,

Photo: Michelle Lord

The News serves South County with two editions, one in Boca Raton, the other in Delray Beach.

finance, society, entertainment, sports and travel.

COMMUNITY VOICE

P.O. Box 17975
West Palm Beach 33416   471-1528

Community Voice, published monthly, calls itself "your alternative lifestyle magazine" and presents news and stories of interest to the gay and lesbian community. Each issue's "Community Resource" guide chronicles what's happening throughout South County and highlights Dade's and Broward's gay communities as well.

Local Publications

Palm Beach County has a wealth of local newspapers that do a super job covering smaller cities and neighborhoods. These include the following:

LAKE WORTH HERALD AND COASTAL OBSERVER

130 S. H St.
Lake Worth   585-9387

This publication covers news and events in Lake Worth and central Palm Beach County.

JUPITER COURIER-JOURNAL

800 W. Indiantown Rd.
Jupiter   746-5111

This paper keeps tabs on happenings in Palm Beach County's northern communities.

WEEKDAY

826 Park Ave.
Lake Park   844-2408

Weekday covers news and events in the north-central area of Palm Beach County.

SOUTH FLORIDA NEWSPAPER NETWORK

601 Fairway Dr.
Deerfield Beach   (305) 698-6397

This network publishes the *Boca Raton Monday Times, Boca Raton*

Thursday Times, Boynton Beach Times and *Delray Beach Times*. Areas of coverage include northern Broward and southern Palm Beach counties.

Arts and Entertainment Publications

RED HERRING
931 Village Blvd.
West Palm Beach   478-0381

Red Herring focuses its coverage on the West Palm Beach area but catches other parts of the county as well.

This self-proclaimed "Journal of contemporary arts and issues" keeps tabs on arts and entertainment news in the West Palm Beach-Lake Worth area and occasionally goes a bit north or south to cover events or personalities of interest.

It's published bimonthly from October through June and monthly in July, August and September, but it provides monthly listings of who's playing at clubs in the Orchid City (West Palm Beach) as well as a comprehensive activities calender.

XS
200 E. Las Olas Blvd.
Fort Lauderdale   (305) 356-4943

An independent product affiliated with the *Sun-Sentinel*, XS is a rollicking, no-holds-barred arts, entertainment and Internet weekly that covers Broward and Palm Beach counties. The magazine's interactive hotlines allow you to listen to excerpts from hot local bands to determine if you'd like to hear more.

XS offers information about area restaurants, clubs, sports bars, cof-

feehouses, art exhibits, support groups and volunteer opportunities.

Niche Publications

SENIOR LIFE
1515 N. Federal Hwy., #300
Boca Raton   736-8925

Senior Life is a monthly publication covering news and events of interest to Palm Beach County's over-60 population.

NEW DIRECTIONS FOR BETTER LIVING
P.O. Box 17865
West Palm Beach 33416   471-7046

New Directions is a monthly newspaper presenting information on health, nutrition, wellness, empowerment and environmental issues. It provides listings of events throughout the county for people interested in those areas and others.

Radio

One of the advantages of living in southeastern Florida is access to the incredible number of radio stations catering to a wide variety of tastes. Because South Florida is flat as a flounder, you can get great reception from stations miles away.

Here's what's available on the AM and FM bands, by category:

AFRICAN-AMERICAN
WEDR 99.1 FM (99 JAM)
WRBD 1470 AM

ADULT CONTEMPORARY/ SOFT ADULT CONTEMPORARY
WPOW 96.5 FM (POWER 96)
WFLC 97.3 FM (COAST)
WRMF 97.9 FM
WHYI 100.7 FM (Y-100)

WEAT 104.3 FM
WHQT 105.1 FM (HOT 105)

WJBW 99.5 FM
WMXJ 102.7 FM (MAJIC 102.7)

CLASSICAL

WQCS 88.9 FM
WXEL 90.7 FM
WTMI 93.1 FM (Plays jazz late at night)

COUNTRY

WKIS 99.9 FM (KISS)
WIRK 107.9 FM

EASY LISTENING

WAFG 90.3 FM
WRLX 92.1 FM
WLYF 101.5 FM (LIFE)
WHLG 102.3 FM

JAZZ

WLRN 91.3 FM (also National Public Radio)
WDBF 1420 AM (Big Band)
WLVE 93.9 FM (LOVE 94)

LATIN/TALK

WAQI 710 AM
WRFM 830 AM
WXDJ 95.7 FM
WQBA 1140 AM
WCMQ 1210 AM
WKAT 1360 AM
WOCN 1450 AM
WQBA 107.5 FM

NEWS/SPORTS/TALK/INFORMATION

WQAM 560 AM (Sports talk, game coverage for Florida Marlins baseball)
WIOD 610 AM (Sports talk, game coverage for Miami Dolphins football)
WSBR 740 AM (Business/financial)
WINZ Newsradio 940 AM (News and sports, game coverage of Miami Heat basketball)
WEAT 850 AM
WVCG 1080 AM (Elevator music and talk)
WJNO 1230 AM
WBZT 1290 AM
WPBR 1340 AM
WFTL 1400 AM

OLDIES

WMRZ 790 AM
WOLL 94.9 FM

RELIGIOUS/INSPIRATIONAL

WLVJ 640 AM
WAYF 88.1 FM
WRMB 89.3 FM
WMCU 89.7 FM
WCNO 89.9 FM
WEXY 1520 AM

RHYTHM AND BLUES/GOSPEL/ETHNIC

WMBM 1490 AM (Gospel music)
WAVS 1170 AM (Rhythm and blues, Caribbean)
WLQY 1320 AM (International music, mostly Haitian)
WSRF 1580 AM (Ethnic music)
WPOM 1600 AM

ROCK

WKPX 88.5 FM
WVUM 90.5 FM
WZTA 94.9 FM (Alternative rock)
WKGR 98.7 FM
WSHE 103.5 FM (Alternative rock)

OTHER

WWNN 980 AM (Motivational/health talk)

Television

As with radio, Palm Beach County benefits from an abundance of electronic media outlets in Dade, Broward and Martin counties that augment local channels and offer viewers a fantastic selection.

SOUTH FLORIDA'S MAJOR TV STATIONS AND THEIR NETWORK AFFILIATES:

WPBT Channel 2 (PBS), North Miami
WTVJ Channel 4 (NBC), Miami
WPTV Channel 5 (NBC), West Palm Beach
WCIX Channel 6 (CBS), Miami
WSVN Channel 7 (FOX), Miami
WPLG Channel 10 (ABC), Miami
WPEC Channel 12 (CBS), West Palm Beach
WLRN Channel 17 (PBS), Miami
WPBF Channel 25 (ABC), Palm Beach Gardens
WFLX Channel 29 (FOX), West Palm Beach

WBFS Channel 33 (Independent), Miami
WTVX Channel 34 (Independent), Palm Beach Gardens
WDZL Channel 39 (Independent), Hollywood
WXEL Channel 42 (PBS), Boynton Beach
WHFT Channel 45 (TBN), Pembroke Park

Cable Service

Your life won't be terribly restricted if you don't have cable to augment your network television coverage, but most folks do because the advantages cable offers are tremendous and the reception is clearer. Our selection of stations here is excellent, drawing from the Palm Beach and Miami markets, but cable opens up a vast array of possibilities, from MTV and VH-1 for the young and hip to CNN, ESPN, The Travel Channel, Cinemax, HBO, The Sci-Fi Channel, Comedy Central, C-SPAN and much more. Here are the cable companies covering Palm Beach County:

ADELPHIA CABLE
Highland Beach and
Palm Beach Gardens   930-2225

CABLEVISION OF MIDDLE FLORIDA
Belle Glade   996-3086

COMCAST CABLEVISION
General information   391-7550
Boca Raton   391-7550
Boynton Beach   478-8300
West Palm Beach   478-8300

LEADERSHIP CABLEVISION
Delray Beach, Boynton Beach, Gulfstream
and Ocean Ridge   272-2521

TELE-MEDIA CO.
West Palm Beach   588-5553
Century Village area of Boca Raton and
parts of Boynton Beach   482-2500

WEST BOCA CABLEVISION
Boca Raton west of Military Tr.   483-4300

Inside
Places of Worship

Even if you hail from a galaxy far, far away, your soul can find a home in Palm Beach County. Not counting the solitary supplications of early pioneers, who often prayed up a storm for deliverance from rattlesnakes, the region celebrates more than 100 years of organized religion.

Your presence and religious preference are welcome, whether you're Jewish, Mormon, Jehovah's Witness, Baha'i, Greek Orthodox, Roman Catholic, Protestant, Unitarian, nondenominational, interdenominational, charismatic, Pentecostal or Apostolic — traditional, modern, liberal, conservative, purist, interpreter, independent, metaphysical, scientific or so-called original thinker.

The number and variety of houses of worship accommodate the diversity of people the region attracts. Folk who relocate here often want to replicate the spiritual style and substance they were previously accustomed to, and area churches and synagogues reflect that desire.

We suggest newcomers check the Yellow Pages for exact times of services and seasonal variations. For current highlights in South County, see Friday editions of *The News*. Religious happenings around the Palm Beaches also appear Fridays in *The Palm Beach Post*.

Boca Raton's Church Row

When sinners and saints go marching along Church Row, a stretch of Yamato Road between Military Trail and St. Andrews Boulevard, eyes are likely to widen at the unlikely neighbors with little use for fences. Running west from Patch Reef Park are consecutive driveways for **St. Mark Greek Orthodox, Congregation B'nai Israel, St. David Armenian, First Baptist** and **Spanish River**, a Presbyterian congregation.

Worship is an ambient force in a region of spiritual communities that combine year-round activities with seasonal swells. Historically, some congregations met in private homes until they could afford to build chapels. Today, people visit friends and family at churches and synagogues throughout the region — geographical lines tend to blur between Boca, Deerfield and Delray when it comes to worship — and newcomers often are introduced to cultural programs, festivals and the performing arts in the social halls.

Boca and its 'burbs support nine Catholic parishes, including **St. Joan of Arc**, which opened its doors in 1959. For many years, St. Joan was the largest parish in the southeastern United States. Today, with 13,655 registered members representing 5,200 households, Msgr.

John McMahon's parish remains the largest in the five-county Catholic Diocese of Palm Beach.

The area from Palm Beach to Miami constitutes the second-largest Jewish population in the country, with a baker's dozen synagogues just in Boca-Delray. With snowbirds, the rounded population is 166,000 for Boca-Delray; 93,000 from Boynton on north; 206,000 for North Broward County; 76,000 for South Broward; and 166,000 for Dade County. By comparison, the largest Jewish population in the United States is 1.4 million in the New York metropolitan area.

The first Jewish house of worship in South County, Temple Beth El, opened in 1967.

Earlier, worshippers traveled to Palm Beach's **Temple Emmanuel**, organized in 1963. Prior to the dedication of its first temple and a later, Moorish-style structure on North County Road, the congregation met in Guild Hall of the Episcopal Church of Bethesda-By-The-Sea.

Temple Beth El, headed for the past 18 years by Rabbi Merle Singer, set a progressive pace by providing religious guidance and instruction, as well as educational advancement and Hebrew instruction. Temple Beth El operates a religious Kindergarten through 12th grade school and coordinates special programs for singles, youth groups, sisterhood and brotherhood. The congregation has taken a leadership role in the cultural community almost from the outset, and organizes and presents its own performing arts series.

A new temple was built last December on Montoya Circle for suburban **Boca Raton Synagogue**, honored for its growth and community service by the Union of Orthodox Jewish Congregations of America.

Rabbi Sam Silver reads from the Torah at Temple Sinai in Delray Beach.

The Jerusalem Sphere, created by Frank Meisler, is a prominent fixture on the Richard and Carole Siemens Campus.

Eyes Turned
Heavenward Early On

Union Congregation Church, organized around Easter 1894, celebrated its centennial last December in new facilities on Summit Boulevard in West Palm Beach. Its original site at Olive and Datura streets was a bellwether, prompting other churches, including **St. Ann's Catholic** and **Holy Trinity Episcopal**, to open downtown prior to the turn of the century. Around 1895, Henry Flagler added a nondenominational chapel to the grounds of his landmark Royal Poinciana Hotel.

As early as 1893, the Styx area of Palm Beach had two black churches — Mt. Olive Missionary Baptist (now called **Tabernacle**) and Bethel African Methodist Episcopal (now **Payne Chapel A.M.E.**). Riviera Beach folklore also mentions an Oak Lawn prayer mission as early as 1892. Farther south, black churches also flourished in Delray Beach, where **present-day Mt. Olive Missionary Baptist** opened in 1896.

Lake Worth, as it was known in the late 1880s, garnered a blessing from the Episcopal Bishop of Florida who agreed Palm Beach could support a mission. An upstate-New York vicar volunteered to minister in the winter of 1888; services were held in the tiny frame schoolhouse. In spring of 1889, a pioneer, recalling Bethesda parish in Saratoga Springs, named the colony's modest chapel **Bethesda-By-The-Sea**.

Subsequently, Bethesda-By-The-Sea expanded twice, including a Moorish-style mission and the 15th-century Gothic edifice and gardens that grace South County Road today.

Early congregations in Delray included Methodist, Lutheran and Presbyterian sects. Reports around 1910 describe Dr. S.S. Gibson, pastor of Gibson Memorial Baptist, who rode his Ford Model T south to Deerfield Beach to lead Sunday afternoon prayer meetings in a private home. By 1913, Deerfield Beach had a church of its own named **The Baptist Church**.

Smaller than the black communities in many neighboring towns, Pearl City in Boca Raton drew laborers from Georgia who had moved south to work in the bean fields west of town. They had worshipped in Delray until 1917, when Pearl City opened the **Macedonia A.M.E.** Within the same year, **Ebenezer Baptist** followed suit and, for awhile, the two congregations alternated Sunday programs.

Elsewhere in Boca, Methodists and other Protestant denominations established a stronger presence as soldiers stationed at the **Boca Raton Army Air Field's** radar base returned to settle down after World War II.

Ecumenical
Worship in Boca Raton

Bibletown
Conference Center

An enterprising fellow with a Miami radio ministry arrived around 1950 with a vision about the potential for a Christ-centered destination. "Doc" Ira Eschleman acquired property the military had occupied north of Palmetto Park Road on Fourth Av-

Photo: Stephanie Murphy

This Protestant church on W. Camino Real in Boca Raton reflects the adaptation of Mediterranean Revival architecture prevalent in the area.

Photo: Dick Spenser

Stained glass creates a colorful mosaic backdrop for these First United Methodist Church acolytes-in-training.

enue, establishing **Bibletown Conference Center**.

Widely promoted around the United States, Canada and Europe, Bibletown drew devout pilgrims who attended week-long revival programs of worship, Bible study, sacred-music concerts and fellowship. The grounds were equipped to house visitors within walking distance of the conference center.

Local residents began attending events at Bibletown, and some visitors invested in apartments nearby. By 1958, Bibletown opened a church to accommodate demand. A few years ago, the congregation altered the name to **Boca Raton Community Church** — still interdenominational and fairly straightforward in its goals.

Says one longtime volunteer: "Our purpose is to make known that Christ lived among us as a man, that He died on the cross, arose from the dead and joined His Father in Heaven. We're waiting for His return, so our purpose is to tell people they need to be saved."

To that end, Bibletown operates a private school, an expanding missionary network and year-round worship and Sunday school programs.

Joint Ventures

Aside from Bibletown, Boca Raton's religious community has shown its ecumenical side in other ways. Temple Beth El, for example, co-founded the **Daily Bread Food Bank** with St. Joan of Arc, its neighbor across Fourth Avenue. Another joint venture is the annual crop walk to feed the needy. Finally, the Rev. Nancy McCarthy, last year's president of the Standing Committee of the Diocese of Southeast Florida, points to the elder day-care program — a collaborative effort between B'nai Israel and Ebenezer Baptist — as another interfaith success.

Inside
South Florida's
Weather and Climate

To chilled-to-the-bone folks from the North and Midwest, there's a word about the in-season climate and weather in South Florida: gorgeous. Stay here a little longer (through the summer especially) and learn another word: humid. A resident of Phoenix attending a summertime convention in the Palm Beaches will go from three-digit temperatures at home to the mid-80s in Florida and complain about the heat. It's the humidity, the moisture in the air, that makes that heat stick to you.

Here in paradise, there are some definite caveats concerning our weather and climate. The first deals with exposure to the sun. The second relates to hurricanes.

Prickly Heat or a Full-Scale Sunburn?

Sun-seekers and people who spend excessive hours outdoors learn there's a price to pay for that gorgeous tan. On a daily basis, sun and humidity cause discomfort and damage to thousands of South Floridians and visitors, one sufferer at a time.

When you get your first dose of South Florida-style heat and humidity, particularly in the summertime, you feel the full oppressive brunt of the heat. After about two weeks,

though, your body begins to make accommodations. Through a process called acclimatization, people find they sweat more readily and their cardiovascular systems deal more effectively with the heat. Until then, though, the unacclimatized should drink extra fluids and avoid exertion.

Sunshine, too, has its problems. First, let's discuss the A-B-Ds of exposure to the sun. We'll start with D, as in Vitamin D, which every 3rd grade student is taught we get from sunlight. Don't try to rationalize a blistering sunburn by saying you did it for the Vitamin D; your diet should provide you with more than enough. Too much exposure to the sun has immediate and long-lasting consequences. Ultraviolet-A rays cause the skin to age; ultraviolet-B rays cause burning. Both can cause skin cancer, but ultraviolet-B rays are more damaging. Additionally, there's a greater incidence of malignant melanoma, a type of skin cancer that accounts for up to 75 percent of skin cancer deaths, in sunspots such as South Florida, Hawaii, Arizona and Southern California. To minimize your chances of UVA and UVB damage, here are some suggestions:

*Avoid sunlight when the rays are most intense — between 10 AM and 3 PM.

Photo: Michelle Lord

A portable fan can help beat the heat.

*Wear clothing that minimizes your exposure, such as long-sleeved cotton shirts, long pants instead of shorts, socks with shoes and wide-brimmed hats. Generally speaking, eschew all but cotton clothing during hot periods (although the outdoor retail industry has developed synthetic materials that function at least as well). Cotton acts as a wick and absorbs sweat.

*If you plan to be in the sun, use a sunscreen with a sun protection factor (SPF) of at least 15. Apply the first coating at least 15 minutes before you go outside, and remember to reapply every hour or immediately after swimming or sweating heavily. Choose a sunscreen that is PABA-free and alcohol-free.

*Finally, remember to protect your eyes from the rays too. Choose gray or green lenses that block at least 99 percent of UVB rays, 60 percent of UVA rays and 97 percent of visible light.

Hurricanes and Tropical Storms: Be Prepared

Here's a tale of two storms and the damage they inflicted upon South Florida.

August 24, 1992: Hurricane Andrew barreled into southeastern Florida like a runaway freight train

A few drops of rain don't dampen spirits in South Florida. Children still can find splashing in puddles just as much fun as being drenched by the sun's rays.

Photo: Michelle Lord

An umbrella is just as useful at warding off the sun's rays as it is at warding off rain.

loaded with pig iron. Originally, it appeared the storm's eye would come ashore near Hollywood, but just before reaching land, the storm suddenly veered slightly southward, away from the densely populated Ft. Lauderdale-Hollywood-downtown Miami area. The storm's sustained winds of 145 mph turned thousands of homes in southern Dade County into pickup sticks and left behind $20 billion in damage.

November 14-16, 1994: Tropical Storm Gordon lollygagged across South Florida, toppling small trees and signs and causing minor structural damage and considerable flooding. Unlike Andrew, which blew through the area with uncommon speed and left little water in its wake, Gordon's slow sojourn left lots of water and water damage, destroying about a third of South Florida's winter vegetable harvest, worth an estimated $200 million or more.

Compared to Andrew, Gordon wasn't much of a storm, but it left lots of damage. The moral: Don't take tropical weather systems lightly. They all demand respect.

Andrew and Gordon have helped remind South Floridians how important it is to prepare for the June 1 to November 30 hurricane season. The beginning of this season is a good time to give your hedges, trees and large shrubs a good pruning. Dense foliage

Insiders' Tips

June 1 through November is hurricane season. Be prepared: Stock up on supplies such as batteries, flashlights, candles, first aid supplies, bottled water and canned goods.

A Hurricane Primer

Here's what all those hurricane terms tossed around by TV meteorologists mean:

Types of Storms

Tropical wave: An area of low pressure in the tropics or subtropics.

Tropical depression: An undefined storm system packing winds of 38 mph or less, with little or superficial rotary motion.

Tropical storm: A large storm system with defined rotary movement and winds from 39 to 74 mph.

Hurricane: A large, well-defined storm system with distinct rotary motion, a defined eye and winds of 74 mph or more.

Hurricane Categories

Category 1: A minor hurricane with wind speeds of 74 to 95 mph. Storm surge is 4 to 5 feet, and barometric pressure is 28.94 inches or more. Causes minimal damage; most wind damage will be of a horticultural or minor structural nature.

Category 2: Winds are 96 to 110 mph, storm surge is 6 to 8 feet, and barometric pressure is 28.50 to 28.93 inches. Causes moderate damage.

Category 3: All storms from this point on are considered major hurricanes. Winds are 111 to 130 mph, storm surge is 9 to 12 feet, and barometric pressure is 27.19 to 28.49 inches. Causes extensive damage.

Category 4: Winds are 131 to 155 mph, storm surge is 13 to 18 feet, and barometric pressure is 27.17 to 27.90 inches. Damage is severe.

Category 5: Winds exceed 155 mph, storm surge is greater than 18 feet, and barometric pressure is less than 27.17 inches. Results in widespread, catastrophic damage.

Storm Alerts

Tropical storm watch: Issued by the National Hurricane Center in Coral Gables, Florida, when a tropical storm could threaten an area within 24 to 36 hours.

Tropical storm warning: Issued when a tropical storm is expected to hit the area within 24 hours.

Hurricane watch: Issued when a hurricane is expected to hit a specified coastal area within 36 hours.

Hurricane warning: Issued when sustained hurricane-force winds are expected to hit a specified area within 24 hours.

acts as a sail; thorough pruning and shaping allow wind to pass through the foliage with minimal effect.

Before a hurricane forms, make plans for what you'd do if one were to threaten the area. First, choose adequate shelter — the rest of your plans will be for naught if you don't have a safe haven. Another step is assembling a suitable hurricane kit. The first need is for suitable first-aid supplies, a reserve supply of medications for those who take them regularly and a sufficient supply of baby food and other baby supplies.

Early in the season is also the right time to obtain a new supply of nonperishable food items. With modern packaging, there is a wide selection of canned, bottled, freeze-dried and crystallized foods and beverages.

Then there's the hardware and supplies you'll need to keep on hand, from rolls of duct tape and nails to flashlights, batteries and matches. When a hurricane threatens, there's invariably a rush on these items at the stores. Planning ahead keeps you out of a potentially long line at the hardware store and lets you concentrate on your storm preparations instead.

Stay extra alert during the hurricane season. Keep an eye on daily local and regional weather patterns and forecasts. When a hurricane is identified, WTVJ Channel 4 in Miami is probably your best overall source of information. Should a hurricane threaten, most South Florida television stations hook up with radio stations to provide constant coverage.

Many communities compile and distribute hurricane preparation guides and supplies checklists. Other good sources of information are the American Red Cross and each county's Office of Emergency Preparedness.

Service Directory

Important Numbers

Emergency

Regardless of where you are, 911 is the number to call in an emergency for police, fire or medical assistance.

Non-emergency

The 37 municipalities and the unincorporated areas Palm Beach County serves have non-emergency numbers for administrative inquiries.

POLICE

Boca Raton	338-1333
Boynton Beach	732-8116
Delray Beach	243-7800
Lake Worth	586-1611
Palm Beach	838-5454
West Palm Beach	837-4000
Palm Beach County Sheriff's Department substation	276-1301

FIRE AND RESCUE

Boca Raton	395-1127
Boynton Beach	375-6035
Delray Beach	243-7400
Lake Worth	586-1171
Palm Beach	838-5420
West Palm Beach	835-2900
South Palm Beach County	278-9970

Palm Beach County Services

County Information Line

If you call 355-6848, or toll-free from South County, 930-5125, a recorded message tells you how to retrieve information on county commission meeting schedules, agenda highlights, parks, library programs, road closings and other useful details.

County Citizen Services Line

Call 355-4314 or toll-free, 930-4314, 24 hours a day, seven days a week. If you call weekdays between 8 AM and 5 PM, staff members can assist; on weekends, evenings and holidays, leave a message and someone will call you back. The Citizen Inquiry Line in Boca Raton is 393-7914.

Courthouses

PALM BEACH COUNTY COURTHOUSE
401 N. Dixie Hwy.
West Palm Beach   355-2431

The new $125 million complex welcomed departments at long last in spring 1995: the judiciary, including civil and criminal divisions of Circuit and County Court; administrative staffs; Probate and Juvenile Courts; custody investigations; youth affairs; victim services; witness management; jury assembly; interpreters; and courthouse security. Most departments not housed in the courthouse are in the Governmental Center, also in downtown West Palm Beach.

SOUTH COUNTY COURTHOUSE

200 W. Atlantic Ave.
Delray Beach   *274-1400*

This complex is open 8:30 AM to 5 PM Monday through Friday. For procedures to obtain or renew your passport, call 274-1586.

Property Appraiser

GOVERNMENTAL CENTER

301 N. Olive Ave.
West Palm Beach   *355-2866*

SOUTH COUNTY
ADMINISTRATIVE COMPLEX ANNEX

501 S. Congress Ave.
Delray Beach   *276-1250*

Homestead Exemption is available for owners who apply by March 1 each year for property they own as of January 1. This pertains to primary residences only. The $25,000 exemption reduces the amount of your assessment and saves you about $500 in property taxes annually. To register, visit the Property Appraiser's office from 8:30 AM to 5 PM weekdays.

Bring along your property deed, driver's license, car registration, voter's registration if you have it, and Social Security number.

Tax Collector

GOVERNMENTAL CENTER

Main Office:
301 N. Olive Ave.
West Palm Beach   *930-7926*

Hours are 8:30 AM to 5 PM Monday through Friday excluding holidays.

Mailing Address:
John K. Clark, Tax Collector
P.O. Box 3715
West Palm Beach 33402-3715

Once you're vehicle is registered, you can easily renew by mail — and don't forget to include the emissions test results.

SOUTH COUNTY
ADMINISTRATIVE COMPLEX

345 S. Congress Ave.
Delray Beach   *276-1225*

Offices are open 8:30 AM to 5 PM Monday through Friday.

SOUTH COUNTY
ADMINISTRATIVE COMPLEX ANNEX

501 S. Congress Ave.
Delray Beach   *276-1200*

Mobile units of the Tax Collector's office follow a rotating schedule from 10 AM to 3 PM weekdays except holidays. Call toll-free, 930-7926, for a recorded schedule of stops.

Vehicle Registration

Palm Beach County requires an emissions control inspection before you can renew. Inspection centers are at 3185 S. Congress Avenue, Delray Beach; 2600 High Ridge Road in Quantum Park, Boynton Beach; and 751 S. Congress Avenue, West Palm Beach.

Hours for testing are 7 AM to 6 PM Tuesday and Wednesday, 8 AM to 6 PM Thursday and Friday, 8 AM to 2 PM Saturday. No inspections Sunday, Monday and holidays.

Bring your old registration and $10 in cash for the drive-through process; bring along music, a good book or a laptop for the wait.

Utilities

TELEPHONE SERVICE

Southern Bell   (toll-free) 780-2355

Call with questions about new residential lines, billing matters or changes in existing service. If you call from outside Florida or outside Southern Bell territory, call (800) 753-2909. For business or commercial lines, call 780-2800 or (800) 753-0115.

ELECTRIC

Florida Power & Light Company   395-8700

WATER AND SEWER

Boca Raton Water Department   393-7750

City residents pay a minimum deposit of $80, and water bills are bimonthly.

Palm Beach County
Water Utilities Department   278-5135

Billing for sewer service is included in the water bills.

Other Resources

Better Business Bureau of Palm Beach County, 2247 Palm Beach Lakes Boulevard, West Palm Beach, 686-2200 or (800) 394-2201.

Palm Beach County Division of Consumer Affairs provides public access to records about complaints against businesses in the county. For information, call 233-4820 or 276-1270 from South County.

Postal and Shipping Services

U.S. Postal Service

MAIN POST OFFICES

2800 N. Military Tr.	
Boca Raton	994-2700
1530 W. Boynton Beach Blvd.	
Boynton Beach	738-5220
14280 Military Tr.	
Delray Beach	498-8504
4151 Lake Worth Rd.	
Lake Worth	964-1102
3200 Summit Blvd.	
Palm Beach	697-2100

Call the respective listed numbers for ZIP code information.

Package and Document Shipping

FEDERAL EXPRESS

Here are some choices for speedy shipping, including two with Saturday service:

FedEx Station, 5900 Park of Commerce Boulevard, Boca Raton, 8 AM to 7:30 PM Monday through Friday, 8 AM to 5 PM Saturday.

FedEx Service Center, 2621 N. Federal Highway in Paseos Plaza, Boca Raton, 9 AM to 7:15 PM Monday through Friday.

FedEx Drive-Thru, 2255A W. Hillsboro Boulevard in the Shops at Hillsboro, Deerfield Beach, 1:30 to 6:30 PM Monday through Friday.

FedEx Service Center, 1145 Barnett Drive, Lake Worth, 8:30 AM to 7 PM Monday through Friday, 8:30 AM to 5 PM on Saturday.

For information on drop-box locations and latest pickup times, call (800) Go-FedEX or (800) 238-5355.

UPS

Authorized shipping outlets can be found at Mailbox International, 153 E. Palmetto Park Road, Boca Raton, 392-2805; Pony Mailbox, 8903 Glades Road, Boca Raton, 488-3344; Mailbox International, 29 South County Road, Palm Beach, 833-8933; and RSVP, 277 Royal Poinciana Way, Palm Beach, 659-9077. For UPS general information, call (305) 427-9922.

Miscellaneous Information and Services

Alcoholic Beverages

Florida's legal age to drink or purchase alcoholic beverages is 21. In addition to chain stores and independent merchants, most supermarkets, convenience stores and neighborhood grocers sell beer and wine.

Animal Services

BOCA RATON ANIMAL SHELTER
21287 Boca Rio Rd.   *482-8110*
The shelter is open 10 AM to 4 PM Monday through Friday, 10 AM to 3 PM on Saturday. Call for emergency animal pickup within the city limits and for information about adopting a pet or finding a lost one.

Beach Conditions

To find out about ocean swimming conditions, call 393-7989. You'll hear information about air and water temperatures, whether the surf is up and the status of seasonal pests in the water such as sea lice or Portuguese Man-O-Wars — the former, you can't see; the other is deceptively gorgeous. Definitely avoid both!

Marine Safety Operations, 80 S. Ocean Boulevard, 393-7820, is the headquarters for Boca Raton's lifeguards.

Beach Permits

Permits are on sale at the **Boca Raton Community Center**, 150 N.W. Crawford Boulevard, one block west of City Hall and north of Palmetto Park Road; or the **James A. Rutherford Community Center** at Patch Reef Park, 2000 Yamato Road, just west of Military Trail. The centers are open 8 AM to 10 PM weekdays and 8 AM to 5 PM on Saturday. Also, on weekends, permits are on sale at the **Park Ranger Station at Spanish River**. (See our Beaches chapter for additional information.)

Boating Safety

For information on marine safety instruction, call the **Delray Beach Power Squadron**, 272-5493, or **Flotilla 51**, U.S. Coast Guard Auxiliary, 844-9252.

Cable Service

ADELPHIA CABLE
Highland Beach and
Palm Beach Gardens   930-2225

CABLEVISION OF MIDDLE FLORIDA
Belle Glade   996-3086

COMCAST CABLEVISION
General information   391-7550
Boca Raton   391-7550
Boynton Beach   478-8300
West Palm Beach   478-8300

LEADERSHIP CABLEVISION
Delray Beach, Boynton Beach, Gulfstream
and Ocean Ridge   272-2521

TELE-MEDIA CO.
West Palm Beach   588-5553
Century Village area of Boca Raton and
parts of Boynton Beach   482-2500

WEST BOCA CABLEVISION
Boca Raton west of Military Tr.   483-4300

Driver's Licenses

Offices are open 7 AM to 6 PM Tuesday through Friday. Locations are 14570 S. Military Trail, Delray Beach; 3220 S. Federal Highway, Fort Pierce; 1299 W. Lantana Road, Lantana; 3185 PGA Boulevard, Palm Beach Gardens; Florida Highway Patrol Station, 1839 E. Main Street,

Photo: Sophie Brandstrom

During the season, sea turtles can be spotted on South Florida beaches. This one, however, can be spotted at the Gumbo Limbo Environmental Complex in Boca Raton.

Pahokee; 8495 Federal Highway, Port St. Lucie; 4320 S.E. Federal Highway, Stuart; 668 U.S. Highway 1 N., Tequesta; and 571 N. Military Trail, West Palm Beach.

To obtain a Florida driver's license or to have one renewed, either walk in at any of the aforementioned locations and wait in line, which can sometimes take an hour or longer, or make an appointment. For information, call (800) 303-7288.

Fishing Regulations and Licenses

Florida Marine Patrol, 624-6935, has information on saltwater fishing regulations. The Florida Game and Freshwater Fish Commission is the place to call about a fishing license, 640-6100. See our Fishing chapter for more information.

Recycling

Boca Raton Sanitation Department collects garbage and bundled trash twice a week. Unbundled yard clippings are collected every other week. The zone pickup schedule is available in the lobby of City Hall. The city provides recycle bins and collects newspapers, plastic, glass and aluminum cans. For information on the weekly pickup schedule, call 393-7867. Twice a year, the city schedules a bulk collection of items such as furniture and appliances. If you live in the unincorporated area, County Sanitation Department handles garbage and trash pickups. For information on county programs, call 471-2700 or 278-1717.

State of Florida Regulatory Agencies

OFFICE OF THE COMPTROLLER
(800) 848-3792

Florida regulates industries such as lenders including state-chartered banks, securities brokers, cemeteries and investment advisers.

DEPARTMENT OF PROFESSIONAL REGULATION
(800) 342-7940

The agency oversees contractors doing work such as roofing, air-conditioning and electrical repairs.

DEPARTMENT OF INSURANCE
(800) 342-2762

This Florida department regulates rates and insurance agencies and investigates fraud.

Voter Registration

Voters must register for city, county and national elections up to 30 days before election day. You are required to be a U.S. citizen and age 18 or older by the time of the election. You may register at the local City Hall from 8 AM to 5 PM weekdays or the Southeast County Administrative Complex, 345 S. Congress Avenue, Delray Beach. For information, call 393-7742 or 276-1226.

Weather Information

The National Weather Service offers a local forecast 24 hours daily at 686-5650. If you like to monitor four winds-seven seas happenings in other time zones, The Weather Channel appears on most cable TV systems serving the county:

Comcast Cablevision	*Channel 39*
West Boca Cablevision	*Channel 26*
Comcast Boynton	*Channel 28*
Continental Cablevision	*Channel 30*
Leadership Cable	*Channel 41*
Telemedia	*Channel 21*
Gulf and Pacific	*Channel 44*

For information on hurricanes, call 393-7800.

Welcome Centers

The **Palm Beach Convention and Visitors Bureau** has offices at 1555 Palm Beach Lakes Boulevard, Suite 204, West Palm Beach, (800) 554-7256.

Wellness Programs

BLOOD PRESSURE SCREENINGS

Boca Raton Fire Department, Station #1
1151 N. Federal Hwy., Boca Raton

Free blood-pressure screenings are offered here on the first Tuesday of each month from 9 AM to 5 PM.

Other station locations in Boca Raton include One S.W. 12th Avenue, 100 S. Ocean Boulevard, 351 N.W. 51st Street (Yamato Road), 2333 W. Glades Road and 1901 Clint Moore Road.

Index of Advertisers

Index

ORDER FORM
Fast and Simple!

Mail to:	Or:
Insiders Guides®, Inc. **P.O. Drawer 2057** **Manteo, NC 27954**	**for VISA or** **Mastercard orders call** **1-800-765-BOOK**

Name _____

Address _____

City/State/Zip _____

Qty.	Title/Price	Shipping	Amount
	Insiders' Guide to Richmond/$14.95	$3.00	
	Insiders' Guide to Williamsburg/$14.95	$3.00	
	Insiders' Guide to Virginia's Blue Ridge/$14.95	$3.00	
	Insiders' Guide to Virginia's Chesapeake Bay/$14.95	$3.00	
	Insiders' Guide to Washington, DC/$14.95	$3.00	
	Insiders' Guide to North Carolina's Outer Banks/$14.95	$3.00	
	Insiders' Guide to Wilmington, NC/$14.95	$3.00	
	Insiders' Guide to North Carolina's Crystal Coast/$12.95	$3.00	
	Insiders' Guide to Myrtle Beach/$14.95	$3.00	
	Insiders' Guide to Mississippi/$14.95	$3.00	
	Insiders' Guide to Boca Raton & the Palm Beaches/$14.95	$3.00	
	Insiders' Guide to Sarasota/Bradenton/$12.95	$3.00	
	Insiders' Guide to Northwest Florida/$14.95	$3.00	
	Insiders' Guide to Lexington, KY/$14.95	$3.00	
	Insiders' Guide to Louisville/$14.95	$3.00	
	Insiders' Guide to the Twin Cities/$12.95	$3.00	
	Insiders' Guide to Boulder/$12.95	$3.00	
	Insiders' Guide to Denver/$12.95	$3.00	
	Insiders' Guide to Civil War in the Eastern Theater/$14.95	$3.00	
	Insiders' Guide to North Carolina's Mountains/$14.95	$3.00	
	Insiders' Guide to Atlanta/$14.95	$3.00	
	Insiders' Guide to Branson/$14.95 (12/95)	$3.00	
	Insiders' Guide to Cincinnati/$14.95 (9/95)	$3.00	
	Insiders' Guide to Tampa Bay/$14.95 (12/95)	$3.00	

Payment in full (check or money order) must
accompany this order form.
Please allow 2 weeks for delivery.

N.C. residents add 6% sales tax _____

Total _____

Who you are
and what you think
is important to us.

**Fill out the coupon and we'll give you
an Insiders' Guide® for half price ($7.48 off)**

Which book(s) did you buy? _____

Where do you live? _____

In what city did you buy your book? _____

Where did you buy your book? ❑ catalog ❑ bookstore ❑ newspaper ad

    ❑ retail shop ❑ other _____

How often do you travel? ❑ yearly ❑ bi-annually ❑ quarterly

    ❑ more than quarterly

Did you buy your book because you were ❑ moving ❑ vacationing

    ❑ wanted to know more about your home town ❑ other _____

_____

Will the book be used by ❑ family ❑ couple ❑ individual ❑ group

What is you annual household income? ❑ under $25,000 ❑ $25,000 to $35,000

    ❑ $35,000 to $50,000 ❑ $50,000 to $75,000 ❑ over $75,000

How old are you? ❑ under 25 ❑ 25-35 ❑ 36-50 ❑ 51-65 ❑ over 65

Did you use the book before you left for your destination? ❑ yes ❑ no

Did you use the book while at your destination? ❑ yes ❑ no

On average per month, how many times do you refer to your book? ❑ 1-3 ❑ 4-7

    ❑ 8-11 ❑ 12-15 ❑ 16 and up

On average, how many other people use your book? ❑ no others ❑ 1 ❑ 2

    ❑ 3 ❑ 4 or more

Is there anything you would like to tell us about Insiders' Guides? _____

_____

_____

Name_____Address _____

City_____ State _____ Zip _____

**We'll send you a voucher for $7.48 off any Insiders' Guide© and a list of available
titles as soon as we get this card from you. Thanks for being an Insider!**

BUSINESS REPLY MAIL

FIRST-CLASS MAIL PERMIT NO. 20 MANTEO, NC

POSTAGE WILL BE PAID BY ADDRESSEE

THE INSIDERS GUIDE
PO BOX 2057
MANTEO NC 27954-9906

We're More Than Just A Pretty Face...

Subscribe Now!
6 Issues for $19.95

Name_____ Telephone_____

Address_____ Apt._____

City_____ State_____ Zip_____

❑ Payment enclosed ❑ Bill me later ❑ Mastercard ❑ Visa ❑ American Express ❑ Discover

Card Number_____ Expiration Date_____

Signature_____

In Canada and Mexico, add $28; in all other countries, add $40. Please allow 6-8 weeks for receipt of the first issue. Payment in U.S. currency drawn on a U.S. bank must accompany all foreign orders.

IGBR-95